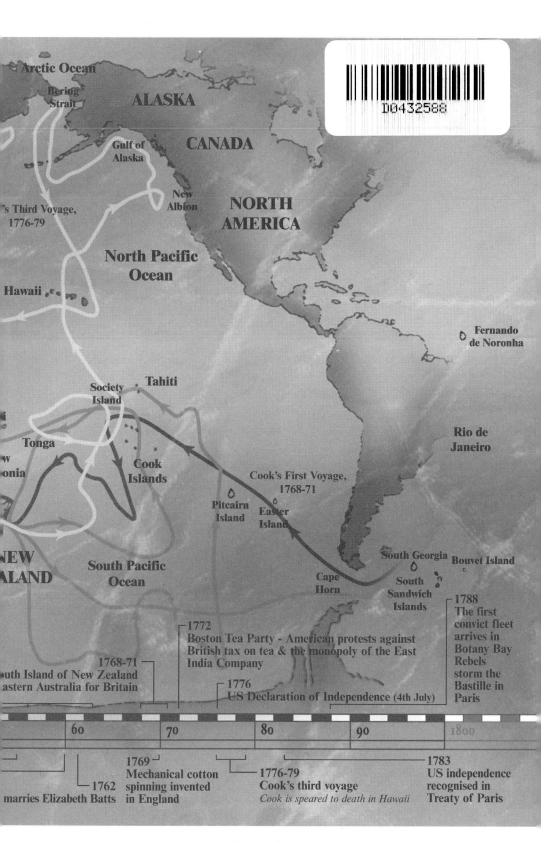

Arctic Ocean

Bering Strait

ALASKA

Gulf of
Alaska

CANADA

New
Albion

NORTH
AMERICA

's Third Voyage,
1776-79

North Pacific
Ocean

Hawaii

Fernando
de Noronha

Tahiti

Society
Island

Tonga

Rio de
Janeiro

w
onia

Cook
Islands

Cook's First Voyage,
1768-71

Pitcairn
Island

Easter
Island

NEW
ALAND

South Pacific
Ocean

Cape
Horn

South Georgia

Bouvet Island

South
Sandwich
Islands

1788
The first
convict fleet
arrives in
Botany Bay
Rebels
storm the
Bastille in
Paris

1772
Boston Tea Party - American protests against
British tax on tea & the monopoly of the East
India Company

1768-71
uth Island of New Zealand
astern Australia for Britain

1776
US Declaration of Independence (4th July)

60	70	80	90	1800

1769
Mechanical cotton
spinning invented
in England

1776-79
Cook's third voyage
Cook is speared to death in Hawaii

1783
US independence
recognised in
Treaty of Paris

1762
marries Elizabeth Batts

CAPTAIN COOK

OBSESSION AND BETRAYAL IN THE NEW WORLD

Vanessa Collingridge

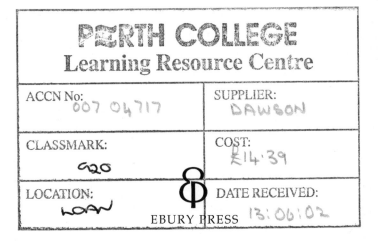
EBURY PRESS

First published in Great Britain in 2002

10 9 8 7 6 5 4 3 2 1

First published by
Ebury Press
Random House
20 Vauxhall Bridge Road
London SW1 2SA

Random House Australia (Pty) Limited
20 Alfred Street, Milsons Point
Sydney
New South Wales 2061, Australia

Random House New Zealand Limited
18 Poland Road, Glenfield, Auckland 10
New Zealand

Random House South Africa (Pty) Limited
Endulini, 5A Jubilee Road
Parktown 2193
South Africa

Random House UK Limited Reg. No. 954009

www.randomhouse.co.uk

A CIP catalogue record for this book is available from the British Library

ISBN 0 09 187913 2

Papers used by Ebury Press are natural, recycable products made from wood grown in sustainable forests

Typeset by Textype, Cambridge
Printed and bound in Great Britain by Biddles Ltd, Guildford and King's Lynn

Jacket design by the Senate
Author photograph by Katy van Dyck

Every effort has been made to clear relevant copyright permissions. Please contact the publisher with any queries.

In Memory
Of
Glennis Allison
&
William Caleb Gould

Who taught me the value of dreams.

ACKNOWLEDGEMENTS

his book would never have happened without the help and inspiration of a whole host of friends, fellow-Cookophiles and supporters from around the world who it would take another book to mention individually but to whom I offer a heartfelt collective 'thanks'. However, the following people have provided particular assitance and/or sanity. Firstly, my now-extended family of Collingridges near and far – in Australia: Winsome, Edith, Ruth, Dick and also David for their constant help and encouragement; my parents, Gordon & Irene, my numerous brothers and sisters, in-laws and outlaws; a profound thanks to the wonderful Cecily Collingridge, Family Archivist Extraordinaire, without whom this book would have been about 200 pages slimmer; special thanks to Susan Gore, Winsome, Dick, Cecily and Cecily's brother, Peter and his wife Jane, for allowing me access to 150 years of Collingridge correspondence.

In New Zealand, Huw Mitchell, Fiona King and their boys, Gus & Luc, provided me with limitless hospitality, encouragement and diversion from the first germ of the idea through to its completion. To John Allan: what can I say but a heartfelt thank-you for the constant stream of materials, ideas, comments and humour; likewise, John Robson, who has generously assisted in every possible manner with my research and also Ken Scadden of the Museum of Wellington City and Sea.

In the UK, thanks must go to the Captain Cook Study Unit, especially Cliff Thornton and Alwyn Peel who provided their knowledge, resources and contacts; Adrian Webb and Sharon Nichol at the UK Hydrographic Office; Tony Campbell at the British Library Map Room; David Clive King for his genealogical research into the family of Captain James & Fiona King; the family of Cook Museums at Whitby, Great Ayton, Marton and Statithes; Habie Schwartz and Brenda McCreery for help with French translations; also Dr Jack Langton at St John's College, Oxford, for 15 years of support and encouragement. A very personal thanks to my much-missed friend and former cameraman, Rob Hill, who was always there to talk to and share the moment – also, to a special little miracle boy, Rory Leanord and his precious family, Pat, Al and Stewart, for reminding us all of what really matters.

In Australia, my love and appreciation to my old friend, Julie Black & new friends Louise Langdon, Ted and Marguerite Webber, Bill Goodchild with his incredible two-thirds scale model of the *Endeavour*, Riemer Brouwer, Stuart Duncan and my fellow-crew members on the HMB Endeavour Replica, among whom Ian Connop deserves a special mention for providing rare books, factoids and much-needed laughter. Thanks also to Bill Tully at the National Library of Australia, Dr Peter Kuch at the University of New South Wales, Dr. Bill Ward of the famous "lead weight", Bill Richardson for his counterpoint theories, and for the assitance from the team at Trailfinders and their paradisal Bloomfield Lodge, north Queensland.

In Hawaii, the author, CCSU member – and now treasured friend, Ellie Nordyke, welcomed me into her home and her family: Ellie, you're an inspiration! Thanks also to Barbara Dunn at the Hawaiian Historical Society Library and to the world-wide Cookophile Community at *CaptCook@yahoo.com*.

Two remaining sets of people have made fundamental contributions in the lifetime of this book: my friends/agents at Take 3 Management – the wonderful Vicki McIvor & Sara Cameron – and the fabulous team at Ebury Press, especially Hannah MacDonald and Matthew Parker: thanks for your help in turning that original scribbled and sellotaped map of ideas into something more readable. . .

Finally, to my beloved and very long-suffering partner, Al, for helping me (just) keep my sense of humour over the last year and retaining his sense of what's important when my own was lost in books and papers.

Ness Collingridge,
December 2001

*Details from Guillaume le
Testu's map of Jave la Grande*

CONTENTS

Preface   1

Introduction   9

1. Beginnings: James Cook's story   13

2. Beginnings: George Collingridge's story   21

3. A Taste of the Sea *James Cook* 1745   27

4. Italian Lessons *George Collingridge* 1867   31

5. 'Mr Cook's Genius and Capacity' *James Cook* 1755   35

6. 'The Happy Foresight of Mr Collingridge'   52
   George Collingridge 1870

7. The King's Surveyor *James Cook* 1762   59

8. In Search of Paradise *George Collingridge* 1872   64

9. The Surveyor's Art *James Cook* 1763   67

10. Trouble in Paradise *George Collingridge* 1879   77

11. 'To the Southwards'   82

12. Preparations *James Cook* 1768   105

13. The Voyage of the Endeavour *James Cook* 1768   117

14. Tahiti *James Cook* 1769   129

15. The 40th Latitude *James Cook* 1769   143

16. Botany Bay *James Cook* 1770   161

17. Jave La Grande *George Collingridge* 1883   168

18. Shipwreck! *James Cook* 1770   175

19. 'A Calamitous Situation' *James Cook* 1770   188

20. 'The Immortal Banks' England 1771   207

21. The Dieppe Maps *George Collingridge* 1883   223

22. 'Further than Any Other Man' *James Cook* 1772   228

23. The End of The Great Southern Continent   233
    James Cook 1773

24. Terra Australis Cognita *George Collingridge* 1885 258

25. The Dinner Party *James Cook* 1775   265

26. Closing the Loop   287

27. The Final Voyage *James Cook* 1776   290

28. The Secrets of the Maps *George Collingridge* 1895 299

29. Alaska *James Cook* 1778   306

30. Obsession and Betrayal *James Cook* 1779   327

31. Kealakekua Bay, 2001   343

32. The End of Ambition England 1780   347

33. Troublesome George Collingridge & the   352
    Ideas Revolution

34. Heroes, Heretics and The Great Whodunit   361

Select Bibliography   369

Index   371

PREFACE

N THE FLAT LIGHT, it was hard to make out where the water ended and the sky began. The bay lay slumped like a drunk, wedged between an oil refinery and a disregarded shoreline. Graphite tankers littered the horizon while water trickled from the stony streams of the wasteland into the murky sea. Everything was grey; everything was soul-less.

This was Botany Bay, the first landing site of Lieutenant James Cook: explorer, mariner and navigator *extraordinaire*. Two hundred and thirty years ago, the piercing colours of nature had stopped his men in their tracks: everywhere was vibrant, green and lush with diaphanous streams, pink and purple shellfish, black people and strange animals. His men were breathless at the wonders of this alien landscape that unfurled before them. They paused here for seven days, inhaling the blend of woodsmoke from native fires and the intoxicating balm of damp, foreign earth, before pushing on up the eastern coast of this new land that would become Australia.

Two centuries on, would he even recognise the place? He had come in search of discovery: the Great Southern Continent, the *provincia aurea*, mythical land of golden promise. He didn't find it and later, by proving it didn't exist, he smashed the fantasy that had driven men for millennia. Instead, his discoveries founded a new colony for the Great British Empire where men would stamp their footprint on the land and create new myths and fantasies of their own, while the soil nurtured the dreams of the millions who followed.

A century later, George Collingridge, a distant relative, came to that pioneering colony in search of new adventures. His father bade farewell in an emotional letter: 'I hope you find your paradise'; instead he found a continent suspended in artifice, shored-up by legend. His own voyage was in search of the truth behind that legend – and his discoveries brought one of the main pillars for the fragile edifice of colonial identity crashing to the ground. But he found that rewriting history is a dangerous game.

I must have been four, or maybe five years old when my mum brought home the weekly pile of reading books from the library. One of those was about a little girl called Millie Molly Mandy. She used to run things called 'errands' – it was the first time I'd learned the word. But more important than what she did was where she lived. On the inside cover of the book there was a map of Millie Molly Mandy's world: a few streets, some shops and a post office. I was transfixed by that map, etched in red, in child-like hand. It contained another universe, lying waiting to be explored. A secret universe, packed full of promise, and holding its breath for me.

A few years later, for my seventh birthday, my aunt and uncle sent me the book that became the catalyst for my obsession. Called *Peru – Land of the Incas*, it told of an alien civilisation and its fatal clash with Spanish invaders. I learned another new word – 'conquistadors' – men with a passion for discovery, in praise of their God and of their King. And even when the book was closed, my eyes stayed open to those who left the safety of what was known to chase the horizon and near-certain death, for glory, duty – or just for the thrill of it.

I read about Cortés, Columbus, Magellan: those who rewrote the rules and redrew the map of the world – they became my heroes, and my inspiration. Maps became my Bible.

Like most people growing up in Britain, I'd been introduced to James Cook at school. I can still remember the sketchy drawing of his death in my textbook – though it showed him dying a hero's death – hopelessly outnumbered, facing the crowd with resolute bravery, and going down fighting. We were told he'd discovered Australia and died in Hawaii, which made him Very Important and worthy of our study. We copied out his story, drew our own picture, then filed him away in that part of the brain consigned to store all that stuff they tell you at school. I wasn't interested: he wasn't Spanish, had no Latin fire in his belly and hadn't even met an Aztec, let alone an Inca. He certainly didn't count as being a *real* explorer. Cook was English – where was the romance in that?

Then a few years later, tucked away at a museum exhibition on discovery, I saw a line that stilled my heart. En route to the coffee shop, I chanced upon a small display of six laminated boards that told of the life of Captain Cook. I stood and read them, more out of casual curiosity than interest. I told my companion to go ahead and get in the coffee queue while I skimmed the boards. I didn't plan to be long and, in effect, I wasn't. But time and meaning are rarely doled out in equal sizes: those next few minutes were to change the course of my life.

The boards spoke of his journey from lowly beginnings to mighty achievements yet it wasn't so much the public glory that caught my attention; instead, a small paragraph – almost an end-thought – snatched my breath and left me motionless. It read simply, 'Though Cook's public life was filled with glory, his personal life was marked by tragedy. Of his six children, not one survived. His mournful wife outlived him by another fifty years, burning his letters before she died to keep some small vestige of her husband's memory just for her'.

The tragedy of those words tore through my nonchalance. I had dismissed the man from my hall of fame as his story seemed too shiny, too manufactured: James Cook – explorer and discoverer, great sea captain and hero of the British Empire. There had been no grit or strand of raw passion in the well-worn tale, nothing but the blinding gleam of a too-polished icon. But here was the scratch that exposed something of the private soul that lurked beneath the gloss. This friction of public glory and personal grief created that first spark of electricity to bring the man to life; here – just possibly – was a real person, with real emotions and hidden passions. Captain James Cook had me intrigued.

From that one reference, my interest grew. Yet, as I learned more about The Greatest Explorer of All Time, I was almost unaware of the hold that he was developing over me. Before long, I had become something of a Cook Bore. I read anything I could find on the man but the tale was always the same: with quiet control, he coolly conquered the seas, ridding his crews of scurvy and dying a tragic Titan – yet the tragedy and drama always came from the situation rather than the man himself who appeared as a two-dimensional discovering machine. I asked my fellow Cookies, 'Do you think you would have *liked* the man?' and they replied that, yes, they would have respected him … but like him? Without more of a sense of him as a person, that was too hard to say. Scouring the literature, there are plenty of references to him as being genial, he certainly earned the devotion of his men *and* his bosses, he was even known to have cracked a joke or two – but as for the inner world of James Cook, what did we know of that? It was still a blank space on the map.

So I tried to get under his skin, to find what drove him to go 'further than any other man' but he seemed to frustrate me at every turn. Other than his logs and journals, there is relatively little written in his own hand, and much of what exists is related business. Partly, this lack of emotional outpouring was a facet of the times: the eighteenth century wasn't known for baring its soul, particularly if you hailed from the working classes;

what's more, although Cook had received some formal education, he was not a confident writer until relatively late in life, and even then he was never really an easy one. So, in terms of personal papers in his own hand, there was very little to go on.

In terms of official documents, there was thankfully more on offer in terms of quantity, if not illumination. His dealings with the Admiralty are reasonably well-preserved, his journals and logs still survive in their various drafts, and of course there are his numerous published and unpublished maps and charts. Occasionally, more of these turn up in a dusty corner of the archives (the man was nothing if not prolific), sending Cookophiles into a spin. But while ploughing through these went some way towards resuscitating the man behind the myth, the snatch of words from the museum still haunted me: what did we really know of the mind and motivations of James Cook? What drove him to set off into unknown waters in leaky ships with press-ganged crews? What went through his mind, alone at night in his cabin, when his ship floated like a plank of relic driftwood on the dark and distant ocean? These were questions without satisfactory answers and until they could be solved, James Cook would remain a too convenient and silent icon, one that could be manipulated by admirers and enemies. It was time to give the man himself a voice, time to explore the uncharted recesses of the explorer. I employed the stealth tactics of a forensic psychologist: if the primary evidence wasn't there, I'd have to piece together the jigsaw from distant shreds across time and space.

The man himself may remain an enigma, but his public achievements are a national boast. In three epic voyages, Captain Cook discovered more of the Earth's surface than any other man. Not only was he prolific as a seaman, he was also highly acclaimed as a scientist, cartographer and surveyor. He laid down his finds with exactitude, proving beyond all doubt what did and did not exist and forging the new era of scientific navigation that helped jettison some of the romanticism from eighteenth-century thought. Quite simply, James Cook was the greatest explorer in the history of our planet.

Yet underneath the plaudits lies an untold story as remarkable as any of his achievements. In the rigid hierarchy of eighteenth-century society where your status was cast at birth, this farm labourer's son rose to join the monarch on the face of the world's banknotes. Renowned on land as the Great Explorer, at sea he was loved by his men, many of whom never left his command. He conquered scurvy (albeit unwittingly), instilled a sense of honour in his crews and in turn won their respect. In all the years of his command, he rarely lost a man through preventable disease or accident.

But as significant as all his discoveries was his attitude towards the indigenous groups he met. Defying the colonial zeal of the day, he treated them with a decency that shattered all convention – and taught his men to do the same.

This is the real legacy of James Cook, the enlightened explorer. He was a true pioneer – socially, geographically and culturally. His principles were instilled in those who travelled with him, who themselves went on to chart new lands and discover new peoples. In a world embittered by conflict and xenophobia, Cook's philosophy remains as valuable today as it was two hundred years ago.

Yet Cook was not the typical hero of his day. He didn't fit in eighteenth-century society – and it was this 'edginess' that captured my attention. What's more, he *knew* he didn't fit in and it was this feeling of being an outsider, a loner, which helped propel him beyond the horizon. Too big for life on the land, he created his own world on board his ship – a world that he could control – and then he set sail, leaving his past, his family and his grief behind him. Each time he returned, he had remoulded himself, drawing on his reading, his conversations and his experiences, so that he changed himself as much as he changed the map of the world. But what use is finding something new if no one else gets to hear of it? To become a hero, you need to return – and Cook needed his homeland as much as Britain needed its icon.

This is the real story of Captain James Cook – and the ultimate tragedy of his violent death. His nemesis came when he could no longer control his world; from the moment he fell face down in the foaming waters of the Hawaiian shoreline, his reputation was picked up and moulded by others pursuing their own agendas so that he became both hero and villain. The story of Cook is really as much about how we manipulate history as it is about the man who set out to sail the oceans in the name of science and discovery. It's a tale of ambition, friction and the journeys we make as individuals and nations.

While it's easy to nod approvingly at his achievements, it takes a certain imaginative leap to appreciate just how truly remarkable they were at the time. Most of today's Earth has already been discovered, save the odd cave system, deep ocean trench or jungle interior. Satellites can peer with steely resolution into the dark recesses of virgin forest, turning up a coca plantation where humans have allegedly feared to tread. And for the modern explorer, a hand-held Global Positioning System is always there to spew out co-ordinates, while phones and radios can alert the rescue plane in case of accidents, danger or running out of Kendal Mint Cake. In today's world, you're never really alone like Cook was.

Getting inside the mind of an eighteenth-century adventurer therefore becomes a challenge in itself. It's necessary to imagine setting off into vast oceans of nothingness, armed with half-drawn maps that tail off into blank spaces. The nearest parallel in terms of modern explorers would be men like Yuri Gagarin or the American moon-landing team: they were launched in unproven technology into the darkness of a new and mapless world, but they had the back-up of teams of scientists.

I was once invited to Russia's Star City where I asked a group of cosmonauts what it was like to go into space. Their eyes glazed over, came their simple reply: 'You can never understand unless you've been there!' While it wasn't exactly the answer I was looking for, it summed up the gulf between us mortals and those who set their goals beyond the known horizon. No, they said, they were not scared – they had a job to do and, if anything, were excited. I should not have expected them to react how I would; after all, they were highly-trained alchemists, turning hot adrenaline into cool action and, while I would have been excited to be alongside them on the launchpad, I know my dominant emotion would have been of fear.

Yet even those who have explored the universe cannot recreate the enormity of what the early explorers faced: in theory at least, today's space adventurers can always communicate with home. When Cook was killed at Kealakekua Bay in Hawaii, it took eleven months for the letter containing news of his death to come across northern Europe to reach first the Admiralty, and only then his widow.

The odds of dying on a US space mission are less than 3 in 100; scroll back to the 1700s, and the chances you'd never make it home from your voyage of discovery were more than 50:50. Up to a half of all sailors on known sea routes could die of disease, drunkenness or drowning before the ship made it home again, if it made it back at all, hence the need for vast quantities of so-called 'pressed' labour – men and boys scooped off the streets or out of the taverns and bundled onto a departing ship to make up the numbers. These men were untrained, unfit and presumably unhappy at their fate – hardly the highly-skilled teams that NASA puts together.

So here we have James Cook, setting out into the unknown with a rag-bag of crew, a posse of gentlemen scientists who know nothing of the sea, and a ship that's barely a hundred feet long. Put yourself in his sea boots: what on earth made him do it, not once but three times; what made him want to discover more of this earth than any other man, to go further than anyone before him, or perhaps as far as it is possible to go? There may not be much left to discover in the way of land, but there was plenty in his mindset and motive to propel me.

My own journey of discovery was in search of James Cook the man; it was a journey that would take me twelve thousand miles and five hundred years, far out of my comfort zone of maps and into the jungle of history. The academic in me made me obsessed with fact; the little girl remained obsessed by passion. I was swamped by dates, ashamed by my ignorance and astounded by the grip that one man had on so many people. I rolled into the houses of those who had spent their lives studying navigation, cartography or even the man himself and brazenly exclaimed, 'Tell me about James Cook!' – but without exception, everyone did. Two hundred years have failed to erase his name from the meme of western civilisation, and – though some hailed him hero and others heretic – every single person I spoke to recognised his place in world history.

Then, as my research progressed, infilling markers like the developing British Empire, the rising power of the Navy and the growing passion for science, I slammed headfirst into another man for whom the personal and public had collided – but this time, I was more than just observer: our collision was brutal and highly emotive. In an instant, my world up-ended. This man was my distant cousin George – another explorer, though like me he had made his discoveries in books and ancient maps. In tracing his remarkable passage, I toured once more through the familiar atmospheres of passion and ambition, the voids of knowledge and the black holes of truth. The more I learned, the more he became the foil to Cook's trajectory – the night sky to Cook's rising star. Now, in place of one man and one story, there were two, with me sandwiched uncomfortably in between – and, where we should have been separated by geography, history and place in society, our stories were now fused into one – a tale of obsession and betrayal in the New World.

Portuguese caravel by George Collingridge, from
The First Discovery of Australia, *1895*

INTRODUCTION

HE STORY OF the three of us – James, George and me – starts calmly enough at four o'clock in Oxford on a cold, spring afternoon. I'd arrived breathless at the School of Geography library, my bicycle still caked in mud from the river where I'd been rowing less than half an hour before. Ditching the bike against the railings, I adjusted my sprint to a purposeful stride, burst through the doors of the library, then – digging out my reading list – I headed straight for the catalogue. This was the other side of being a student: my essay was due the next morning and I hadn't read a single book.

I was meant to be looking up references on fossil fuels and climate change. The list was long, I was tired, impatient and hungry, the light was fading and the library was about to close. 'Coleman, Coles, Coleton', no sign of the book I was after. A restless line was building up behind me as I flicked scowlingly through the pile of cards. 'Collard, Collier, Collingridge'. Collingridge? No one in our rather large, extended family had written anything that I was aware of. But there it was, in black and white, albeit now faded to a sepia brown: 'Collingridge, George: The Discovery of Australia, 1895 (Outsized)'.

Forgetting my essay, I left the queue and headed to the 'outsized' shelves. And there it was – slumped wearily against a pile of altogether smarter books. I carefully pulled it out. The book itself was large and heavy with a dusty cover the colour of ox-blood and indented gold writing. It looked like it had lain there for a thousand years and wouldn't mind resting for a few thousand more. I laid it flat on the large, leather-topped table, opened the front cover and entered another world.

There was plate after plate of exquisitely drawn maps, interleaved with fine tissue and old-fashioned print, detailing some long and involved story of Pacific pioneers. As I leafed through the introduction, the spine yawned and stretched sleepily. Carefully, I prised open each grudging page, stunned by what was in front of me. Here was the work of another geographer, another Collingridge, but from an altogether different time and place.

Magical hand-drawn maps unfurled before my eyes, taking me back to the story-books of my childhood; each chapter began with an illumination that almost rivalled the *Book of Kells*. Taking a closer look, the scope of its history was broad indeed, stretching from Ptolemy and his ancient though enduring view of the world, through to dense pages on Magellan and my hero, James Cook. Reading this last name made me smile – to think that this strange Collingridge had the same interests as me! But by now the library was preparing to close and I didn't have time to do much beyond flicking through the pages laden with text and maps; although my curiosity had been aroused, I certainly hadn't absorbed the enormity of what lay before me. For me, it was just a beautiful book about early Australia by a Collingridge who – by some Grand Coincidence – was also a geographer.

I heaved the book shut and sat for a moment in quiet reverence. Collingridges are few and far between – they are usually connected. So here we were, dozing ancestor and distant descendant, resting on a table in the school of Geography. I filed George Collingridge under 'Interesting Miscellaneous'. I had found my box of delights.

Ten years on, the memory of that book would still be with me.

I'd been living out of a suitcase for years, had had only two days off in over two months, was wrung out and exhausted and badly needed a holiday. With that delicious prospect in mind, I collapsed into the arms of my airline seat for six weeks Down Under. I think I slept the whole way there – certainly, when I staggered out of Sydney airport, the kiss of warm air and the chirruping frogs did little to rouse me from my daze. It took until morning when I woke in a strange hotel for me finally to realise that I'd arrived.

Like a child opening her first chocolate wrapper, I inhaled the excitement of what lay ahead: of course I would dig up more on the mysterious George but he was really just tangential to the whole exercise; I was here to pursue a private passion to follow in the footsteps of Captain James Cook, from Botany Bay, via New Zealand to Hawaii.

My first port of call was the Maritime Museum in Sydney's Darling Harbour. Here, I spent days wandering through the exhibits, absorbing the context of the voyage of the *Endeavour*. I learned the structure of who discovered what and when, from the accidental discoveries of the Dutch to their planned forays around the coast; I traced the piratical adventures of the English buccaneer, William Dampier, slowly building up the jigsaw of continental form – and then revelled in the drama of Cook's own explorations along the dangerous eastern seaboard. And when my head was too full of facts, I relaxed among the books and postcards in the museum shop.

As I meandered through the merchandise on the last day of my visit, I picked up a book on the history of Australia, flicking through the index for the section on James Cook. I scanned through the list of 'C's, as I had done more than ten years before in the closing minutes of the University Library. I never got as far as 'Cook', for there – just above – was his name in black and white: Collingridge, George – p182.

The sales assistants around me were tidying the shelves, closing up the till, pulling down the shutters while my eyes scanned the pages for George's name; and then came the lines that transformed my quest:

> Although he received much vitriol at the time, it seems George Collingridge experienced a terrible injustice; in fact, his theories on the discovery of Australia are now gaining widespread acceptance.

Much vitriol? For what? What 'terrible injustice' had cast George as a wronged man? And more worryingly – if official history claimed that Cook discovered the east coast of Australia, what had George said about the man who had brought me ten thousand miles to follow in his track? It was one thing to discover an interesting ancestor; it was quite another matter when that ancestor turned troublesome.

The two room cottage at Marton in Cleveland where
James Cook was born, 27 October 1728

1
BEGINNINGS: JAMES'S STORY

HERE WAS NOTHING in his humble birth to indicate James Cook would rise to be a national, even international icon. In fact, all the omens pointed towards quite the opposite – a life of grinding drudgery and social obscurity where the only record of his name would be in the births and deaths pages of the parish register. He was born on 27 October, 1728 – a time when men were meant to know their place and, for the young James, that place was among the rural labouring classes.

At the top of the social pyramid, King George II had just replaced his father on the throne, Purcell, Bach and Handel were the height of fashion and ladies' crinolines had reached a ridiculous six feet in diameter. England was thus ruled by a German Protestant, Scotland had joined an uneasy union with England (though many on both sides of the border would have preferred a catholic Stuart King to be the British monarch); a Dane – Vitus Jonassen Bering – had just discovered the Strait between Asia and America; Europe was finally at peace after decades of war, and a third of the world that we know today was missing from the map.

But all of that would have been irrelevant to the Cooks in their small, clay cottage in the farming village of Marton. Their lives were ruled by sunrise and sunset, oppressive poverty and the boss's word. James's parents were of good working stock: his father – also James – was a Scottish day labourer from Ednam, near Kelso. Early biographers wrote that when James senior had left Scotland to travel south in search of work, his mother had exclaimed, 'May God give you Grace!' Whether true or not, it makes for a romantic legend: arriving in Yorkshire, he had fallen in love with Grace Pace, who hailed from the nearby village of Thornaby, and they were happily married for the next forty years.

After marrying in Stainton-in-Cleveland in 1725, the couple moved to Marton in Cleveland where James senior found work as a labourer on Mr

Mewburn's farm and it was here, in a tiny, dark, two-roomed clay cottage, that James junior was born. He was the second of eight children, of whom four would not make it to adulthood. As this fair-haired babe grew into a tall, strong child, his world consisted of not causing any bother to his continually pregnant mother, running errands in his bare feet and helping his father with the animals. While this did not necessarily render him a member of farming community for life – William Dampier, the English pirate-explorer who blazed a trail in the Southern Seas in the dying years of the 1600s, had had a similar upbringing – the chances of breaking out of the mould were slim. Under normal circumstances, the closest young James would have ever come to the sea would have been watching the masts of the sailing ships on the River Tees which, at that time, flowed just three miles away. However, his parents had aspirations for their children; recognising that James was bright, they sent him to learn his alphabet with Mrs Walker, whose husband farmed Marton Grange. According to the later reports by the Walkers, this was given in exchange for errands and help around the farm; whatever the payment, it was the start of a life-long passion for learning that shaped his character and his future. Moreover, it was perhaps the earliest suggestion that there was something about the boy that marked him out as special.

When James was eight, his father won promotion to a job managing Aireyholme Farm which was owned at that time by Thomas Skottowe, the Lord of the Manor, a few miles away in the village of Great Ayton. By all accounts, the years his son spent here were happy ones: although a few miles out of the village itself, their new home was larger and more comfortable and, perhaps best of all for the young James, it lay in the lea of the magnificent Roseberry Topping. This hill is the king of local landmarks – the largest peak in Yorkshire's North Riding, rising sharply and symmetrically from the gently rolling green of the landscape into a bold conical spire. The perfect balance of the hill is only upset at the summit, now as crooked as a hooked nose. Folk say this damage is recent and man-made, the result of hundreds of years of working layers of ore embedded in the hill. This hill became James's playground in the rare hours he had away from his work, and tales from his contemporaries suggest he was as happy here in company as on his own.

Over two hundred and fifty years on, that hill became the signal that I had reached Cook Country. I was *en route* to the former village of Marton to visit James's birth-place, long since absorbed into the new town – and now metropolis – of Middlesbrough. Finding Marton is no mean feat: there is little to betray its rural origins beyond the stately grounds at next-door Ormsby Hall and there is even less trace of the cottage where Cook was born, let alone a blue plaque gracing its façade. The cottage was demolished in 1786 by Major Rudd to make way for an impressive hall and 'pleasure grounds'. Rudd was not totally blind to the significance of the site – he planted a willow tree on site where the cottage had stood. However, like the Cooks' cottage, his stately home did not have a long future either: just fifty years later, it was gutted by fire then it, too, had to be demolished.

Next on the land was the wealthy ironmaster, Henry Bolckow who had made his fortune treading the same path as the inventors and entrepreneurs James Watt and Matthew Boulton (the latter was born a few days before Cook and would go on to design the commemorative medals for his Second Voyage). Bolckow built the state-of-the-art Marton Hall in the mid-nineteenth century, complete with hot running water pumped from the nearby boiler-house. Again, Cook's name lived on: to mark the spot where baby James made his first journey into the world he erected a huge granite vase and, ironically, it is the vase not the Hall which survives today. At his death, Bolckow gifted the grounds to the new industrial town of Middlesbrough and today they comprise the beautiful Stewart Park, a 'rare breeds' zoo and the new Captain Cook Birthplace Museum which celebrates the life of the explorer *extraordinaire*. The little church nearby still holds the registration of young James's birth, but beyond that, there is little to tie his spirit to the area.

Not so Great Ayton: there, rows of terraced houses, shops and stone cottages jumble together, accreting in layers of historical styles that form a kind of architectural geology; the streets are patently not designed for cars, and the pace of life is barely more than a gentle amble. Here, the young James Cook is everywhere – in the buildings, in the sights and sounds of the village and in the landscape's geography. I picnicked on the village green in the shadow of a statue of the young Cook who would still, no doubt, feel at home here today. So strong is the feeling of yesteryear that when a horse and carriage trotted by, I hardly noticed: the clacking of hooves on ancient roads seemed the most natural thing in the world.

In fact, very little has changed since the 1730s: Aireyholme Farm where James senior became the bailiff is still in operation, some of the key characters' houses are family homes to this day, and the beautiful twelfth-century All Saints Church where the Cooks worshipped still stands, though now a memorial stone for Grace and James senior lies quietly in the churchyard.

On the other side of the village, a few miles out, lies Roseberry Topping. Climbing up its steep sides, it is easy to see why he loved it so much: the huddled buildings of the village below glisten like fresh-laid eggs in an ants' nest. Here, the blustery wind becomes your playmate, nudging you into an endless game of tag – the perfect place for a boy who rarely got time to himself. It was probably his childhood forays up this hill that set the pattern for the years of exploration to come: whenever he arrived in foreign parts, one of his first actions would be to climb to the top of the nearest peak, look down at the lie of the land and take his bearings. The hill can be a bleak and lonely place at times and, even on a warm summer's day, there is still an edge in the wind that reminds one of nature's potency. The fact he chose to spend his free time in this barren isolation shows a self-reliance and a freedom of thought that would be alien to most small boys. It gives a strong hint, too, that he was happier striking out into a new world – a world according to his rules and observations – than occupying the known world of others.

One day, the young James led a group of boys to the summit of the hill where he could name every village and hamlet in the vista below. When it came to going back down again, the boys elected to go one way but James was adamant about going the other. What's more, he would not only go down *his* way but he would be first to reach the bottom! Even when all the boys went the other way, he continued on his path with the characteristic single-mindedness and determination that would mark him out for life. This was typical of young James – but what happened next taught him that exploring alone was not without its dangers. He saw a jackdaw flying into a nest wedged in a crack in the rock and, following it up the crag, he grabbed on to a sapling, pulled himself up to the nest, collected some of its eggs which he put in his cap, then he put the cap in his teeth and began to climb back down. However, this proved rather more dangerous than he had imagined: the sapling he was holding on to suddenly began to come loose from the rocks and he slid perilously down the crag. Luckily, he was not alone on the hill: a soldier on watch for signs of Jacobite invasion from Scotland heard the cry and Cook was rescued, somewhat chastened no doubt, but allegedly having lost none of his courage or adventurous spirit.

More tales from this time allude to his developing strength of mind, although all of them fit a little too nicely into the folk legend surrounding the young explorer to be trusted as pure fact. But romanticised or not, there is probably an essence of truth in some of them that makes them worth adding into the story of his childhood. For example, John Graves in his 1808 *History of Cleveland* paints an interesting picture of the boy who would change the face of the globe:

It appears that he was never much regarded by the other boys … and was generally left behind in their juvenile excursions; a circumstance which can only be attributed to his steady adherence to his own plans and schemes, never giving way to the *contre-projets* of his associates. This, instead of conciliating their regard, naturally rendered them averse from his company. It has been asserted by those who know him at this early period in his life, that he had such an obstinate and sturdy way of his own as made him sometimes appear in an unpleasant light; notwithstanding which, there was something in his manners and deportment, which attracted the reverence and respect of his companions.

James senior was by now impressing his employer, Thomas Skottowe, with the quality of his work – but it was not only the father who caught the Lord of the Manor's eye. Skottowe was a wealthy man – a member of the gentry rather than a yeoman-farmer – and he no doubt saw it as his duty to scatter largesse amongst the villagers where he could. Great Ayton also boasted a rare amenity in the villages of the day – a sometime charity/sometime fee-paying or 'petty' school with space for twenty to thirty pupils, all taught by a single master. This had been established as far back as 1704, partly to teach Christian principles and obedience to the working classes and partly, perhaps, in reaction to the increasing popularity of Quakerism. This had been given a boost by the Toleration Act of 1689 which removed penalties to members of non-conformist religions and they were now growing to the extent that they were worrying traditional Christians who saw them as seducing believers away from the English Church. Of all these 'new' types of faith, Quakerism had taken the strongest hold in the north of England and by the time the Cooks moved into the village, it was well-established in Great Ayton. Not only that but it also had a high-profile sympathiser there — Thomas Skottowe, the Lord of the Manor.

Skottowe was a regular member of the Church of England – a memorial to him graces the wall of the ancient All Saints chapel in the village. However, he was also a non-conformist and even had a small non-conformist chapel at his home in Ayton Hall; this suggests that he was progressive in his ideas as well as his religion – perhaps progressive enough to think outside the rigid confines of the eighteenth-century society when it came to education and self-improvement. It is also pertinent that, although the Cooks certainly worshipped at All Saints, over recent years historians have highlighted their Quaker links, with the suggestion that Grace Pace may have come from a Quaker family. Certainly, the future career of James was given a firm footing by the close-knit members of this faith but whether it was a religious kinship or like-mindedness, a recognition that 'there was a something' in the young boy that warranted investment, or most likely a combination of the two, Thomas Skottowe decided to pay the penny a week for him to attend the Great Ayton school.

Here, he learned reading, writing, arithmetic and, of course, the catechism – most probably by rote with strict discipline and little in the way of fun. It may also have been at school where he came across the story of Robinson Crusoe, published in 1719–22, written by another non-conformist, Daniel Defoe. This immensely popular story capitalised upon and further stimulated the public's hunger for information about the exotic lands across far-off oceans; it would certainly have whetted a young boy's appetite for travel and adventure. Other reports from his contemporaries in the village allege that he was more interested in sums than literature, having a 'remarkable facility in the science of numbers'; this was soon borne out by his first job as a shop-boy and, later still, his talent for surveys and navigation. However, there is no indication that he was a shining genius, even though he acquired this reputation within a few years of joining the Navy. For the meantime, he clearly kept his head down and studied as hard as any young boy would, when forced to sit still in a cold, dark schoolroom, learning enough to give him a sound platform for his real education – a self-taught one – in future years.

From Great Ayton's marriage records, it seems that few of the village's girls were educated out of illiteracy – most brides signed their names with a cross, making it likely that the school was mainly 'boys only'. There is also no evidence that any of James's brothers attended the school, so he must have been clever enough and lucky enough to have caught the attention of the benevolent Mr Skottowe. Or perhaps not: one intriguing suggestion coming from the village of Great Ayton is that Thomas Skottowe might not have been quite as altruistic as he first looked. With a nod and a wink, I was told to look closely at the portrait of Cook compared with the portrait of Thomas Skottowe's son, John, of roughly the same age. John went on to become Governor of St Helena and a fine seaman in his own right, aided by the connections of his father but, then again, Skottowe also used his connections with the Admiralty to further Cook's career. Was it possible that Cook was Skottowe's son? The dates would seem to cast doubt on the whisper: James had spent his first eight years in the village of Marton but then his father must have known Skottowe before the move in order to get the job. James senior had stood out enough to capture his future boss's attention – had Grace Cook done the same? If she was a Quaker, this would be most unlikely – and it is even less likely that James senior would move closer to the source of marital strife. Meanwhile, the portraits show two strongly-featured men, both from the same village – two men not dissimilar in appearance.

For the next four years, James was a regular attendee of the school, probably under the tutelage of a William Rowland. Rowland had been granted an archbishop's licence in 1738 to teach a 'petty' school in Great Ayton, though from the parish records he appears to have been living in the village for some years before that. There is a striking similarity in the copperplate handwriting of both Cook and Rowland, exhibited alongside each other at the Captain Cook Schoolroom Museum that now occupies the site where young James would have received his lessons.

Cook finished school, aged twelve, to help his father on the farm. Although he barely refers back to his Great Ayton days in the surviving papers and records, there were some legacies from his rural upbringing. When he made his travels in later life, he would take a healthy supply of farm animals and seeds with him which he would help establish in the new lands he visited for the benefit of the natives and returning sailors. The privations of his early life also stood him in good stead with Navy food – he could stomach even the poorest fare and was famous for his open mind when it came to experimenting with the strange local produce they encountered en route. But beyond these, he was no rose-tinted romantic and never one for looking back; childhood was just a necessary stepping-stone onwards and upwards.

It was not just the young James who was ready to move on; the countryside itself was changing. By the middle of the eighteenth century, the industrial revolution was getting underway, bringing new develop-ments in terms of technology, employment and social confidence. While these were most visible in the emerging towns and cities, they also transformed much of the British countryside. Rural villages now sported a whole host of industries and for those with the brains and the ambition – and of course the right connections – it was occasionally possible to break the mould of your parents' lives. As for the young James, he was about to take a step that would take him off the farm forever.

Plaque in the 'Collingridge' church

2
BEGINNINGS: GEORGE COLLINGRIDGE'S STORY

EORGE'S STORY could not start more differently than Cook's. One hundred and nineteen years after the great explorer was born in Marton, 150 miles away to the southwest and a million miles in terms of his social standing, George Alphonse Collingridge de Tourcey was born in the small, rural village of Godington in Oxfordshire. His parents, William Collingridge and Louisa Maguire, had met in the nearby village of Hethe, where her cousin, Alfred Maguire, was the first Catholic priest in the new chapel. This had been part funded a few years earlier by the extremely religious and wealthy Collingridge family, whose names and portraits adorn the stained-glass windows and fill the graveyard to this day.

A damp mist hung in the air. At first, I couldn't see the church, so heavily was it cloaked by the tall, dark hedges and over-hanging trees, and I drove past several times before finally spying a few gravestones. This discretion would have been essential in the days of religious strife but now its presence is sewn into the ancient fabric of the village. Entering the churchyard was like entering the *Secret Garden*: the chapel that stood before me was small and neat with long stained-glass windows reaching down the sandstone walls. I walked through the long, wet grass: the graveyard was positively groaning with dead Collingridges, their stones in a proud line (the older ones developing a decided list to starboard). I still get a shock to see my name written down when it doesn't relate to either me or my immediate family, yet here there were rows upon rows of us, with first names repeated through successive generations. So much for a secret garden – this was a secret history that I knew nothing about. I hastened towards the church.

Ringing the doorbell, I waited rather sheepishly on the doorstep of the adjoining manse, planning my spiel about my quest to seek out my ancestors. The door opened and a tall, slim, white-haired man in a dog-collar looked at me with raised eyebrows.

I began to explain who I was but before I got very far, he interrupted, 'You're not another one of *those*, are you?!' With a smile almost too mischievous for a priest, he feigned a heavy sigh and told me to wait while he got the key to the church door.

As he disappeared into the darkness of the hall, I stood there completely fazed: was our family really that infamous here? Moments later, he reappeared and before heading back into the manse gave me a quick lesson in how to jiggle the key in the lock. As the door swung open and the cold air enveloped me in its stillness I had my answer: I stepped inside into a celebration of Collingridge Piety – as far as I was concerned, an oxymoron if ever there was one, and one as conflicting as my emotions. The place was both alien and intensely familiar: I've never met a Collingridge that I haven't known all my life, yet here they were on walls, plaques, stones and windows. The whole place was heaving with Collingridge ghosts. Wandering around, it was all too much to absorb: strange saints, strange symbols and even stranger relatives.

Collingridge is an old and well-documented name, with records dating back as far as the early 1400s. Our antecedents have links even further back to Bancho, Thane of Lochaber, and to the Normans of William the Conqueror. As with most old English families, true blue blurs into French navy the further back you go, though some have claimed connection with the ancient kings of Scotland and Ireland. More surprising than these grandiloquent claims are tales linking us to Sir James Tyrell – the alleged murderer of the Princes in the Tower for which he was beheaded in 1502, and to the explorer, Sir Richard Burton, the first white man to penetrate Mecca. Whatever the truth on that score, it seems the Collingridges have never shied away from exploration and drama; rather fittingly, one version of our coat of arms carries the legend, 'Dum Micat Sol' – 'While the sun shines!'. Although it rarely seems to have done us much good, the spirit of adventure appears to flow deep in our veins. But something had happened in the eighteenth century that caused a break in the records – and by the time the family reappears, one family had spawned seven branches, all living within a few miles of each other but with different religions and different future paths. My side had lost their riches, been forced to convert to the Protestant faith and were now living in Finmere and Tingewick while George's had stayed wealthy, Catholic and around Godington. We knew the other sides existed; we had even heard of the Collingridge church, but each branch had developed in silent parallel. Until now.

George's mother, Louisa Maguire, had come to Hethe Church to visit her priestly cousin but instead found him fencing with a fierce-looking opponent. Looking first at her cousin, then at his dashing young combatant, she took refuge behind James, declaring a little too confidently that the Church would protect her; as it turned out, her faith was not misplaced: she ended up marrying James's friend, William, and they were blessed with five children – Charles (who himself became a priest), then Alfred, George, Arthur and Mary (all of whom became artists).

They moved into neighbouring Godington, where the large, stately farm which became their family home still stands, tucked away at the end of what's more accurately now a hamlet, surrounded by a duck-filled moat and acres of rolling fields – a scene of bucolic bliss. The house itself is grand in that quiet, very English kind of way – an assemblage of substantial buildings, pink plaster, black beams and Cotswold stone, built over different ages and then adjoined. A secret underground tunnel connects the house to a tiny nearby church, which in its time has been either Catholic or Church of England, depending on the religious affiliations of the more powerful local families.

George was William and Louisa's third child, born on 29 October, 1847 – 119 years after the birth of James Cook and during a time of deep change across Europe, particularly for Catholics. The Irish Potato Famine had wreaked huge devastation; France, Italy, Hungary and Germany were working up to revolutions and Marx and Engels were writing the first Communist Manifesto. Meanwhile Britain was more settled: Turner was the rising star in the world of art and the Brontë sisters published *Jane Eyre* and *Wuthering Heights*. In theory at least, Catholic emancipation was well underway. Yet other troubles beset the Collingridges: within three years, the family were forced to leave their home – according to family legend – after an unsuccessful law-suit against the Duke of Buckingham, with whom they were involved in a land dispute. The Duke had run up thousands of pounds' worth of debt from high living and sought to reclaim this by demanding back-payments for lands allegedly his. William and Louisa challenged that they held any such lands, but lost the case and their home as a result. On 21 September, 1850, a notice was published in the *Bucks Herald* by William's solicitors, regretfully announcing an auction of his 'extensive and highly bred cow stock' along with his sheep, horses, pigs, crops and agricultural instruments. The family left farming for good and moved to London.

Three years and two more children later, William and Louisa clearly hadn't settled into urban life and so made the radical decision to emigrate to France. This was technically illegal at the time – British children were forbidden from receiving a Catholic education, though naturally this law was impossible to police. They arrived in Paris in late autumn and the boys were signed into Mr Dummond's Private School, near to the Arc de Triomphe. By now George had developed into a spirited boy of six, with a sense of high drama and the good humour that would stay with him all of his life. One of his earliest recollections of the time was watching the French soldiers pass under the Arc de Triomphe on their return from the Crimea – a sight to widen the eyes of any small child with its colour and pageantry, discipline and honour, sweeping past to the rhythmic crunch of their marching boots. Only later would he learn that the reality of war was far from glorious.

An account appeared in the press the following year of a fire which had terminated Mr Drummond's Educational Establishment. It gives an early indication that George was no ordinary boy:

> The boys, surrounding the flaming Ecole, were crying out, 'L'anglais va être brulé!' ['The English boy is going to be burnt!']. But L'Anglais was quietly taking his hat off the peg – where somebody had placed it beyond his reach – standing on a chair which he had procured in order to reach it. By this time the fire had burnt a lot of the other hats and had extended to the wooden stairs, so that when L'Anglais arrived at the top landing the flames were escaping through the steps in front of him – the only exit from the upper storey. Mr Drummond stood at the foot of the stairs, waiting for L'Anglais to put in an appearance if he was ever coming. Catching sight of him through the dense smoke and flames, he called out to him to jump, which L'Anglais did, and was caught in Mr Dummond's powerful grasp.

Other reports suggest some worryingly familiar character traits: a rampant imagination, deep-rooted artistic nature, a certain fondness for romantic missions and a rather less than focussed approach to his work. If these can be encoded in a gene, then it still flows though Collingridge blood today, being both our strength and our fatal flaw. Piecing together the facts of George's life was like seeing the traits of my own family rolled into one. At times, it was astounding to see the parallels, and at other times, deeply unnerving.

The young British émigré managed to surpass himself in his studies, going on to the Pension Petit Jesuit School in Vaugirard and finally to the Latin Quarter as a student at Académie des Beaux-Arts in Paris. Here, he began studying architecture under Viollet le Duc, life-drawing with Chapon and landscape painting with Harpignies, a member of the Corot school. With typical fervour, George fell in love with Corot's work and boldly sought him out to see if he would accept him as a pupil. Despite the fact the great master generally refused to teach, he could not withstand the charms and persistence of the young *Anglais*: George would not take no for an answer. Finally, Corot, having taken a reciprocal interest in George's work and finding the young man to his liking, granted the rare favour of inviting him to watch him paint.

As the relationship grew, they began taking excursions together into the countryside to observe the landscapes and discuss the importance of nature *in situ* – something Corot summed up as taking 'a bath of nature', in the twilight after sunset (*'entre chien et loup'*). The experience was clearly profound: a quarter of a century on, a reviewer of Collingridge's work remarked that 'he was the first, and is probably the only artist still to perceive and to portray that marvellous, delicate, lace-like fringe which the eucalyptus-clothed mountain ridge makes against the dying light of the sky'. George was passionate about landscape painting for the rest of his life.

However, the young artist's real talent lay in the popular art of wood-engraving. This was the period before photography had taken off and every printed illustration had to come from an engraved block which would then be sent to the printing press. The work was immensely finicky, time-consuming – and lucrative. Six months after signing up for lessons with the master engraver Horcholle, he was supplying local and national newspapers and earning more than his master! But just as George was finding his feet as a commercial artist, European politics turned his world upside down.

By the late 1860s, Garibaldi's fight to unify Italy as a republic was well under way; for the Collingridges, this became a threat against the Pope and therefore a threat against their faith. Alfred, the second oldest of the Collingridge boys, had already signed up as a Papal Zouave to defend the honour of Rome, and George – an impassioned young man of twenty – resolved to follow suit. Casting off his aesthetic ambitions for the mantle of Catholic fervour – and swapping his £10 a week illustrator's wage for a soldier's pay of under a penny a day – he went off to Italy to fight against Garibaldi.

APRIL 1767.

Diftances of ☽'s Center from ☉, and from Stars weft of her

Days.	Stars Names.	12 Hours.			15 Hours.			18 Hours.			21 Hours.		
		°	′	″	°	′	″	°	′	″	°	′	″
1		40.	59.	11	42.	34.	44	44.	9.	51	45.	44.	35
2		53.	32.	7	55.	4.	24	56.	36.	16	58.	7.	45
3		65.	39.	18	67.	8.	27	68.	37.	14	70.	5.	39
4	The Sun.	77.	22.	36	78.	48.	58	80.	15.	1	81.	40.	46
5		88.	45.	20	90.	9.	27	91.	33.	21	92.	57.	0
6		99.	52.	6	101.	14.	34	102.	36.	52	103.	59.	1
7		110.	47.	42	112.	9.	6	113.	30.	25	114.	51.	40
6	Aldebaran	50.	36.	10	52.	4.	5	53.	31.	57	54.	59.	44
7		62.	17.	43	63.	45.	10	65.	12.	34	66.	39.	57
8	Pollux.	31.	25.	48	32.	53.	11	34.	20.	40	35.	48.	12
9		43.	7.	5	44.	35.	4	46.	3.	8	47.	31.	15
10		17.	51.	57	19.	20.	36	20.	49.	26	22.	18.	27
11		29.	45.	36	31.	15.	26	32.	45.	26	34.	15.	35
12	Regulus.	41.	48.	49	43.	19.	55	44.	51.	10	46.	22.	35
13		54.	2.	11	55.	34.	36	57.	7.	12	58.	39.	59
14		66.	26.	28	68.	0.	18	69.	34.	20	71.	8.	33
15		25.	4.	34	26.	39.	23	28.	14.	26	29.	49.	44
16	Spica ♍	37.	49.	37	39.	26.	14	41.	3.	5	42.	40.	8
17		50.	48.	40	52.	26.	59	54.	5.	31	55.	44.	15
18		64.	1.	2	65.	41.	3	67.	21.	18	69.	1.	48
19		31.	37.	14	33.	19.	7	35.	1.	13	36.	43.	32
20	Antares.	45.	18.	29	47.	2.	10	48.	46.	5	50.	30.	12
21		59.	14.	6	60.	59.	31	62.	45.	11	64.	31.	2
22		73.	23.	37	75.	10.	43	76.	58.	2	78.	45.	31
23	β Capri-	33.	17.	26	35.	4.	38	36.	52.	4	38.	39.	45
24	corni.	47.	41.	9	49.	29.	53	51.	18.	44	53.	7.	40
25	α Aquilæ.	65.	57.	35	67.	29.	54	69.	2.	36	70.	35.	39
26		78.	24.	51	79.	59.	9	81.	33.	29	83.	7.	45

Lunar distance tables from the Nautical Almanac, 1767

3

A TASTE OF THE SEA

James Cook 1745

ROUND TWELVE miles from the village of Great Ayton lies the small fishing village of Staithes – a jumble of terraces, narrow lanes and shops, tumbling down the gorge of Staithes Beck in ramshackle style towards the sea. Its location made it perfect for two lucrative sources of income – fishing and smuggling, despite the best efforts of the officers from Customs and Excise. But man is no match for geography: the twin headlands of shale and ironstone cliffs cup the community in their hands, keeping the whole affair almost hidden from the sloping moors that lead to it, let alone from the outside world. Staithes has little need for the land behind it: its eyes are turned firmly towards the sea.

It was to this infamous village that James made the long walk from Great Ayton in 1745. Staithes must have been a total contrast to the relative peace of Great Ayton. Here the noise of the gulls alone would have warned of the different pace of life: their urgent cries are amplified in the echo chamber of the rocks and blend with the crashing wind and waves. But the most recurrent sound in Cook's new world would have been the jingling bell as his next customers came through the door, for his first job away from home was as a shop-boy for William Sanderson. Sanderson was related to Thomas Skottowe by marriage – and no doubt had received a glowing report of the young man. He ran the local grocery and drapery store and would have been glad to take on a new recruit who was both sober in temperament and good at maths. James worked in the shop by day and slept under the counter at night, and in his limited spare time, he took the opportunity to go out with the local fishermen and learn something of their craft. By now, he was a strong young man of six feet, naturally fit, with large hands, piercing brown eyes and a regal nose adding to the serious air about him. He was an earnest and able pupil.

In Staithes, even inside his shop, Cook would have been steeped in the sea. It would have been in the fabrics and foodstuffs he sold, the conversation at the counter and in the smell of the air as customers came and went. It is hardly surprising that he could not resist its call. One apocryphal tale from his early biographers suggests that the end of his land-lubbing days came with the 'South Sea Shilling' episode: a customer had paid for some goods with a coin issued by the South Sea Company and Cook was so transfixed by the piece that he swapped it for one of his own shillings. But Sanderson had already seen the exotic coin and questioned its absence, accusing Cook of theft and thereby driving the headstrong young man to quit his job and head to sea. However, the tale is as unlikely as it is romantic: shilling or no, the sea had already permeated Cook's bones. It had widened his perspective on the world and his mind was made up – he would make a career as a sailor. And rather than be angry at losing his employee, when Cook broached leaving his job in July 1746, Sanderson found him an apprenticeship as a merchant sailor at the busy port of Whitby – something he would surely not have done for a thief. What's more, he held the young man in high enough regard that he took him there himself.

The two men travelled together the seven miles down the coast where Sanderson introduced James to John and Henry Walker. The two brothers were well-respected Quaker ship-owners at the port and they liked the look of the tall, steady man who now stood before them. John Walker took on dozens of apprentices and was renowned as a firm but fair master; anyone falling behind his high expectations was soon dismissed but everyone knew that any sailor trained by the Walkers would be an expert in his trade. And here was the eighteen-year-old Cook – older than most recruits, educated and with a reputation for hard work. They looked again at the young man: he was attentive, sober and with a confident stance that no doubt was trying hard to beat down the nerves: he would do well. An elegant, illuminated legal document was drawn up with the same terms used for over one hundred and fifty years, in which Cook promised not to play dice, cards, bowls 'or any other unlawful game', or 'commit fornication nor contract matrimony'; in return, his master vowed to instruct and teach his apprentice 'in the trade, mystery and occupation of a mariner' and 'find and provide meat and drink, lodging and washing'. Signing him up as a three-year servant, John Walker unwittingly laid the foundations for both a legend and a life-long friendship.

Cook immediately moved into the attic of his master's four-storey house in Grape Lane. His new home was under the apex of the roof where he lodged with the other apprentices, sometimes more than ten at a time. For him in particular, this proved a testing environment: at six foot tall, the sloping roof and beams were another painful reminder of his land-locked status. There are no surviving records of his thoughts or feelings at this time; he seems to have mixed well enough with his fellow apprentices but the only enduring friendship he forged was with John Walker himself. James was different from his peers – uncommonly serious, focussed and studious. There were no windows on to the dark, narrow lane at the front: the only sights and sounds came from the attic windows which looked down on to the arterial River Esk that bisects the town and gives it its lifeblood. Along with the other apprentices, this would have been his waking view – complete with rowing boats, sailing ships and the renowned Whitby 'cats' used to ferry coal between the Tyne and the Thames. The boys would rise early and then head downstairs and out of the back of the house where stood a working shipyard bordering the quayside; here Cook studied the boats and their trades until he knew them all intimately.

For much of the time, though, his view would have been of open water: as much as possible, training was 'on the job', sailing on the trade-routes of the North Sea down to London and out to the ports of the Baltic and Channel, with cargoes of coal, wood and produce. London alone demanded over a million tons of coal each year; to satisfy this demand, a thousand ships would have to make ten return trips to the capital annually, as well as all their other ports of call. But it wasn't just the pace of trade that made life pressured for the mariner: the North Sea coasts were notorious for their shifting banks, strong tides and sudden storms, providing a challenge for even the most experienced navigator. The art of swinging the lead to gauge the depth and the composition of the sea floor would soon have become second nature to the young apprentice. Drake had learned his seamanship in these tricky waters and now it was Cook's turn.

His first recorded voyage was as 'servant', aged nineteen, in the *Freelove*: a Whitby 'cat' or sturdy coal ship. These workhorses of the ship-world were designed with a broad, flat bottom for navigating the treacherous Eastern Coast and also to make it easier to heave it up onto dry land to unload. Somehow, the ship fits Cook's character – steady, reliable, nimble when need be and well-suited to the job. By the time he left the Walkers, he knew this type of vessel inside out, having sailed and even overseen the construction of them during his time with the Walkers. Little did he realise that the Whitby cats would soon deliver him his future.

His apprenticeship, meanwhile, left little time to dream of that: when back from sea, he lived at Grape Lane and studied the skills of the mariner, learning the principles of navigation by instruments, charts and the stars, maritime law, and the efficient loading and running of a merchant ship. Cook was clearly popular in the Walker household. In fact, their elderly house-keeper, Mary Prowd, seems to have taken a shine to the young man, making sure he had enough candles to light his work and enough food to sustain him. When he returned, years later, after his first voyage of discovery, she was told to treat him with respect and call him 'Captain' or 'Sir', but on seeing him, she forgot all this in her enthusiasm and cried out instead, 'Oh honey James, how glad I's to see thee!' It's a rare glimpse of the family atmosphere that warmed the Walker household, for although strict and austere in appearance according to Quaker teachings, it had a benevolent and genuine heart.

The friendship of the Walkers would have been a welcome break from the hard mental and physical labours of being an apprentice. During the long winter months when not at sea, he would be splicing ropes, repairing sails and carrying out maintenance on his master's fleet of ships – at least until the light faded and then he would head inside to study. However, this food for the mind was probably more palatable than the food he had for his stomach once he waved goodbye to Whitby: along with their tea and sugar, on board they were allowed just one pound of salt-beef a day, which was dragged behind the ship in a net to wash the salt away and soften it for eating. These meagre rations had to keep the crew going as they worked their shifts five hours at a time, though it must have stood Cook in good stead for the years of exploration that lay ahead. Officers on his voyages of discovery marvelled at his strong stomach, which could tolerate even the most rancid or unappetising of foods.

The three years of Cook's apprenticeship passed quickly into five more years of increasing responsibility. John Walker was pleased with his recruit and no doubt the feeling was returned. But, just as Great Ayton had opened up his ears to the siren's cry of the sea, the waves breaking in Whitby harbour brought news of lands across seas more distant still. James Cook had matured into a confident and driven young man with good skills, a good reputation and a good boss – but he wanted more. He had passed his examinations to be a 'mate' in 1752, taking over that position on the *Friendship* and yet, when Walker offered him the job of 'Master' just two and a half years later, Cook turned him down. Most sailors would have leapt at the chance, but this twenty-six year old had other ideas: he was going to join the Navy.

4

ITALIAN LESSONS

George Collingridge 1867

THAT 'L'ANGLAIS' was going to fight in the French-run Papal Army, in Italy, against the Italians begs the question, 'Why?' Sure enough, the revolutionaries were affronting his faith but this was also the little boy who had been so impressed with the returning Crimean troops marching through Paris; now here he was, not ten years later, getting dressed up himself in dashing military garb: bright blue breeches, bright white gaiters reaching halfway up the shinbone, white smock jacket with gilt buttons – and a scarlet sash five yards long! The Papal Army clearly had no desire to hide its colours.

Italy was in turmoil, if you could call it 'Italy' at all: more accurately, it was a collection of different people with different languages and markedly different cultures, divided into independent states for the last thousand years. The only thing that united the people was a disillusionment with the ruling élite who abused their power and held them in servitude. But where once the idea of a unified Italy seemed nothing but a distant dream of intellectuals, it was now growing as a mainstream populist cause, to the dread of the state governors, Popes and Kings who had ruled their mini-empires with an autocratic hand.

The movement for *Risorgimento*, or rebirth, had been gaining ground since 1860, under the strong leadership of the patriotic but uneducated soldier-cum-revolutionary, Giuseppe Garibaldi. He may have been described by one of his contemporaries as having 'a heart of gold and the brains of an ox' but here was a figure to inspire the hard-nosed farm-labourer as well as the romantic. From lowly origins, he had risen through bravery and passion to become the popular leader of the movement for Italian unity and a more democratic, egalitarian society for all. To Victor Emmanuel, who would become the first king of a unified Italy, Garibaldi

The Collingridge coat of arms

was a useful instrument of war. To the Collingridges who kept a close eye on the unfurling drama, he was a dangerous enemy of God.

The aim of the politicians was to make Italy one nation and break the power of the Pope; for the people, the battle was for the end of feudalism and a more democratic society. For both groups, Garibaldi was the lynchpin. At home and overseas, the *Risorgimento* was given an added boost by composers Verdi, Donizetti, Bellini and Rossini who used their music to popularise the democratic cause. In fact, some commentators put Verdi as the musical figurehead of the *Risorgimento*, the letters of his name conveniently spelling out the initials of the pro-unification King, Vittorio Emanuele, *Re D'Italia*. Britain lent its official support, though presumably with the exception of its Catholics and Collingridges. Meanwhile, the peasant farmers of Italy welcomed Garibaldi as the man who would offer them deliverance – as much from their feudal overlords as from the divisions of what should have been one nation.

The Pope at this time held huge power and vast lands reaching from the boundaries of Tuscany and Umbria, throughout all of Rome to just north of Teano and Naples, where the Bourbon Kings held sway. Clearly, this did not coincide with Garibaldi's plans for universal Italian popular democracy – he made no secret of his plans to 'liberate' the Papal States and include them in the new Republic.

Defending the Papal States was the small French army of Zouaves. In his book, *Tales of the Papal Zouaves*, published in 1899, George talks wryly of the 'cosmopolitan' and almost rag-bag nature of the Papal Forces, who were drawn from all the Catholic countries. The official language of the army was French, though for many soldiers this was totally incomprehensible, leading to a 'certain confusion … that, albeit very amusing at times was not always conducive to perfect discipline'.

George's brother, Alfred, was already with the Zouaves. His letters home are the most revealing of all, stinging with a poignancy unknown to their author as he talks about 'finishing that game of chess' when he next sees George, and promotion in two months' time, if he is 'still here'. From Viterbe, on 20 January, 1867, he writes to his parents:

I got the newspapers you sent (of the 1st, 2, 3 and 7th of Jan). I found them very interesting; several of the Zouaves asked me to lend them to them. But what is said about the Zouaves provoking the people is quite untrue. Everywhere the Zouaves have always been very peaceful with the people. When the French soldiers were at Velletre, there were 13 killed when on faction (so I was told) and during the time we were there, no accident of the kind occurred; and now since we are at Viterbe, we have been all the while on very good accord with the inhabitants. Of course there are plenty of revolutioners. A few days ago at Rome a Zouave was stabbed in the neck and killed in a moment; we don't know yet how it happened, whether in the street or in a public place. They seem to begin to be tired of waiting. I heard yesterday evening of other murders but I know nothing for certain. The assassin is now in the hands of the police. I dare say we shall hear about it in the newspapers. I knew the Zouave that was killed very well. He had served in the French army, and was one of our instructors at the exercises at Velletre. Many think that the revolution will break out at the Carnival.

I think the French government dislikes very much the Zouaves, on account, perhaps, of the political opinions of many amongst them, such as those of nearly all the French nobility.

They say we are going to Rome at the end of this month. I shall be glad to leave Viterbe, where we are like in prison. At Rome we shall not be let to go out of the town either without permission, but there is more distraction than here and plenty of nice walks …

I shall put this letter in the box for you to get it sooner. You asked me how I should like my letters to be addressed. I don't mind at all. Simply A.J.L. Collingridge, 2nd Battalion, 2nd Company, Viterbe.

Good bye my dear Papa and Mama

Believe me your affectionate son

A.J.L. Collingridge

Six months after this letter was written, Alfred, aged just twenty-one, was fatally wounded at the battle of Monte Libretti. He died in October and was buried at Nerola where a monument still marks his grave.

In such a tight-knit family, Alfred's death ruptured their lives. For a heartbroken George, the life of the soldier had lost its gloss. The culmination of his own war years came at Mentana: here, despite Republican troops greatly outnumbering the Zouaves, Garibaldi was squarely defeated. By the end of his service, George had been awarded two mentions for 'distinguished bravery', had been decorated with the Mentana Cross, the Cross of St Gregory the Great and the Bene Merenti Medal. In all, George had seen seventeen engagements; he'd received not a scratch.

Without his brother, the accolades meant little to this artist-turned-warrior. He was discharged from the Zouaves on 22 June, 1869, into a Europe teetering once more on the edge of war. After a brief sketching trip around a southern Italy still feeling the ructions of political change, an older, wiser George returned to the family home in Paris. However, before he had time to restart his artistic career, Franco-Prussian relations descended into bitter conflict.

5

'MR COOK'S GENIUS AND CAPACITY'

James Cook 1755

HERE HAS BEEN much speculation as to why someone as calculated as James Cook should take the radical decision to join the Navy. His only reported comment on the matter was that 'he had a mind to try his fortune that way'. True enough, there were press-gangs active in both Whitby and London, on the look-out to force fit young men to enlist, and with mounting political tension between Britain and France over who owned the colonies in North America, these gangs would soon be doubling their efforts as the Navy prepared for war. However, Cook's rank in the Merchant Navy conferred some protection to his freedom as, theoretically at least, he should have been immune from being pressed. Some biographers have said that the prospect of war was the very reason for him to enlist (after all, nationalist fervour and support for the King have spurred many a young man into the forces – 100 years later, George Collingridge would do just that in the name of his God) but beyond unquestionable loyalty to the Admiralty and Crown, there was nothing extreme about Cook's patriotism.

The move, though, does seem odd: here he was, in the midst of his twenties, giving up promotion and security for the devil and the deep blue sea. Admiral Vernon described the Navy as 'manned by violence and maintained by cruelty'. Even Samuel Johnson famously commented that being at sea was like being in prison – but with more chance of drowning! And yet here he was, voluntarily leaving the Merchant Navy with its better pay and conditions of service, to get demoted in rank in the Royal Navy at a time when he was as likely to be shot and sunk as die of scurvy.

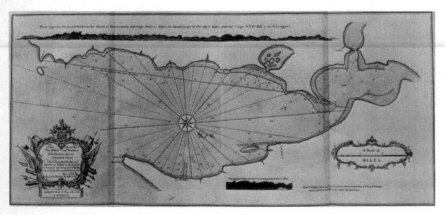

Draft of the bay and harbour of Gaspé, Cook's first published map, 1758

Whitby is now part of the twenty-first century landscape but the sunsets still glow tangerine-orange into the horizon, transforming the long shadows into a matt, flat grey-blue. It's a pretty town, busy by day but fading with the light, comfortable but quiet – the kind of place that's for the homely rather than the progressive; the kind of place that cannot hold on to those with dreams.

Cook had seen the world beyond these shores, in his reading, his travels and in the conversations of other sailors. He had come a long way from the drudgery of his father's life and had already had the courage to escape the constraints of the shop counter. He knew he was not cut out to be a bystander: he was young, quick-witted and hungry for learning. The mood of the country and the timing was right. Commodore Anson had just given the Spaniards a drubbing in the Pacific, returning home laden with gold to a hero's welcome; James couldn't achieve that by staying on Whitby cats in the cold seas of Northern Europe.

Cook knew the known world was not only getting larger but, for the first time, it was just possible to seize opportunities and be part of the new order by merit and not just by birth. His own father had done something of the kind, rising from farm labourer to manager, but he was still dependent on the lord of the manor for a roof over his head. James wanted more than that: he had been ill-fitting all his life until he found his home on the sea. This would now be his route to the status and security a second son could only dream of, a sense of finally belonging in his own right and on his own terms. He would also qualify for a share of the bounty from captured ships which could amount to a considerable sum – an ordinary sailor could earn an extra £100 per ship – and Cook planned to be much higher up the scale than that.

But there was more to this ambition than pay and promotion: he yearned to push against the boundaries of his world and nudge them outwards – and for this, the perfect vehicle was a boat, the perfect landscape nothing more than water. On land, he had travelled until he reached the shore; when that wasn't enough, he had pushed out into the shallow seas of northern Europe; what he wanted now was to strike out into the ocean.

So here again is the small boy who resolved to follow his own path, only this time it would lead him far from the crags of Roseberry Topping. His need for adventure was the start of the obsession of the mountaineer or astronaut – to conquer the heights *because they are there*, and the Navy represented a free pass to the base camp. He knew in his heart that he was good: it takes a certain confidence of mind to risk a life laid out before him for an empty canvas of potential. On 17 June, 1755, he left his ship at

Wapping and volunteered.

The risk paid off – and quickly. By 25 June, he had joined the fourth-rate HMS *Eagle* – fourth-rate because she only had sixty guns. A frustrated Captain Hamer had been given urgent command of an unready, undermanned ship whose skeleton crew, to make matters worse, would barely have earned their place at the bottom of the barrel. Hamer complained bitterly to the Admiralty, 'I do not believe there is a worse man'd ship in the Navy'. But what was bad news for Hamer was good news for Cook: it took less than a month for his skill to be recognised and he was promoted to 'Master's Mate' – his former rank in the Merchant Navy.

Meanwhile, in the political arena, events were in hand that would lead to the Seven Years' War. Its scope would be deep as well as wide: its battlefields were as far apart as Europe, India and North America and its legacy would set the pattern of colonialism for the next hundred years, along with Britain's world hegemony. The key player as far as Cook and the Navy were concerned would be the War Minister, William Pitt the Elder. A bullish but brilliant strategist, he rescued Britain's ailing overseas fortunes and famously declared, 'I am sure I can save this country, and nobody else can!' Pitt's skill lay in realising that if it wanted to retain and expand its overseas colonies, Britain had to think big, and that meant forming a coherent foreign policy along with a strong military and maritime base. In a matter of months he reorganised the Army, built up the Navy and, by doing this, set the British stamp on the emerging map of the New World.

In Europe, the tensions were initially between Austria and Prussia who were battling for control over the rich province of Silesia in modern-day Poland. Silesia's wealth rested on its rich coal-mining and textile industries. These had been the magnet for Frederick II of Prussia to invade in the 1740s and it was now the attempts by the Austrians to win the province back that pulled the trigger for the ensuing Seven Years' War. As tensions escalated, Europe divided its loyalties with Prussia and Britain on the one side and Austria, France, Russia, Sweden and latterly Spain on the other.

Four thousand miles away in the prized and valuable India, it was left to Britain's Robert Clive to take on the French, who had come dangerously close to controlling the region. Two years older than Cook and with a similar strength of purpose, Clive had propelled himself through self-education from 'difficult boy' and querulous young man to someone Pitt described as a 'heaven born general' renowned for his superb guerrilla tactics. Throughout the early 1750s, the growing hostilities between the British East India Company and the powerful French traders and colonists in the subcontinent drew him from his trade interests into a broader, military sphere and, by the time Cook had joined the Navy, Clive was on his way to India again with sufficient troops to expel the French once and for all.

While Britain was set against France in both Europe and India, the other key battlefield was North America. Here, too, the French were proving troublesome: although hopelessly outnumbered by the British and lacking the economic base in the West Indies, they had potent support from the local Indian populations, and the pre-war skirmishes appeared to be going France's way. Back home, the British fleet did what it could by disrupting France's Atlantic supply-lines, even before the official declaration of war, and it was into this environment that Cook launched his naval career – though if he thought he would be thrown immediately into the fray, he was to be sorely disappointed. His first enemy was the weather; the second was the apparent reluctance of his Captain to be in combat. The *Eagle* was only on patrol between Ireland and the Scilly Isles for little over a month before it was damaged by a 'Monstrous great Sea' and had to return to Plymouth for repairs. However, even after the ship was classed as fit to sail again, Captain Hamer made excuse after excuse to postpone his departure. Eventually, the Admiralty lost patience and replaced the disgraced officer with a rising star in Navy ranks, Captain Hugh Palliser. It was a move that would have a profound effect on Cook's career.

Like his Master's Mate, Palliser was a Yorkshireman, though five years Cook's senior and with a background littered with glory, honour and prestige. He already had experience in the waters around India, North America, the West Indies and Europe, and was thoroughly decent, highly capable and energetic. To him, playing cat and mouse with French ships in the Channel would prove little more than a game, albeit one where the loser faced death.

The *Eagle* left Plymouth on 8 October, 1755, roaming its hunting grounds on and off for almost the next two years and collecting the occasional French scalp along the way. As well as the bounty from captured ships, which was apportioned according to seniority (a lieutenant might receive a bonus of over ten thousand pounds this way), Cook also won further promotion to Boatswain, the temporary command back to Plymouth of the French *Triton* and, by June 1757, he had sat and passed his examinations to become a 'Master'. Although it was not officially a commission, the Master was one of the most powerful people on the ship. He had full responsibility for all navigation and would receive more pay than anyone barring the captain. The eighteenth-century writer, Ned Ward, described the holder of this position in the 'Wooden World' of 1707:

> He is a Seaman every bit of him, and can no more live any while on dry land than a lobster; and but for that he is obliged sometimes to make a step ashore, to a new-rigg, and to lay in a cargo of fresh Peck and Tipple, he cares not though he never see it.

However, Cook's education had extended much further than just seamanship: by now he had witnessed the un-glorious death and destruction of fighting at sea, and the steely grip of sickness which picked off the *Eagle*'s motley, underskilled crew by the score. It was now Palliser's turn to complain to the Admiralty about the quality of crewing and supplies. He had lost twenty-two men in just one month to disease through, he thought, the cold and wet conditions his men had to endure; he therefore demanded the Admiralty provide them with extra food and clothing. Cook must have paid attention, as he would repeat – and similarly win – the same fight himself a few years down the line.

Meanwhile, Cook's days on board the *Eagle* were coming to an end. Promotion meant he had to leave the ship and bid a temporary farewell to his captain. He paid a short visit to his parents in Yorkshire, then joined HMS *Solbay* for a few months' patrol of the Scottish coast, looking for smugglers and more French bounty. It was hardly the dashing first 'Master's' appointment he would have hoped for, but it can be no coincidence that it was also at this time that he began to add swirls and flourishes to his signature on the log: here was a man who was growing in status and quietly pleased with himself. He was also deeply impressed by the landscape on this one and only trip to Scotland and the isles, remembering place-names to be given out to future discoveries.

If he was content enough with his appointment to the *Solbay*, his next position must have been the best birthday present ever, for on 27 October, 1757, he was made Master of HMS *Pembroke*, a five-month-old ship with sixty-four guns, under the much-admired and 'truly scientific gentleman', Captain John Simcoe. This, at last, was a real ship with a real mission – not just in the waters of Europe, but in the murky waters of imperial politics on the other side of the Atlantic ocean.

Britain was now officially at war with France at home and overseas but although Clive was making progress in India, things had not been going so well in North America. The strong union forged between the French and the Native Americans initially through the fur trade had been reinforced by the mutual enmity against the British, who cut down the forest hunting grounds of the Indians and nudged the boundaries of so-called New France. Apart, the two factions would have presented less of a threat; together they were proving formidable.

William Pitt now realised he needed a concerted effort to turn the situation around. He knew that fighting in remote lands was as much to do with communications and supplies as military might, and so resolved to wipe out the French convoys before they reached the hungry battalions of soldiers. At the same time, he would also build up the British naval force for a full-scale attack. But where in the developing colony was their Achilles heel? One look at the emerging maps of the continent was enough to solve that: the key to cutting supplies and devastating the French fortresses was the main artery into New France – the St Lawrence River. Pitt set down his strategy: the *Pembroke* and its new Master were to sail as part of the British Fleet across the Atlantic and into the jaws of the enemy. For Cook, this is where his real naval career started: he had done his preparation, served his time and proved his worth. At last, he was about to take his ship into the unknown – what lay ahead was a chance at fame, riches and glory.

As Master of the ship, Cook was in charge of navigation, sounding for depth, equipment and general management, along with the keeping of a precise log; he would have had little time to rest but after years of steadily learning his trade, looking out over the decks of his colliers onto the North Sea, he must have reflected on how far he had come in career terms as well as geography. His view as he stood at the helm would have still been blue water, but this time it was the Atlantic Ocean, and he was facing the longest journey of his life.

It had taken until the end of February 1758 before they had finally left Plymouth with eight other ships – including Palliser's *Eagle* – to join the fleet of Admiral Boscawen. Despite a neck injury years earlier from fighting the French, 'Wry-neck'd Dick', as Boscawen was commonly known, was highly regarded as a man to get the job done. It was now down to him, along with General Jeffrey Amherst of the Army, to deliver New France to the British. However, even these war-horses could not control every eventuality, least of all the weather and disease. The crossing was plagued by stormy seas, contrary winds and devastating scurvy, but while the ship could withstand the former, there was nothing they could do to keep the latter from steadily picking off the crew. Scurvy was an accepted evil of life at sea, killing more men than war ever did. It strikes after a month and a half of dry rations with ominous, tell-tale signs: first your gums swell and bleed; this gets worse until your teeth fall out.

By now, however, your limbs and joints are painfully stiffening until they, too, turn a ghoulish blue-black from the blood that is seeping out from veins under the skin and in the muscles. As the days and weeks progress, the slightest movement is agony – not that you have the energy to even try to move with anaemia sapping your strength away until you lie, black and bloated, praying for the release of death.

Cook must have been horrified to see his men dying in droves. In all his years in the Merchant Navy, he had never witnessed anything like this: John Walker insisted upon due care and attention in the victualling of his ships but the Navy took no such care and was now reaping the grim penalty.

By the time they arrived in Halifax, Nova Scotia, at the beginning of May, twenty-six men were already dead and many more were rushed straight into hospital. Then five men deserted the *Pembroke*. A final, galling blow came when the fleet departed Halifax to take on the French at Louisbourg and his now grossly undermanned ship was left behind. Despite his despair at missing out on the action, it must have been quite a sight – one hundred and fifty-seven ships sailing out of the harbour, fired up with nationalist pride, cannons blazing in salute and ready for battle. Cook watched as they disappeared into the thick and ghostly fog that shrouded the Gulf of St Lawrence, frustrated not to be amongst them and no doubt cursing the disease that had laid his men low and deprived him of sharing the moment.

In all, it took another week before he had sufficient crew to set off in the Admiral's wake, the *Pembroke* cutting a lonely figure as it sailed the two hundred miles to the Gulf of St Lawrence after the British fleet.

Louisbourg had been founded by the French in 1713 and named in honour of Louis XIV. Situated on Cape Breton Island at the mouth of the Gulf, it had immense strategic importance as guard-dog for the inland colonies in Quebec and Montreal, as well as its economic role in the fur, fishing and shipbuilding industries. By the time the British fleet approached in 1758, this crucial stronghold for the French had become the most heavily-fortified settlement anywhere in North America. Its four thousand population had been swelled by three thousand troops manning two hundred cannon, and there were another three thousand men on the warships in the harbour – a clear sign that France was not about to give up its base without a fight.

But not everything was going France's way; a combination of ship fever and blockade by the British back home had prevented the French fleet from bringing food into the town – and the few ships that made it through had sacrificed their guns to bring in more grain. The soldiers were hungry and there was no chance of outside relief. What's more, when Cook arrived on 12 June, the British were already in place: a young but brilliant Brigadier Wolfe had made a successful landing to the southwest the day before and was already preparing for the bombardment.

For the Master of the *Pembroke*, it was a new and no doubt terrifying scene. Instead of chasing ships in open water, this was a slow and calculated game of stealth to be played move by move, attack by counter-attack, against a background of stifling tension and the foulest of weather. Amherst and Boscawen made a perfect union for land and sea attacks: the Navy carried the troops and ammunition ashore in convoys to reinforce Wolfe's men, who had already stormed their first French battery and were pressing on to the besieged fortress of Louisbourg itself. By now, enemy fire was exacting heavy losses. Then the French blocked the harbour by sinking four of their own ships, but the British merely waited for a dark night and then rowed in to set fire to the remaining vessels. The fire on the water was mirrored by fire on the land from burning barracks and fortifications. Thick smoke mingled with the mist, rain and fog, blurring the boundaries between night and day in the ceaseless pounding of guns. Then, on 26 July, after five long weeks of being under siege, the French Governor surrendered. Amherst and Boscawen had blasted the St Lawrence River wide open and the British were primed to wrest North America from the grip of France.

When Cook stepped ashore the next day, the devastation of Louisbourg would have been only too apparent. It was here at Kennington Cove that Wolfe had made his bold landing seven weeks before but this time, traipsing amidst the debris of battle, he had an altogether more friendly encounter. A young army officer, of about his own age, was peering along the top of a small table, mounted on a tripod, taking what looked like measurements. As Cook watched interestedly, he would jot down remarks in his pocket book then go back to his contraption. Eventually, Cook's curiosity got the better of him and he struck up a conversation with the man, who turned out to be one of Wolfe's own men – Lieutenant Samuel Holland, military engineer and surveyor. He explained to the ship's Master that he was making a plan of the land and its encampments, and showed him how – by taking angles off certain fixed points – it was possible to reproduce the landscape exactly on paper.

Cook was a keen mathematician and had already learned the rudiments of trigonometry and coastal surveying from Captain Palliser on the *Eagle*, but this was something new and, to Cook at least, it was nothing short of a miracle. On returning to his ship, he told Captain Simcoe about the young officer; Simcoe immediately invited Holland on board to demonstrate his surveying techniques over dinner. He ended up staying not only overnight but, with the blessing of the Captain who was too unwell to attend, took Cook and two 'young gentlemen' with him the next day to continue his instruction and work. From then on, the Great Cabin of the *Pembroke* was transformed into a cartographic studio and the three men became firm friends united by their passion for translating subjective views into hard, graphic fact. Cook had found his *forte* – and that chance meeting would, in turn, change the course of world history. War may have been his duty but nothing ignited his soul like the coasts that now took shape on the large fibrous sheets of blank paper.

Unwittingly, Cook had stumbled into one of the great periods of change in naval history: the rise of scientific navigation. Until then, seamen had relied more on written 'sailing directions' than charts, although they were often bound together in the same large book. The problem with charts was age-old: how to represent a spherical earth on a flat piece of paper and cope with the distortion that this caused. The Flemish cartographer, Gerardus Mercator, solved the first part in 1569 with his 'Mercator Projection' which flattened the world out according to a grid of longitude and latitude and then, thirty years later, Edward Wright, the English mathematician, solved the problem of distortion by publishing tables of correction. However, the Navy like all seafarers was slow to catch on: Cook's training would have been using 'plane charts' which took no account of the curvature of the earth and based their gridlines on rhumbs – lines that corresponded to the directions of the wind. Moreover, they were rarely used for plotting courses which was still done by 'dead reckoning'. This estimated the ship's position from direction and distance travelled (from the compass and the log), rather than using landmarks or celestial navigation.

Against this atmosphere, the charts that emerged from the pens of Samuel Holland would have been like gold to an alchemist: here at last was a means of plotting the ebb and flow of the coastline which could be achieved with scientific rigour. The method would not be generally available for another twenty years when Murdoch Mackenzie would publish his *Treatise on Maritime Surveying* and a young man called Alexander Dalrymple would divulge his *Essay* on the subject. Until its principles were adopted, navigation was still largely based on guesses and experience – there was no reliable means of determining longitude and the quadrant had only been used for measuring latitude since 1731. The importance of what Cook was now experiencing and the impact upon him cannot be overstated. This was a phenomenal advance, and his genius lay in recognising it.

Meanwhile, the siege of Louisbourg had lasted so late into the summer that phase two of Pitt's strategy – to win Quebec for the British – would have to be postponed until the following year. Simcoe and Wolfe were alone in calling for the campaign to continue, but they had their own reasons, perhaps, for wanting to push on. Both men were dying – Simcoe of an unspecified malaise, Wolfe of tuberculosis – and neither would want to leave unfinished business.

In the end, Pitt agreed that the forces should withdraw for the winter, save for a few harrying attacks on French settlements around the Bay of Gaspé a little further upstream. While these communities were no great risk in themselves, they were able to provision the enemy with food and supplies, so three battalions under Wolfe and a squadron with the *Pembroke* were sent to finish off the rather unsavoury business of ridding the French threat from the Gulf of St Lawrence. Fishing boats were sunk, guns were destroyed and prisoners were taken – not the kind of mission that anyone would choose, least of all James Cook, who would rather study his books than raid civilian settlements. His mind was still intrigued by his recent acquaintance with Samuel Holland; the potential of his new-found knowledge whirled around his brain and sharpened his eye and, whether suggested by Simcoe or off his own bat, he somehow managed to find the time to practise using his skills with instruments borrowed from this friend and tutor.

The result was a masterpiece of surveying: a small but brilliant coastal survey of 'The Bay and Harbour of Gaspey'. A few feet wide and about a foot tall, it lays out the narrow bay and its hills, coastline and waters using five different colours. But this is no artist's impression – it may not have used the classic gridlines of the Mercator projection but the measurements are precise and a compass rose nestles neatly just inside the bay entrance to correctly orientate the incoming navigator. Although unsigned, this remarkable chart is clearly in Cook's hand: the writing spiders across the paper and dates it to 1758, around the time of his thirtieth birthday. One can only imagine how proud he must have been when it lay completed on the table before him – and more still when it was engraved and published the following year in London, presumably through the efforts of Captain Simcoe. The chart now rests in the archives at the Hydrographic Office in Taunton, Somerset. Gently unrolling it today, it still has the power to stop your breath as if you were unfurling Picasso's first painting from playgroup, only this is art, science and history combined, and the effect is one of sheer beauty.

By the end of September, the squadron returned to Louisbourg and then retired to Halifax for the long winter. Boscawen and Wolfe went back to England for the sake of their dwindling health, leaving Amherst in charge of the remaining British forces. The next six months would drag with that suffocating inertia that turns disagreements into feuds and feuds into riots. Although the harbour itself remained ice-free, the winter of 1758–9 was the coldest on record. The men's breath froze almost before it escaped their lips and the desperate need to keep warm led many to stay too long at the inns. Penned in by floating bergs, there was little escape from the town itself, adding to the mood of claustrophobia. Beyond routine maintenance, the men had little to do. A steady line of sailors 'departed this life', through illness or no-doubt drink-induced accident; Cook's log wearily reports these events along with the changing weather, an occasional stabbing, a fatal fire and regular drunkenness. There is nothing in his words to suggest that, for him at least, the oppressive winter was a blessing in disguise, but then there was no official reason why he had to log his growing friendship with Samuel Holland and his growing passion for the science of surveying.

When weather and time permitted, Cook and Holland would go out with their instruments to make detailed recordings of the St Lawrence, as much borne of obsession as of requirement. Once the light had faded they would return to tell Captain Simcoe of their exploits and discuss the techniques they were reading about or employing in the field. Although ill-health prevented him from being an active part of their team, Simcoe was a clever, well-educated man who could neatly explain in seaman's language the finer points of astronomy and spherical trigonometry. He must have thanked the day the Admiralty assigned Cook to his ship, for here was a man of equal talent and interest to himself, if not of equal rank or birth. But what did that matter when they sat discussing the day's work, books in hand, around the table of the Great Cabin of a night? The three men formed a tight-knit group, kept warm by the fire of their passion for learning.

It was also about this period when Cook first started compiling the other great navigational aid of the time, called 'Sailing Directions'. These were written guidance to seamen, warning of dangers, advising courses and giving reference points to help ships travel safely in unknown waters. They are large sheets of paper, folded and bound into books and, as far as Cook's were concerned, inscribed with careful copperplate writing on pencilled lines, with all the flourishes and graphic art to make them as much items of beauty as tools of the trade. And they *were* much-needed – at the time, the charts and directions for sailing in the Gulf of St Lawrence and up the St Lawrence River were somewhat haphazard affairs, lacking in detail and inaccurate in the detail they did manage to supply. No wonder that Holland reports Simcoe's frustration, expressed to the naval powers-that-be, that a full survey of the region was essential – and then his advice to Cook to brush up his skills so he could become the person to do it. It was wise advice indeed and, under Simcoe's watchful eye, the amended Chart of the St Lawrence began to take shape.

However, as the productive winter melted into the spring of 1759, other priorities came once more to the fore; the reason for the fleet braving the cold and ice was to make an early start for phase two of Pitt's strategy in North America: the capture of Quebec.

Any hope of swift action was again thwarted by the weather; it took until May for the waters outside the harbour to be unlocked but at least the weather was not partisan, having cut off French supplies as well as British warships. However, as the thaw freed the ships to sail again, Captain John Simcoe's health deteriorated further and he finally passed away on 15 May, *en route* to Quebec. For Cook, this was losing a friend and mentor as well as his commander; his burial at sea was accompanied by genuine sadness and 'a salute of twenty guns, half a minute between each gun'.

Also slipping into the St Lawrence, very much in secret and very much alive, was a squadron of ships led by a rising star in the French Navy. Louis-Antoine de Bougainville was Cook's junior by just one year and their careers would develop in bizarre congruence with both men exploring the Pacific, and Bougainville almost beating his English rival to Australia. But all that was a decade in the future. In the meantime, not only did the Frenchman sneak his ships into the harbour at Quebec, he also managed *en route* to intercept some letters from Amherst that outlined the entire British campaign.

The Québequois acted quickly: the sixteen-hundred troops shored up the town's defences, then removed all navigational aids and markers from the St Lawrence to cause maximum difficulty for the enemy in reaching them by water; finally, they positioned their batteries, dug in and waited for action. In turn, the British were making slow but steady progress up river. Without charts to assist them, Cook and the other Masters spent the journey continually 'sounding' for depth and the type of riverbed that lay beneath. The river was narrowing perilously as they drew closer to Quebec; after a journey of almost four hundred miles, they were about to enter a section of the St Lawrence called the Traverse – and to do so blind would be suicide. At each side, the banks turned into towering cliffs and the waters in the channel were strewn with islands, rocks and shoals just waiting to snare a careless sailor.

Just when they were facing having to inch their way through the Traverse, they managed to capture several French pilots. It was made clear to them that they should guide the British fleet through the dangerous shoals or die. They chose the former, and by 27 June, 1759, in what had been a remarkable feat of navigation, all the ships safely completed the final stage of their long journey to Quebec.

The fortified city now lay before them, high up on the cliffs and surrounded by army barracks and guns. Since Louisbourg, Wolfe had been promoted to general and was now back from England and in charge of the army campaign. Despite his confidence, however, it was clear to everyone that Quebec would be a tough nut to crack. Leading the French was the eminently capable General Montcalm. He had more troops than the British and Americans combined, and furthermore, he had the strategic advantage of an almost impregnable base.

At the foot of the cliffs, a short distance away, lay a British fleet spoiling for action yet stymied for a good site to land. In order to plan their attack in this unforgiving environment, they needed an accurate survey. Soundings had to continue, yet from much smaller boats that could weave along the craggy shoreline and dodge the enemy snipers. This was dangerous stuff, yet vital preparation for the final military push. Captain Palliser, still of the *Eagle*, knew just the man to take part. At his suggestion, James Cook was assigned to the job.

For several nights in succession, Cook and a group of other Masters headed out under cover of darkness, taking their soundings and making their survey of the river. It was in this scientific pursuit that he first came face to face with death: one night, just as he was finishing his measurements, he was spotted by a canoeful of Indians and French gunmen who went racing up behind him. Realising he could not escape by water, Cook made for one of the islands in the channel, by all accounts leaping out of the bows and onto the shore as the Indians were leaping into the stern. Just in time, the ferocious noise of the attackers roused a nearby posse of British soldiers who rushed over and chased the Indians away. It was a narrow and very lucky escape and Cook was later praised by the Admiralty for performing the survey 'in a manner that gave complete satisfaction to his officers but with no small peril to himself'.

But the dangers were not over for Cook and his fellow attackers. The French might not have reckoned on the British getting through the Traverse, but they still had one ace up their military sleeve: fire-ships. This ancient form of warfare was now deployed on the men on the St Lawrence: coming towards them like a ghastly apparition was a squadron of flaming ships, filled with tar and pitch, exploding with bombs and old weapons and racing down the river at a nightmarish pace. Some of the ships in the British front row struggled to escape the fire-ships' deadly touch and then, just in the nick of time, the wind blew two of the flaming pyres onto the shore while the others were snared with grappling hooks and towed out of harm's way.

Montcalm, meanwhile, was playing for time. His troops might have outnumbered the British, but they were poorly trained and starving from being under siege first by sea-ice and then from the enemy fleet. He knew he needed to delay battle until the autumn snow and ice returned and did his work for him, forcing the British to evacuate for fear of being trapped. But General Wolfe had other ideas. While the Navy bombarded Quebec, he was still busy looking for landing sites to get his troops into action.

Summer pressed on with more fire-rafts from the French and more hell-raising by the British. The fleet sailed up and down the river, forcing Montcalm's men continually to change their defensive positions. August came and went. Quebec was set on fire while the British lost several ships to enemy guns – and all the time the weather was getting cooler. By now, Wolfe was getting desperate.

On 13 September, in what Cook logged as 'moderate and cloudy weather', the *Pembroke* and other ships from the fleet made a fake landing at Beauport, a little downstream from the city. Meanwhile, Wolfe and the main contingent of five thousand men landed just beyond Quebec at the Heights of Abraham. A day of bitter fighting ensued: by evening the enemy was, Cook wrote, 'Tottally Defeated' and, on 18 September, Quebec finally capitulated. As the British raised their flag, both sides counted their losses, including General Montcalm for the French and General Wolfe for the British.

When news of the victory finally arrived back home in Britain, the relief was palpable. Britain had proved her might on land as well as sea, spawning a new era of colonialism. It seems Great Ayton also took part in the celebrations. The Churchwarden's book records the cost: '*For ringing on account of Good News 1/-*', with the wry addendum of 6d '*For mending bell-rope*'.

For James Cook, it would be another three long years before he would hear the Great Ayton bells ring for himself. He was in the process of being transferred onto the larger HMS *Northumberland* where he gained a new boss – Lord Colville – yet another captain who would become a life-long friend and mentor for this very special young Master. Remaining behind with around three and a half thousand sailors, he spent a second winter in the freezing grip of Halifax Harbour, with little to occupy the time other than disciplining his bored and frustrated men and continuing his beloved surveys and studies. He must have missed the companionship of Samuel Holland and Captain Simcoe as he waded his lonely way through Euclid and his astronomy books, heavy-going even for one with a solid education and all the more challenging for a man with just four years of formal schooling.

Still, there was plenty of time to get to grips with the knottier parts of his learning: it took until late spring for the ice to recede enough for the Navy to leave the harbour for Quebec, which they finally managed on 22 April, 1760, the very same day that, in London, the 'Draught of the River St Lawrence' drawn up by Cook, Holland and Simcoe, was being recommended to the Admiralty. It was accepted and published by Thomas Jeffreys of Charing Cross, the leading British cartographer of the period. Meanwhile, summer came and went, with the official military action being supplemented by Cook's unofficial surveying action. He returned to Halifax for another long winter and, in January, 1761, Lord Colville granted him a bonus of fifty pounds for his 'indefatigable Industry in making himself Master of the pilotage of the River of St Lawrence &c' compared with his usual salary of six guineas a month.

More surveys and sailing directions continued, some of which are still available at the Hydrographic Office in Taunton where it's possible to chart Cooks growing confidence as well as skill. The work is clearly a labour of love, often beautifully coloured with graphic detail; the survey of St John's Harbour, for example, even depicts a wonderfully-drawn gibbet situated a little way out of town and no doubt ready for the sailors who took their boredom a step too far. However, the best prize of all came on 7 October, 1762, when the *Northumberland* finally sailed out of St John's Harbour and headed for home.

Cook had spent almost five years out of the country; the Britain he now returned home to was vastly different in both mood and modernity. Just ten years previously, when the modern calendar was adopted dropping eleven days from the year, there had been riots in the streets as people thought their lives had been shortened; now Britons looked eagerly to the future. George III governed over an established Empire; the Industrial Revolution was gaining pace; James Brindley had ushered in the Canal Age with his new route from Worsley to Manchester and Josiah Wedgewood had set up his first china factory. The atmosphere was one of progress and expansion.

James Cook, that son of a farm labourer, had also changed: he had found his niche, somewhere his perfectionism and attention to detail would be valued, somewhere he could exercise his brain but, perhaps most of all, somewhere he could be judged by his own merit rather than the rank of his birth. And his efforts had not gone unnoticed. Letters to the Admiralty and comments by his mentors refer directly to the Master of the *Northumberland* and his survey-work in glowing terms; and if ample proof were needed that here was a man who used every spare minute of his time, the armfuls of charts and sailing directions which Cook brought back to Britain would have convinced even the most cynical naval officer of his worth.

The journey home took just nineteen days and he collected a pay-packet of £291 19s 3d, worth well over £21,000 today; but, once again, the monetary value was far exceeded by the sum of his now-impressive reputation. Lord Colville addressed the Admiralty on his behalf:

> Sir ... Mr Cook late Master of the Northumberland acquaints me that he has laid before their Lordships all his draughts and Observations, relating to the River St Lawrence, Part of the Coast of Nova Scotia, and of Newfoundland.
>
> On this Occasion, I beg leave to inform their Lordships, that from my Experience of Mr Cook's Genius and Capacity, I think him well qualified for the Work he has performed, and for the greater Undertakings of the same kind. – These Draughts being made under my own Eye I can venture to say, they may be the means of directing many in the right way, but cannot mislead any.

However, the rather perfunctory comment of 'Recd' by the Admiralty Secretary belies the importance of such a letter. Indeed, plans were already crystallising in Admiralty minds about the future for this man of 'Genius and Capacity'.

6

'THE HAPPY FORESIGHT OF MR COLLINGRIDGE'

George Collingridge 1870

HILE GEORGE was still fighting for the Pope in Italy, Count Otto von Bismarck was plotting more political strife further north in Europe. Just as Italy was undergoing its *Risorgimento*, the 'Iron Chancellor' was dreaming of creating a vast, united Germany – which would also increase his own personal power. His plan was to foster a series of strategic alliances between the various German states, then test them with a string of orchestrated wars against their neighbours. Denmark and Austria were the first pawns in his game, then he cast his eyes to France.

The perfect opportunity presented itself in 1870. The throne of Spain lay vacant and a little-known Prussian Prince stepped forward to stake his claim. The French Emperor, Napoleon III, reacted with fury at the expansionist stance of its neighbour and, although the claim was withdrawn within days, France was still deeply concerned. Napoleon sent an ambassador to meet with William I of Prussia at the German spa-town of Ems. The ambassador requested that the claim to the Spanish throne should never be renewed but William refused and, précis-ing the conversation, sent a polite but firm telegram to Bismarck, detailing his position and confirming that the crisis was now over. However, Bismarck had other ideas for Franco–Prussian relations. He published the now infamous Ems telegram – but in a vastly edited form, deliberately changing the refusal into a clear insult to the French. It had the desired result: on 19 July, 1870, after his ambassador's return, an outraged Napoleon III declared war on Prussia. Little did he know that it would not only end in his own downfall but that of the French Second Empire as well.

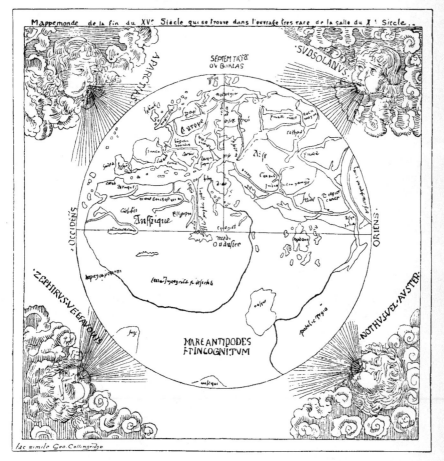

George Collingridge's reproduction of La Salle's Mappemonde,
from The First Discovery of Australia, *1895*

Before the French had even mobilised their forces, a combined German army had crossed the border. Other German states now united behind William as emperor of a single German state, with Bismarck its chief warlord. The invading armies were unstoppable, far outstripping the French in artillery, communications and strategy. In the Battle of Sedan, in September 1870, Napoleon III was captured along with large numbers of the French army. The next prize in the Germans' sight was Paris.

George may have fought with the French in the Papal Army, but this was no religious war; it may have been that they were still too pained by the loss of Alfred or perhaps they didn't feel French enough to risk their lives in the nationalist cause, for although the Collingridges were intensely political, this time they shied away from direct involvement. Family legend has it that, as the German army surrounded the capital, they escaped from the city on the very last train.

The Collingridges sought sanctuary in London, taking on a house in Belgravia. It was an emotional time for this close-knit and almost bohemian family: their international lifestyles and passion for European politics that had previously brought them so much entertainment now caused them nothing but anguish. Likewise, they had left behind their friends and colleagues, their home and their jobs for a London they found sterile and formal. They tried to put a brave face on the move, finding new work as quickly as they could, but their letters of the time hint at a deeper grief and concern for each other that was greater than their concern for themselves. Charles, the oldest son, may have been in Rome but he was not immune from the family's despair: '... Mary asks me to vote for going back to Paris, but it appears that all except poor Mamma have a better chance in London ...'.

Their sister was struggling to find pupils for her art and music tuition; meanwhile, George and Arthur were much luckier: they could bury their anxiety in their engraving, working on bookplates or for *The London Illustrated News* and the grandest journal of all, *The Graphic*. The two brothers had always been inseparable, whether painting in Paris, fighting in Italy or now working in England where they made an unbeatable team. The work itself was painstaking. George was at the top of his profession – he and his brother were regarded as the cream of Paris – yet, using anything up to a hundred and fifty tools, including gravers, burins, scoopers, tint tools and burnishers, it would take two days of working flat out to produce a block measuring eight inches by six for a newspaper. For the same picture to appear as a bookplate, much finer work was required and the brothers would devote a full two weeks to the engraving. However, there was no shortage of work or, it seems, the money to reimburse them handsomely, but even that was not enough to stop them dreaming of returning to Paris.

Across the Channel, their friends and adoptive countrymen had gone through the jaws of hell. With Napoleon III now captured, the Germans had brought Paris under siege by September 1870. Though the vast majority of the French now regarded Napoleon as a failure with no right to remain Emperor, the Parisians endured the siege, hoping for rescue by what little remained of the decimated French troops. But they reckoned without the weather: the savage winter that followed was as potent a force as any army in history and slowly but surely added to the general cup of discontent.

Inside the city walls, as the population struggled to keep warm in the bitter cold, rampaging disease compounded the desperate shortage of food and society began to break down. For the few who could afford to eat out in restaurants, new and exotic types of cuisine appeared on the menu – elephant consommé, camel 'roasted in the English Style', civet of Kangaroo – even 'cat on a bed of rats' – all the desperate product of the local zoos. For the poor, there was no such recourse: they simply grew hungrier and angrier with an upper class keen to surrender to save themselves from financial ruin and a provisional French government equally anxious for a settlement, believing that the Germans would then grant them better terms.

On 27 January, 1871, after the last hope of deliverance by the French army had been thwarted, Paris finally gave way. Bismarck granted an armistice and a new National Assembly was elected to ratify the peace. But neither the Germans nor the French had reckoned on the fury of the working people of Paris. The Franco–Prussian war may have officially come to an end, but a new, bloody episode in the city's history was only just beginning.

Furious with what they saw as 'selling out' to the Germans, the poor rose up against the new regime and the old enemies of élitism and religious bigotry. The Prussian siege of Paris gave way to angry street riots and the self-imposed holing-up of the Paris Commune. A Revolutionary Government was set up to run the city. This consisted of ninety-two 'members' from the middle and working classes, united in the fight to rid France of both the Germans and the corrupt upper classes.

Meanwhile, the leader of the new National Assembly, Adolphe Thiers, had fled the city for the relative safety of Versailles where the official Government was now in session. He decided the only solution to bring down the mutinous Commune was attack and, for six weeks from 15 March to 26 May, 1871, Paris was bombarded by French government troops. Historic buildings were destroyed and central Paris became a wasteland, yet even as the death toll climbed ever higher, the French Government was unrepentant: Paris must be brought back under the control of France, at any price, even if that price was the lives of innocent French citizens.

Under their military leader, Charles Delescluze, the Communards fiercely defended the city against the Government's continual bombardment. However, on the evening of 21 May, while the faithful were attending a concert and rally in the Tuileries Gardens, a Government sympathiser strolling near the Point du Jour Gate noticed the entrance was unguarded. Hastily climbing the ramparts and waving an improvised white flag, he ushered in the Government troops and launched the start of 'La Semaine Sanglante', the infamous 'Bloody Week'.

In the seven days of vicious fighting that followed, thousands of Parisians, including women and children, were massacred by the French forces. Some of these were Communards – a schoolmistress, Louise Michel, led a band of twenty-five independence fighters defending the hill of Montmartre – but many more were innocent civilians, caught up in the street violence. As the government troops pushed their way through the city, the Communards burned what they could not defend. However, this did little more than slow down the inevitable. Montparnasse Station fell, followed by Montmartre and the south bank of the Seine.

Both sides knew the end was in sight. Before surrendering, the Communards executed their hostages, including the Archbishop of Paris. Then, after four days of bitter combat, at around 7 p.m. on 25 May, Charles Delescluze mounted an abandoned barricade and stood there, silhouetted against the setting sun, until a single bullet took him down. The battle for Paris was over.

The next day, heavy rains put out the fires while the Government troops extinguished the last of the Communard resistance. The revolutionaries were captured, rounded up in their hordes and marched through the city to Versailles. Many never arrived – they were executed along the way and their bodies dumped in trenches. By the time the Government had regained control of Paris, French troops had massacred around twenty thousand people.

The city to which George and his family returned was thus a very different Paris. Whole streets seemed to be inhabited only by old women. As for the men – those who had the money or contacts to escape had fled, leaving the working classes to be annihilated in the fighting. By now, the capital's industry had been decimated at every level; more than half the decorators, plumbers and cobblers had disappeared, while much of the fabric of the city centre was burned or blown up beyond recognition. Paris had become a ghost town, eerily quiet save for the echoes of grieving.

But George and his family had known only too well what to expect. Their friends had kept the family as up-to-date as sieges would allow with the sad news from the capital, letters that add an achingly personal slant to the military story. A close friend, Emile, wrote of the isolation felt by those who stayed behind in Paris. His letter of 14 February, 1871 – two weeks after the end of the Prussian Siege – gives an insight into the strength of French feeling against the Germans:

> More than once we have thought of you and of the happy foresight of Mr. Collingridge, that you left Paris, where, since you have asked, you would not have found a very pleasant stay; in the first place for five months an almost incessant bombardment; and always very noisy, sometimes even somewhat dangerous for the mostly innocent inhabitants; sad and useless cruelty; and I say it without boasting, the Prussians would never have entered Paris, even if there had been 10 million of them, if it had not been for the starvation, which had let them in, and they know it very well ... Like you I hope we will see each other again this summer. But from now till then? In Paris we are waiting for something strange shortly ... I hope that which we most fear will not be realised. But!!......'

Charles, George's oldest brother and an ordained priest, was in Rome during the bombardment but kept them well-versed in the sad twists and turns of the Communard revolution through contact with his friends and colleagues. Writing to Arthur, on 9 April, 1871, he says,

> I have received a letter from Monsieur Jocard which is full of horrors. Can you imagine that C. Villedieu and Raoul de Kerolan have been killed? Here is part of the letter ...
>
> The poor Villedieu died at Vincennes at the beginning of the siege, from the effects of his wounds, in which he was involved. Raoul de Kerolan died also from the effects of his wounds at St Germain-en-Laye in the month of November. He was enrolled in the 'Francs Tireurs'. We fear that Villette is dead, his regiment was among the first engaged, and as it was horribly decimated, we have reason to believe that our poor friend has been killed. Guelen has been taken prisoner, I do not know what has become of him
>
> Theology continued to take place at St Sulpice even during the bombardment, but all the students (i.e. 90) followed their courses as external students, as the cells were occupied by the sick. Mr Jocard was

occupied looking after them. 12 Sulpiciers are dead. This is the news, which makes me very sad.

A letter to his parents on the same date is just as telling.

Paris, taking it in a general point of view seems to form a republic apart from the rest of France – its customs are not those of France, its religious feelings, etc. France despises Paris and Paris despises France. Just now the news from Paris is of the worst kind – the Red Republicans are getting wild, killing the Jesuits etc etc. I shall wait for confirmation of the news, the Archbishop in prison etc ...

By the time the Collingridges returned, the Archbishop was long-dead, the victim of a Communard firing squad. Their home was badly damaged by shell-fire and George's studio had been completely wrecked. Along with the thousands of other Parisians, they set about rebuilding their lives once more.

But what kind of life did George now want? He had played out his youthful vigour on the battlefields of Italy, he had seen honour, pageantry and death abroad and now at home, and knew that war was less about glory than pain, suffering and worthless destruction. He had been a soldier by duty and perhaps by *naïveté*, but he had never been one by instinct. Instead, his instinct was to pick up the pieces of his life as an artist, to throw himself into his work and draw, pen and paint his soul back to health. With every brushstroke, he recovered his spirit; with every engraved line, his focus returned. Art had long been his passion; it now became his salvation. And, like the Master of Her Majesty's Ship *Northumberland*, over a century before, it would be the pen and not the sword that would now lead him to adventure and, much later, discovery.

The two men's journeys that had started out so polarised were drawing ever closer through a sea of ink and paper. Cook had overcome poverty, Collingridge exile and war – but both men knew the chaos of their worlds could be given order on the canvases in front of them. As the map of their futures began to take form, they could now use their art to shape their destiny, never knowing that those destinies would become entwined.

7

THE KING'S SURVEYOR

James Cook 1762

THROUGHOUT LATE autumn and early winter 1762, the Thames-side communities of Shadwell and Wapping were their usual throng of activity. Ships crowded into the Pool of London, spilling their cargoes into wharves and docks that echoed to the sounds of accents from the length and breadth of Britain and all over the world. Huddling into every square foot of space on the waterfront were shops and warehouses holding any conceivable product that could be of use to this sea-faring community – from rope-factories and chandlers to breweries and timberyards. And a short walk up the streets rutted with mud and manure lay the alehouses where the workers took their rest, their food and often their lodgings. Here was where deals were struck and labour hired against a background of drunkenness, gambling, swearing and fighting. If nothing else, this was where real life happened in eighteenth-century London – a city where the Government passed draconian laws to promote public order and young girls sold their bodies for less than a shilling a time.

James Cook knew all the premises along the waterfront, those to frequent and those to avoid. His friend and former boss, John Walker, had made good contacts in the Pool of London through the Quaker community who were responsible for running some of the most successful businesses in the area, and these contacts had become James's own. Among them had been *The Bell Tavern*, located near the river on the corner of Wapping High Street and Brewhouse Lane. With a good reputation as a safe and honest place for Walker's visiting seamen, it had probably provided lodgings for Cook when he was in the Merchant Navy. It may also have been here that, a decade earlier, he met a young girl of around ten years old, who would prove his match in both strength and character.

Illuminated letter by George Collingridge

In the cold, dark days of winter 1762, Cook was back in lodgings in the area, preparing once more to leave for North America and the campaign against the French. The *Northumberland* was cleaned and repaired ready for resupplying, but by now Europe was tiring of war. Eventually, on 3 December, hostilities officially came to an end. The Seven Years' War was effectively over and Britain was now at peace.

Cook was now a man of means and standing and, at thirty-four years old, it was high time he found himself a wife. He knew he would not have to look hard: less than eight weeks after arriving at Spithead, he walked up the aisle with Elizabeth Batts, age twenty-one, who spent the next seventy-two years as Mrs James Cook. Some commentators have thought this an impetuous move for one so steady as the young seaman; others have taken it as a sign that he pursued his goal with focus and application! However, the truth is probably that he had known Miss Batts and her family for more than a decade, and had already marked her out as a good companion and devoted partner.

We know relatively little about Elizabeth – she was an intensely private woman, loyal in the extreme and quietly supportive of Cook's every move. As one might expect from a man as sure of himself as James Cook, the woman he chose to be his wife was level-headed, sensible and eminently capable. From the public records, it is known that her parents, Mary and Samuel Batts, had owned the well-run and respectable *Bell* tavern and boarding house. They also seem to have owned a wharf in Execution Dock, which would have added to the family's reputation and finances and put them in even closer contact with the men of the Merchant Navy; it would certainly have given Elizabeth a view of life well-grounded in reality. One thing is certain: she was no pampered princess.

When she was just three years old, Samuel Batts had died. Her mother thought a tavern an unsuitable place for a young child to grow up and Elizabeth was therefore sent to live with friends in the Barking countryside, a few miles out of London, until Mary remarried two years later. Her new husband was John Blackburn, a forty-year-old sailor who gave up the sea to help run *The Bell* and raise Elizabeth as his own.

For the next five years, they lived there as a family, running the alehouse and providing lodging for itinerant sailors like the young James Cook and his fellow Whitby crewmembers. The strongest suggestion that Cook met his future bride here comes from the artist, John Constable, whose uncle sailed with Cook on his second and third voyages. In a letter dated 1833, he wrote 'When Captain Cook stood sponsor for a little girl in Barking Church he said, "If this infant lives I will marry her".'

Although the date of her baptism makes that impossible as it puts Cook still on the farm in Great Ayton, he could certainly have been lodging in the capital at the time of her confirmation, as he was by then making regular trips down to the Pool of London with the coal trade.

Historians may not agree on how the future couple first met but it seems more likely that Cook would have 'stuck to his plan', as he famously did from early childhood, than rashly select a wife after only a few weeks' acquaintance. It is hard to imagine Cook playing Casanova – he was not a man of flowery language, extravagant gestures or obvious emotion; fulfilling a verbal contract is far more his style and, from the clearly happy union they achieved in spite of the challenges of separation, one suspects that he believed in sticking to his marriage vows just as strongly.

The possibilities that Cook knew Elizabeth for most of her life are strong: after *The Bell*, the family lived next door to another alehouse a short distance away in Shadwell where we know James spent a good deal of time. In fact, on his marriage licence in 1762, he is listed as being a resident of St Paul's in Shadwell.

Ironically, however, if he did come back from Canada looking for his intended bride, he would have been disappointed as Elizabeth was nowhere to be seen. One can only imagine the frustration of waiting five years for the reunion, only to have it postponed. He eventually tracked her down to Quaker friends in Barking and, once he found her, he was not going to let her go. He proposed almost immediately and, to his immense relief, she accepted.

At twenty-one years old, Elizabeth knew she was ready for marriage: she was realistic, used to the ways of sailors and prepared for the gruelling separations they would face over the long years ahead. She must also have looked proudly upon the man she had watched develop from apprentice to master mariner, entirely through his own merit. She was from a respectable family, and here was a respectable man, tall, gentle and with prospects as strong as his ambition to achieve them. He would make a fine husband, she would make a suitable wife and together they would make an excellent team.

James Cook was well acquainted with Elizabeth's friends and hosts in Barking – James Shepherd was a business partner of his old boss, John Walker, and they jointly owned a number of Whitby colliers. The house itself was a grand affair, brick-built with five bedrooms and five attics, so there was plenty of room to accommodate the war-weary mariner and he moved in with the family until 21 December, 1762. Then, he and Elizabeth walked across the meadow to St Margaret's Church in Barking where, under special licence from the Archbishop of Canterbury and the minimum of fuss, they became Mr and Mrs James Cook.

As befits the custom of the day, there are no records of any relatives attending the wedding, nor of any friends. Of the three witnesses to the marriage, one was the Parish Clerk and the others seem to have been casual acquaintances. The rather low-key event was not out of the ordinary – for many of their social class, weddings were a mere formality, and with Cook having at least Quaker sympathies if not their faith, he would not have been looking for ostentatious displays of pomp and ceremony.

Similarly, the concept of the honeymoon was meaningless to most newlyweds of the eighteenth century, and there was no time for one anyway: the happy couple moved into Elizabeth's parents' old house in Upper Street in Shadwell, but had only lived there for four months when James received the inevitable news that he was once again needed overseas. One wonders if he already knew that Elizabeth was pregnant when, in April 1763, he joined HMS *Antelope* and headed once more across the Atlantic to Canada. There was, however, a major difference between his previous trips and this: for the handsome fee of ten shillings a day – Palliser's pay as Captain of *The Eagle* – he was now appointed not as Master but as a supernumerary:

> In order to be employed in making surveys of the coasts and harbours of the island, and for making drafts and charts thereof.

James Cook was about to become The King's Surveyor.

8

IN SEARCH OF PARADISE

George Collingridge 1872

N THE DAYS before photography, the illustrators and engravers were among the best-known people in the art world. Their plates would be published in newspapers, books and the flourishing magazines, providing some of the only graphic images to fire the imagination of the reader. The leading illustrator of the day was a Frenchman named Gustave Doré, who would be immortalised for his extraordinary plates for Dante's *Inferno*, Coleridge's *Ancient Mariner* and the Bible. He was so prolific that he would frequently employ up to forty artists to engrave his work and make it ready for the printing press – and among this élite band of engravers was the young Englishman, George Collingridge.

By 1872, George was back working in Paris at the very top of his profession. Along with work for the newspapers and journals, including *L'Illustration* and *Le Monde Illustre*, he also engraved some plates and decorative tail pieces for Michelet's *Histoire de France*, which stretched to a massive nineteen volumes. Much of his work was engraving the paintings of Doré and also of the so-called 'Prince of Black and White', Daniel Vierge. George worked with Vierge on the *Histoire*, the French copy of *Don Quixote* and they would again be paired up for the highlight of George's European career: the marriage of Spain's Alfonso XII to Princes de las Mercedes in 1878.

When *Le Monde Illustre* decided to cover the Royal Wedding, it wanted the best illustrators it could find. Vierge was the obvious choice as the artist, and he wanted the top engravers of the day. George was selected, along with two other engravers of international standing. The work was hard but it formed one of the most memorable periods in his life

Illuminated letter by George Collingridge

and the subject of later reminiscences. The artists were invited as guests of the King to the Royal Bull Fight and were an integral part of the marriage pageantry, but they were under no illusion that they were there solely to enjoy themselves. Vierge made a colourful companion: George described him as 'witty as Whistler' and used to living in a blaze of glory. He would sketch the grand nuptial scenes – the ceremony, the fiestas, the fights at the Plaza del Toro – then at night, George and his colleagues would be given the drawings to engrave, working through the night to finish the blocks in time to reach the printing presses of Paris.

To a young man with a taste for adventure, the Royal Wedding was manna from heaven. The opulence of the occasion must have seemed surreal in comparison to war-torn Paris: he later told stories of how the fountains of Madrid actually spurted out wine instead of water, which the poor took away by the bucket-load. However, his favourite scene was at one of the bull fights when all the nobility were asked by 'Royal Command' to ride into the ring in full regalia: the colours, robes and spectacle stayed with him for the rest of his life.

Meanwhile, the trip to Spain had renewed George's wanderlust and the Royal Wedding was followed by a sketching tour of Britain, extending up to Orkney and including 'every lake in Scotland'. He returned to a France which disillusioned him. Though the third Republic was gaining ground in France with the anti-clerical République des Camarades, George was now less fervent in his religion than he had been in his youth. All he would say to friends was that it seemed 'not the best country to live in' anymore. There is little in his letters or reported conversations to suggest a more concrete reason for his next course of action.

One suspects that he was undergoing a general life reassessment: he had turned thirty, was already professionally at the top of his tree, and – although he stood to make a lot of money – he was not the kind of man to spend the rest of his life ploughing the same furrow. Letters between him and his father reveal that he was searching for something new, somewhere he could have his heaven on earth, with all the drama, discovery and passion he craved. His father William gave him his blessing; the letter survives today:

> If you find it paradise, all is well – if not, you will have made your experience – and you are not obliged to remain longer than circumstances require.

William was saying goodbye to his son, knowing that it might be forever.

9
THE SURVEYOR'S ART
James Cook 1763

HE START OF June 1763 saw Cook arrive into a damp and driech Newfoundland. The coast was shrouded in mist and fog and the mosquitoes attacked every inch of bare flesh. For the Navy, however, these were mere irrelevancies and the proud surveyor was just as eager to start work. He was immediately dispatched to the islands of St Pierre and Miquelon, just off the southern coast. Although Britain had won Canada, the Treaty of Paris which marked the official end to the Seven Years War laid down certain terms and these included the handing back of these islands to the French as a base for their fishing trade. However, before this was done, the Admiralty wanted a full survey to see exactly what Britain was giving up – and what it was obtaining.

This was more than just an exercise in mapping: the island of Newfoundland had been developed since the 1400s, partly due to location and partly for its wealth. Its immense strategic value came from being the most easterly part of North America: the capital, St John's, is closer to Ireland than it is to Winnipeg, and that made it a first port of call for transatlantic trade and communications. The other reason for Newfoundland being so highly prized was its geographical situation just off the Grand Banks. These were – and still are – some of the most important fishing grounds in the world, famous for their cod and appalling weather. Here, the cold Labrador current meets the warmth of the Gulf Stream and it was said that the seas actually bubbled with fish. The local fishing industry was worth thousands of pounds a year, and every nation wanted a piece of the action. Dried fish comprised a large part of the Mediterranean diet in particular, and was also becoming more popular in Britain; all you needed was a boat and somewhere to land and

Captain Cook's signature

process your catch – which is exactly what St Pierre and Miquelon now represented to the French.

The Governor of Newfoundland was Captain Thomas Graves. He was a genial man who had sailed with Cook to Quebec and had witnessed first-hand the 'genius and capacity' of this amateur surveyor. Graves was good friends with Captain Palliser and Lord Colville, and they all agreed that Cook's talent should not go to waste in what he called 'a country at present little known'. After much bureaucratic wrangling for materials and assistants, 'Mr James Cook, a Person well skilled in making Surveys' was kept busy for the next seven months, charting much of the six thousand miles of coastline and harbours in Newfoundland, until the threat of winter's ice forced him to return. In fact, unbeknown to Cook, the task would occupy him for the next four years.

Traditionally, and if they could be bothered at all, sailors would make a 'running survey' of the coast, with observations taken solely from the deck; Cook's uniqueness lay in the fact that he knew how to conduct a survey from the land as well as from a ship. That original meeting with Samuel Holland had led to a mastery of all the technical equipment needed for the job, and the firm grounding in academic theory to back it up. The end result was stunning even to the experienced eye of the Admiralty: the charts were not just unparalleled in their accuracy, some of his measurements were relied upon by sailors and chart-makers for the next two hundred years, and many were only finally bettered when digital satellite mapping came along in the late twentieth century. Without doubt, Cook's time in Canada was the highlight of his surveying genius, spawning most of his finest and most beautiful work. But they are also valuable historical documents: aside from their cartographic information, they provide a window into the vulnerability of these tiny settlements, thousands of miles from home, served by a ship-based colonial governance and battling against the elements. The early pioneers were truly a brave and determined bunch, as the tightly-knit geography of their villages bear witness.

For the time being, however, Cook was desperate to swap the cruel Canadian winter of 1763–4 for the warmth of family life. Whilst working in the familiar harbour of St John's, he had received word that Elizabeth had given birth to a boy. It is no coincidence that, with the blessing of Captain Graves, he raced back to England on the pretext that he would achieve more work there. He arrived home when the baby was just seven weeks old and, soon after, they baptised the child 'James'. The pressures of combining a new job with a new family must have been immense; nevertheless, what little evidence there is points to the Cook family home as immensely happy and to 'Mr Cook', as Elizabeth always called him, as a proud father.

Meanwhile, it was soon clear that their current lodgings were too small for the enlarged household, particularly one where he was working on the vast Newfoundland charts, so he took on a small end-terraced house, two-up two-down, a short distance away in London's Mile End. It was respectable though certainly not grand – the stench of the gin distillery next door saw to that – but at least he was surrounded by his fellow seamen or those involved in trade, making for a sociable if smelly community. The new house had only recently been built and he kept on the lodgings in Shadwell for another year, perhaps to have a quiet space in which to finish the surveys for the Admiralty.

It may have taken thirty-six years but Cook had now transformed himself from a barefoot son of the rural working class to respected and urbane professional. By his side was an educated wife, the beginnings of a family and the stamp of social approval. He may have worked hard for his rise in status but he was also exceedingly lucky: the eighteenth-century passion for science and learning had created a slipstream for those with the talent and Cook was perfectly positioned to seize the advantage.

The next few years were to settle into a regular pattern of winters in Britain, where he would draw up and complete his surveys, then he would head back to North America for the summer to pick up at the exact spot where he had left off the previous season. His goal – and his orders – were to chart every bay and promontory of Newfoundland, no mean task considering its size and the coast that wriggled busily along the shoreline, but the task suited his meticulous nature and his desire for exactitude. He believed that laying the land down precisely on paper was somehow making it real; it was no longer a casual sketch that could mislead, it was committing nature to the rigours of science – value-free, raw facts. However, he was not naïve: he knew from his work on the St Lawrence that while the data itself may be value-free, the charts and maps themselves were intensely political. Maps were power: they laid claims over dominions and proclaimed 'this is our land – you may steer by it, but you may not have it'. And when it came to the New World, the pen was indeed mightier than the sword, for what is the point in fighting if you don't know what you are fighting for?

For Elizabeth, too, there were new rhythms to blend into. The solitary role of the Navy wife became ingrained in her day to day, looking after her expanding brood with the help of Cook's cousin, Frances Wardale, and keeping house until her husband returned. At least the patterns of James's work meant that winter was now something to look forward to, and meantime she had the benefit of being near friends and relatives: in such a sea-faring community, there were plenty of other wives in the same situation. Being intelligent, reasonably educated (from the quality of her letters) but also used to life in an alehouse, she had the experience and capacity to deal with most of the things life threw her way, not least being a single parent for long stretches of time. The prospect did not seem to faze her: when Cook sailed again for Newfoundland on 7 May, 1764, she was already pregnant with their second child.

Once in Canadian waters, he took command of his first ship, at the suggestion of his old friend, Captain Palliser. The *Grenville* was a smallish vessel specially kitted-out for surveying and called after the Prime Minister of the day, the hapless George Grenville. Cook must have felt it was like another child to him, and they stayed a team for the rest of his time in Canada, even ferrying him across the Atlantic and back home again for the winters.

Cook's second season as the official surveyor proceeded smoothly, continuing the work along the northern coasts. They fell into an easy if relentless routine – he would go ashore with his flags, theodolite and other surveying equipment, position the flags, take his readings to 'lay down' the land while, offshore, the small boats would go out to sound the water; then, back in his cabin, he would marry the two to create the survey on paper.

All was going well until, on 6 August, disaster struck:

> Came on board the Cutter with the Master who unfortunately had a Large Powder Horn blown up & Burst in his hand which shatter'd it in a Terrible manner and one of the people that stood hard by suffered greatly by the same accident and having no surgeon on board Bore away for Noddy Harbour where a French fishing ship Lay, at 8 sent the Boat in for the French surgeon at 10 the Boat returned with the Surgeon, at 11 Anchord in Noddy Harbour in 6 fathom water.

Quite what Cook was doing with a Large Powder Horn is not clear, though it was most likely for defence against rogue Indians or Frenchmen, or to signal the boats working just offshore. More important was what it meant: Cook was now without the use of his critical right hand which had been ripped open from his thumb down to his wrist. The gash took over a month to heal during which time he could do little if any surveying. He was lucky to be left with just a scar and not more permanent damage. Fifteen years down the line the injury would take a more macabre significance. It was this scar that helped to identify his hacked-up body on a black, volcanic beach in the Pacific.

The reality for Cook was now one of overseer, rather than participant. The frustration must have been overbearing as he watched others doing his work with less skill and application: it may have been their job but this was his obsession, in all its tedious repetition, and now it was stripped away from him. The men, too, felt the effects of the accident. Increasingly bored with the reduced workload, they became drunk and unruly. Eventually, things got out of hand and the ringleaders had to be punished for 'Drunkenness and Mutiny'. They were made to run the 'gantlope' – a traditional punishment that gave us our term 'running the gauntlet', whereby the offenders would be marched at swordpoint between two rows of sailors who had to hit them with a knotted rope. Surprisingly for Cook, also among those he had to punish was his senior hand, Peter Flower. This was clearly aberrant behaviour on the part of this fellow supernumerary and surveyor's assistant: he was devoted to Cook and never left his side until his own death in Rio at the start of the first voyage of discovery.

By the end of August, scarred hand or not, Cook was back at work. It was not only his own obsession to get the job done; in Newfoundland the summers are short and the winters come snapping at the heels of the darkening September nights, so it is not surprising to see in the ship's log that on 14 September,

> PM the Mastr with the Cutter went on shore with five Days provisions, in order to go on with the Survey.

By the start of October, with the daylight dwindling and the men working non-stop, one of the boats ran into an underwater shelf. It may have been this event or the general acceptance that conditions would only get worse that propelled Cook to return to St John's and from there, leave for England.

He made it through some appalling storms to reach London by 12 December, 1764, where he immediately wrote to the Admiralty asking that the ship should lie at Deptford rather than the usual Woolwich. This was not only more convenient for his new house in the East End, it would also mean he could combine work on his beloved surveys with his equally beloved family. He had good reason: just as he arrived home – and just fourteen months after his first son was born – Elizabeth gave birth to their second boy, Nathaniel. It must have been quite a home-coming.

He had precious little time to enjoy his new arrival for all too soon the pressures of work were rearing their head. The *Grenville* needed repairing and he wanted to change her sails from a schooner's to the square rig of a brig, making her more manoeuvrable for coastal surveying. The details themselves are less interesting than the process by which he went about this mission. The written request to the Admiralty was made with all the elegantly-constructed argument of a lawyer: with courteous deference, he acknowledged his superiors' authority but diminished none of his own. His unshakeable confidence in his reasoning and experience clearly impressed the Navy Board and it was no surprise that his request was granted.

Another request that was granted came on behalf of Cook by his friend and sponsor, Captain Palliser. He petitioned the Admiralty to allow Cook to publish the surveys he had made of Newfoundland, which Cook duly did at his own expense. Two beautifully-drawn charts along with sailing directions were available on the market by 1766 – a must for any sailor in those waters, when compared to the unreliable surveys on sale at that time, the main competitor for Cook being a hundred-year-old edition contained in the Mariner's Bible, *The English Pilot*.

The King's Surveyor was kept busy in Canadian waters until the end of 1767, marking down every twist and turn of the heavily-indented coastline. He does not seem to have minded the grinding pressure of season after season, picking up where he had left off when the ice threatened to besiege him. There is no record nor even less suggestion of him turning to drink or women like many men of the sea. In fact, what little detail there is of his pastimes suggests that his pleasures as well as his employment came from the science of surveying. Like a true perfectionist, he read every book he could get his hands on, kept up with advances when back in Britain, and was always on the look-out for news ideas to further his skills.

One of these came about on the 5 August, 1766 when he was surveying in the Burgeo Islands off the southwest of Newfoundland. Cook had long been interested in astronomy ever since he was an apprentice for John Walker and had made his first study of the subject. The leading light in the field was Charles Leadbetter: his *Compleat System of Astronomy* was one of Cook's favourite texts and the author's enthusiasm – and tables of dates – for eclipses had captured the imagination of the young mariner. One such eclipse was due on that day in August and, for James, it presented the perfect opportunity, as Leadbetter wrote in 1728, to

'determine the true Difference of the Meridians between *London*, and the Meridian where the ship then is; which reduc'd into Degrees and Minutes of the Equator is the true Longitude found at sea'.

In those days of 'dead reckoning', precision was a rare dream for most seamen, but Cook was already looking to make his best measurements even better. He noted down his observations of that eclipse with characteristic care, then continued with his day-to-day surveying until he could put his work to good use.

The chance came on his return to London when he pursued an acquaintance with Dr John Bevis, a member of the Royal Society who shared his passion for astronomy. Bevis was clearly impressed with the work of the young surveyor and, after seeking some help with the nightmarish mathematics needed to turn readings into longitudes, he prepared a brief paper for the Society on Cook's Newfoundland observations. It may seem surprising that someone with just four years' formal schooling should approach the Royal Society, but James Cook was no ordinary seaman: he had total confidence in himself and his abilities and, as with Simcoe, Palliser and Graves, the community of scientific gentlemen welcomed him into their midst.

The finished paper may have been brief but the implications were far-reaching. In the short term, it must have impressed the Admiralty who agreed to his suggestion to buy a telescope to work out longitude by the stars. In the longer term, however, it was much more significant: it was not only his passport to credibility among the learned of the Royal Society, it also helped mark him out for the greatest prize of all.

But first he had to finish his Newfoundland survey. It must have been galling when his assistant, William Parker, was promoted from Master's Mate to Lieutenant, leapfrogging Cook who kept his rank as Master, but it gave him the opportunity to work with Michael Lane, another man of talent who took Parker's place. The survey itself progressed relatively quickly as he attempted to finish the entire west coast, hindered only by poor weather and the profusion of islands that must at times have made him feel as though he would never complete his task. At last, however, he returned to St John's and, after a week of repairs to his battered ship, headed across the Atlantic in super-quick time.

But the winds that had assisted him now had the last laugh. On reaching the entrance to the Channel, the weather closed in and the night of 10 November was marked by a most ferocious storm, which drove the *Grenville* onto a submerged shoal. As she pitched and rolled on an angry sea, the crew divested the ship of anything that was not essential to their making land, including stores and ballast. Meanwhile, the ship began to take on water and eventually Cook ordered the men to take to the smaller boats and make for land. Next morning, they returned to the ship and found that she was surprisingly undamaged so that by removing more ballast, they managed to get her afloat and then sail on to Sheerness.

However, among the items that went overboard – either deliberately or by accident – was an Indian canoe belonging to a young gentleman scientist who had been in Canada collecting botanical species for his collection. His name was Joseph Banks and, if Cook did not know him already, he soon would. Their acquaintance could have come about from a variety of sources: Palliser or someone aware of Cook's interest in matters scientific might have introduced the two men, or possibly the contact could have come about through the new mate on the *Grenville* who previously had been on the ship that carried Banks as a passenger. There is no record of the gentleman's reaction to losing his canoe, though it probably caused some embarrassment to Cook when they met a short time later.

A few days after being rescued, the *Grenville* docked in London and Cook returned home to the news that he was once again a father – this time to a daughter named Elizabeth. Rather confusingly, there were now two Jameses and two Elizabeths in the house at Mile End, which seemed that little bit smaller than when he had left the previous spring. He loved his boys but a daughter was something special. Not for her a career in the Navy; she could be a companion for her mother and then a genteel bride.

There were plenty of friends and neighbours to help him celebrate her birth and his return, and plenty of alehouses in which to do it if he could bear to tear himself away from home. Mile End was thriving, as was the whole of London; it was all a great contrast to sleepy Newfoundland.

As well as his family commitments, there were yet more surveys to complete and engravings to oversee. A fourth chart went to the publishers and he did a small piece of private surveying for Captain Palliser, who clearly thought he was the best man for the job. The Admiralty were busy, too, responding to the daily barrage of requests and demands. These included granting Cook the ship's surgeon he had requested (no doubt remembering his own accident a few months earlier) and minuting other changes to the crew of the *Grenville*. They resolved that Michael Lane should replace Cook as Master, and even found a replacement for the now-vacant post of Master's Mate. Just as significantly, it was around this time that the Admiralty also noted down a resolution to prepare a ship to voyage 'to the Southward'. Unbeknown to Cook, it seems that bigger changes were afoot for the King's Surveyor.

Collingridge Point

10
TROUBLE IN PARADISE

George Collingridge 1879

EORGE'S EDUCATION, experiences and lifestyle had been unusually cosmopolitan for a young English man, even one from the upper classes; in fact, his orientation was decidedly international. So in many respects, it comes as no surprise that his next move was out of the playing fields of Europe to the other side of the world. He first thought of Canada, but was convinced by his beloved Arthur, who, along with his other brother Charles, had already emigrated to Australia, to think even further afield and so, on 24 January, 1879, George walked off the gangway of the SS *Lusitania* and onto the shores of Australia.

At the time, the country was made up of a number of separate colonies, the oldest still bearing the name bestowed by James Cook: New South Wales. But more than that, Cook's legacy was buried deep into the psyche of the pioneering population. No longer a dumping ground for British convicts, the Australian settlements were a honeypot to those seeking a better life; the 'new' land was considered empty of culture – Aborigines were largely regarded as an irritating inconvenience; Britain was the motherland, the role-model and the inspiration for the colonists and, in a country perceived as a blank slate until 1770, James Cook slotted into the settlers' mythology as the great white Anglo-Saxon founder and hero of the continent. It did not seem to matter that Cook had sailed just once along its mainland coast, landing only when necessary and choosing never to return. Now he had been manipulated by history to become an Australian icon: brave, with a pioneer's spirit, and, best of all, an Englishman. Britannia not only ruled the waves, she ruled her colonists' hearts and minds as well.

With worrying efficiency for a Collingridge, George had already sent some samples of his work to Arthur, who had arrived in Australia the year before. He was already working there as an artist and had shown his brother's pictures to the editor of the *Illustrated Sydney News*. Before leaving France, George had secured a deal to continue his work for *Le Monde Illustre* while overseas but, on arrival, he was immediately engaged by the Sydney paper as well and, within months, he and Arthur were representing these newspapers as artist-engravers at the great International Exhibition at the Botanic Gardens in Sydney. Despite fierce competition from home and abroad, George took the medal for first prize in 'xilography' (otherwise known as wood-engraving).

Things were going well for George. Within his first year, he had earned over £300 for his wood-blocks, had contracts with the *Illustrated Sydney News*, *The Sydney Mail* and the *Town and Country Journal*, and had produced the largest wood-engraving (of Bathurst, Australia) yet executed in the world.

However, along with expertise, he also brought with him ambition, not just for himself but for the entire Australian art world. It seems everything George did was inclined towards the grand scale. Frustrated by the amateur nature of organisation among local artists trying to exhibit and sell their work, George had an idea. In Europe, he had been a member of many art societies, including *L'Union* in Paris. He translated their rules and regulations into English and, on 22 June, 1880, the brothers convened a meeting of leading artists at the Sydney Coffee House. Together, they suggested that the artists set up a similar organisation to the French society – somewhere to hold exhibitions and act as a showcase for their work. Their colleagues agreed and from this a committee of seventeen drew up the rules for the Art Society of New South Wales, later to become the Royal Art Society. Its inaugural meeting was held on 6 July and the first exhibition was five months later; over a hundred years have now passed and the Royal Art Society is still in existence.

The broad base of George's career and his deep desire to develop art within the colony led to the formation of several journals and pamphlets on the subject. He became editor and publisher of *Australian Art* in 1888, the first magazine devoted exclusively to art, and he also laid out his teaching methods in a series of seven booklets called *Form and Colour*, which took a prospective pupil through lessons in drawing and painting. George had always been interested in teaching. He had done some tuition whilst still in Paris, becoming a Professor of Painting and Drawing at Albert-le-grand College, and now took up posts at several local schools and colleges, as well as teaching pupils in his home.

However, it was as an artist that George was best known, and all the more so after the growing art of photography took over the role of engravings and sent the price paid for woodblocks dwindling to almost nothing. However, George had a magpie brain and a resourcefulness that kept his head – and his morale – above water. Specialising in landscapes and working mainly in watercolours and oils, he continued to exhibit his paintings all over the world, winning more medals and prizes in the process; in fact, his last one-man show was held in 1926, when he was nearly 79, at the gloriously-named Feminist Club Rooms in Sydney. To the Australian art world at least, he was respected for his talent and enthusiasm and also for his sense of historical significance: as well as the enormous Bathurst engraving, he was also the first (with Arthur) to paint the Hawkesbury River area in 1879, Berowra in 1880 and the Jenolan Caves in 1881. The picture of the Caves paints a revealing thumbnail sketch of George's personality: seizing the opportunity to take a few days off, he, Arthur and some friends went to explore the bush around Sydney. Following the course of the Fish River, they noted with excitement that it suddenly disappeared underground. Luckily, they were well prepared: they threw a knotted rope over a thick stalagmite and crawled through a 'kind of window' ninety feet down into the river below, becoming the first discoverers of the now-famous subterranean landscape in the process.

The taste of discovery must have lingered in his mouth. Here was a young man in a 'new' country, energetic, curious and eager to explore the strange world that stood before him. The passion which ruled his soul soon drove him to test his boundaries once more. Perhaps it was the distant memory of his childhood in rural Oxfordshire or his life-long love of nature; more likely it was the quest for new adventure. Whatever spurred him on, he quit Sydney for the bush, taking up a selection of eighty-eight acres on the bend of Berowra Creek which is now called Collingridge Point. A year later, he had built a small stone cottage and a fifty-foot well.

A watercolour by George of Collingridge Point rests on the wall in my study, the generous arm of water nestling a small sail-boat in its crook. It's easy to see why he loved the place, and the endless paintings and sketches of the area stand testament to the depth of his feeling. Berowra was his dream – or so he thought. Here George literally (and gleefully) re-drew the map of the area, discovering another five miles of foreshore, from Still Creek to Calabash Bay, which the Land Department had missed. Collingridge Point itself was so remote from civilisation that if he wanted to go to Sydney, he first had to row the five miles down the river from his home to get to the road-end, and from there he still had to make the four-hour commute into the city. The isolation led him to style himself 'The Hermit of Berowra', though given his cosmopolitan lifestyle, this must have been done with an ironic smile. That sense of humour would prove to be a lifeline in future years.

Meantime, it was no wonder that he thought the place special, for it was to here that he brought Lucy Monica Makinson, whom he married in November 1882. They had been introduced by his brother, Charles – by now a fully-fledged priest, who had been in Australia since shortly before George's own arrival. He was a close friend of the Makinson family, and it seemed natural that George should become one, too. Lucy's family had strong religious credentials: her father had been a rector firstly in the Church of England and then, upon converting to Catholicism, became secretary to the Archbishop. She was a good choice and George clearly adored her.

But despite a new home and family, a successful career and a worldwide reputation, it seems that wasn't enough for Cousin George. He wanted to prove himself, to carve out his own niche as surely as he carved the woodblocks for his engraving. Whatever anyone else did, he wanted to do it better – not for competition with them, but within himself. Like Cook, he was propelled to go further than any other man, but unlike the heroic mariner, he was not escaping from the claustrophobia of poverty and powerlessness, he was stripping off the shackles of comfort and privilege. And if that meant launching out into *terra incognita*, then so be it. Without risk, there was nothing, but *with* risk came the friction of adventure – and it is this that would become the driving force for the rest of his life.

In his travels around Europe, he'd become something of a polyglot and by the time he reached Australia, he was fluent in six languages. One of these was Portuguese, a language practically unknown in his adoptive homeland, yet one that fuelled the fire of a passion that would take over his life and leave him steeped in controversy and intrigue.

There are two stories about the origins of that fire: the official version I read in books and articles; the other came as a bombshell over lunch with his granddaughters. We were discussing his zeal for the geography and history of Australia and how it all started. I asked if it sprang from being asked by the authorities to interpret some legends on a series of early maps – so ran the official version, anyway, for in 1883 the Public Libraries of Adelaide, Melbourne and Sydney had acquired large reproductions of some sixteenth-century maps of the world and they needed the wording translated. 'Oh no,' came the reply, 'it all began when he responded to an advertisement in the newspaper about a Government competition to write the best school history of Australia!' The humble origins of his downfall left me silent. So George was ruined by chasing a newspaper advert! I smiled ruefully: this was the man who had illustrated the French edition of *Don Quixote*, and here he was a few years later, tilting at his own windmills and on the verge of breaking his big, brave heart. For this upper-class Englishman – born of gentility and establishment – was about to pronounce a heresy that would shake the very pillars of history: Captain James Cook may have been the greatest explorer on Earth, but he didn't discover Australia.

11

'TO THE SOUTHWARDS'

ARLY IN THE seventeenth century and continuing for the next hundred years or more, a volcano erupted across Europe and the New World. This was the Enlightenment and it marked an epoch that was one of the most fervent and intellectually exciting in the history of the world. Fuelled by the discoveries of Copernicus and Galileo – and the revolution in disseminating information via the printing press – the pent-up pressure to explain our universe finally exploded in torrents of new ideas about God, nature, reason and the state of Man himself. The mood saturated thinking in politics, philosophy, commerce and the growing field of science, and spawned a raft of public institutions whose very aim was to question the wonders of the heavens and earth. In the Britain of 1660, this gave birth to the Royal Society for the Promotion of Natural Knowledge, the first scientific organisation in the country, and one of the oldest in Europe.

Over a century later, with the end of the Seven Years' War, an exhausted Europe settled down to a period of much-needed stability. Peace breathed new life into the imaginations of her citizens and institutions, who shook themselves and sloughed off the quiet restraint of the war years and looked afresh at their world. This was the culmination of the Age of Enlightenment and for the Men of Science who typified the times, the big event rearing up on the horizon was of astronomical importance. In 1716, Edmond Halley, the Astronomer Royal, had forewarned the Royal Society that a Transit of Venus was due to take place in 1761 and 1769, when the planet would pass across the face of the sun. Halley was already an old man – sixty was a fair age for the time: he knew he would not live to see it; instead he begged the Gentlemen to take up the mission for themselves and study the phenomenon scientifically.

The sense of urgency was not over-dramatic. These transits occur at

MAGALHAENS.

Magellan by George Collingridge

intervals of more than a hundred years, then two occur around eight years apart before there is another century-long gap. The observations of the transit in 1761 had been a disaster – a combination of poor organisation, bad weather and war had seen to that; the gentlemen of the Royal Society knew they had just one more bite of cherry in their lifetimes and they had to get it right.

The Transit was more than just an astronomical curio, it was the key to a wealth of information about the universe, information that would be seized upon by the intensely curious men of science who characterised the age. In the days before reliable time-keeping, the skies were used as a giant clock – and a transit of a planet across the sun provided a natural stop-watch. Observers could start taking their measurements at the precise moment the two discs touched, and – as everyone on that side of the world would be seeing the same thing – this would make sure that their international partners were each taking their measurements at exactly the same time everywhere in the world. The aim in all this was to determine the parallax – in this case, the angle made when two widely-spaced observers look at the sun. Once you know this and the distance apart of the two observers, it should be possible (using some basic trigonometry) to work out the distance between the earth and the sun. This information could then be inserted into further calculations, opening up the whole universe to scientific enquiry.

The relative scale of the universe had become something of a holy grail to astronomers ever since the first half of the sixteenth century when Nicolaus Copernicus had proposed his radical theory that the earth goes around the sun. Over the next hundred years, the secrets of the universe had begun to be unwrapped by men of learning, such as Sir Isaac Newton, Edmund Halley and Galileo Galilei, who spawned an era of experimentation and deduction. Astronomy had the same promise, the same excitement, as the field of genetics does today, turning old ideas on their head and opening eyes to a new way of looking at the world. Instead of trying to decode the Book of Life, they were using radical new technologies like the telescope to decode the workings of the universe. But more than that, these great thinkers were laying down the scientific method that would be used to explain nature's mysteries – mysteries previously assigned to the work of God. If something could be seen, it could be measured, whether it was on earth or further afield in the universe.

By 1767, the gentlemen of the Royal Society were seriously lagging behind their European counterparts in organising the huge international effort to observe the Transit of Venus. National pride – as well as a once-in-a-lifetime scientific opportunity – was now at stake, and at last they stirred themselves into action or, at least, into forming a Transit Committee to work out what they should do next. Top of the agenda was how and where the observations would be carried out. The Astronomer Royal, Nevil Maskelyne, was consulted for the best locations. He concluded that along with the bases at Hudson Bay in Canada and the North Cape in Norway, a defined area in the South Seas would offer the best view of the proceedings and a good counterpart to the observations in the Northern Hemisphere. This southern area formed a trapezium roughly 1,500 miles east of Australia, with the Marquesas at the top right-hand corner and the as-yet undiscovered New Zealand just outside the bottom left. In between lay thousands of miles of empty ocean.

The next job was to find a 'proper Person' to lead the expeditions. There was a handful of suitable candidates, some recommended, some putting themselves forward. Captain John Campbell was a clear contender – a member of the Transit Committee, he had developed the sextant, was a gifted sailor and also a talented scientist – and yet he failed to bite, possibly regarding it as a step sideways or backwards in his impressive naval career (and one with limited opportunity for bounty!) It is hard not to develop an affection for this kind man with his profound interest in scientific matters – and it is no surprise to see him eagerly supporting the inventor, John Harrison, during the development of his chronometers for the Board of Longitude.

Mr Green was another obvious choice for the voyage: he had worked for three Astronomer Royals, travelling with Maskelyne to Barbados in order to test Harrison's chronometer. Although the two men fell out on the voyage, Maskelyne could not cast doubt over his assistant's skills. He would be someone of immense value on an expedition such as this and was assigned to travel to the 'southwards' destination, whatever that would be. Another name that came to fore was the man who would become almost an antihero to Cook and the closest he ever came to an enemy: Alexander Dalrymple.

Alexander Dalrymple is one of British maritime history's most engaging characters – a dashing explorer, hopeless dreamer and a fiercely competitive mischief-maker. Born nine years after Cook to a large and well-to-do Scottish family, he sailed for Madras with the East India Company when just fifteen years old and, once there, devoured any books he could lay his hands on. Like Cook, he had received little in the way of formal schooling but had the intelligence and tenacity to become his own tutor. So, while Cook was in Canada studying astronomy and surveying, Dalrymple was soaking up anything he could find on the South Seas. He became quite expert on matters concerning the region's trade and had grand designs for winning back Britain's economic power in the East Indies, then usurped by the Dutch.

His other grand design, perhaps even an obsession, was to be an explorer, and a famous one at that. Although he had toured extensively within East Indian and Indian waters before returning to Britain as a forceful exponent of British expansion in the region, his credentials as a mariner were highly questionable; he had never served as an apprentice seaman, nor less officially commanded his own ship. The longest time he had spent in open sea was allegedly a mere nineteen days! For Dalrymple, however, the passion was enough. But this was not a passion for astronomy – in fact, he had shown little interest in observing anything other than his own meteoric rise to fame. Dalrymple's dream was to claim his own place in the history books by being the first to discover the land that had inspired geographers for over a thousand years: the mythical land of milk and honey, perfect climate, civilised inhabitants and unimaginable wealth, the Great Southern Continent. This infamous and much-dreamed-of land was believed to lie somewhere in the Pacific Ocean – and a voyage such as the one proposed by the Royal Society was the perfect opportunity to pursue it. John Beaglehole, who edited the definitive collection of Cook journals, captured the mood that so gripped Dalrymple and his forebears:

> Terra australis incognita, the unknown southern land – or, more hopefully, *nondum congnita*, not yet known but in due course to be revealed: the brief words rail a long history, are aromatic with an old romance, as of great folios in ancient libraries, compassing all the philosophical and geographical knowledge, with pages and double pages of maps whose very amplitude and pattern ravish the mind; and they present us also with one of the great illusions. It was an illusion raised by abstract thought, buttressed by fragments of discovery that seemed to fit into a likely pattern, demolished by experienced fact. There is a southern land, of course, and even now it is not fully known; but it was not this of which so many generations dreamed. The Antarctic is the fact which has survived; and the Antarctic is not the *provincia aurea*, the golden and spicy province, the lands of dye-woods and parrots and castles, the jumble of fable and misinterpretation that was piled on Greek reasoning and Marco Polo.

The fabled land grew out of the Ancients' need for harmony in the cosmos. The Greeks and even their predecessors believed in the fundamental principle that the mass of land in the Northern Hemisphere must have a counterbalance in the Southern Hemisphere, or the world would be unstable. As more and more land was discovered in the New Worlds of the north, the imagined continent grew larger in turn; its fate was finally sealed when Europeans gained their first glimpses of the Spice Islands – these must surely be just the outliers to that vast land of potential, a land that was itching to be discovered and harvested, a land that would answer every dream of its conquerors.

The stakes, meanwhile, were high for those who sailed in search of it. Clandestine expeditions set out from Portugal, Spain, France and England, their captains were sworn to silence over details of their routes and their discoveries. A cloak of secrecy swathed the maps of the seas and new-discovered lands, everyone desperate to hide anything that might advantage their international competitors. For the discovering nation, the prize was global supremacy, for the man who discovered it, eternal fame. The Continent must lie in the Southern Ocean, and the race was on to find it.

In Britain, the impetus for finding the Continent was spearheaded by Alexander Dalrymple. He used his impressive connections at the East India Company, the Royal Society and Government to lecture, petition, write and draw up maps supporting his dream and his claim as discoverer-incarnate. The proposed Royal Society and Admiralty voyage was the perfect answer to his hopes for immortality. So sure was he of his position as the most suitable person for the job – and to be fair he had a good deal of support for this view – he even laid down strict conditions to the Transit Committee about how he would take part. Thanking the Council for their 'favourable Intentions', he added that, 'there is but one part of the World, where I can engage to make the Observations'. As if that was not demanding enough, 'it may be necessary to observe that I can have no thought of undertaking the Voyage as a Passenger going out to make the Observations, or on any other footing than that of having the management of the Ship intended for the Service'.

However, the Admiralty had already had one bad experience of putting a non-naval officer in command of a ship. Edmund Halley, the former Astronomer Royal, had presided over the *Paramour Pink* in 1698 to study the variation of the compass. Despite being denounced by his astronomer colleagues for drinking brandy and swearing 'like a sea-captain', Halley was no seaman. After a disastrous and mutinous voyage, he was eventually forced to return home. This incident had scarred the minds of the Admiralty, particularly the First Lord, Sir Edward Hawke, who said that he would 'rather cut off his right hand than permit anyone but a King's Officer to command one of the ships of His Majesty's Navy'.

The Admiralty's position was clear, but that did not stop Dalrymple from using his connections to try to win them round. He not only petitioned the Government directly but, through his brother, Lord Hailes, he asked Adam Smith, the famous economist, to petition the authorities on his behalf. If anyone was going to be sent on a scientific expedition to the South Seas, home of the infamous Great Southern Continent, it was going to be him – or so he thought.

It is strange now to look back on the very different map of the world that Dalrymple and his fellow geographers would have used, with its bizarre mixture of myth and reality. Seventeen sixty-eight was a time of intense maritime activity: the Seven Years' War may have been over but there were still colonies to serve and international trade to pursue. However, while the northern seas bubbled with activity, the maps petered out once they left these busy waters. Mariners knew that the Pacific Ocean was large enough to hide islands, but could its capacious arms hold the earthly paradise that was *Terra Nondum Cognita*, the as-yet unknown Great Southern Continent?

The Pacific Ocean – or great Southern Ocean – was still just being opened up by those who risked their lives for bounty, their King or their God. Beyond the known spice routes, new lands were occasionally discovered but with no sure way of determining longitude and thereby plotting an accurate position, all too often they were as soon lost as found. As the Transit Committee was making its deliberations about would-be participants of the Royal Society voyage, they would have looked at the coastlines sketched out on the charts, knowing that at best they represented a rough guess and at worst the fantasies of those too long at sea, beguiled by ice or cloud into calling 'land!'

Europeans had gained their first glimpse of this vast ocean of potential, fear – but mainly water – around 25 September, 1513, when the Spaniard, Vasco Nuñez de Balboa was crossing the dense jungle and rivers of Isthmus of Panama to conquer the Incas and claim their gold. Climbing up the *cordillera*, and standing 'silent up on a peak in Darien', he saw a magnificent ocean glistening blue and wide beneath him and realised he was looking on a vast expanse of water previously unseen by European eyes. It took another four days of travelling before he finally reached the coast and could wade in and claim the ocean, along with all its islands, for the King of Spain, and it would take almost another four centuries before its true extent was known.

The Pacific is the largest and deepest ocean on the planet, with more than twice the surface area and volume of its nearest rival, the Atlantic.

Stretching from Antarctica in the south to the Bering Strait in the north, it covers a third of the earth's surface – almost 64,000,000 square miles, or 165,000,000 square kilometres; in fact, you could chop up every bit of land from the northern and southern hemispheres, sink them in its depths and still have room for more. When he stood on that Darien peak and stared at the ocean below, Vasco Nuñez de Balboa would have had no conception of the magnitude of what lay before him, still less of how and if Europeans could reach it by sea.

A route into the Southern Ocean was dreamed of long before it was a reality for the kings, sailors and mapmakers of Europe. At the time of Balboa, at the start of the sixteenth century, Portugal and Spain were global super-powers, locked in a bitter fight for maritime, economic and political supremacy in the New Worlds of Africa and the Americas. Portugal had become the most sophisticated seafaring nation in Europe with the scientific and financial support of one remarkable man: Prince Henry the Navigator. In 1419, he had established a centre for leading astronomers, cartographers, navigators and mariners at his base in Sagres; his aim was simple: to expand Portugal's empire into the furthest-flung corners of the earth, something he achieved in his lifetime and beyond through inspiring his mariners onto some of the greatest feats of exploration that the world had ever seen. One of the most significant was the smashing of the taboo on crossing Cape Bojador, just south of the Canary Islands. Located at the western end of the Sahara desert, its Atlantic coastline was famous for its appalling weather and strewn with lethal reefs to ensnare unwary ships. This Cape was the bogeyman of the medieval navigators, abounding in ghastly legends that it was indeed the end of the earth – sail too close and you would simply fall off the edge of the world and down into hell. Given how superstitious people were in the Middle Ages, Gil Eanes' achievement deserves huge respect – both for his navigational skill in crossing of the Cape in 1434, and his bravery and leadership in getting his men to go with him.

But Henry had an even greater goal in sight: his grand strategy was to find a sea-route via Africa to the Spice Islands and thereby defeat the power of the Moors; once he had broken the Moorish monopoly on the spice trade, he knew that politically they would be broken, too, leaving Portugal the most potent nation on earth.

Henry died before his plan came to fruition, though by then his ships had reached modern-day Sierra Leone and possibly beyond. Twenty-eight years later, in January 1488, Bartolomeu Dias passed the Cape of Good Hope – the southernmost tip of Africa – opening up the sea route to the valuable cargoes of the Spice Islands. Until then, trade from these islands had been under the strict monopoly of the Muslim merchants of

North Africa, but Portugal was now set to snatch the prize for itself. Henry the Navigator was finally proved right: the money in terms of gold and spices from such a route was so colossal that it did, indeed, make Portugal the most powerful nation in the Northern Hemisphere.

Spain, meanwhile, fizzed with jealousy, despite its own advances in exploring the east coast of South America. Such was the acrimony and bloodshed between these two Catholic nations that in 1493 the Pope intervened. Calling the two sides together, he looked at the map of the world as it was then known and saw that Spain's lands mainly lay to the west in the Americas, while Portugal's lay to the east with Africa and the Spice Islands. Both regions had their potential riches – gold and silver in the west, spice and silks in the east – and so, like a parent separating fighting children, Pope Alexander VI simply divided the undiscovered world into two. The result was a hypothetical line from Pole to Pole through the middle of the Atlantic Ocean, around three hundred and twenty miles west of the Cape Verde Islands. What lands each nation already had, they could keep, but any future discoveries to the west of that line would become the property of Spain, and anything to the east of that line would be Portuguese. This 'Line of Demarcation', shifted after Portuguese appeals to 1,185 miles west of the Cape Verde Islands (therefore giving Portugal the coast of Brazil), was ratified by both sides in the Treaty of Tordesillas in 1494 and set the pattern for the next hundred years of voyages of discovery. It is the also reason why most of Latin America speaks Spanish, and why you can dance to Portuguese bailar music in Sri Lanka.

However, as time went on and the two warring nations sent more and more ships into the Southern Hemisphere, two further issues arose to muddy the waters of the uncertain geography of the fifteenth-century world. The first was the matter of longitude. As the technology for navigation improved, it became relatively straightforward to determine a place's latitude – that is, how far north or south it was of the Equator – by using a device known as an astrolabe. This became widely used from the Middle Ages before eventually being replaced by the quadrant and sextant. Determining longitude – that is, how far west or east you are of a given point – was an altogether knottier problem. Theoretically, the knowledge of how to work out your longitude by using the moon and stars had been known since the end of the fifteenth century, but the mathematics involved, let alone the need for clear weather, made it wholly unworkable. It took another two hundred years before reliable lunar tables were published, reducing at least some of the calculations involved, and then it took the invention of the first chronometer by John

Harrison in 1735 before a workable mechanical method was available. But in the years after the Treaty of Tordesillas, longitude was arrived at by 'dead reckoning', which was little more than an educated guess. This meant that you never really knew for certain how far east or west you were of the Line of Demarcation, making the zones around the line still something of a free-for-all, with ignorance as your best defence.

The other issue was the world itself: if the earth really was a globe, as geographers were suggesting, then the Line would run over the North Pole to Siberia and then through the blank space of what would be eventually called the western Pacific, but in 1493, those waters were seemingly blocked-off by the Americas and as unexplored by Europeans as the heavens themselves. Even if navigators reached this continuation of the Line, determining whether you were on the Portuguese or Spanish side of it would be little more than a stab in the dark.

All this gave Spain a problem: until El Dorado bore its fruit in the Americas, the major wealth still lay in the spice trade, which was still only accessible by crossing eastwards over the Line of Demarcation into Portuguese waters and then round the Cape of Good Hope into the Indian Ocean. Spain needed its own route into the Great Southern Ocean – and for that, it would have to head west.

Ironically, the passage via South America into the Pacific was delivered by a Portuguese navigator who had defected from his country when he was refused a pay-rise. Born Fernão de Magalhães, the son of a nobleman, Ferdinand Magellan, as he is better known, had taken part in the Portuguese Spice Wars against the Muslims of Africa and India. Though successful in battle, Magellan received a limp that affected him for the rest of his life and when he returned home, he demanded more money from the King in recognition of his part in the victory. The King refused and sent him back to Morocco, where again Magellan petitioned the King. Once more the King refused – and suggested that if he did not like it, Magellan should offer his services elsewhere. It was to prove a costly mistake for Portugal: a furious Magellan took the King at his word and signed his loyalty over to Spain.

His new country immediately recognised his worth. They needed a fearless navigator to open up a west passage to the Southern Ocean, and Magellan was just the man to do it. Spain furnished him with five good ships – a sign of their commitment to both him and the project – and, on 20 September, 1519, in spite of numerous sabotage attempts by the Portuguese, two hundred and seventy men left the safe waters of Europe for an unknown destiny. Magellan realised he was now staking his life against immortality.

Within a week, the fleet had reached Tenerife and, by 13 December, it had ridden the storms to Rio de Janeiro; but it wasn't just the weather Magellan had to worry about. Stopping for supplies on the coast of South America, the crew enjoyed the favours of the local women, who could be 'bought' in exchange for an iron nail. Unsurprisingly, when it was time to sail again, many were reluctant to leave; it was said that even the priests had to be dragged back on board, and the ships themselves were left rather the worse for wear. General discontent was spreading throughout the crews, mingled no doubt with the fear of what lay ahead and, at midnight on Easter Day, 1520, the Spanish sea captains led a mutiny against their Portuguese commander. With cool and steely anger, Magellan turned full vengeance against those who had betrayed him, quelling the mutiny and executing the main agitator whilst leaving another to take his chances on the barren shore.

Setting off for the final push down into what is now Patagonia, he reached the entrance of the Strait that would bear his name. It begins easily enough, with a large entrance and open water, but then degenerates into a maze of channels, rocks and islands with no clear way out. On top of this, the weather can turn treacherous with ice, dense fog and squally gales to make life even more miserable – and Magellan had them all. Here, in the twisting, narrow and shoal-strewn passage, he met with still more mariners' nightmares: one of his five ships was wrecked while another deserted; only the *Vittoria*, the *Concepión* and the *Trinidad* made it through the strait and into open water. On the news that the Great Southern Ocean was in sight, the cool-headed commander reportedly broke down in tears of joy, knelt on the deck and gave thanks to a merciful God.

The men were rewarded for their audacity by an unusually calm crossing of that new ocean, and this gave the Pacific its name; but on board, the curse of the long-distance seaman was taking hold. By now, the crew was wracked with scurvy, stricken by thirst and starving. They had finished the last of the ships' biscuits – soaked through with rats' urine and covered in faeces – and then started on the rats, too, if and when they could be caught. Finally, the desperate crew were reduced to eating sawdust and the sun-baked leather off the yardarms. In all, it was ninety-nine grim days before they made landfall at Guam in the Marianas. Here, at last, they could stretch out on *terra firma* and replenish their bodies with fresh food once more.

When the ships again set sail, it was not for the Moluccas or 'Spice Islands', even though they knew (probably from leaked Portuguese intelligence) the approximate position of this holy grail. Instead, they went to the Philippines, where they could rest safely while the men built up their strength and their supplies. Here they secured a base from which to make the final push to the Spice Islands where they would fill the holds with precious cargo before returning home to glory and riches.

But all that was a year away. Meanwhile, Magellan was making the most of his stay in the Philippines, winning Spain's first alliance in the Pacific and converting the ruling hierarchy of Cebu to Christianity. However, not everything ran so smoothly: some of the Filipinos were less than happy to welcome in the foreigners. Soon the locals' discontent turned into skirmishes with the interlopers and then, two months after arriving in the islands, Ferdinand Magellan was killed in fighting.

From here, the voyage slowly disintegrated: only two of the ships made it to the Moluccas and just one spice-laden ship, the flagship *Vittoria* – under the command of Juan Sebastián de Elcano – made it back via the Cape of Good Hope to Spain. On board were four Indians picked up along the way and a mere seventeen of the original crew, 'weaker than men have ever been before'. Yet they had completed the first circumnavigation of the globe, forging a westward passage to the Pacific, and giving final proof that the Earth was indeed round.

From this point on, the Pacific Ocean became the new hunting ground for international traders. Spanish explorers continued to nudge the boundaries of geography and politics while the Portuguese vainly defended the empires the Pope had declared as theirs – and everyone kept an eye open for the infamous Great Southern Continent. As far as each nation's Policy of Secrecy allowed, philosophers and geographers compared notes with explorers and mariners to lay down the growing map of the southern hemisphere; where no land was known, it was easily discussed in literature or painted in on the maps: it was, after all, surely there, it just had not been discovered yet.

The practice of drawing maps as a confusing medley of fact and fiction was still frustrating navigators in Cook's day. Jonathan Swift had satirised the practice with the lines:

So geographers, in Afric maps,
With savage pictures fill their gaps
And o'er uninhabitable downs
Place elephants for want of towns.

Again Beaglehole sums up the mood nicely: 'Geographers no less than nature seem to have abhorred a vacuum.'

Sometimes, however, it was not the geographers' fault – until Halley and then Maskelyne developed their astronomic tables in the 1700s, determining one's longitude was little more than a guessing game, while latitude could only be measured when skies were clear enough to use an astrolabe, octant or later, a sextant. With explorers unable to give accurate co-ordinates for the lands they discovered, cartographers and navigators alike would have to rely on written journals and their own reasoning. Marco Polo was a case in point – his travels inspired generations of cartographers yet his alleged Locac was really the Malay Peninsula, at the time mistakenly positioned twelve thousand miles to the west and southwest of Java, and ended up being represented as the Great Southern Continent.

At other times, explorers would be 'gagged' to keep their discoveries secret, for fear of the land being plundered or colonised by their enemies. This was evident in the maps of the period after the Treaty of Tordesillas when landmasses appear to have been nudged east or west to better fit within the areas assigned to Spain and Portugal under the Pope's Line of Demarcation. But, as Swift noted with ironic humour, just to make the traveller's life that little bit more difficult, it was also customary for cartographers to make up place names, draw in non-existent rivers and illustrate the mythical lands with scenes from other 'exotic' parts of the world, further blurring the line between what was geographical fact and what was cartographic fiction. In all, until the late eighteenth century, when technical improvement meant that cartography and hydrography were respected as scientific disciplines, maps were the factual equivalent of the *National Enquirer* or *Sunday Sport* newspaper. It is hardly surprising the Admiralty had so much enthusiasm for the meticulous and scrupulous surveys of James Cook.

But even as late as February 1768, with just sixteen months before the Transit of Venus was due to take place, the Royal Society was still assuming Dalrymple would lead the South Seas voyage and furthermore was petitioning the King to stump up the cash. The arguments laid down were persuasive: it would 'contribute greatly to the improvement of Astronomy, on which Navigation so much depends'; most other 'Great Powers' in Europe were sending observers to record the data; and it would 'cast dishonour' on Britain not to take part. Then, almost as a postscript, there was the claim that they needed £4,000 to send the observers around the globe, exclusive of the ship.

Surprisingly, and to the King's credit, he paid up the substantial sum, worth a quarter of a million pounds at today's rates. At last the Royal Society had the money; what it now needed was a ship. This matter was resolved in a Council Meeting on 3 April, 1768: the President read out a letter from the Admiralty, advising the gentlemen that it had bought a Whitby Cat, or collier-ship, for the voyage; it also asked the Society who was going to be on the ship and what instructions needed to be given to the ship's commander.

The scene that followed must have had flies fighting for a space on the wall: the President rather shamefacedly admitted to the Council that, on proposing to the Admiralty that Alexander Dalrymple should command the voyage, he had received the reply that any such idea would be 'repugnant to the rules of the Navy'! Clearly, Lord Hawke had stuck to his word: it would be a Navy man – or his right arm, and a Navy man would be less of an inconvenience.

It is not recorded whether Dalrymple was actually in the room when the President gave the news, but he was certainly in attendance that day and was told in person that his demands for sole command of the voyage would not be met. Dalrymple had lost his chance to become the discoverer of the Great Southern Continent and with it, a national hero. The offer was still there to go along as an observer, but that was as repugnant a suggestion to him as he was to the Navy and, unsurprisingly, this hot-headed wannabe explorer decided to withdraw from the whole affair. With his ego badly dented, the thirty-year-old stormed out of the Royal Society buildings in what can be politely termed a mild rage; the scene had been set for a life-long enmity with whoever had got that command.

It took another two months for the Admiralty to decide officially just who that person should be. In early April, at the personal recommendation of Philip Stephens, the secretary, and Captain Hugh Palliser, the King's Surveyor in Newfoundland was temporarily removed from his post to lead a scientific voyage into the South Seas; James Cook was to be the anointed commander.

Yet another month passed before the Council of the Royal Society discussed the issue of voyage personnel again; this time, however, the atmosphere could not have been more different. True enough, a mariner waited outside the Council chamber but this time the proceedings were mere formalities; there were no histrionics and no surprises. The minutes of that meeting survive in the Society's Library:

Captain John Campbell mentioned that Captain James Cook who now attended will be appointed by the Admiralty to the command of the vessel destined for the observation in the Southern Latitudes, and that he was a proper person to be one of the observers in the observation of the Transit of Venus, Mr Cook was called in, and accepted the employment in consideration of such gratuity as the Society shall think proper, and an allowance of £120 a year for victualling himself and the other observer in every particular.

One assumes that the Royal Society knew that Mr Cook was not yet a Captain and the slip was just a clerical error; the learned gentlemen might well have raised an eyebrow to realise that their Mr Dalrymple had lost his place in the history books to someone still officially only a Royal Navy Master. However, he would remain as Master for just twenty more days: he had finally received his King's commission and, with effect from 25 May, the farm labourer's son could style himself Lieutenant James Cook.

Finding the right man to command the voyage was one issue, the other was to find a suitable place in the Southern Ocean for observing the crucial Transit. This was proving just as much of a challenge for the gentlemen of the Royal Society. The map of the Pacific Ocean was bounded by known trade routes infilled with strange lands visited once and then lost or forgotten, or by mythical lands of milk and honey. It might have been perfect for dreamers and writers – and books like *Gulliver's Travels* were certainly essential reading for anyone with intellectual pretensions – but for their scientific observations, the Council needed somewhere that was easily locatable, as far away from the northern observing sites as possible, and with friendly inhabitants to let the observers carry out their work in peace. The trouble was, unlike Portugal, Spain and the Netherlands, Britain did not have a wealth of colonies in the South Seas, particularly in the zone deemed best for making the observations. Commodore Anson had returned from his Pacific voyage laden with Spanish gold rather than new-found lands, John Byron – grandfather of the poet – had spent twenty-two months circumnavigating the world in search of the Great Southern Continent but only discovered some small and unsuitable islands in the desired region. Captain Samuel Wallis had been away for nearly two years and was still in mid-ocean on his way back to Britain. It was hoped he would bring better news home with him; in the meantime, the search was on for that perfect place. The gentlemen of the Royal Society unfurled their world maps, smoothed them out on the large tables, and stared into the blank space that was the Pacific.

Throughout the sixteenth and seventeenth centuries, both Portugal and Spain had been eagerly carving up the New World between them, according to the will of the Pope. Numerous voyages of exploration and discovery set off in search of gold, new recruits for religious conversion and glory. The Great South Land still motivated men to forsake their homes and head out into the unknown – and mostly to their death.

However, two names stand out from this time for expanding European knowledge of the South Sea: Pedro Fernández de Quirós and Luis Vaez de Torres.

Although he was Portuguese, Quirós had sailed for Spain in 1595 as the navigator for the young and ambitious Álvaro de Mendaña. In a previous expedition in 1567, Mendaña had been searching for King Solomon's mines, which he believed lay west of Peru, probably in the Great Southern Continent. He travelled over 8,000 miles of empty ocean before making land, but it was not upon the mythical shores of Terra Australis; instead, he had discovered the Solomon Islands, no gold and some decidedly unfriendly natives who soon drove them off. Undeterred, he resolved to try once more and, twenty-eight years later, he finally won support for another attempt to set up a Spanish colony there; the only trouble was, he could not find them again. En route, Mendaña did discover and name the Marquesas Islands and then the Santa Cruz group where they eventually settled, but the colony was doomed to failure. Mendaña was dead within a month and the settlers slaughtered by the locals; a few weeks later, the remaining men and women fled to the relative safety of the Philippines under the sober command of the saintly Quirós.

Despite the failure of Mendaña's dream, the fire to find and settle the Great Southern Continent was kept alive by the young navigator. He passionately believed that God had sent him to bring Christianity to the heathen of this bountiful land and, on 21 December, 1605, he once again left the Peruvian port of Callao to sail west. He took with him three ships – his flagship, the *San Pedro y San Pablo*, the *San Pedro* – commanded by the much-respected Luis de Vaez Torres – and a small launch.

It was not an auspicious start: within a few weeks, Quirós ignored the pleas of his small fleet to head towards what looked like distant land. Instead, he headed due west for over seven thousand miles until they came across a large bay in what he believed was indeed the Continent. He duly named it, Austrialia del Espíritu Santo – present-day Vanuatu, just a thousand miles from the Australian coast.

Like a true missionary, he set about creating the Kingdom of God on earth but Quirós's vision was at odds with reality: the colonists were facing punishing terrain and less than happy locals – and, after a tense and difficult month, they put the Kingdom on hold and set off once more in search of the Promised Land. But if they thought their trials would be over, they were wrong; heading out to sea, the strong winds turned into a violent storm which scattered the fleet, leaving Torres' *San Pedro* and the launch without their flagship. They searched for Quirós for a fortnight, not realising he had already returned to Peru; then Torres began the remarkable journey that ensured his place in history.

Rounding Espíritu Santo to prove it was just an island, he then headed southward to search for the Continent. Finding nothing but the Coral Sea, he turned north again and sailed via the Louisiade Archipelago at the south-eastern tip of New Guinea, then made his incredible voyage south of New Guinea and through what became known as the Torres Strait, one of the most treacherous passages in the world. He knew he was charting undiscovered waters, although with no way of measuring longitude and less than accurate latitudes, it is hard today to follow his precise route. What is crucial is that he had proved that New Guinea was an island and not connected to the large continent that lay to the south – the continent we now know as Australia.

Bizarrely, however, when he made it back to Spain via the Philippines, despite his charts, letters and report to the King, the information about this strait was buried in the archives for the next 175 years. The ruling belief of cartographers and navigators well into the eighteen century was that New Guinea formed part of a larger body of land. Other than a brief mention by a Spanish chronicler in 1621, another in the early 1630s and a few maps drawn over the succeeding century, possibly from a leaked or stolen chart, Torres' new-found strait was smothered by the Spanish policy of secrecy and disappeared from view.

But not, it seems, to Lieutenant James Cook. During the British occupation of Manila, Alexander Dalrymple had obtained a copy of the 1630s document describing Torres' achievements which he included in his 1767 pamphlet, *Discoveries made in the South Pacific, Previous to 1764*. He presented one of these pamphlets to Joseph Banks to take on the Transit voyage and it would be the source of a long-running argument between Banks and the ship's commander over whether such a strait really existed.

In the seventeenth century, a newcomer appeared in the southern seas; the Dutch rose as a new European super-power, steadily gobbling up the empire of the Portuguese and nibbling at the edges of the Spanish. However, they were primarily a trading nation rather than one keen for new discoveries. Their strategy was one of sure hits: it was easier to capture existing trading posts than go searching for new ones that might or might not bear fruit. With military efficiency, they eroded Portugal's supremacy in the East Indies and soon captured the region's trade and with it, its wealth. From their base in Batavia (now Jakarta, Indonesia), the Dutch East India Company, or VOC, spread out its fingers to pluck the riches from neighbouring islands and coastal lands.

Dutch ships *en route* to the East Indies had already made a series of accidental discoveries along a strange coastline that was styled as Terra Australis or the South Land, which lay to the southeast of Java. In 1605, Willem Jansz sailed the *Duyfken* to the coastline of the modern-day Gulf of Carpentaria, where he explored the gulf's east coast. Then, in 1616, Dirck Hartog was travelling from Amsterdam round the Cape of Good Hope to Java when he caught sight of a barren island. He landed, gave the island his own name, and spent the next couple of days exploring. There was not much there to capture his imagination and so he nailed a pewter plate to a tree that proclaimed him as discoverer, before continuing on his way to Java. It seems the VOC were equally uninspired when they heard the news – it took another eighty years before the island was revisited by Willem de Vlamingh, who replaced Hartog's plate with one of his own, and sent the original home where it can still be seen in the Rijksmuseum.

Gradually, and mainly by accident when their ships were blown off-course, the Dutch filled in sections of the northern and western coasts of what is now Australia but what was then the South Land. It took until 1642 for the VOC to make any serious plans for exploration, and these were under the vision of the great Governor General of the Dutch East Indies, Anthony van Diemen. His impressive rule began in 1636 and he immediately began consolidating the haphazard trading posts into a commercial empire. From the Spice Islands to Malacca (now in Malaysia), Formosa (Taiwan), Ceylon and India's Coromandel Coast, he brought the spice trade under strict Dutch control – and then turned his eyes to the millions of square miles of potential that lay to the unexplored south.

He may have been inspired to make discoveries when he travelled out to the East Indies with the explorer, Willem Jansz. On 31 July, 1618, they had seen and possibly even stepped on Australian soil, believing it to be just another island. Fourteen years later, as Governor General of the region, he resolved to explore and survey what was already known of South Land, make new discoveries and survey them fully – and find an easy route across the Pacific to South America. It was a tall order.

The man chosen for the job was the experienced and highly capable Abel Janszoon Tasman. Aged thirty-nine, he had spent years sailing the North Pacific and South China Sea and was the clear choice for such a grand and dangerous venture. On 14 August, 1642, a small squadron of ships under his command sailed out of Batavia and then southwestwards towards Africa and the island of Mauritius. This was uninhabited at the time but was known to have a reasonable supply of fresh water, along with the flightless dodo. Here they resupplied and carried out some essential repairs before continuing south to pick up the strong westerly winds that would carry them eastwards towards the Pacific. By the time they reached 49°S – almost on a parallel with Cape Horn – the stormy seas were enough to convince them that no continent lay to the south, and they headed north again. Finally, as night fell on 24 November, 1642, they caught sight of some high mountains about forty miles away. It must have been a tantalising wait until the morning light could confirm that they were indeed looking at a new land – but was it the Great Southern Continent? They named it Anthoony van Diemenslandt after their esteemed Governor General, and over the next few days made one successful and one failed landing on what we now call Tasmania. They saw definite signs of habitation but no people, just beaches turning into dense, dark forests they did not care to explore.

After pushing up the eastern coast of this strange land, they headed once more out to sea and, eight days later, in mid-December, they saw the coast of New Zealand's South Island.

Whereas the inhabitants of Tasmania had not shown themselves, the natives of this new land came out in canoes. A small party of Dutchmen went out in one of the small boats to greet them – to their cost. Four sailors died in the encounter and Tasman ordered the squadron to withdraw, naming the place 'Murderer's Bay'.

Fate continued to be against them as they continued north, with strong winds and stormy seas plaguing their passage north and preventing Tasman from exploring the large 'bay' that was really the passage between New Zealand's North and South Islands into the Pacific that would later be called Cook Strait. After naming the northern cape Maria van Diemen after the Governor General's wife, he left what he believed could be a promontory of the famed Southern Continent and headed over a thousand miles north to Tonga and its neighbouring Fijian Islands, then northwestwards along the top of New Guinea. Here the contrary winds decided their route for them: they would not head back down to answer the question of New Guinea's insularity or explore the north coast of the South Land but instead tracked west back home to Batavia, where they arrived on the 14 June, 1643.

In the ten months of the voyage, Tasman and his men had circumnavigated Australia without ever seeing it. However, by sailing in open water to the south of the South Land, he had also proved that the land so often found by Dutch ships *en route* to the Spice Islands was not part of the Great Southern Continent. Van Diemen's Land was possibly part of the south coast of the South Land but what if the land he had styled 'Staten Landt' really *was* the northerly projection of the Great Southern Continent? The thought did not excite the voyage's sponsor; in fact, van Diemen was not a happy man. Tasman had failed to resolve the issue of whether New Guinea was an island or part of the South Land, had not made contact with the people of Van Diemen's Land and had failed to pursue good relations and trade with the inhabitants of Staten Landt. The Governor General angrily complained to his VOC directors in the Netherlands that

> Tasman has not made many investigations regarding the situations nor form and nature of the discovered lands and peoples, but in principle has left everything to a more inquisitive successor.

Tasman was given the chance to redeem himself in a second expedition in 1644, during which he was to explore and chart the northern coasts of the South Land to determine whether or not a passage lay to the south of New Guinea, providing a short-cut into the Pacific. If a passage did exist, he was to make his way through it and then down the east coast of the South Land to see if it was continuous to Van Diemen's Land, before following the coast back round to Batavia. If there was no such short-cut, he was to travel around the coast of the South Land, charting and exploring as he went.

The ships left in February but, once more, Tasman took non-discovery to an artform, failing to find any channel to the south of New Guinea; instead, he explored the Gulf of Carpentaria before heading around Arnhem Land, past the Kimberleys then down the west coast to Ningaloo. He returned to Batavia having found nothing of any consequence, 'only poor, naked people walking along the beaches; without rice or many fruits, very poor and bad-tempered people in many places'.

Tasman's reputation is not helped by the fact that there are no known surviving journals or charts from the voyage, but a year or so after his return, the information from his explorations gave rise to a modified map where, instead of Terra Australis or South Land, appeared the revised coastline of the land called for the first time 'New Holland'. However, as Joan Blaeu's *c.*1650 Chart of the Pacific Ocean shows, in between New Holland and the Pacific coast of the Americas lay vast expanses of nothingness, punctuated only by the tiniest of islands and the symbolic ships of the nations that dared to explore the void. The Dutch had added little to the map of the world.

One hundred years later, in May 1768, the Royal Society was staring into that same empty space. Cook was signed up, along with the esteemed Mr Green, but still there was nowhere to send them for their observations. The situation was getting desperate. By 19 May, Cook had agreed his Society gratuity of 100 guineas (just over £100, or £6000 today) to command a voyage to a location as yet unknown; then, the next day, Captain Samuel Wallis arrived home.

In twenty-one months, the *Dolphin* under the command of Wallis and its companion ship, the *Swallow*, under Philip Carteret, had travelled the world in search of the Great Southern Continent. Always one step ahead of their French rival, Bougainville, they rounded Cape Horn into the Pacific. Foul weather had separated the ships in the Magellan Strait and while Carteret returned home via Pitcairn Island and the Philippines, Wallis tracked northwest then west across the South Sea. After many more weeks of sailing in an empty ocean, he began to encounter a scattering of atolls – rings of coral reefs forming rocky islands – most of which seemed uninhabited apart from hundreds of seabirds. Then, far to the south, and through a blanket of cloud, he and his men saw what they thought must be the tall mountain peaks of the Continent itself. At last! Wallis would go down in history as the discoverer of Terra Australis Incognita. But within minutes of their rejoices, the thick cloud shifted and hid the peaks from view. Night fell with the ship drifting ever-closer to the atolls and men waiting anxiously for dawn; when it came, they could not see the Continent but there was something all the more astounding to capture their attention: long canoes filled with beautiful native men and women peppered the water, gradually gaining confidence to come up to the ship. Wallis realised that his crew were the first Europeans they had ever seen, and gently sailed the *Dolphin* along the coast until he found a break in the reef leading into an expansive harbour.

The land was an earthly paradise: food and fruit abounded, there was fresh, sweet water, ample wood and the natives were increasingly warm and welcoming; in fact, some of the women were a little too welcoming. They were happy to give sexual favours in return for the iron which their island lacked and the men so enthusiastically took up the offer that the *Dolphin* was stripped of its nails and nearly fell to bits. Whatever the effect on the ship, the men thought that they had arrived in heaven. During the next five weeks, Wallis took possession of what he called King George's Land, the island of Tahiti. The purser took precise astronomical observations to determine the exact position of the island – latitude 17°30'S and 150°W longitude using 'Dr Masculines Method which we did not understand'! However, the observations were good and when laid down on the chart, provided a sure reference for future visits.

Then Wallis made sail for Britain with news of this 'large, fertile and extremely populous island', charting some other smaller new islands along the way and little realising the significance of his discovery.

The point was not wasted on the gentlemen of the Royal Society. As soon as they received word of the island, they knew they had found their perfect place. It lay almost at the heart of Maskelyne's area in the southern hemisphere for the best observations of the Transit. There was no doubt whatsoever: Cook and his scientific voyage would be heading to Tahiti.

The Admiralty was doubly pleased with the choice of location. Not only would it provide a suitable base in the Pacific, but it also provided an opportunity to make other explorations in the area, explorations that might open the way to that distant horizon spotted by the men of the *Dolphin*, twenty leagues to the south.

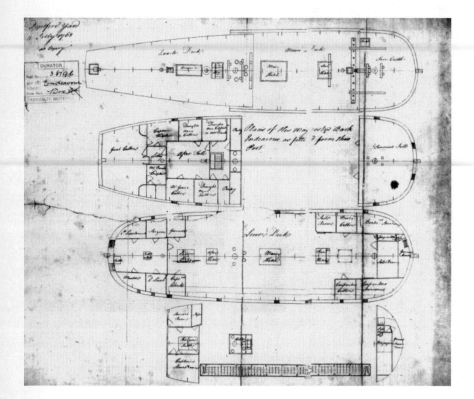

The Admiralty plans of The Endeavour

12
PREPARATIONS

James Cook 1768

HE SHIP that would convey the gentlemen and sailors southwards had by this stage already been purchased by the Navy Board. The *Earl of Pembroke* was a Whitby cat – sturdy, flat-bottomed and ideal for the job. She could carry the necessary year-long supply of food, could take the odd knock and was less likely to ground herself when sailing close to the coast. If the Clippers would in later years be the greyhounds of the seas, the Whitby cats were its bulldogs, with their blunt noses, strong shoulders and workaday appearance. And if dogs sometimes look like their owners, the *Earl of Pembroke* was a fitting ship for the look and the character of Lieutenant James Cook. It was an added piece of serendipity that not only did she sail like a dream, Cook had learned his trade in just such a vessel and could handle them as though they were an extension of himself.

Meantime, although she was just under four years old, there was much work to be done to prepare her for the long years ahead: she needed new masts, to be sheathed with a thin layer of extra planking over her bottom to protect against 'worm', refitted and given 'six carriage guns of four pounds each and eight swivels'. She was also to be classified as a 'Bark' and given the new name that would become symbolic of one of the most famous voyages in history – the *Endeavour*.

To many people, the classification of the ship as a 'Bark' is an unusual and slightly odd choice. The word comes from the Latin word *barca*, meaning 'ship's boat' and is a variant of the old French word, *barque*, but in the eighteenth century the term was used by the Navy to denote any small ship with a broad stern and three masts. And the *Endeavour* really was small. At just 106 feet long (and only 97 of those being in-board), she was the length of three double-decker buses, and was one bus-length wide; squat rather than elegant, her collier-origins had left her more functional than pretty. She had no lady figurehead – she was too low a rating for that; in fact, she had little decoration save for the two carved carrickheads on either side of the windlass that looked stoically back to the stern. Instead, to a modern eye, she would give the impression of being grossly over-engineered: the decks crowded with small boats and cannon, heavy, square sails tethered to yard arms thicker than a man's waist and 27 kilometres of rope cobwebbing across a rigging that stretched forty metres high.

Endeavour was hardly a grande dame of the ocean but at least she would be perfect for the rough conditions they would meet *en route*. For their £2,800 – around £170,000 today – the Navy had got themselves a fine ship.

The Admiralty were keen to get the necessary repairs and refits to the *Endeavour* underway as quickly as possible – not for them the lengthy bureaucracy of learned gentlemen's committees, at least, not on this occasion. Contemporary reports say that all other naval business was swept to one side so that the work on the bark could be completed as a matter of urgency. But not everything was going the Navy's way – and not everyone responded to Admiralty orders, as they were all too soon to find out. From January 1768, a rumble of discontent over low wages and high prices began to reverberate through the communities along the riverside before eventually boiling over into 'tumults and riots of the Seamen of the River'; whole industries went on strike – the coal-heavers, weavers, watermen and, by the beginning of May, the workers in the dockyards, too, leaving the *Endeavour* literally high and dry. There was nothing the Navy could do: when the workers down-tooled, she was left languishing in dry dock, her seams bursting open in the hot sun, until the pay dispute was resolved. It would have been a frustrating combination for the Admiralty to contend with: striking workers on top of the inertia of the Royal Society; after all, they were men whose wish was generally someone else's command.

By the middle of May, however, the men in the yards resumed their work and *Endeavour* was finally allowed back into the water for the serious business of preparing to set sail. Cook still had the occasional visit to the Royal Society but beyond that he seized upon the few slack weeks to invest in his family, cramming in as much time as he could with Elizabeth and the children before the long voyage ahead. Within the safe confines of the household, emotions were beginning to bubble – excitement at the prospect of the expedition, anxiety over the last-chance observations, concern about leaving his family for years or maybe forever. His children were just four, three and one: would he ever see them again? He may have been used to leaving but this was something entirely new for all of them.

As for Elizabeth, she had spent her whole life saying goodbye to sailors passing through her parents' inn and lodgings and was used to James's absences, but this time the future was more uncertain. He might not have been heading out in wartime, but who knew what the South Seas held in terms of danger as well as promise? The romance spawned by mariners, writers, artists and poets could do little to quell the sharp anxiety that now lurked deep inside her, though what little we know of this strong, intelligent and practical woman suggests she kept it to herself.

Two days after his commission as Lieutenant, James met with the ship that would become his home and – little by little – with the crew and gentlemen who would become his new family. There is nothing to suggest that he had played a part in choosing the vessel – the *Endeavour* was signed up for the voyage long before he was, and he never makes mention in letters or journals of joining the Navy search for a suitable ship. However, he would have thought her a suitable choice; after all, he had learned his trade on the Whitby cats and knew them well. It must have been a comforting omen to come face to face with his future and feel secure in the manner of its delivery. One can imagine the pride with which he stood before her, lines rattling, workmen shouting, all the noise of the yard – and her glorious hulk of a body being pummelled into shape. There is no doubt that he was pleased at the sight of her.

What he thought of his crew was another matter: in all, they were to number ninety-four men – fifty-five seamen, twelve marines, one astronomer, fourteen officers of all types and nine 'gentlemen' – all mostly under the age of thirty, with Cook having little or no choice in the motley bunch who came aboard. The seamen may have been young but at least were all experienced sailors, unlike the crews of 'pressed' men with whom he had sailed to Canada. A handful he already knew – eighteen-year-old Peter Flower was the supernumerary he had had to discipline in Newfoundland, Thomas Hardman and William Howson were Able Seamen from the *Grenville*, Isaac Smith, Elizabeth Cook's sixteen-year-old cousin also from the *Grenville*, and John Charlton, who had previously been Cook's servant.

His officers were similarly committed: second-in-command was twenty-nine-year-old Lieutenant Zachary Hicks, from Stepney in London, who had been at sea since his early teens; he joined the *Endeavour* on 3 June, carrying with him the deadly bacteria of consumption which would steal from him his life but not the immortality of his name, which would be given to the first land sighted in New South Wales. The Third Lieutenant was an American, John Gore – at thirty-eight years old, he was well-qualified for the post; not only that, he knew the South Seas as well as any sailor having already circumnavigated the world twice aboard HMS *Dolphin*, under the command of John Byron and then Samuel Wallis. He would achieve notoriety for his hunting skills, which kept the officers' table well-provisioned and also bagged him the first kangaroo ever shot in Australia. The Master was another member of the *Dolphin* crew, twenty-two-year-old Robert Molyneux, as was the Mate, Richard Pickersgill, then just nineteen years old but a talented surveyor and draughtsman whose charts stand testament to his skill and productivity. Together, they were responsible for navigation, stores, ballast, safely using and stowing the anchors – and looking after the beer.

Below Richard Pickersgill was Charles Clerke, the twenty-five-year-old Essex man and Second Master's Mate. He had first gone to sea at the age of twelve and had also sailed the *Dolphin* under Byron before spending time in the West Indies. One of the great characters of the crew, he endlessly entertained the men with jokes and stories, many from his previous travels around the world. Like Cook, he had been 'published' by the Royal Society – his 'Account of Very Tall Men, Seen near the Streights of Magellan' recounted sightings of men 'certainly nine feet if they don't exceed it' and was printed in their *Philosophical Transactions* in 1767. Much-loved by his fellow crewmembers, he in turn became a devoted friend and colleague to Cook, accompanying him on all three of his voyages.

Other notable men included William Monkhouse, Surgeon (whose Mid-shipman brother, Jonathan, would later save the ship), and his excellent Mate, William Perry – they were responsible for the health of the crew, although this was a topic for which Cook also had a passion and deserved most of the credit. Much of the success in keeping the crew healthy was down to diet – and in part due to the culinary abilities of the ship's cook. Here, the ship's commander battled with the Navy with varied degrees of success. His first appointment was a man – chef would be too strong a word – called John Kelly. Cook was not impressed, complaining to the Navy that he was 'a lame infirm man, and incapable of doing his Duty without the assistance of others; and as he doth not seem to like his appointment, beg you will be pleased to appoint another'. But if Cook thought that would improve the situation, he was wrong; sure enough, the Navy discharged John Kelly but in his place came John Thompson. Another objection was raised 'as this man hath had the misfortune to loose his right hand'. However, one-handed or not, the Navy refused to budge and Thompson eventually proved himself a very able cook.

Along with this one-armed chef came an ancient sailmaker. John Ravenhill was an 'old man about 70 or 80 Years' and 'generally more or less drunk every day'. Unsurprisingly, he was not to survive the voyage, though the cause was nothing more sinister than old age; until then, he stayed in perfect, pickled health until the day he died.

A few Able Seamen are notable from the muster rolls. The American James Magra was 'one of those gentlemen, frequently found on board the Kings Ships, that can very well be spared, or to speake more planer good for nothing' – and yet he was the first to raise the idea of settling Australia as a colony, recommending Botany Bay as the best site and suggesting that Tahitian women should be brought there as mistresses for the marines! Changing his name to Matra, and no doubt his image with it, this velvet spokesman ended his days as British Consul at Tangier. Charles Praval (or sometimes Proval) was a talented artist, while Isaac Smith was similarly talented at surveying and drawing charts.

Other family members on the muster roll were James Cook (age five, servant) and Nathaniel Cook (age three, Able Seaman); however, they were present in name only, residing at home with their mother whilst on paper they were earning a few years' experience to help them gain a Lieutenant's rank in later life. Although this was strictly illegal and could have earned their father a court martial, the practice was widespread. It is, however, one of the few times that Cook was seen to break the rules. The youngest legitimate crew member was only twelve years old – Isaac Manley later gained notoriety as the last surviving crew member of Cook's first voyage, dying as an Admiral of the Red in 1837, at the ripe old age of eighty-one.

Not much is known about the seamen whose names are listed on *Endeavour's* muster roll though Cook grew to respect and praise them, and many joined him on his next two voyages around the world. His log records their achievements and, frequently, their misdemeanours and punishments; sometimes they kept their own journals, which give a colourful sense of the voyage that was to come, but sadly these are few and far between. However, there was another group of men on board, men with literary skills and a well-trained eye: the civilians.

On the same day that Cook was brought before the Royal Society to discuss his future, a Mr Charles Green was also waiting outside the council's door. This thirty-three year old had much in common with Cook – both were Yorkshire farm lads, both had a passion for astronomy – and they were to become loyal friends as well as colleagues. Green had pursued his heavenly obsession through the Royal Observatory at Greenwich and, despite the falling-out in Barbados with the Astronomer Royal during the testing of Harrison's chronometer, he was one of the first to be officially signed up for the transit voyage with a fee of two hundred guineas a year, and was to prove invaluable in the help he gave to Cook in taking readings to determine latitude and longitude of both land and ship.

Cook had less in common with the other major signing by the Royal Society, though the man would have the greatest influence on him of anyone encountered in the entire voyage. Joseph Banks was fifteen years younger than James Cook but was worlds ahead in terms of experience, education and social class. They had encountered each other before – though perhaps not in person – when Cook carried his Indian canoe home from Newfoundland, before promptly losing it in British waters in the storm off Sheerness. One can only imagine what the commander thought of this young gentleman when they did finally meet: Banks was large in size and large in character – he was over six feet tall, handsome, dark-haired and strongly featured, with the signs of good living already filling out his frame; a gentle giant and genial member of the upper classes, he was, however, used to getting his own way – and, make no mistake, this was going to be *his* voyage.

To be fair, he was born for an opportunity like this. From his arrival in the world on 13 February, 1743, he lived life to the full, gaining a reputation at Eton for being good at having fun and useless at work. According to one schoolfriend, 'Joe cared mighty little for his book' but this carefree young boy was to have a damascene conversion: in the summer of 1757, aged fourteen, he was returning to school after an evening swim in a local river when he was awe-struck by the beauty of the swathes of wild flowers. From that moment he read everything he could about the emerging world of botany and a short while later had set up his first herbarium.

His exuberance now had a focus. After somehow leaving both Eton and Harrow schools with a breath-taking ignorance of even basic learning, he went up to Oxford where he gained 'a reputation for his love of botany and his ignorance of the classics'. It did not seem to bother him. When he failed to find a tutor to suit his needs in Oxford, he simply went to Cambridge and brought one back with him. To his mind, anything was possible if you had contacts and money – and luckily for Banks, he had both in quantity. When his father died and he gained his inheritance, he bought property in London where he quickly became a shining star of the social and scientific scenes, despite leaving Oxford without his degree. Among his friends was John Montagu, fourth Earl of Sandwich, who was to become a life-long supporter of both Banks and Cook.

Meanwhile, obsession continued to grow and he devoted both time and money to his new library and expanding plant collection. Some reports suggest that his passion made him a little too focussed for his own good; stories abound of him becoming so dishevelled that one day, when out plant-hunting in a ditch, he was mistaken for a vagrant or thief and arrested; the matter was only cleared up when he was brought before the magistrate, explained himself and was immediately released with profuse apologies. But soon all the ditches of Britain were unable to contain him and in April 1766, he eagerly took up the offer by the Earl of Sandwich of a berth on HMS *Niger* to Newfoundland.

Newfoundland offered the young naturalist a whole host of new plants, insects and animals to whet his appetite and swell his collection, and by all accounts his botanising was ceaseless. His friend Lieutenant John Phipps of the *Niger* remarked: 'He works night and day, and lets the mosquitoes eat more of him than he does of any kind of food, all through eagerness!'

He returned home at the end of the summer season, boxes creaking at the hinges to contain his haul of wildlife, rocks, anthropological notes on the Eskimos and even an Indian scalp. These would be duly painted by a talented young Scottish artist called Sydney Parkinson, whom Banks hired for the task. But he brought home from Newfoundland something far more significant than just samples and curiosities: he had caught the travel bug that would inspire him to launch his most ambitious plan yet.

While other men of his age and standing were heading off for their Grand Tours of Europe, this passionate naturalist had altogether more elaborate designs. At first he planned a pilgrimage to Sweden to see his hero, the botanist Carl Linnaeus, who had devised the now-universal system for classifying every plant on earth; then, through his membership of the Royal Society, which had finally been endorsed while he was in Canada, he heard talk of a journey to somewhere far more exciting – a voyage to the new lands of the South Seas. He had already read the anonymous account of Commodore Byron's voyage around the world and was captivated by the promises the New World held for a young man interested in science: flightless birds the size of lions, flowers as big as a man's face and sting-rays the size of table-tops; his Garden of Eden lay waiting for him. His mind was made up; even before a ship and crew were procured, he proposed himself and a 'Suite' of assistants for the voyage, proffering a reported sum of £10,000 – worth over half a million pounds today – as proof of his commitment. It was to be the best investment he ever made.

When asked why he was not going on a Grand Tour, he allegedly retorted with true grandiose camp, 'Every blockhead does that, my Grand Tour shall be one round the whole globe!' However, the Admiralty were not so sure that they wanted this headstrong young gentleman on one of their long Naval voyages; it took a great deal of time and some brokering by Banks's friend, Lord Sandwich, as well as the Royal Society, finally to secure his place. It is interesting that the latter great institution made reference to his 'large fortune' before any mention of his capacity for 'natural history'. Clearly, money talked – even in the rarefied world of the learned.

The Admiralty made him sweat. It was not until 22 June, 1768, that Banks and his entourage of seven artists, scientists and servants were officially awarded their place on the ship. Whatever Cook's reaction to this swelling of the ranks, he kept it to himself, despite the fact it meant that accommodation on the *Endeavour* had to be reorganised. He must have taken a further deep breath when Banks decided he wanted yet another man, his new Swedish friend, Dr Daniel Carl Solander. And what Banks wanted, Banks got. Dr Solander was duly welcomed on board.

Banks's team was an ambitious part of his Grand Plan for a scientific expedition rivalled by none. It included three scientists (including himself), two artists and four servants – not forgetting his two greyhounds (one bitch and a dog) to accompany the nanny goat that had already circumnavigated the world (after all, the gentlemen would be requiring milk for their coffee).

Dr Solander's last-minute appointment was down to a chance conversation at a London dinner party. Another member of the Royal Society, Solander was the star pupil of that eminent botanist, Carl Linnaeus. The two men collaborated on several projects and Linnaeus even adopted Solander as a son when his father died, although their relationship cooled when Solander refused to return to Sweden. Quiet by nature, brilliant by reputation and loved by everyone he met, he was the perfect foil for the ebullient Banks. He listened carefully as the Englishman spoke of his forthcoming trip, then allegedly Solander jumped up and proclaimed that he, too, would venture to the South Seas. A great scientific partnership had been born.

The third of the scientific party was another Swede, Herman Spöring – three years senior to his fellow countryman at thirty-eight years old, with a broad and very useful range of talents. He was a surgeon, watchmaker and botanist who had been working with Solander at the British Museum in London. Officially, he joined the expedition as secretary; unofficially, he became both scientist, instrument-repairer and an exquisitely-talented voyage artist. He accompanied the official artists – the ghostly and serious

Sydney Parkinson, and the quietly genial Alexander Buchan – another Scot, employed as a draughtsman. These five men were accompanied by four servants – two from Banks's country estate in Lincolnshire and two black servants, as was the fashion of the time.

The scientific community and London society watched the proceedings with fevered interest and plenty of gossip. Mr Banks and his entourage were the subject of the day – a position Banks would have relished. However, one can imagine the sailors' reaction to this circus loading its equipment on board; there would have been many a raised eyebrow over the boxes, cases, instruments, papers and enough natural history books to create a library fit for the King. Unlike the average sailor who was lucky if he owned a second change of clothes, the English Gentleman did *not* travel light.

However, there was one item in that library that would have been of extreme interest to the mariners, at least those who were able to read. This was Alexander Dalrymple's 1767 pamphlet on *Discoveries made in the South Pacific* containing a map of the tracks of every explorer in the region, which the aggrieved would-be commander had presented to Banks. Clearly, Dalrymple had hoped that his own tracks would be added to those of the great explorers; it is no surprise he omitted to give a copy to a certain Lieutenant James Cook.

Little by little, the ship's complement stowed their luggage: ninety-four people and the menagerie that was to provide fresh food and entertainment on board – Banks's two greyhounds (which were to sleep on cushions in his cabin), three cats to keep down the inevitable rats, seventeen sheep, four pigs, twenty-four chickens, hens and other birds and the infamous goat. She had gained quite a reputation on her previous voyage around the world with Wallis, providing an endless supply of milk and, on one occasion, emptying the deck of visitors by headbutting their behinds; she would add to her reputation on the forthcoming voyage, becoming probably the most famous goat in all the world.

Fresh food would be at a premium on board, despite the veritable farm that was to cluck, bah and oink its way to the South Seas. As a result, the men were given the standard issue of Navy rations, which basically meant a pound of biscuit (about five pieces) and a gallon of beer every day. This was supplemented with 4 pounds of salt beef per week, 2 pounds of salt pork, 3 pints of cereal grains, 6 oz of butter and 12 oz of cheese. Nutritionally, this was fairly meagre pickings, doing little more than keeping the men alive and permanently tipsy, but for many the food on board would be more regular and plentiful than they ate on land. Mondays, Wednesdays and Fridays were deemed 'Banyan' or meatless days, when the salt beef or pork would be replaced by sloppy pease pudding and onion; this conserved the precious meat and used the 'portable soup' – concentrated meat juices that were boiled into a jelly or even a hard lump – as flavouring.

However, the crew of the *Endeavour* were at an advantage over most of their fellow seamen: Cook had seen the devastation caused by scurvy in his first crossing of the Atlantic and it had made a profound and lasting impression on him. He was also personally overseeing the victualling of the ship and, ever the scientist, made sure he did everything in his power to keep his crew healthy. The Admiralty was also keen to use the voyage for experimentation, and furnished him with a year's supply of sauerkraut for every man on board in addition to the twenty pounds of onions and malt wort, in an attempt to keep the disease at bay. Joseph Banks, naturally, brought his own concoction of citrus juices preserved with brandy that he was to try after developing scurvy a few months into the voyage. His information was up-to-date – Nathaniel Hulme, a graduate of Edinburgh's medical school, only published his ideas in 1768, recommending citrus fruits, vegetables and 'scurvy grass'. However, despite the fact that it rapidly cured Banks's symptoms, he never recommended it to others.

The definitive link between diet and scurvy had been made as early as 1753 when the Scottish Naval surgeon, James Lind, showed that taking orange, lemon or lime-juice could cure and even prevent it. Even then, the idea was not new – the Dutch had realised the importance of citrus juices almost two hundred years before – but, despite Lind's 1754 *Treatise* on the subject and subsequent papers, it was slow to be taken up by the Navy and was only finally adopted as policy in 1795. Meantime, the disease was killing more sailors than ever died in combat, and this meant that ships frequently had to be given twice the amount of crew to cope with the inevitable loss. Little wonder, then, that on this scientific voyage the Admiralty were keen to try anything that might reduce the death toll. As for Cook, like all sailors he knew that the disease was cured when they ate fresh food, but thought that good health was as much to do with personal hygiene and warm, dry clothes as lemon juice so, along with the remedies, he asked the Navy to provide ventilators for the lower decks, thick woollen 'Magellan' jackets and 'Fearnought' canvas waterproofs for the men.

The fitting-out, victualling and crewing of the *Endeavour* took until the end of July 1768, leaving less than a year to get to the Southern Ocean and prepare for the Transit. By then, the atmosphere must have been a heady mixture of mild panic, nerves and excitement but Cook stayed ostensibly calm and controlled, reporting nothing in his log book but the usual 'common Occurrences'. One wonders what Elizabeth thought of the proceedings; though busy with the children and heavily pregnant with number four, she could not escape the sights and smells of the same sea that was to carry her husband to the other side of the world. His cousin, Frances Wardale, had moved into the house to help her, but she was no substitute for James. Childbirth, like exploring, was a dangerous occupation; the odds were high that neither of them would see out his return.

And then the moment arrived: on Saturday, 30 July, the Lords of the Admiralty signed Cook's official instructions. They were detailed as secret, and comprised two parts: one set was for immediate effect – that he should depart Gallions Reach for Plymouth, where the sailors would all receive two months' wages in advance, then he should make for Madeira to collect some wine before proceeding 'round Cape Horn to Port Royal Harbour in King George's Island', arriving there by late April to May, 1769, to prepare for the Transit on 3 June. The second part of Cook's Admiralty Orders was to remain sealed until the Transit observations were complete, for this was no ordinary scientific voyage. The British Government and the King had another plan in mind for Lieutenant James Cook, a plan that had to remain a secret from any other nations encountered on the way – a plan *so* secret it had to remain officially confidential even to the voyage commander himself. That plan, if successful, would make Britain the richest, most powerful nation in the world.

On Saturday, 6 August, while a pilot steered the *Endeavour* through the tricky reaches of the Thames, Cook said a final farewell to his family and took a coach to Deal where he joined the ship and set sail for Plymouth. He would never get to see his third son, baby Joseph, born on 5 September and dead within a month. Elizabeth had now lost her child, along with her husband; life must have seemed bleak indeed as she shivered in the lonely shadow of her husband's rising glory.

Meantime, Cook arrived in Plymouth where he collected the last of his supplies and men, including Joseph Banks, who had been at a London opera with his fiancée and a friend when the messenger brought news of the ship's imminent departure. He promptly drank himself into a stupor, and arrived two days later at the ship, still the worse for wear. As the final preparations were made, Cook read his crew the Articles of War – a seemingly endless list of dos and don'ts concerning discipline, worship and punishment that was more convention than inspiration. However, it did little to dampen the men's spirits – they were buoyant, happy with their two-months' wages and eager to get sailing. At last, on Friday, 26 August, the squally weather cleared; they slid the lines off the bollards and headed out into the open water. Cook's journal entry gives little insight into his emotions, though it is hard not to imagine a feeling of immense pride and achievement lurking behind his dry, stoical words:

At 2pm got under sail and put to sea having on board 94 persons including Officers Seamen Gentlemen and their servants, near 18 months provisions, 10 Carriage guns 12 Swivels with good store of Ammunition and stores of all kinds. At 8 the Dodman point WNW Distt 4 or 5 Leagues. At 6am the Lizard bore WNW1/2W 5 or 6 Leagues Distt. At Noon sounded and had 50 fathoms grey sand with small stones and broken shells.

13

THE VOYAGE OF THE ENDEAVOUR

James Cook 1768

HE DEPARTURE OF the *Endeavour* was marked by frenetic activity amongst the sailors, and violent seasickness for Joseph Banks. For four days the normally avuncular gentleman did little but vomit and groan – and, just when he thought he had found his sea-legs, they sailed right into the middle of a hard gale which sent him staggering back to his cabin. He would never make a good sailor.

For Cook, the thrill of actually being under sail – on his own expedition – was almost breathtaking. He inhaled the aroma of fresh paint and newly-planed wood, saw the glint from the polished brass of his instruments and looked through the proud rigging that smothered *Endeavour* like the webs of a million spiders. Any last-minute nerves were quashed by the relentless demands that now presented themselves: not only was he getting to know many of the characters with whom he would share the bark for the next three years but he was sailing a new ship in deteriorating weather. The storm hit on 1 September, causing some slight damage to the rigging, washing the boatswain's boat overboard and drowning 'between 3 and 4 Dozen of our Poultry which was worst of all'. A small boat they could do without, but fresh food was going to be priceless. Cook knew his priorities well.

The storm blew itself out in a day or so, leaving the crew to concentrate on getting acquainted with each other and doing their normal day's work in shifts of four hours at a time. Cook was already taking careful note of the ship's position, becoming puzzled and frustrated when his observations went awry:

Kangaroo engraving after Stubbs

Found the Variation by the mean of 5 azth to be 2140'W, three degrees more than it was found to be yesterday, which I cannot account for, as both Observations appeared to me to be equally well made.

Not only was it in his nature to be so precise: for him personally, there was much riding on this Transit voyage. The Royal Society and the Admiralty had chosen him to lead it because of his skill in conducting observations – it was embarrassing and humiliating to be seen to get things wrong. Cook was a perfectionist and had long made up his mind that his voyage would set the standard of naval good practice. This was his chance to shine, and nothing was going to get in the way of him making a good impression.

As they sailed further south, the weather grew warmer, and humid air hung in the sails. Almost three weeks after leaving Plymouth, the ship arrived at its first port of call – Madeira: island of wine – but things got off to an unfortunate start: 'owing to the carelessness of the person who made it fast', the anchor slipped in the night and one of the men sent to retrieve it was carried down to the bottom of the sea. Cook was less than pleased and had to impress a young American sailor from one of the ships in the harbour to take the drowned man's place. While there is no record of anyone specifically being blamed, Cook did not take long to assert his authority on the ship. Two days later, having taken on board fresh supplies, Henry Stephens and Thomas Dunster were punished with twelve lashes each for refusing to eat their allowance of beef. The crime may seem trivial to us, but it was the start of an obsession with diet that would mark out Cook as one of the most scientific navigators the Navy had ever known. Cook's crew were slowly realising his passion about their health and his determination not to lose a single man to the preventable disease of scurvy. And, just as importantly, he was stamping his mark as a commander whose word was law; only later would he would swap corporal punishment for cunning with remarkable effect.

Having taken on 20 pounds of onions per man, 270 pounds of fresh beef, a live bullock weighing 613 pounds, replacement poultry, 10 tons of water and 3,032 gallons of wine, they took advantage of the fine weather to set sail for Rio de Janeiro, their next stop *en route* to Tahiti and the Transit of Venus. Meanwhile, the Gentlemen had also been busy: they had decamped to stay at the British Consul's house for the duration of the visit and had spent their days botanising like excited children. Along with all the official provisions, there came aboard almost seven hundred plant specimens, all neatly stored away in their cabins.

As the hills of Madeira dissolved into the clouds, a change came over the captain and his crew. There was now two months of unbroken sea before their next port of call and, like a long, slow exhalation of breath, they settled down into the comfortable routine of ocean sailing. Cook put the men on eight-hour watches where they would get more rest and, along with their sauerkraut and portable soup to protect against scurvy, the men were issued with 'Hooks, Lines, Slops and Tobacco' for recreation; the crew had their first indication that their Lieutenant Cook was going to prove a firm but genial commander.

For many including the captain, their southward track was taking the ship into unknown waters and they observed the changing birds, insects and sealife as acutely as Banks's own men. The weather was also getting warmer than Cook had ever experienced and he made keen note of the compass variation and the strange currents that nudged their course. Like a detective on the scent of a crime, he pieced together his observations of latitude, longitude and distance travelled until he was able triumphantly to enter in his journal:

> At Noon found the ship by the Observ'd Latitude 7 miles to the southwards of the Logg, and by the observed Longitude 30' to the Eastward of yesterdays Observation; and as these Observations for finding the Longd if carefully observed with good Instruments, will generally come within 10 or 15 Ms of each other and very often much nearer, it therefore can be no longer a doubt that there is a current seting to the Eastward. Yet we cannot have had this current long because the Longitude by account and that by Observation agree to day but yesterday she was 28' to the westward of the observation.

Nothing if not precise, Cook had come across the Counter Equatorial Current.

Meanwhile, if any of the men thought that their captain would leave them in peace to enjoy the quiet, steady sailing, they were in for a rude awakening – and rank was no exception. To keep them all exercised, and to show who was boss, he ordered the Mates and the Midshipmen to practise their small arms drill. The results were embarrassing. The astronomer, Green, observed wryly, 'they behaved much like the Londn Trane Band [volunteer militia] with their muskets sometimes on one Shoulder and then on the other!' Regardless of whether or not it improved their skill, it proved hugely entertaining for the watching seamen. A fortnight later the seamen were similarly ordered to 'scrape and clean between decks, which Mr Pickersgill (only) having the spirit to refuse was order'd before the Mast'. The devil would find no idle hands on HMB *Endeavour*.

Relief came for everyone on 26 October, 1768; though cloudy and breezy, Cook worked out from his observations that they had at last crossed the Equator, and that could only mean one thing: everyone who could not prove upon a sea chart that they had crossed 0 latitude before had two stark choices – to pay up four days' rations of rum or, according to ancient custom, be ducked in the sea. The officers duly gave up their rum, as did Banks and his Gentlemen. They even made settlement to save the cats and two greyhounds who were on the list of those qualifying for initiation rites; then the names were submitted of the victims who would either not pay up or who fancied a refreshing dip in the ocean and, as the Bosun whistled a suitable tune, they were each suspended in a chair from the mainyard before being unceremoniously dunked in the foaming waters. All took their fate with 'great Spirit and gave universal Satisfaction' and the evening was spent in drinking and merriment.

By now, Cook had settled into the rhythms of the ocean and his men were settling down with a captain they were growing to respect. His towering frame – six feet high – was almost always on deck, scouring the horizon or scrutinising the rigging, pulling the crew up for slack lines or shoddy work but doing so with an air that he knew it could be done better as he had done their job himself. It was not arrogance that drove him but a growing confidence in his own ability, and the steadiness of character that had marked him out as a man to be trusted now permeated the ship. The men were in safe hands – and they knew it. Here was a man they could respect, a man who knew what he was doing and a man with an almost uncanny instinct for the best way to do it. He may have kept his distance but his heart and mind were embedded in the very fabric of the ship.

The *Endeavour* passed without incident from the airless heat of the equatorial doldrums to the breezy beaches of Brazil. If the captain had celebrated his fortieth birthday on 28 October, 1768, it was not commented upon in any of the crew's journals. Cook was in his element – he had a good crew, a good ship and the chance to prove himself to his superiors: the voyage was gift enough.

On 13 November, *Endeavour* anchored in the harbour at Rio de Janeiro to restock with fresh food and water and carry out some routine maintenance on the ship. The Viceroy there was unable to grasp why they should want to observe the Transit, and assumed they – and Banks's entourage in particular – were spies, and insults were traded from ship to shore.

One final event marked the sorry episode: Peter Flower, that 'good and hardy seaman' who had been with Cook 'above five years', fell overboard and was drowned. It was a sad and personal loss, in no way compensated by the taking on of Manoel Pereira, a Portuguese replacement. The dead man's friend and captain bid Rio a glad goodbye.

Their passage down the coast of South America was marked by violent storms and monstrous seas, which made the fine and fresh weather on Christmas Day, 1768, the greatest gift of all – excepting the copious amounts of alcohol that somehow appeared on the scene. Cook makes no mention of the festivities until the following day, when he notes wryly:

> At Noon the Observed Latitude 26 Miles to the Southward of the Logg- which I believe is chiefly owing to her being generally steerd to the Southward of her Course yesterday being Christmas day the People were none the Soberest.

As ever, Banks can be relied upon to give a more colourful picture:

> Christmas day; all good Christians that is to say all hands get abominably drunk so that at night there was scarce a sober man in the ship, wind thank god very moderate or the lord knows what would have become of us.

But Banks underestimated his captain: Cook would have known that the weather was going to be calm and accordingly would have turned a blind eye to the drunkenness on his ship and may even have encouraged it. He knew as well as any that there was a time to work and a time to play – and on long voyages in particular, his men needed the chance to relax. Being a good commander meant understanding men as much as understanding ships, and, in the Navy of the eighteenth century, being relaxed meant being completely drunk.

As they increased their latitude towards Tierra del Fuego, and the temperatures plummeted, Cook issued his secret weapon: fearnoughts. These heavy, felted jackets and trousers kept out the worst of the inclement weather but there was more to this than the men's personal comfort. Cook still believed that cold and wet conditions contributed to diseases like scurvy, so the clothing was as much part of his health-drive as to improve his crew's cheer. Not that they could swaddle themselves permanently in the fearnoughts until they reached warmer climes; they were still expected to wash and change regularly as well as keep the decks spotless and well-aired. A clean ship is a healthy ship, and so it was to prove.

As for *Endeavour*, she handled even the biggest seas with staunch resolve. Even Banks was prompted to comment on her 'excellence':

> Shipping scarce any water tho it blew at times vastly strong; the seamen in
> general say that they never knew a ship lay too so well as this does, so lively
> and at the same time so easy.

But as the weather worsened, she needed more in the way of sailing and
reluctantly Cook put the men on 'watch and watch' – that dreaded rota of
four hours on, four hours off, throughout the day and night. No one
would be getting much in the way of rest while the seas remained so
fierce.

New Year's Day, 1769, was quietly celebrated off the Patagonia coast.
Banks's journal talks of the hopes for success in the coming year; Cook
makes no mention of the day at all. For him, the date, just like any
other, was marked by measurements of latitude and longitude, records of
the wind and weather, and '4 sets of observations between the Sun and
the Moon'. For this man of the Enlightenment, science was more
dependable, more black and white, more comfortable than the
vicissitudes of human nature.

The Gentlemen, meanwhile, were becoming more and more excited:
the more southerly the ship sailed, the more interesting the wildlife
became, both in and out of the sea, and their enthusiasm began to rub off
on the crew. Even Cook began to take note of the different species that
passed their way and soon most of the journal-keepers were noting down
the day's finds. Banks's botanising was proving contagious. One of the
most mentioned creatures were the 'small red Crawfish' that littered the
sea so densely and (according to John Bootie, the Midshipman) 'you could
not tell the Colour of the water'; certainly, Sydney Parkinson was glued to
his paintbrush, while Francis Wilkinson –the Master's Mate – assiduously
records that they were 'the Same Kind we Pass'd by in the Dolphin Last
Voyage in the same Latid'. It must have been quite a sight as the same
phenomenon was mentioned by Lord Anson in his voyage journal, and
also by William Dampier, the English buccaneer and explorer who saw
them in the Falklands around seventy years earlier.

The next sight to assail their eyes was even more enthralling – land. On
11 January, through the clear skies of morning, they made out not only the
shores of Tierra del Fuego, but also what seemed to Cook to be smoke
signals from the inhabitants. It was well over a month since they had seen
anyone other than their colleagues, and the locals here seemed more
friendly than those at Rio. To Banks's great delight, Cook decided to find
a harbour in the Strait of Le Maire where they could take on more wood

and water before the passage around Cape Horn, but the decision was easier made than acted upon; the weather turned foul, and they were faced with violent currents and beset with fearsome rocks. When the Gentlemen were ready to burst with excitement, Cook put them ashore by boat for some South American botanising while he plied up and down, looking for a way through the current; and as soon as they returned – well satisfied with their haul – he took the ship into the Strait.

The Strait of Le Maire lies between Staten Island and the southeastern tip of Tierra del Fuego, a short hop from Cape Horn. It had been discovered in 1615 by the Dutch explorers, Willem Schouten and Jakob Le Maire, who were looking for an alternative route into the Pacific that avoided the Strait of Magellan – at the time under a strict trade monopoly by the Dutch East India Company. Sailing south of the Magellan Strait, they discovered this longer but much safer route, with its deeper waters and sandy bottom providing access into the Pacific via Cape Horn, and named it after Schouten's birthplace in Hoorn. This six-hundred-mile strait became the most popular westerly route from the Atlantic to the Pacific until the opening of the Panama Canal four centuries later and, poor weather notwithstanding, it was also the route now taken by Lieutenant James Cook.

On 15 January, 1769, Cook anchored in the Bay of Success and went onshore to look for a watering place. Almost immediately, they were greeted by the first of the many indigenous peoples they would encounter on the voyage. The Fuegians were remarkably friendly and clearly used to visiting ships but to Cook they were 'perhaps as miserable a set of People as are this day upon Earth'. Other than the animal skins they wrapped up in for warmth, the men were naked and the women wore just a fur loin-cloth over their black-painted bodies; and despite the fact they lived on the coast, they appeared to have no boats. However, the Fuegians had two characteristics which would prove to be almost universal amongst the indigenous people they would meet over the next three years of the voyage: a love of beads and a love of thieving. Banks in particular was fascinated – he had been to Newfoundland and seen the people there, but these were the first real anthropological curios for his attention. Cook was also used to the Canadian Indians, in fact, he had almost been killed by them, but these jovial Fuegians were like a window into the Stone Age, living just as they had done for hundreds if not thousands of years. He noted down their characteristics like he would a strip of land: precise, descriptive, but without emotion.

Over the next five days, Banks's men went collecting, the crew replenished their stocks of wood and water and Cook surveyed the bay. It would not have been easy: blinded by snow showers and with his fingers freezing on to the metal instruments, the captain worked as fast as he could to complete his survey in time for Banks's return and before the weather deteriorated further.

Meanwhile, the Gentlemen were having problems of their own. Hiking off into the hills, they were so caught up with their botanising that they failed to leave enough time to return before nightfall and, as the snow battered their bodies into submission, they had no option but to make some bearable camp for the night in what little shelter they could find. Tom Richmond, one of Banks's black servants, was so cold he lay down and refused to go any further, even though he was only a quarter of a mile from where the others had made a fire; he was therefore left with George Dorlton, the other black servant, a sailor and one of Banks's greyhounds to guard him. Only too late did the Gentlemen realise that they had also left their supply of brandy with the group. At midnight, leaving the servants drunk on the ground, the sailor staggered on to join the men at the fire. A miserable night ensued but gradually the snow showers cleared and at first light the Gentlemen returned to the servants' meagre camp: the dog had survived but both of the men had frozen to death. A weary party collected the greyhound, crawled back to the ship and recounted the whole sorry tale to an anxious Cook.

Robert Molyneux, the Master, wrote of the servants' death in his private journal:

> This was a heavy loss to Mr Banks as they were both very useful … However he had the Satisfaction in his late Excursion to make a Valuable Collection of Alpine & other Plants Hitherto unknown in Natural History.

While the others went straight to their beds, the irrepressible Banks went out fishing, 'without Success', as Molyneux wryly adds. For the mariners on board, the Gentlemen were proving as curious as their specimens. Four days later, on 21 January, Cook weighed anchor and braved the gales to round Cape Horn.

The passage around the tip of South America was not made easier by sailing into the jaws of the stormy wind, though Cook still made time to observe and record novel features such as 'New Island', so named 'because it is not laid down in any chart'. Thankfully, he would prove more imaginative as the voyage wore on. Meanwhile, for the first time, Cook was sailing in areas little known to Europeans and along with the longitudes and latitudes, distances and compass bearings, his journal records a growing fascination with the actual process of discovery. His entries become tales of his attempts to decode the snatches of coastline only visible through the cloud or the ribbons of current that waylaid his navigation. His role becomes that of the geographical detective, piecing together the fragments of evidence with the strands of his own knowledge, plotting his observations, then cautiously deducing the map of the alien land and seascape that lay outstretched before him. He notes every detail with meticulous care: these are entries born of obsession. He could have sailed far out to sea, out of danger of rocks and tides; instead, he hugs a coastline that sailors have feared for four hundred years to make a sound survey for those who might follow.

Cook's entry on rounding the Horn runs to almost five pages as he lays out his reasons for believing that the land they had seen really was the Cape. He cites the arguments of his opponents before dismantling them one by one like the most skilful of lawyers until only his theory remains standing, only too aware that his judge was the Admiralty. Though he could not say for sure that the Cape was indeed an island, in the quarter hour of clear weather before the fog once more descended he fixed the Horn at Latitude 55°59'S, Longitude 68°13'W. Cape Horn is, in fact, the southernmost tip of Horn Island, its official position 55°59'S, 67°16'W: in all that bad weather and with the crudest of instruments, Cook's instincts were not only piercingly accurate, his observations were just one degree longitude out.

With typical cool confidence, he takes this as read, adding in his journal:

> I can now venter to assert that the Longitude of few parts of the World are better assertain'd than the Strait of Le Maire and Cape Horn being determined by several observations of the Sun and Moon, made both my self and Mr Green the Astronomer.

His biographer, John Beaglehole, adds his own addendum: 'There was no trivial boasting about this. It was a careful statement of fact.'

And so it was.

Two and a half long months were to follow as the *Endeavour* traversed the vast open waters of the Pacific, from the icy storms of 60° South – two-thirds of the way to the Pole – to the warm sun of Tahiti. There was no sign of land, no relief from the miles of blue, just the monotony of working the ship that was now their prison as much as their home. More than anyone, Cook knew that any call of 'land' was nothing but a mirage: there was no land here, no mythical continent; he felt its absence in the swell, in the roll of the ship, in the cold observations of the ship's position.

After eight weeks of the same work, the same food and the same faces, the atmosphere on board had become intense. A marine, William Greenslade – twenty-one years old and painfully quiet – stole a sealskin he had been coveting; his crime was discovered and his colleagues turned against him but rather than endure their censure he stepped over the side and into the ocean. It took half an hour for anyone to notice he had gone, by which time he was lost in the watery depths.

Time dragged. The only change from day to day, week to week, was the steady warming of the air that whipped in their faces, slammed rain into their eyes or nuzzled their weather-beaten cheeks. As conditions improved and the sailing became easier, Cook reorganised the watches into three groups to give the men eight hours between shifts instead of the stupefying four. Soon they would be in the tropical paradise of King George's Island – Tahiti – land of beautiful women, abundant food and sun-kissed beaches. Their desire was so strong, they could almost smell its fragrance in the breeze.

Birds appeared on the horizon and then a piece of driftwood. On 4 April, Banks's servant, Peter Briscoe, sighted the Pacific atoll they named Lagoon Island. More land was spotted but although they drew close to shore, Cook was adamant they sailed on. On 10 April, the heavens exploded with thunder and lightening. The next day, through the fleshy light of the sunrise, they saw the tall peaks of Tahiti.

The locals came out to greet them in their canoes – a few familiar faces to the men who had been here with the *Dolphin* but many others bearing gifts of coconuts and the outstretched arms of welcome. Two days later, on a whisper of wind, Cook sailed HMB *Endeavour* into the broad smile of Matavai or 'Royal Bay'.

As his men lowered the anchor, he breathed a sigh of relief and reflected back on the incredible seven and a half months since the previous summer when he had bade farewell to Plymouth: it had been a long voyage – from the temperate climate of Europe to the freezing wastes of 60° south and onwards to the balmy heat of the tropics. At a time when ships could lose around half their complement through scurvy, his crew had remained healthy and strong. They had lost just five men, four through accident and one through probable suicide. Not a single person had died of sickness – an achievement as great as their rapid passage round the Horn and due in Cook's mind at least to the careful ministrations of Mr Monkhouse the Surgeon and the giving of 'wort' made from malt. In this he was entirely wrong – the prevention of scurvy was due to the vitamin C in the fresh foods they had eaten and the stored supplies like the sauerkraut that he had coaxed the men into eating. How he managed the latter is a proof that his talent for decoding the workings of the world also extended to understanding the minds of his fellow man:

> The Sour Kraut the men at first would not eat until I put in practice a Method I never once knew to fail with Seamen, and this was to have some of it dress'd every Day for the Cabbin Table, and permitted all the Officers without exception to make use of it and left it to the option of the Men either to take as much as they pleased or none at all; but this practice was not continued above a week before I found it necessary to put everyone on board to an Allowance, for such are the Tempers and disposissions of Seamen in general that whatever you give them out of the Common way, although it be ever so much for their good yet it will not go down with them and you will hear nothing but murmurings gainest the man that invented it; but the Moment they see their Superiors set a Value upon it, it becomes the finest still in the World and the inventer an honest fellow.

Cook is no autist: his 'genius and capacity' lay as much in his skills of leadership as in his surveying and navigation – and it was this rare combination of qualities that had just propelled this quiet, sober Yorkshireman to complete so successfully the first leg of his first-ever long ocean voyage.

14

TAHITI

James Cook 1769

HE ISLAND OF Tahiti has fired European imaginations since it first became known through the visit in 1767 by Captain Samuel Wallis and by Bougainville the following year. A century later, it would supply the palette and inspiration for the artist, Paul Gauguin, whose sensual paintings of island life stamped their mark on the nation's image abroad – colours so sharp they pierce the heart, beautiful women promising the world with their eyes and the languid palms scattering shadows in the sand: little wonder that, for Cook and his men, it was the embodiment of a true island paradise.

The largest island of the Society Islands, it lies almost midway in the Pacific Ocean between Peru and Australia, forming part of the Windward Group (or Îles du Vent) of French Polynesia. Unlike its atoll neighbours, this is no lagoon island: its verdant cloak is slung over giant volcanoes whose jagged, ancient peaks form the centrepiece of a land shaped like a figure-of-eight, swollen at the north end. The island may cover more than four hundred square miles but much of the interior was and still is undeveloped: these mountains provide a formidable barrier to anyone trying to penetrate inland. Instead, they are home to a riot of tropical vegetation and myriad streams, the largest of which feeds down into Matavai Bay at Tahiti's north end. All around the coast, narrow fertile plains fringe the mountains like a grass skirt, edged in sands that change from black to coral, and it was here that the Polynesian communities made their homes, looking outwards to the sea.

Cook had arrived perfectly on schedule: the Transit was due to take place on 3 June, leaving him a full seven weeks in which to set up camp ready for his observations. He knew something of the land and people

Views of Tahiti by Captain Cook

from the *Dolphin*'s journals and from the accounts of men like John Gore, who were here for a second time, and what he knew told him that humans could pose more of a worry than all the planets in the firmament. Even before they disembarked the ship, he therefore read to his crew a List of Rules, first of which was:

> To endeavour by every fair means to cultivate a friendship with the Natives and to treat them with all imaginable humanity.

Other than that, the rules were mainly concerning trade – to protect the stocks and supplies on the *Endeavour*, to standardise the rate of exchange with the locals and to somehow try to protect both the islanders and his men against sexual disease and prostitution. The favoured currency of the islands was metal: because there were no natural ores on the island, it could be traded at a premium; a single knife or a nail could buy a woman a night, though as Magellan, Wallis and others had found to their cost, while the sailors may have ended up happy, too much illicit trade and the nail-less ship would be almost falling apart by the time they left.

Cook, however, made the situation perfectly clear: he was not prepared to tolerate dissension or disorder – anyone found breaking the rules would be subject to harsh punishment, from fines to floggings or worse. The desire for strict control is not surprising. Cook and the observers were here to do a job, a job entrusted to him and for which he had ultimate responsibility, and on the success of which he would be judged by his superiors on his return. On board the ship, it was easy enough to control the men. His position was assured and his word was law. But on land there were many more factors in the frame – another culture with its own rules and social mores – and to him at least, these were unknown. Nothing must get in the way of him completing this crucial stage of the mission. He must assert his authority over those on the ship, and also over those on the land.

His first task was to go onshore and secure provisions. While they were on land, they needed to conserve their dry supplies and their health, by eating fresh foods. According to reports from the *Dolphin*, this should not have been a problem: the *Dolphin* crew had been exceptionally well looked after. But some disaster seemed to have befallen the island since that previous visit and the land and its people appeared decimated. Cook's disappointment was palpable – so much for the island of plenty. At least there was water and wood, though he made sure that not a branch was cut down without the say-so of the locals.

Little by little, Cook gained an idea of the social structure of Tahiti, aided in no small way by Banks. The officers and Gentlemen would talk long into the night over what they had seen and understood of island life. Banks was a man of learning and Cook made an eager student, though the complexities of life without obvious Kings and Queens, with the strange taboos, customs and language, challenged his every preconception. While Cook was the master of all he surveyed at sea, on land it was Banks whose opinions shaped the mind of his captain. Almost eight months in the same ship had broken down some of the barriers of class and education – the men would never be close friends, the social divide was too deep for that – but they were at last beginning to be respectful colleagues.

Meanwhile, there was the serious business of setting up the observatory that Cook attended to 'without delay'. The best space for the camp was Matavai Bay itself: its long sweeping beach gave good access to both ship and shore, while a promontory at the north end offered the perfect spot for the observations, with wide open views away from the usual thoroughfares of human and marine traffic. Cook asked the chiefs for permission to use the space, and the station became known as 'Fort Venus' with the promontory as 'Point Venus'. Both would become the focus of Cook's stay in Tahiti.

It was the duty of the marines to guard the fort, which would also contain Banks's tents and other stores, but as the men were quickly learning, the Tahitians may have been friendly but their ideas over property ownership were decidedly un-European; they stole anything and everything they could, from the pockets of Drs Solander and Monkhouse (who lost a spy-glass and a snuff box) to a musket and even the precious astronomical instruments from the fort. This was not done through malice, and the objects were usually returned, but the constant grind of thievery soon wore down the patience of Cook, who resolved to take hostages in exchange for his goods – a trait that would mark his relations with all the indigenous people he met on his travels over the next ten years, and one that would ultimately prompt his own tragic death.

In the meantime, it was someone else's turn to meet their maker: on Monday, 17 April, Alexander Buchan died from complications of his epilepsy. His death sent shockwaves through the ship and formed the headline for Cook's journal entry:

> Departed this Life Mr Alex Buchan Landscip Draftsman to Mr Banks, a Gentlemen well skill'd in his profession and one that will be greatly miss'd in the course of this Voyage.

Banks, too, was grief-stricken, both personally and in terms of the loss of Buchan's skill:

I sincerely regret him as an ingenious and good young man, but his Loss to me is irretrievable, my airy dreams of entertaining my friends in England with the scenes that I am to see here are vanished. No account of the figures and dressed of men can be satisfactory unless illustrated with figures: had providence spard him a month longer what an advantage would it have been to my undertaking but I must submit.

If nothing else, Banks was not afraid to show his true colours, though he had sensitivity enough to convince Cook of the merits of a burial at sea in order to avoid offending the Tahitians. Then, not willing to miss out, he passed the burden of picking up the artistic pieces to poor Sydney Parkinson, Banks's overworked natural history artist and the deadly-serious but multi-faceted administrator, Herman Spöring.

Work on the fort continued apace. Cook and Green tried to get in some astronomical practice by observing an eclipse of Jupiter's first satellite but the perfect weather in this island paradise – so consistently good that Cook had stopped recording it – could still prove as capricious as its people. In the event, clouds swept in, obscuring the proceedings and putting paid both to the observations and their determination of longitude. In all, it was an ominous start to their astronomical pursuits in Tahiti and another lesson in what could and could not be controlled.

On Sunday, 30 April, Cook gave the men their first half-day off, though it seems not many chose to spend the day in worship of anything other than the local women, whom Wilkinson notes were 'very kind in all Respects as Usal when we were here in the Dolphin'.

The men also got the chance to observe the religious practices of their hosts, after the death of a local man. His body was laid out in a flimsy wooden structure nearby to the villagers' houses, with food and water provided, presumably for the corpse. The surrounding area was avoided by the locals who grew decidedly uneasy when the crew went in for a closer look, not realising the significance of *tapu*. The grisly spectre left Cook intrigued, though it also underlined his views of religion in general – and perhaps explained the lack of Sunday worship on his ship:

If it is a Religious ceremony we may not be able to understand it, for the Misteries of most Religions are very dark and not easily understud even by those who profess them.

Here was a man for whom faith was a matter of duty; by choice, he would believe only what he could observe with his own eyes.

The Fort was ready by the beginning of May and the astronomical instruments were taken ashore with due ceremony and set in place, heavily defended by cannons, swivel guns and around forty-five armed men. The edifice was like a small garrison, complete with forge, bakery, workshops for the sailmaker and cooper, along with the Gentlemen's tents, all surrounded by high walls and a ditch. Cook was satisfied with its construction, thinking it impervious to the light fingers of the Tahitians:

> I now thought myself perfectly secure from anything these people could attempt.

It did not take long to receive a stark lesson in the dangers of underestimating the skills of his hosts:

> This morning about 9 oClock when Mr Green and I went to set up the Quadt it was not to be found, it had never been taken out of the Packing case … and the whole was pretty heavy, so that it was a matter of astonishment to us all how it could be taken away, as a Centinal stood the whole night within 5 yards of the door of the Tent where it was put together with several other Instruments but none of them was missing but this. However, it was not long before we got information that one of the natives had taken it away and carried it to the Eastward.

The quadrant was one of the most essential pieces of equipment for observing the Transit; to lose it would be a disaster. Banks and Green immediately rushed to see Tepau, a chief with whom they had become friendly, and although it was clear he had nothing to do with the theft, he not only knew who had taken it but where the quadrant now was. The men gave chase across the island where they at last found the quadrant bruised rather than broken, and thankfully intact.

On the way home they met Cook coming to help in the search with a group of marines. His first reaction had been to detain all the canoes in Matavai Bay and take the high-ranking chiefs hostage; however, on discovering that the chiefs were innocent, he went to join Banks and Green, leaving orders that none should be troubled – orders that in his absence were disobeyed. The search party returned to find one frantic chief, Tuteha, imprisoned in the Fort and clearly in fear of his life. A crowd of distraught Tahitians had gathered outside and the whole scene was one of chaotic emotion. Cook knew he had to act quickly: Tuteha was immediately released to a tearful crowd, though it took some time to reassure him that he would not be put to death. It had been a harsh lesson in cross-cultural conflict, and one that took time, apologies and gifts to finally resolve.

Cook was now learning the frustrations of working in an alien environment: the thin veneer of friendship with the locals was based on flimsy understanding and, at times, little more than goodwill. Even the thick walls of the fort could not protect them from the realities of mixing these two very different sets of peoples, each with their own hierarchy, their own laws and their own customs. The point was reinforced the next day when Tuteha's servant came asking for reparation, only to be followed by a woman holding a pale-coloured child, the product of too much mixing between the crew of the *Dolphin* and their friendly hosts. The need to find a balance between constructive friendship, exploitation and annihilation would prove a constant theme that pricked the captain's conscience for the rest of his career.

It took several days to repair the damaged relations between Tuteha and Cook, by which time the quadrant had been fixed and the finishing touches put to the observatory. There was now less than a month to go before the Transit on 3 June and the waiting game was proving tense. To help pass the time and smooth over any lasting ruffles, Cook and his men went on the social offensive, attending celebrations, making axes for the locals out of spare pieces of iron, watching their wrestling matches and even joking with a Tahitian 'queen' that the doll Cook had given her 'was the Picter of my Wife' – though this move backfired when a jealous Tuteha insisted on having a doll, too! After becoming almost tantrumous until he was given one, the dolls were soon discarded like the playthings of a spoilt child.

Meanwhile, Banks was finding the Tahitians more than amenable: one day, a man and two young women appeared at the Fort, laid down some plantain trees and spread some cloth on the ground, while the women stripped off their clothes from below the waist and performed a dance in front of him. The interpretation was simple – to place the region's women at the disposal of the handsome gentleman. It was an offer he appears to have willingly taken up.

By now, the Transit was drawing ever closer and a stasis descended over the party. There was little to do but maintain the *Endeavour*, guard the Fort – and wait for 3 June. The oppressive stagnation was only made worse by the weather, which grew ominously cloudy and wet. To pass the time, Cook and the Gentlemen went visiting around the island. They camped out overnight, taking

as much care of the little we had about us as possible knowing very well what sort of people we were among, yet notwithstanding all the care we took before 12 oClock the most of us had lost something or other, for my own part I had my stockings taken from under my head and yet I am certain I was not a Sleep the whole time.

It seemed nothing was safe from the pilfering hands of the locals. It wasn't evil, just a mischievous game, though the effects were tiresome just the same.

They returned on the evening of 29 May: there were now just four days to the Transit. It was time to make the final preparations. Although the weather was clearing, Cook was becoming increasingly concerned that the mission rested on so few shoulders and so he decided to train Banks's Gentlemen in the art of observing: more observers meant more chance of success – and it was success that he wanted more than anything.

At last June arrived and, with it, a change in pace. With adrenaline flowing, Cook flew into action dispatching Lieutenant Gore with Dr Monkhouse and Herman Spöring to make their observations on an offshore island, along with Banks and some Tahitian helpers; next day, Lieutenant Hicks, Charles Clerke and Richard Pickersgill and others were sent 'to the Eastward', armed with another set of instruments and orders to do the same. A hush of tension filled the Fort, infusing itself into the gentle breeze that nuzzled the Pacific islands.

Dawn broke on Saturday, 3 June, 'as favourable to our purpose as we could wish', wonderfully clear with not a cloud in the sky. Cook and Green checked and double-checked the telescopes, the astronomical and journeyman clocks, the troublesome quadrant, then settled down with their notepads and waited in silence for the Transit to occur. Eight o'clock, nine o'clock ... the suspense rose with the temperature, a record 119 degrees. Everyone was ready, everything was perfect.

At 9.21, the planet Venus nudged its way towards the sun; the men held their breath, ready to start their observations the moment the discs eased into contact. Standing stock-still, they screwed up their eyes to make out the exact moment when the two discs touched. But then disaster: unknown to Cook and Green, unknown even to Halley, the esteemed Astronomer Royal who had first suggested the observations, a dark smudge called a penumbra surrounded the planet, blurring the outline and with it the precise moment when Venus began to cross the sun. The men were distraught. For six hours, through the burning midday sun, they watched the little black spot creep across the sun's face, knowing that they had probably missed the true start and waiting for the same confusion to mask the exact moment the two discs separated. With a sinking heart, Cook compared their results: Gore and Monkhouse were confident in their numbers, as were Hicks and Pickersgill. Trouble was, the results did not match.

We very distinctly saw an Atmosphere or dusky shade round the body of the Planet which very much disturbed the times of the Contacts particularly the two internal ones. Dr Solander observed as well as Mr Green and myself, and we differ'd from one another in observeing the times of the Contacts much more than could be expected.

Eight months' travel, a reported ten thousand pounds, one hundred people – for what? They agreed a compromise set of results; nothing more could be done. Without precision, the observations were meaningless. A weary Cook said no more about it.

If the crew thought the Transit would mark the end of their stay on the island, they were wrong, and no doubt thankful for it as well. While the captain and the Gentlemen had been attending to their observations, the seamen and marines had been attending to matters of the flesh. By now, they were well aware of the value of iron nails in procuring creature comforts and some seem to have made the most of island hospitality, as the dour but gifted artist, Sydney Parkinson, noted in his journal:

> Most of our ship's company procured temporary wives amongst the natives, with whom they occasionally co-habited; an indulgence which even many reputed virtuous Europeans allow themselves, in uncivilised parts of the world, with impunity; as if a change of place altered the moral turpitude of fornication: and what is a sin in Europe, is only a simple innocent gratification in America; which is to suppose that the obligation to chastity is local, and restricted only to particular parts of the globe.

The matter came to a head when Cook was alerted to the theft of over a hundred and twenty pounds of nails from the ship's stores. Archibald Wolfe was found with his pockets still bulging but refused to name his accomplices. Not only was the crime serious in itself, it also broke the list of rules concerning trade with the locals and risked seriously disrupting the currency used for their transactions; Wolfe was duly given two dozen lashes, the most serious punishment doled out thus far.

But there was another concern for Cook. His crew were going down with what he called 'Venereal distemper', which had swept through the ship and was now affecting over a third of the complement. Although the islanders attributed the disease to two ships – presumed Spanish – which had called at the island about a year ago, that was small comfort to Cook who had meticulously checked his men for any disease a month before arriving in Tahiti. He was realistic enough to accept he could not prevent contact altogether as his men were needed on shore every day; he also knew the temptations that faced them when 'the Women were so very liberal with their favours' but the frustrations were obvious:

> All I could do was to little purpose for I may safely say that I was not assisted by one person in ye Ship.

What Cook did not know was that the infection was not a sexual disease at all but yaws – a highly contagious skin complaint known throughout the Pacific islands and caused by a bacterium entering the body through a cut or abrasion, triggering small, red, crusted lesions like raspberries. It was treated the same way as syphilis and other venereal diseases – by injections of arsenic to which it seemed to respond.

Meantime, the sex-for-nails scandals were just some of the discipline problems Cook was facing. Two sailors stole some bows and arrows and plaited hair from the locals and received for their troubles two dozen lashes in return; then, there was more thievery from the Tahitians, who took a liking to an iron rake. However, this time, Cook's actions were even more extreme:

> I resolved to recover it by some means or other and accordingly went and took possession of all the Canoes of any Value I could meet with and brought them into the River behind the Fort to the number of 22, and told the Natives then present (most of them being the owners of the Canoes) that unless the Principal things they had stolen from us were restored, I would burn them every one, not that I ever intend to put this in execution, and yet I was very much displeased with them as they were daily either commiting or attempting to commit one theft or other, when at the same time (contrary to the opinion of every body) I would not suffer them to be fired upon.

In the event, the rake was returned by lunchtime and harmony was again restored, but the strategy failed to turn up any of the other missing pieces he had asked for; Banks also doubted the morality of holding the canoes of the innocent when the real culprits were easily known. Whatever the rights and wrongs, it is clear that Cook's intention was to be tough but fair, to set the boundaries of acceptable behaviour with the locals as well as with his own men and to punish those who stepped outside his limits. What emerges is a picture of a just and decent commander who understood human nature and was willing to give a long leash in difficult environments, but a man who also knew his word ultimately had to be law: his responsibilities lay in getting his job done and getting it done efficiently; anything that interrupted that was to be dealt with swiftly and seriously.

The job he now had in mind was more familiar than observing the heavens: setting out in the pinnace with Banks and a local man, he began a circular tour of the island during which he could make his sketches and surveys of the coast. This was above and beyond the Admiralty's orders but surveying was to Cook what botanising was to Banks – a sport of passion. Moreover, after the upset of the Transit and the frustrations of both his men and the locals, it provided him with something foolproof and controllable once more.

They made their observations and measurements on foot and by water, pushing eastwards around the island until their guide became anxious. He explained that they had reached the domain of his enemies and was only reassured when Cook loaded his gun with ball. However, they met with only friendliness as they pushed their way south, noting some good 'safe and commodious' harbours *en route* and sleeping in chiefs' houses or under canvas on the shore. Their one mistake was not taking more food with them: they had reached the end of the breadfruit season and spent much of the time with nothing to eat at all despite the goodwill of their hosts.

As they journeyed around the coast, the landscape changed from beach to cliff and then to woodland; all around was the constant roar of the reef in their ears and the glistening sunshine in their eyes. Passing around the south of the island, they paused for a while at a gigantic marae – a sacred pyramid built of red stones and coral which towered into the sky – a 'wonderfull peice of Indian Architecture and far exceeds every thing of its kind upon the whole Island'. Then it was back up the west coast to Matavai Bay, where they arrived at the Fort on the evening of 1 July, having completed 'something more than 30 leagues' in just six days. As ever, the result on paper was impressive but played down by its surveyor:

> The Plan or Sketch which I have drawn, although it cannot be very accurate yet it will be found sufficient to point out the Situations of the different Bays and harbours and the figure of the Island and I believe is without any material error.

It was, of course, a stunning piece of work – a work of art and science that was used to inspire, guide and reassure navigators for the next one hundred years.

By the beginning of July 1769, the *Endeavour* had rested in Matavai Bay for almost three months. Banks had finished his botanising within the first three weeks and had spent the rest of his time conducting anthropological studies, particularly among the more beautiful women of the island. Beyond sorting out the stores and new supplies for the ship, there had been little in the way of work for the crew who had settled into an easy routine of light duties and easy living. With Cook's return, all that changed: the men were to leave their 'wives' and return to the ship. They would be sailing within a few days. For some, the shock was too great.

Two marines, Clement Webb and Samuel Gibson, were found absent next morning. Cook was surprisingly phlegmatic with what amounted to desertion by the men, noting in his journal:

> As it was known to every body that all hands were to go on board on the monday morning & that the ship would sail in a day or 2, there was reason to think that these 2 Men intended to stay behind, However I was willing to wait one day to see if they would return before I took any steps to find them.

When they still had not returned by the next morning, it was time to act. He learned that the men had headed up into the mountains with their 'wives' but none of the locals would say exactly where the marines were. In what was becoming usual practice for Cook, he decided to take as many chiefs hostage as he could and hold them as a bargaining tool for the men's prompt return. It did not take long to learn the men's whereabouts and he immediately dispatched two of his men with a small group of Tahitians to collect Webb and Gibson and bring them back to the ship. But they, too, failed to return. In what was fast becoming a comedy of errors, Clement Webb suddenly reappeared with the sorry tale that the party sent to retrieve them had been seized upon, disarmed and were now themselves hostage in the hills. As soon as they heard this, the chiefs – still under captivity – dispatched yet another group of their people with a second contingent of men from the *Endeavour*, with the warning that they feared for their lives if Gibson and the rescue party were not returned intact. The mêlée took until seven o'clock the following morning to resolve, whereupon Sergeant Gibson and the remaining men were brought back to the ship – minus their weapons which took several more hours to recover. In all, it had been a shambolic and irritating affair: everyone expected Cook to erupt with rage; instead, he remained almost unerringly calm throughout.

When I came to examine these two men touching the reasons that induce'd them to go away, it appear'd that an acquentence they had contracted with two Girls and to whome they had stron[g]ly attache'd themselves was the sole reason of their attempting to Stay behind.

His cool response paid off: Gibson became one of his most loyal devotees, signing up for the next two voyages, earning promotion and proving himself an able and much-loved colleague. If nothing else, in the eleven months they had spent together, Cook had managed to retain his inscrutability.

Of more concern than his deserting marine was the impact of the desertions and ructions on their relationship with their hosts. After three months of bridge-building, they were about to leave with their friendship turning sour, all because of the 'folly' of Gibson and Webb. However, it was now time to go – the season was drawing on, the harvest was over and food was wearing as thin as the Tahitians' patience for their curious visitors.

After one final social offensive by Cook and Banks which went some way to mending fences, on 13 July the *Endeavour* weighed anchor and sailed out of Matavai Bay. On board were the two runaway marines, now severely chastened, and joining the crew a young Tahitian priest called Tupia and his young servant, Taiata. Tupia had formed a strong friendship with Banks, proving himself intelligent, a first-class translator and invaluable for his knowledge of the wider geographical area, and when the time had come for the men to leave, he had asked to come aboard. Cook eventually agreed to the man's request. The captain's reasons were sound enough:

We found him to be a very intelligent person and to know more of the Geography of the Islands situated in these seas, their produce and the religion laws and customs of the inhabitants then any one we had met with and was the likeliest person to answer our purpose; for these reasons and at the request of Mr Banks I received him on board together with a you[n]g boy his servant.

Banks's reasons for wanting Tupia were similarly in character:

The Capt refused to take him on his own account, in my opinion sensibly enough, the government will never in all human probability take any notice of him; I therefore have resolved to take him. Thank heaven I have a sufficiency & I do not know why I may not keep him as a curiosity, as well as some of my neighbours so lions & tigers at a larger expence than he will probably ever put me to; the amusement I shall have in his future conversation & the benefit he will be of to this ship, as well as what he may be if another should be sent into these seas, will I think fully repay me.

With that, on the fine morning of Thursday, 13 July, the expanded complement set sail from Tahitian waters. In the short term, Cook wanted to explore the islands that Tupia had tantalisingly described as lying within a few days' travel, where they would find more provisions and more land to lay down on their growing chart of the Pacific. It was almost a year since they had left home but, before they finally headed back, there was another, important set of orders to fulfil, orders laid down in that second, secret packet of Admiralty Instructions that was to remain sealed until the Transit observations were complete.

These are what Cook now turned to, reading and re-reading the words in the cramped confines of his cabin. He had already guessed the broad outline of the lines that lay before him – it had long been the source of gossip and speculation amongst the chattering classes of London – but the thrill of unravelling the message contained in that year-old ink still raced through his veins like Madeira's heady wine. The thick sheets of fibrous paper could never hope to contain the weight of the mission that now lay ahead for Lieutenant James Cook and his crew: they were to continue their voyage – and go in search of the Great Southern Continent.

15

THE 40TH LATITUDE

James Cook 1769

OR ALMOST A month, Cook had been making a
detailed investigation of the islands that Tupia unfurled before him. He
had charted, sketched, landed, traded, studied and socialised with their
inhabitants, writing up the results in his journal with his usual rigour and
scientific air of detachment. But as the wind shifted around to the east on
9 August, it was time to go.

Banks drew a line under their Tahitian explorations and looked into the
future with characteristic romance:

> We again Launched out into the Ocean in search of what chance and Tupia
> might direct us to.

Banks was a friend of the thwarted Dalrymple and, like that other
dreamer, believed a Continent must surely exist. As for Cook, his intent
was there before him, clear and straightforward, in the sealed packet from
the Admiralty: here, there was no room for romance – his orders were
thorough and systematic:

> Whereas there is reason to imagine that a Continent or Land of great
> extent, may be found to the Southward of the Tract lately made by Captn
> Wallis in His Majesty's Ship the Dolphin (of which you herewith receive a
> Copy) or of the Tract of any former Navigators in Pursuits of the like kind
> … You are to proceed to the southward in order to make discovery of the
> Continent abovementioned until you arrive in the Latitude of 40, unless
> you sooner fall in with it. But not having discover'd it or any evident signs of
> it in that Run, you are to proceed in search of it to the Westward between

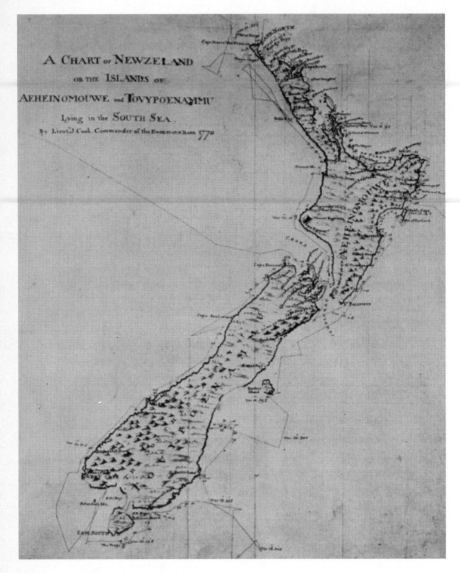

A chart of New Zealand 'or the islands of Aeheinomouwe and Tovypoenammu lying in the South Sea,' by Captain Cook

the Latitude before mentioned and the Latitude of 35 until you discover it,
or fall in with the Eastern side of the Land discover'd by Tasman and now
called New Zealand.

He accordingly set his course due south and left the paradise islands
behind them. Doubting the existence of any such mythical continent,
Cook was prepared for months of nothing but sea: the men were fit and
healthy and the ship was bursting with provisions, though unaccountably
the animals taken on at Tahiti refused to eat and literally hung their heads
and died soon after leaving the island shores. Tupia was likewise sceptical
that the Continent existed – he knew most of the islands that were in the
locality, and had travelled as far west as Tonga. He had already proved his
worth by predicting their arrival at Rurutu, five days south of Tahiti, and
Cook now paid close attention to any information he gave.

On 16 August, they saw 'the appearance of high land to the Eastward' and
they temporarily changed course towards it. Was this the high land that had
so convinced Wallis that the Continent lay just beyond him? Two hours later,
the mirage revealed itself: the peaks were just clouds, and they steered south
once more, into the gales and big seas of the South West Pacific.

The island birds and sharks gave way to albatrosses and whales, while
comets and waterspouts 'the breadth of a Rain Bow' were a poignant
reminder of their frailty in this vast, empty ocean. By now, Cook's journal
becomes a daily monotony of weather conditions, route and wildlife
skimmed over by most biographers, but there is a manner of his entries in
these blank, uneventful periods that makes them invaluable in
understanding the man behind the ship's captain. In the space created by
the lack of action, his personality is given room to breathe: his choice of
words and expressions give the impression of someone perfectly at ease
with themselves and their world – even if that world is a few planks of
wood in the middle of the ocean. He describes the birds that come into
view with a passionate curiosity, noticing and recording every detail with
wonderment as if he had never seen a bird before. Here is an
environment where he feels utter contentment and completely in control:
he has a plan and a method to achieve it; nothing else gets in the way.
Here is a man at peace with himself, a man who is doing what he loves
best of all: commanding a fine ship on a mission of discovery.

With each increasing degree in latitude towards the pole, the weather
worsened: gales became 'very strong gales', squalls became 'heavy squalls'
– and still they pushed southwards. September arrived with violent
tempests: Banks went strangely quiet as conditions deteriorated; Sydney
Parkinson grew increasingly concerned.

The sea ran mountain-high, and tossed the ship upon the waves: she rolled so much, that we could get no rest, or scarcely lie in bed and almost every moveable on board was thrown down, and rolled about from place to place. In brief, a person, who has not been in a storm at sea, cannot form an adequate idea of the situation we were in.

By now, the men's hands were freezing on the rigging while horizontal icy rain stung at their eyes as they kept their bearing southward. Thirty-seven degrees latitude became thirty-eight; thirty-eight turned into thirty-nine, and then, at last, the golden forty – with no Continent in sight, nor any indication of land nearby. Cook looked at the swell to the south, then up at his tattered sails, and then ordered the ship to stand Northward.

Little by little, the weather improved – gales turned to squalls and hail to drizzly rain. Within a fortnight, the exhausted crew were once again lulled by gentle breezes and fair weather; malt wort was issued to those showing signs of scurvy and the men were exercised with small-arms drill.

Normality returned and Cook set his course directly westward to seek the coast of New Zealand and fulfil the second section of his orders. He never forgot to look for signs of the Continent but the huge swell from the south convinced him that no land existed there, despite the frequent sightings of driftwood and seaweed that presaged land nearby.

Within days, land birds appeared and Banks wasted no time in shooting those that dared to stray too near; he even took down an albatross transgressing the seafarers' superstition that it would bring bad luck. There was no limit to the Gentlemen's collecting passions, particularly in the tense anticipation that they would soon see a coastline – perhaps the coastline of the Continent itself.

Its shores remained elusive until 2 p.m. on 6 October when Nicholas Young, high up on the masthead, excitedly called out 'Land!' – and won himself a gallon of rum and the honour of having the point called 'Young Nick's Head'. It took another day for the high mountains to be clearly in sight, with smoke rising from the slopes as clear evidence that the land was inhabited – but what land was it? Banks, as ever, was confident:

Much difference of opinion and many conjectures about Islands, rivers, inlets &c. but all hands seem to agree that this is certainly the Continent we are in search of.

Cook, however, remained silent in his thoughts, merely observing and noting down the facts of position, weather, depth, coastline and the activity on the ship. He knew that his latitudes and longitudes were close to those of Abel Tasman for the west coast of New Zealand – and here he was on the eastern coast of an unidentified stretch of land. Tasman had thought the land he discovered ran northwards to what he had styled 'Cape Maria van Diemen' but he also thought it might run south-east to connect with Le Maire's Staten Land off Cape Horn – and so he had called his newly-discovered land by the same name.

As for Cook, he knew that New Zealand was not connected to Staten Land; he also had just proved by the empty ocean to the east it was not part of Dalrymple's conjectured Continent – though it could still be part of a continent lying immediately to the south. There was only one way to find out: his orders as well as his inclination spurred him to make a full investigation of the land, its coastlines and people, or at least as full an investigation as his deteriorating ship, crew and supplies would allow. He immediately turned his attention to a suitable landing-spot.

The visit got off to a hideous start. The first meeting between his men and the fearless inhabitants of this strange new land ended in disaster when one of the native men was shot dead trying to steal one of the *Endeavour*'s boats. On hearing the gunfire, Cook went immediately to the site of the shooting, only to find the dead man's body sprawled on the ground. He stared heartbroken at the crumpled figure: this was against everything he had hoped for and warned of. Retiring to the ship, he vowed to make amends.

Next morning, Cook tried again to show they had come in peace, taking a small party of men, with Tupia as translator, to meet the people of this strange land at the river near the site of the previous day's killing. But instead of a *rapprochement*, the assembled group of warriors on the far side of the water leapt up and rolled their eyes in a war dance, a sure sign that they were not to be meddled with. Tupia called out to the warriors that the men had come as friends to collect water and to trade; much to everyone's surprise, the warriors understood him perfectly and twenty or thirty swam across to meet them, with Tupia warning his shipmates to take extreme care. His caution was justified: just as the two parties began to make exchanges, one of the warriors snatched a sword from the astronomer, Mr Green, inciting his band to more mischief. Cook knew he had to keep control: his men were hopelessly outnumbered and, although armed with muskets, they could easily be overpowered. He reluctantly gave the order to fire upon the thief – first with small shot that only momentarily stopped him and then with ball that took him to the ground, bleeding. A few moments later, he was dead.

If Cook thought this would stun the band into submission, he badly misjudged them – the dead man's colleagues merely swooped down and picked up the sword and attempted to carry it off until one of the Gentlemen finally snatched it back and the warriors ran off empty-handed in a hail of small-shot. Though shocked, the men marvelled at the bravery of these people who seemed to have no fear of death. Meanwhile, their commander went on to search for water, resolving to make a fresh start at building a friendship. He would not end as Tasman had – leaving nothing but bloodshed and bad memories: in what his Master called a 'generous christianlike Plan' he vowed to 'take them on board and by good treatment and presents endeavour to gain their friendship'.

Heavy surf prevented Cook's boat from landing a second time but if he could not get to the Maoris, the Maoris *could* get to him. Two canoes approached his boat from further out to sea but when Tupia called out in friendship, they began to paddle away. In an attempt to shock them, Cook gave the order to fire the muskets over their heads, but once again, they failed to respond as he thought: instead of surrendering or jumping overboard, they picked up their spears, stones and paddles and began to attack his men. Things were getting out of hand. There was now the risk that his men would be injured, or worse, so reluctantly Cook gave the order to fire directly at the canoeists and two or three more were killed. At last, three jumped into the water from where they were picked up by his men and treated with

> all imaginable kindness and to the surprise of every body became at once as cheerful and as merry as if they had been with their own friends.

However, for Cook, this was no compensation for the débâcle of the last two days and his disastrous start to relations with the indigenous people of this unknown coast. He had been given his orders and 'hints' from the Admiralty to help him deal with the native people he was to meet *en route* – hints that seem remarkably modern in spirit – but recent events had made a mockery of these in effect, if not in sentiment. As he wrote draft after draft for his journal entry, his mood was sombre:

> I can by no means justify my conduct in attacking and killing the people in this boat who had given me no just provocation and was wholy ignorant of my design and had I the least thought of their making any resistance I would not so much have looked at them but when we was once a long side of them we must either have stud to be knockd on the head or else retire and let them gone off in triumph and this last they would of Course have attributed to their own bravery and our timorousness.

Banks was more concise:

> Thus ended the most disagreeable day My life has yet seen black be the mark for it & heaven send that such may never return to embitter future reflection.

The following day they went ashore once more, taking with them the three native men who by now seemed reluctant to leave. The intention was to cut wood for the ship back at the river but a group of a hundred and fifty to two hundred armed warriors suddenly appeared on the other side. With Tupia doing some fast-talking, they brokered a gift-giving exercise which seemed to go well, and then a somewhat cautious Cook called upon his men to leave before the day turned sour. At least they could now leave on reasonable terms. Next morning, at 6 a.m., they left what Cook had hoped to call 'Endeavour Bay' but changed its name to 'Poverty Bay because it afforded us no one thing we wanted'.

The ship once more headed south, past the verdant mountains with their snow-covered tops and the green rivers that cut through the forests to the shoreline. They saw more canoes and met with more of the natives, in one encounter hearing the ghoulish tradition of eating one's enemies ... there was clearly more to this lush, green country than met the eye. By 15 October, the ship was almost becalmed in the light breezes of a large bay when they were again approached by some canoeists wanting to trade. One man stole some red cloth which he had gestured he wanted to exchange for, but if that was not frustrating enough, Tupia's servant boy was grabbed from the side of the ship and carried off towards the shore. This caused outrage amongst the Gentlemen and crew who had grown fond of the child and they immediately fired at the canoe, hoping that the boy would jump overboard and swim to safety. In the mêlée that followed, around three more natives were killed before the boy was finally rescued, half-drowned, terrified and exhausted, from the water. Cook named the nearby white cliffs 'Cape Kidnappers' and the bay itself 'Hawke Bay' after Edward Hawke, First Lord of the Admiralty, and then set off once more to the south.

By 17 October, the winds were still light though the temperature was dropping, the further south they sailed, along with Cook's resolve to keep exploring in that direction. Around lunchtime, the niggling concern that he was wasting time became too loud to ignore and he made the decision to turn north once more into better weather and more likely discoveries. At the bluff head he called Cape Turnagain, at latitude 40°S, he tacked and stood 'to the Northward'.

The mood now changed from the excitement of new discovery to serious and scientific exploration. Cook was in his element: he had a plan to survey and chart the coastlines and no doubt prove his secret theory that this land was indeed part of Tasman's Staten Land, or New Zealand as it had become known, and not the famous Continent. Standing a little further out to sea, they again met with the people of Poverty Bay who this time at least seemed friendly and, a little further north at Anaura Bay, he put in for land. He had some success here trading with the locals for sweet potatoes and scurvy grass, but learned that the best wood and water were in a neighbouring bay. On their arrival at Uawa, today's Tolaga Bay, the men investigated a small cove, now called Cook's Cove, and found almost everything they could want – friendly locals, good trade, plentiful wood and water and for the Gentlemen, a profusion of wildlife that sent them into ecstasy.

Meanwhile, Cook and Green were busy with their observations, fixing their position at 180°47'W and 38°22'24"S, climbing hills to take in the view (just as Cook had done as a young boy on Roseberry Topping) and taking soundings out in the bay. But he was not too busy to consider the long-term health of his men. Their final hours onshore were spent collecting wild celery and scurvy grass, reasoning that it could be added to

> Portable Soup and Oatmeal every morning for the People's breakfast, and this I design to continue as long as it will last or any is to be got because I look upon it to be very wholesome and a great Antiscorbutick.

His instinct was spot-on, and the vegetables did more to reverse the signs of scurvy than any amount of Dr Monkhouse's malt wort.

Five days after anchoring, Cook once again pushed northwards and, on 30 October, rounded the headland he called with more uncanny instinct East Cape 'because I have great reason to believe that it is the Easternmost land on this whole coast'. From here the coastline swept round into a stretch that seemed 'both fertile and well inhabited' and accordingly Cook named it the 'Bay of Plenty', but by now, he was more interested in finding a suitable site at which to observe the forthcoming Transit of Mercury. This was not the result of a new obsession with Transits themselves, rather his long-time obsession with precision: if he could get an accurate observation, it could be used in turn to determine the longitude of their position, making his chart even more exact.

At last he found what he was looking for: a safe anchorage with friendly natives for trading and a good site for making his observations, which gave the place its name of Mercury Bay. They stayed here for eleven days, taking on plentiful supplies of seafood, wood and water, studying the habits of the locals, repairing the ship and conducting detailed surveys of the area. Green and Cook considered the Transit a success – in fact, everything seemed most satisfactory. The only blot on their stay was the shooting by Lieutenant Gore of a man who 'stole' some cloth that caused Cook some concern on a moral level. They were not to know that the Maori system of exchange was not always immediate, and what appeared to the Europeans as theft was merely a half-transaction to be completed in a day or maybe even a week or two. Even if they had understood the rituals of trade in this unknown country, it would not have been of much benefit – Cook was keen to keep pushing on around the coastline, so the ship would probably have moved on before any reciprocity was completed.

However, misunderstandings were on both sides but at least the humanity of this tall, white man was not wasted on the local people. Their strong oral tradition meant that over a hundred years later, John White's *Ancient History of the Maori* (1887–91) was able to record the impression Cook made on a small child called Te Horita Taniwha:

> There was one supreme man in that ship. We knew that he was the lord of the whole by his perfect gentlemanly and noble demeanour. He seldom spoke, but some of the goblins [the British were at first taken for creatures from another world] spoke much. But this man did not utter many words: all that he did was to handle our mats and hold our mere [greenstone war club], spears, and wahaika [a sort of club] and touch the hair of our heads.

John Beaglehole picks up the theme in his *Life of Captain James Cook*:

> The boys did not walk about, they were afraid lest they should be bewitched, they sat still and looked; and the great lord gave Te Horita a nail, and Te Horita said *Ka pai*, which is 'very good', and the people laughed. Te Horita used this nail on his spear, and to make holes in the side boards of canoes; he had it for a god but one day his canoe capsized and he lost it, and though he dived for it he could not find it. And this lord, the leader, gave Te Horita's people two handfuls of potatoes, which they planted and tended; they were the first people to have potatoes in this country.

The tenderness with which both parties refer to each other is all the more remarkable given the fact the locals clearly fought severe and frequent wars; moreover, it was here that they confirmed to Cook their custom of eating their enemies, yet Cook merely notes down this trait as he would their sleeping or living arrangements: there is no judgement and no moralising, he just recorded it as fact.

By 15 November, 1769, even the friendship of the locals and the profusion of delicious oysters could not detain Cook any longer: he cut the name 'Endeavour' in a tree along with the date, and took possession of the place for George III, albeit without first asking the consent of the locals, then set sail once more around the coastline of the Coromandel Peninsula (so named by the Navy more than fifty years later). Rounding the promontory he named Cape Colville after his old commodore, he followed the coast southwards into the deep bay of the Hauraki Gulf, then northwards again up the indented sweep of the northeast coast, past the Bay of Islands, surveying and charting as he went and doing what research into the local peoples and terrain the time and weather could afford. They did, however, get close enough to observe the heavily tattooed buttocks of some locals along the way – and to find them comparable to the 'Backsides [of] the Inhabitants of the Islands within the Tropics'.

Occasional 'insolence' from the Maoris was mirrored by some members of his crew: at the end of November, he had to punish Matthew Cox, Henry Stevens and the Portuguese replacement seaman, Manuel Pereira, with a dozen lashes for 'leaving thier duty when ashore last night and diging up [sweet] Potatoies out of one of the Plantations'. Cox was particularly aggrieved and launched an ill-fated legal action against Cook on his return, but the commander was as strict with his men as he was with the locals: it was not only important for him to *be* even-handed; he had to be *seen* to be even-handed as well.

Meantime, another battle on his hands was against the weather that now toyed with him like a predator, teasing him with calms and then lashing at him with all its furious might. Throughout the whole of December he was at its mercy, struggling to keep his surveys going and the ship pushing northwards through the capricious winds. That he managed to sustain his surveying at all is remarkable; the fact that he did so with a skill and detail that shocked even his competitors is astounding.

Also astonishing is the fact that on 16 December, when Cook was fifty miles out to sea, fighting the winds to get around the North Cape, another ship was hugging the shore – a French ship, under the command of Captain Jean François Marie de Surville. He had come from India's Pondicherry in June 1769, looking for a mythical Pacific island full of riches, just at the time that Cook was preparing for the Transit. He reached as far as the Solomon Islands before the desperate health of his ailing men forced him to turn sharply south to look for fresh supplies. He had arrived in New Zealand two months after Cook on 12 December with sixty men dead and the rest so sick from scurvy that they could barely man the boats. Landing to get fresh food, he fell out with the natives and was hit by a tempest that damaged the ship. His explorations in New Zealand cut short, he limped back to Peru where he drowned just off the coast. The two captains – one an explorer, one an adventurer – never met or even saw one another.

Meantime, at last the winds were kind to Cook and his men on the *Endeavour*: appropriately enough, on Christmas Eve the clearing skies revealed the island which Tasman had named The Three Kings, removing the last shred of doubt that this was indeed the Dutch's Staten Land and not the Continent. On Christmas Day, Cook fixed the island's position before dining on the goose pie which Banks's gun had provided the day before. According to that great hunter, this was eaten

with great approbation & in the Evening all hands were as Drunk as our forefathers usd to be upon the like occasion.

– and on 26 December:

This morn all heads achd with yesterdays debauch.

However, there was no chance to sleep off their hangovers: the mounting breeze soon cleared their blurry minds as it turned to gales and then to a hurricane. The ship was blown west, northeast then to the southwest on the 'prodigious high' sea but Cook was determined to fix the position of North Cape and Tasman's Cape Maria van Diemen, and not even a hurricane would get in his way. Holding it in his sights like a bird of prey, he jockeyed for position for six long days and then, at last, he had it: in one of the most incredible displays of his 'genius and capacity' – not to mention his tenacity – he fixed North Cape at 34°22'S and 17°35'E and Maria van Diemen at 34°30'S, 172°42'E, positions that were barely a few minutes out.

By the first week in January, the gales subsided and at last Cook could come in close to land and have pause for thought. His sailing around the Cape had been a superb mixture of caution and daring – but for what? The coast he now explored was 'most desolate and inhospitable', one to avoid at all costs in the future, he mused. He pushed on south into better weather and more promising geography until, on 16 January, he anchored in 'a very snug Cove' in a wide bay-like area where they rapidly caught over three hundred pounds of fish and found a

fine stream of excellent water, and as to Wood the land here is one intire forest.

He had reached the beautiful coastline that was to seduce him and lure him back to its bosom time after time, the region he would call Queen Charlotte Sound.

Here at last was a place where he could drag his battered ship on shore for an overhaul and give his men their land-legs. They had been sailing almost continually for over a month, through some of the fiercest storms his crew had ever seen and everyone now needed fresh food and rest. Everyone, it seems, except Cook. He had Tasman's scent in his nostrils – this must be near the site of his predecessor's 'Murderers' Bay' but the local people who came to fight and then to trade said that

> they never either saw or heard of a Ship like ours being upon this coast before them: from this it appears that they have no Tradition among them of Tasman being here.

No wonder Cook was confused: Murderers' Bay was just seventy miles away but the Ngati Tumatakokiri people who had lived there – who had been responsible for the killings – were now themselves being wiped out by their enemies. Although Cook was right to put faith in their oral histories, few now remained to pass on the stories of the white men who had come on a giant ship, and the Maori who did were scattered in a hopeless bid to save their own lives.

However, if he wanted proof of their thirst for blood, he was not long in finding it:

> Soon after we landed we met with two or three of the Natives who not long before must have been regailing themselves upon human flesh, for I got from one of them the bone of the fore arm of a Man or a Woman which was quite fresh and the flesh had been but lately pick'd off which they told us they had eat, they gave us to understand that but a few days ago they had taken Kill'd and eat a Boats crew of their enemies or strangers, for I believe that they look upon all strangers as enemies.

Unlike the other journal-keepers who pour shame on the practice, Cook relays this information with a detached air of scientific inquiry quite remarkable for his time: he relates how he challenged a local man 'in order to be fully satisfied of the truth of what they had told us', saying that the bone came from a dog rather than a human to see his response, but this evoked strong disagreement from the man who symbolically chewed at his own arm to prove his point; Cook then observes men and women actually eating from the bone – after which he is convinced. There is never the slightest suggestion that he condemns the people's tradition, merely that this is part of their world and to be recorded by him as he would the weather or the profile of the coast.

Two days later, his journal entry further underlines this remarkable ability to accept people for who and what they are, without prejudice:

> The natives came along side and sold us a quantity of large Mackerel for nails pieces of Cloth and paper, and in this traffeck they never once attemptd to defraud us of any one thing, but dealt as fair as people could do.

Such a comment coming off the back of what any man of the Enlightenment must have viewed as a repulsive habit, reveals some of Cook's greatness as a humanitarian explorer: he well understands that what *he* feels is not important; his job and his inclination are to transmit to his bosses at the Admiralty and Royal Society what he sees of this alien land with its strange people and even stranger practices. However, by following these orders with such honesty and integrity, we can glean even more insight into the mind of this great explorer. It is these moments of intended and unintended analysis – all too frequently glossed over by commentators pursuing the story of his adventures – which add the third dimension to his achievements. These are not mere points on a chart or co-ordinates for geographical discovery. They are new markers in the growing map of Cook as a human being that is being in-filled with each new experience. Cook may have shaped the map of the world, but that world also shaped the man he became and charting this journey is just as intriguing and crucial to gain a sense of the man behind the legend.

After making a thorough survey of the area, Cook knew it was time to give his men some free time. His stocks were replenished and the boat was now in reasonable repair; they could now relax and look about this beautiful and promising land. At this stage, he still believed they had found an inlet – albeit a large one of which no amount of exploring in the small boats could trace the far end. His curiosity was insatiable. The coastline was heavily indented with bays and good harbours; inland were wood-covered slopes, hills and freshwater rivers; offshore lay a profusion of hilly islands. The complexity of the area tugged at his sleeve and drew him out in the boat and up the tallest hills to bring the confusion into order. The notion grew in his mind that while he might be looking at a vast inlet running southwest, to the southeast lay another expanse of water that could indicate a strait connecting as far as the 'Eastern Sea'. Was Tasman's land a large island – and if so, was the land to the south an island too, or connected to a continent? Like a giant puzzle, he assembled his survey little by little, piece by piece, with the meticulous care of a man obsessed by detail.

Meanwhile, the relations with the local men and women were proving both friendly and fruitful. His crew had as much fish and scurvy grass as they could eat and they traded happily with their own possessions for whatever they desired. By the end of January 1770, Cook's work was done: he left markers of stone and iron at the top of the tallest hills, and set up carved boards telling of their arrival along with the date. Hoisting the Union Flag, he took formal possession of Queen Charlotte Sound and the adjacent lands in the name of the King:

> We then drank Her Majestys hilth in a Bottle of wine and gave the empty bottle to the old man (who had attended us up the hill) with which he was highly pleased. Whilest the post was seting up we asked the old man about the Strait or passage into the Eastern Sea and he very plainly told us that there was a passage and as I had some conjectors that the lands to the SW of this strait (which we are now at) was an Island and not part of a continent we questioned the old man about it who said that it consisted of two Wannuaes, that is two lands or Islands that might be circumnavigated in a few days, even in four. This man spoke of three lands, the two above mentioned ... and for the third he pointed to the land on the East side of the Strait, this he said was a large land and that it would take up a great many moons to sail round it.

It seemed that, once again, those wishing to discover the Great Southern Continent were about to be disappointed – and their commander was the man who would place solid fact where myth once prevailed.

Their departure was delayed by bad weather until the first week in February, during which time Cook checked again the truth of what the old man had said and found it confirmed by others: there were two large islands, North and South, along with the much smaller one where they now lay at anchor. Tupia then asked the man if he had ever seen a boat like theirs before, and received a strange reply: no, he had not personally, but his ancestors had told him that a smaller vessel had come from a distant land called Olhemaroa that lay to the north –and four of the crew were killed. This tallied with what Cook had been told by the locals in the Bay of Islands but could he rely on what was clearly an old tale? Banks's version of the tale records

> 2 large vessels much larger than theirs, which some time or other came

here and were totaly destroyed by the inhabitants & all the people belonging to them killd

and says that Tupia knew of the island from which the explorers had come, though the Tahitian put only the name, not the island, on his map. So where was 'Olhemaroa'? And just who was it who had been here before? Were they referring to Tasman or some other visitors from this unknown land at an unknown time? Cook could gain no more information so, with the question hanging in his mind, he prepared to set sail through the strait.

The passage was strewn with shoals, islands and dangerous currents that contrasted starkly with the beauty of the land but as they neared the eastern sea once more, the strait widened and they could concentrate less on the sailing and more on observing the wooded headlands and mountains that flanked them on either side. He gave no name to the strait itself – its title, Cook Strait, was conferred by Joseph Banks, who by now held his captain in the highest esteem.

As they left the eastern end of the strait to once again push north up the coast of the North Island, the officers began to doubt that they were indeed skirting an island – perhaps it was a continent after all, extending southeast between Cape Turnagain – the southernmost point of their original east coast explorations – and Cape Palliser at the eastern entrance to the Strait. Cook, however, was firm in his belief and set out to prove his men wrong in the only way he knew – not by argument but by sailing north to survey the coast.

The weather did not help his cause: it was hard to make out the trend of the shore through the hazy cloud and mist, but at last the skies cleared revealing the familiar lines of Cape Turnagain, whereupon Cook gently but firmly made his point:

I then called the officers upon deck and asked them if they were now satisfied that this land was an Island to which they answer'd in the affirmative and we hauled our wind to the Eastward.

It was now time to resolve the only query that remained in Cook's mind: was the land to the south an island as the locals had told him, or was it connected to a larger body of land? He sailed south past the mountain range of Kaikoura, then down to a large peninsula he thought could be an island. Here, Lieutenant Gore was fixated with the idea that he had seen land to the southeast; Cook was convinced it was just cloud but once more vowed to prove the truth, if nothing else to show his explorations were completely rigorous. They spent a whole day in search of 'Mr Gores imaginary land' before heading south once more with his lieutenant duly chastened.

As they made their way down the coast, the weather degenerated into gales and heavy squalls, and the air became so hazy they quickly lost sight of the land. As the ship was blown this way and that, the men became firmly divided into two camps: those who wanted the land to be an island, so they could finish surveying it and head home, and those who wanted to find their Continent. Banks was firmly amongst the latter; Cook still believed that the land was insular.

Tracking southwest, the weeks rolled by and February turned into March. The weather still blew foul and the dangers were compounded by underwater ledges which Cook named 'the Traps because they lay as such to catch unwary strangers'. However, for the Continentalists, time and hope were running out as the ship bore steadily westwards before finally turning north again up the west coast. There was no continent, only two large islands. Cook's only error had been not realising that the land he had called South Cape (now called South West Cape) was the cape of a small island rather than of the larger South Island itself.

Banks was downcast:

> Blew fresh all day but carried us round the Point to the total demolition of our aerial fabrick calld continent.

The sombre mood amongst the Continentalists was, however, temporarily lifted by the birthday celebrations for one of the officers, where the cook served up roast hind quarters of dog, with a pie made from its fore-quarters (its crust made of the dog fat) and a haggis from its 'viscera'. Sydney Parkinson, ever delicate of mind and spirit, looked on in bewildered disdain.

With hopes of a continent shattered, Banks now returned to the theme of his botanising – and once more got into a dispute with Cook over the naturalists' desire to land and make their studies. However, Cook had his eye to the wind that was blowing in the wrong direction to put into any harbour, no matter how enticing they looked. The captain clearly felt under siege from the Gentlemen, writing into his journal a strong defence for his decision to keep sailing rather than putting in to 'Doubtful Sound', so named because of the risk that, once inside, they might never have got out. There was certainly no chance to moor on the inhospitable coast – the sheer sides of the snow-capped mountains slid straight into the sea, 'without,' a crew member wrote, 'the smallest beach or landing-place'.

By the time he wrote his entry for 21 March, he was sailing the same coastline that Tasman and his pilot, Visscher, had charted, one hundred and twenty-eight years before. Unlike Cook, they were blessed by better weather, and Visscher's chart, particularly around Cook's Cape Foulwind, shows the extra detail that could have been gained by sailing closer to the shore. For Tasman's successor, the weather of March 1770 was so bad that he even missed some of the grandest peaks in the Southern Alps, one of which now bears his name. Frustrated, he knew his survey of this stretch of coastline would be incomplete but there was little choice but to stand out to sea in such risky weather. Instead, he pressed on up the west coast until the land trended once more to the east past Tasman's Murderer's Bay to Stephens Island and the larger D'Urville Island, and then the coastline grew suspiciously familiar: he was back where he started, looking out to Queen Charlotte Sound. The circumnavigation had taken almost two months of non-stop sailing but now it was complete; the Continent myth had been laid bare and in its place was a survey and chart of two large islands that would become classics in the art and science of cartography.

Cook's obsession had borne sweet fruit in terms of navigation, though the botanists looked sourly at the loss for their exploring passions. Though he might well have used his own mantra that 'the sea is certainly an excellent school for patience', Banks was far from pleased. However, nothing could be done: this was a voyage of discovery, not of natural science.

His commander used the four days at anchor in the Strait to replenish the stocks of wood and water – something they did with ease in the spot that was to become a regular stopping point on later voyages. He also wrote up his notes on the country and people in general, apologising that they would only contain conjectures owing to the small amount of time spent in any one place. However, one thing is certain:

> The situation of few parts of the world are better determined than these Islands are being settled by some hundreds of Observations of the Sun and Moon and one of the transit of Mercury made by Mr Green.

This was no empty boast: Crozet's 1783 account of Marion du Fresne's voyage to New Zealand substantiates his claim:

> As soon as I obtained information of the voyage of the Englishman, I carefully compared the chart I had prepared of that part of the coast of New Zealand along which we had coasted with that prepared by Captain Cook and his officers. I found it of an exactitude and of a thoroughness of detail which astonished me beyond all powers of expression, and I doubt

much whether the charts of our own French coasts are laid down with greater
precision. I think therefore that I cannot do better than to lay down our track
off New Zealand on the chart prepared by this celebrated navigator.

In under three months, Cook had surveyed and charted 2,400 miles of
coastline; he had landed at just eight sites in all – six on the North Island
and two on the South – and, though Banks had complained of the lack of
landings, he and Dr Solander were leaving New Zealand with four
hundred new plants. Cook's job, at least according to his Admiralty
Instructions, was now complete. It was time to go home. Or, at least, any
other navigator would have thought so.

His Instructions were to choose the best way back to Britain for his ship
and his supplies. Returning to the ship on the evening of 30 March, he
called upon his officers to give their suggested routes and listened to the
pros and the cons of each variation in passage home. He listened out of
diplomacy as much as genuine interest: his mind was already made up, his
decision crystallised from the thoughts that had been rolling around in his
head since he gave the order to sail past Doubtful Sound – and his plan
was as audacious as it was inspired.

He rejected returning east via Cape Horn – even though the suggested
track would prove or disprove the existence of the 'imaginary continent' –
because the ship was not strong enough to keep in high latitudes in
winter. Likewise, the ship was in too poor a state to sail directly west to the
Cape of Good Hope, and anyway 'no discovery of any moment could be
hoped for in that rout'. No discovery of any moment. In those words he
laid his intentions bare: it was not just surveying and charting that now
fuelled his obsession, it was discovery.

That night, he wrote up the notes for his journal detailing what the
'officers' had decided – and they had, of course, decided on his own plan:

It was therefore resolved to return by way of the East Indies by the
following route: upon leaving this coast to steer to the westward untill we
fall in with the East Coast of New Holland and then to follow the deriction
of that coast to the northward or what other direction it may take untill we
arrive at its northern extremity, and if this should be found impractical than
to endeavour to fall in with the lands or Islands discover'd by Quiros. With
this View at day light in the morning we got under sail and put to sea ...'

On 31 March, HMB *Endeavour* slipped through the angry water past
Cape Farewell and left New Zealand forever.

16
BOTANY BAY

James Cook 1770

T WAS NOW almost twenty months since the *Endeavour*
had slid out into the English Channel; nineteen months since the death of
the baby boy that Cook had never seen and seventeen months since they
were in Rio and were able to send letters home. Few other mariners had
sailed in the waters of the South Pacific, even fewer had crossed the
Tasman Sea that now stretched endlessly around them. The only feelings
that penetrated the loneliness and isolation were relief that they were
now on their way back to Britain and tingling excitement that their
journey would entail almost certain adventure.

As he sailed westwards from New Zealand, Cook had little idea what to
expect of the voyage ahead. He was now convinced that a Continent did
not exist, in these seas at least, but with huge areas still unexplored, one
thing alone was certain – that they would make discoveries. This was now
his aim, his obsession: to clear up fantasy and fiction and leave behind
only fact. In essence, he was doing Tasman's route in reverse, sailing west
to chart the unknown east coast of the land styled 'New Holland' by the
Dutch. Its north, south and west coasts were laid down with confidence
but the geographers of the day knew nothing of the east coast. Whether it
stretched in an unbroken line from Van Diemen's Land (modern-day
Tasmania) to New Guinea or was made up of a series of islands was now
the subject of considerable debate and conjecture aboard the *Endeavour*.

Before they had left home, Alexander Dalrymple had sufficiently
buried his pique to give Banks an early copy of his pamphlet on
discoveries in the Pacific. Amongst the papers and charts was so-called
evidence that as far back as 1606, Luis Vaez de Torres had made a voyage
in which he had found a strait separating the continent from New Guinea

Chart of Botany Bay, Isaac Smith after James Cook

and the other islands of modern-day Indonesia. Banks was convinced; Cook was more sceptical. There was, however, a further piece of evidence: in the volumes of the French intellectual, Charles de Brosses, which detailed explorations in the region – there was a series of maps by Gilles Robert de Vaugondy, which not only showed there was a strait, but seemed also to show that 'the Spaniards and Dutch' had at some time in the past few hundred years 'circumnavigated the whole of the island of New Guinea as most of the names are in these two languages'. But if previous expeditions had passed this way, why were their discoveries not recognised? In New Zealand, Cook had heard stories from the Maoris about previous visitors from far-away lands, with their strange manners and big ships. Could it be that he was only here to chart the lands already discovered by his forebears?

Whatever his private thoughts, Cook was not a man to live off rumour or romance; he believed his instincts, his learning and most of all his own eyes, and they showed that there was a confusion about the Pacific lands that needed to be cleared up: that was his job – to set the record straight for the Royal Navy and his fellow seamen. Politicians and dreamers could do what they will.

Meanwhile, the southern seas were looking kindly upon the *Endeavour*. She made good progress in benevolent winds across the blue water to New Holland while, on board, the men settled into a steady routine of keeping their course, catching up on maintenance – and even a spot of bird-shooting for Banks and the Gentlemen. But once the land-birds appeared on the horizon, the weather turned foul: the winds changed direction, the waves slammed the bows and stormy rain battered the sails. As the clouds crashed down and the spray flew up, there were few clues for the look-outs trying to determine what was land, what was sea and what was weather: the curtain of water wrapped them tightly in its blinding folds.

Inside his cabin or pacing the deck, Cook stared at the readings on his instruments. He knew he was already a degree further to the west than Tasman's coast – and yet no land was in sight. He would not and could not know that Tasman had located his coast of Van Diemen's Land three degrees too far east. All he could do was to ride the storm as best he could and hope he was not pushed too far to the north. His hope was futile: instead of heading towards Van Diemen's Land, they were now aiming directly for the large stretch of water that separates Tasmania from mainland Australia, the Bass Strait.

With all the spray blending into rain blending into stormclouds, it was impossible to see what lay ahead, although they knew land must be near.

Then, almost three weeks after leaving New Zealand, the sunrise brought the news he had been longing for: at 6 a.m. on 19 April, Lieutenant Zachary Hicks looked about 15 miles away to the northeast and spotted land. They had reached the mysterious east coast of New Holland. Cook turned the ship towards the shore and named the cape 'Point Hicks'.

Although he knew that Van Diemen's Land must lie to the south, it was not visible from the New Holland coast and to go looking for it would be taking the ship and her crew in the opposite direction to home. His mission was clear: to make his discoveries *en route* back to Britain; the galling question of whether Van Diemen's Land was an island or part of the much larger body of land called New Holland would have to remain unanswered, at least for the moment. Here was land heading in the right direction and that was Cook's priority.

And so began what would turn out to be four months of charting the coast and seas of this new-found terra firma. To the best of his knowledge, his ship was the first that had ever sailed these shores and he bathed in the flurry of adrenaline: this was his discovery, or so he passionately believed. Setting his course northeastwards, he once more began the painstaking task of continuous surveying, though at least this time he was aided by much better weather. Clear skies offered good visibility while easier winds allowed him to take the *Endeavour* within two or three miles of the shore as he began the long process of mapping, naming and claiming the coast for Great Britain. At Cape Howe, called after the man who would become First Lord of the Admiralty, the land veered northwards and so did Cook, keeping clear of the surf that fringed the water's edge. In his caution, each night for safety he headed out to sea before coming back towards the shore each morning – after all, who knew what dangers lay in these uncharted waters?

For ten days he sailed non-stop, observing the 'promising aspect' of the grassy hills and wooded plains that lay to the west. Banks was more undecided on his view of the land, describing some parts as having 'the appearance of the highest fertility' while others seemed stark and bare: 'it resembled in my imagination the back of a lean Cow, covered in general with long hair, but nevertheless where her scraggy hipbones have stuck out farther than they ought accidental rubs and knocks have entirely bard them of their share of covering'. However, the sun was now shining, the weather was warm and there was no sign of hostility from the few natives spotted on the shores. Their fires had given the first indication that the area was inhabited and it was up to Cook to negotiate with them to take the land in the name of George III. As for Banks and Dr Solander, they were itching to explore what new delights lay in store for them amongst the trees, plants and flowers in this strange and alien place.

On 27 April 1770 they made their first real attempt to land but were forced back by the surf; they resolved to try again the next day. Dawn broke to reveal a large bay, sheltered but wide. It was perfect. By afternoon, they were sailing along its shoreline under the watchful eyes of the Gwiyagal Aborigines: men, women and children, whose stark-naked bodies were painted with broad white stripes; their reactions ranged from caution to nonchalance to total disregard: they continued fishing and cooking totally unmoved.

As for Cook, he and his crew stayed on the ship while they ate their own meal, casting askance eyes at the natives onshore. The tableau was all very polite, somewhat embarrassing and mildly ridiculous. Everyone was clearly trying to behave as if nothing unusual was happening, yet here was a huge ship full of ghostly white interlopers, dressed in strange regalia, and doing ... nothing.

But the men could not hold off for long. As soon as lunch was over, Cook, along with Isaac Smith, Banks, Solander and Tupia, climbed into the boats and made their way to shore. As they approached, women and children on the beach slid away into the trees; just two men were left who attempted to repel these strange white men seemingly intent on invading their coast.

Tupia called out in peaceful greeting but they shouted back in a language he did not understand. By now, the men on the shoreline were turning angry. Cook fired a warning musket between the two men but this merely drove them back to where they had laid their spears. Cook fired again with small shot. Some pellets struck one of the warriors but he merely picked up a shield to defend himself and retreated towards the trees.

The water grew shallow, Cook's boat had beached. A moment of silence stretched between its crew and this ancient land. Cook knew the significance of what was to follow; he turned to Isaac Smith, the cousin of his Elizabeth, and quietly gave his order, 'Isaac, you shall land first'. The mystery of that great South Land was about to be demolished.

The party combed the beach, looking at the meagre bark huts and finding a group of small children quaking behind a shield. They gave them some strings of beads and quickly moved on, picking up the scattered darts that lay on the ground and examining the paltry canoes, the worst Cook had ever seen. There were signs of habitation but none of the fresh water the men so badly needed. They retired to the boats and rowed back to the ship.

Next morning they landed again and found the children's beads lying abandoned in the sand; the 'Indians' were nowhere to be seen. The men went in search of wood and water, finding both in good supply, along with a profusion of shellfish still cooking on smouldering fires. There was enough here in terms of food, water and wood to make staying worthwhile, at least for a few days. Cook immediately set out in one of the small boats to survey the sweep of the bay and as far inland as he could strike; Green set his eyes to the measurement of latitude and longitude. Botany Bay slowly etched its trace onto the map of the world.

Meanwhile, Banks, his Gentlemen and even the greyhounds were in botanical heaven, collecting all manner of new species from the sea, land and air. They combed the sands and mudflats, the mangrove swamps and woodlands, the waters and the canopies, comparing hauls and fevered with excitement. Even Cook was smitten with the 'variety of very beautiful birds' that flocked to this magical bay. It seemed as though every man could now attend to his passion, the only sadness being the death of the Orcadian seaman, Forby Sutherland, from the consumption that had gripped him since the Straits of Le Maire.

Each day was crammed with activity; each night the men swapped stories about this new land and its people but the 'Indians' themselves stayed elusive. Though shaking fists and flying darts needed no translation, Cook pursued their acquaintance by following them unarmed into the woods, having first made sure that their darts were not poisoned. The information he gleaned was purely observational – painted naked bodies, lank black hair, dark brown skin – and neither words nor gestures would tempt the people to come near; in fact, 'all they seem'd to want was for us to be gone'.

If contact with the locals was rare enough, even more curious was the brief sighting of a bizarre creature that hopped like a rabbit and left grassy dung like a deer. But it disappeared without trace within moments of coming into view, leaving the party baffled. More lingering an impression came from the profusion of giant stingrays brought in by Lieutenant Gore who chose the fish for his sport. With two of them weighing almost 600 pounds, there was more than enough meat for even the heartiest appetite.

For Banks in particular, the place was bursting with potential for colonisation – a good harbour, some fertile soils, lush vegetation and a bounty of fish and meat. Of all the discoveries they had made on their voyage, this was his Eden; of all the promises whispered in his ears by the South Sea breeze, this was the one to which he pledged his heart.

The ship now groaned under the weight of fresh supplies and the enormous haul of the botanists that took up every inch of spare space in the great cabin and spewed out into the adjoining rooms. It was time to move on. Banks's men collected their final treasures together and Cook carved an inscription of their visit on one of the trees. But what should he call the place? His instinct was to honour the giant fish, so loved by Lieutenant Gore. The name Stingrays Harbour was thus laid down – and then amended; surely it was better to honour the men who so rejoiced in the wealth of natural species here? Botanist Bay? Botanists' Bay? And then the name that was to become the most famous in the land – Botany Bay.

As dawn broke on the morning of 6 May – and much to the relief of the watching Gwiyagal, the *Endeavour* weighed anchor and slipped out of the harbour on a gentle breeze before sailing northwards up the coast.

17
JAVE LA GRANDE
George Collingridge 1883

NE HUNDRED YEARS after the death of Captain James Cook, George Collingridge had stepped off the *Lusitania* into a colony buzzing with enterprise and pioneer spirit. Within a few years, he had woven himself into the fabric of Sydney – a city that now swarmed with merchants, colonists, seamen and the normal wharf-life of crime and prostitution. However, less than a century after the arrival of the first fleet of British settlers, the ties back to the mother-country were still deeply embedded in the colony's soul – the fashion in London became the fashion in Australia, whether in ideas, manners or clothes; the Duke of Edinburgh was invited to open the International Exhibition, and Britain was still regarded by many as 'home'.

Superficially, Sydney had all the trappings of a major city: large buildings, reasonable transport, even leisure facilities. The zoo was gathering the last of its animals and curiosities, while, down in the harbour, the world champion sculler, Ted Tricket, was pulling the crowds at the regattas. It wasn't exactly Henley but it was a start. However, underneath this veneer of social contentment and civilisation, the government was worrying about an 'alarming increase in infant mortality' and the growing numbers of Chinese immigrants. Flogging, which had been abolished in 1877, would soon be reintroduced to control the burgeoning population and law and order were high on the agenda. Not all was well in the land of opportunity but, good or bad, the ever-changing stories in the news kept George employed with plenty of lucrative jobs.

One of his earliest and best-known engravings for the *Sydney Mail* was of a group of thirty townsmen rounded up by the infamous Australian bushranger, Ned Kelly. He and his gang had spent the last few years

A woodcut by George Collingridge of his home, library and studio

causing mischief in the South, holding up banks and kidnapping townspeople and playing cat and mouse with the police. Things came to a head in June 1880, when the gang captured the town of Glenrowan, including the local policeman. A trainload of police stormed the inn where the gang was holed up and, in the showdown that followed, all the members of the gang were either killed or captured. George's picture took pride of place in the newspaper reports and was still being used over forty years later.

Meanwhile, he launched himself into his artistic and social excursions with typical vigour and style, spending his free time riding out into the bush and capturing the new landscape in pencil or watercolours. How different the scenery must have been from the familiar vistas of Europe – and how alluring the native Aboriginal people would have looked to the artist's unaccustomed eyes. There are two possible reactions when faced with something new – to try to recreate the security of the familiar or to take up the challenge to engage with change. For George, however, there was only one realistic option. Since his arrival in France as a six-year-old boy, he had learned to embrace new cultures and countries; he had done the same on his travels in Italy, Spain, England and Scotland, absorbing their languages, landscapes and histories into the jewel box of his experience and imagination. It was therefore almost inevitable that he would be seduced by this strange land where eucalyptus trees shimmered like belly-dancers against the blood-red earth and the biggest blue sky he had ever seen – but what riches lay glinting in its navel?

If George had been interested in making his fortune, he would have flocked to the new gold and silver mines that were cutting deep into the belly of the colony. In 1883, a German migrant, Charles Rasp, discovered one of the world's richest deposits of silver, lead and zinc in a mountain range called Broken Hill, nearly 600 miles west of Sydney. But George was interested in riches of a more enduring kind.

It was no surprise that this artist-turned-warrior and explorer should turn his enquiring mind to his adoptive homeland. He certainly had no reason to be hidebound by the colonial convention of looking only to the motherland – for him, the pastures of England had been quit too long ago to tug at his heart and soul, while France remained too unstable to be a bedrock for any sentiment. Even the last few members of his family were gradually making their way across the ocean to join him and his new wife, Lucy, in the continent. He had married a second-generation settler: they would make Australia their home, and that meant, for George at least, it was time to get acquainted with its roots.

Collingridge was not the only one to want to dig deep into Australia's past: around that time, the Government launched a competition for the best history text for New South Wales's schools. From the moment he read of the challenge, George was hooked: he had, after all, worked on numerous books and now here was the perfect opportunity to combine professional skill with a private passion for exploration and discovery, only this time the journey would be his own – and not over seas but through the mountains of journals and maps.

In 1883, as Mark Twain's travel books and Stephenson's *Treasure Island* were taking the Northern Hemisphere by storm, Indonesia's giant volcano, Krakatoa, blew its top in one of the most catastrophic eruptions in history. The blast was heard over two thousand miles away in mainland Australia, where George was preparing his own explosion in the field of cartography.

The public libraries of Adelaide, Melbourne and Sydney had recently joined forces to purchase a strange set of world maps – or mappa mundi – from the British Museum. They were facsimile copies of what looked like French maps – one dated to 'before 1536' but unsigned, one dated 1550 by Pierre Desceliers and another (in two parts) from Jean Rotz's *Boke of Idrography* which was gifted to Henry VIII of England and dated 1542. Not only were they an expensive use of public money, they purported to show early representations of Australia – almost 250 years before Cook first mapped its shores.

The press went wild – the maps were fakes, the money an outrage and anyone who was duped into seeing Australia in the misshapen slab of land was a fool. For George, the maps would have been sufficient draw in themselves but the furore now made viewing essential. The three vast charts were in archaic hand, with that strange witches' brew of myth and reality that led sailors to new lands of riches and old terrors of shipwreck and starvation. The maps were objects of outstanding beauty; the question was, were they real – and if so, what secrets lay buried in the faded ink?

According to the experts at the British Museum, there was little doubt that they were indeed genuine documents from the time of the early Renaissance – Jean Rotz's *Boke* had lain in the Royal Library since 1542, while the authorless map of 'before 1536' bore the coat of arms of Henry the Dauphin who later became Henry II of France. This last map had become known as the Dauphin or Harleian map, after Edward Harley, the Earl of Oxford and one of the principal Lords of the Admiralty. Curiously enough, it had been Edward Harley's passion for world geography and exploration that had encouraged him to send William

Dampier out to 'New Holland' in 1699. On Harley's death, however, the precious map was stolen by one of his servants and later came into the possession of Dr Solander, who gave it to Joseph Banks, who in turn had it gifted to the British Museum. However, even if the maps themselves were genuine, there was nothing to prove they were based on genuine information – and it was this point that vexed the residents of Adelaide, Melbourne and Sydney: what possible use could a set of old maps be when they were drawn over two hundred years before James Cook discovered the east coast and first stepped on Australian soil? Everyone knew that *he* had been the real discoverer of those shores! What did anyone else know of that continent in the middle of the 1500s – particularly the French? What indeed! George spread them out on the library table and peered down into the charts that were to become his life.

Looking at these maps today, it is easy to see why George was first enchanted: lying before you is the old world painted with exquisite care and detail – Europe, India, 'Asie la Grande' and 'Afrique', in-filled with winding rivers and tall, green mountain ranges. Stretching out across the land are walled cities, mighty castles and kingly figures, dressed in their traditional robes. In the frozen north of Russia, soldiers joust on horseback while south of the equator, elephants graze the flat plains of what is now Botswana. Their coastlines may be malformed but the lands themselves are easily recognisable, with Europe at its undisputed place, the centre of the world.

The maps lie heavy with pride and purpose: much more than vehicles for geographic facts, they breathe both power and politics. Although the seas are criss-crossed with the starbursts of compass roses and rhumb-lines, no navigator would have used them, let alone have taken them near a ship. They were meant instead for the great libraries of kings and queens who wanted a record of their domains; they were also a form of flattery or instruments in geopolitical war and empire-building – for along with the well-known lands of old, they also contained the sketchy outlines of the New World: a squat South America styled 'La Terre du Bresill', the great continent of 'Canada' that reaches down to the Gulf of Mexico and – lying between 'La Mer Pacifique' and the 'Mer des Indes' in the latitudes where Australia should be – a vast block of land, called simply 'Jave La Grande'.

Jave La Grande: what strange country was that? It could not be a grossly enlarged Java as an island called 'Jave' lies just to the north with the other Spice Islands. Everyone knew of the Spice Islands, source of the phenomenal wealth of Arab traders, then the Portuguese and later still the Dutch. But who had heard of the continent called Jave La Grande?

The maps still have the power to take your breath away. The sheer beauty is overwhelming – it takes a few seconds to take in their size and scale, then many more to focus through the textured layers of colour and ornament to the detail that languishes inside. I traced the outline of its geography like a lover's face: I had spent years learning how to examine things like this with cool scientific rigour and geopolitical critique but all that was now impossible. Instead, I stared and let them fill my eyes: here was a piece of living history, the touch-paper for a great debate that would span the centuries and wrap the onlooker in medieval skulduggery and modern controversy. Little wonder that George was seduced.

Unknown to George, the history of controversy had first started almost a hundred years before. A few years after Cook's death, the Dauphin Map had come to the attention of Alexander Dalrymple who still retained his passion for the South Seas. By now, of course, James Cook had cleansed the official map of the region of nearly all the fantastical lands that Dalrymple had supported, leaving him thwarted, angry and longing for revenge. He looked carefully at the strange shape and position of Jave la Grande – could it be an early map of the land they now called New Holland? He compared its shape with the modern map of the continent – a map whose east coast had been allegedly discovered and charted by his sworn enemy.

In 1786, Dalrymple published a small pamphlet on the geography of the region, which contained a brief but explosive analysis of that peculiar map – an analysis that was yet another dagger into the heart of Captain James Cook.

> I have a manuscript in my possession, belonging to Sir Joseph Banks ...
> The very curious manuscript here mentioned is painted with the Dauphin's Arms. It contains lost knowledge; Kerguelen's Land seems plainly denoted; the east coast of New Holland, as we name it, is expressed ...

The 'lost knowledge', he claimed, was of Australia itself. But not only was he alleging that Cook had not been the first European on that continent's eastern shores, he gave a strongly-worded insinuation that the great navigator was a cheat and a liar! Dalrymple knew that Banks had been given the map by Dr Solander – and both men had sailed with Cook on his first voyage of discovery – but had they taken the maps with them on the journey and, more importantly, had Cook seen the map before claiming to have 'discovered' New South Wales?

The mischief-making delighted Dalrymple. At last, here was a chance to damage the reputation of a man who'd eclipsed his own – and, what's more, he could do it under the guise of pursuing a historical truth. But there was much more to his argument than just spite. While he had no evidence of plagiarism, there were, he noted, 'curious circumstances of correspondence' between Cook's chart of the east coast and the east coast of the Dauphin's Jave la Grande.

Cook's 'Bay of Inlets' seemed to correspond in location with the Dauphin's 'Baye Perdue' while his 'Bay of Isles' seemed to match the Dauphin's 'Riviere de Beaucoup d'isles' in both geography *and* name.

The argument over the names on the maps continued with the work of Cook's former lieutenant from his third voyage, James Burney, who was busy writing his history of Pacific exploration. He came up with the most 'curious correspondence' of them all:

> By extraordinary coincidence, immediately at the latitude of thirty degrees, the coast is named COSTE DES HERIAGES answering in climate and name to BOTANY BAY.

Had Cook been using the Dauphin Map to guide his explorations? It seemed plausible given the similarities in the names on both charts but he always made reference to the maps he took with him, cursing their cartographers when the coastlines became fantasy and gaining as much satisfaction from announcing his corrections as he did from his discoveries. It is highly unlikely that – on this occasion – Cook decided to cheat and lie, but his accolade of 'discoverer'? Well, that was now in question.

18
SHIPWRECK!
James Cook 1770

FTER LEAVING the lush and vibrant world of Botany Bay, Cook continued to push his way up the east coast of New South Wales for another fortnight before making landfall. For the most part, he was blessed with fine weather by day and some beautiful nights when the moon shone silver, and he seized the opportunity to keep skirting the bleached outline of the coast without having to stand off for safety. This was good sailing – he could barely have asked for more.

As he progressed steadily north, the line of the shore was translated onto paper; he took latitude and longitude, the trend of the coast and its salient features, committing them as geographical fact to his unravelling chart. His eye was not infallible to hidden detail – he sailed past Sydney and Newcastle Harbours without realising their magnificence – but the general survey was the work of genius, giving praise to the lives of famous men or painting an air of familiarity to this strange land. Smoky Cape (a headland on which he saw fires), The Three Brothers (three adjacent hills – the North, Middle and South Brother), the Solitary Islands (islands above Coffs Harbour) and Cape Byron (easternmost point of Australia, named after the explorer John Byron who had circumnavigated the world) – the land of New South Wales was slowly taking shape.

Cook was in businesslike mood, hugging the coast, conducting his survey with unerring focus and plotting the immaculate charts; meanwhile, Banks and Dr Solander were in a race against time to preserve and log the thousands of specimens from their week-long plant-fest at Botany Bay. As they catalogued and described, Parkinson drew and painted: ninety-four sketches in just fourteen days. Alien species spewed from mounds on every surface as the gentlemen pinned, packed and

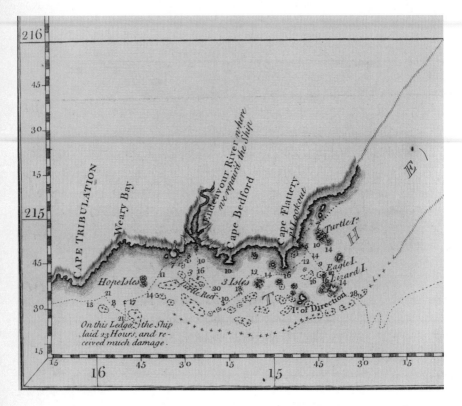

Endeavour reef and river chart, by Isaac Smith after Captain Cook

penned their haul. The mood was intense, the work relentless. Every man had his task; no one had respite.

They saw the occasional signs of life – smoke rising in plumes from the hills of the Great Dividing Range, people gathered near the beach – but there was no more contact, nor did they seek any. Sailing past what he called Point Lookout, Cook did not see that behind this seemingly continuous coastline lay the glorious Moreton Bay, site of the Brisbane River and its namesake city. But his eyes were fixed firmly on the route ahead and the ominous shoals that were to plague his journey. Having carefully navigating up the coast, he approached Fraser Island with its thirty-mile sand bar, Break Sea Spit. Luckily for the ship, the weather was fair enough and the water clear enough to make safe passage through the shallows but Cook was still on his guard. At last, on 22 May, they reached what he described as an 'inviting bay': greener and more lush than the previous miles of shoreline, and with a good possibility of finding fresh water. He decided to anchor for the night, in preparation for landing the next day.

It had been a long stretch up a coast without much in the way of respite. The ever-present islands and shoals meant that Cook had had to keep his wits about him while constantly looking out for fresh water and suitable landing sites. But although he was able to keep his ship under control, the crew were another matter. Knowing that tonight at least they could relax, they hit the drink with a passion.

Cook normally gave his men a fair degree of latitude on these occasions: boys will be boys and sailors will drink. But this time, the crew went a step too far. It may have been the tension of the tricky sailing conditions, it may have been the tiredness of the long journey beginning to catch up with him, but Cook could not contain his fury at the 'very extraordinary affair' that followed, even when writing it up in his journal a day later. It started with the drinking and went downhill from there.

Richard Orton, the captain's clerk and not a man without his faults, had collapsed into bed after supping what must have been a knock-out dose of rum. But he was not alone for long.

> Some malicious person or persons in the Ship took the advantage of his being drunk and cut off all the cloaths from off his back, not being satisfied with this they some time after went into his cabin and cut of part of both his Ears as he lay asleep in his bed!

Winding himself up into a rage, Cook continues:

The person whome he suspected to have done this was Mr Magra one of the Midshipmen, but this did not appear to me upon inquirey. However, as I Know'd Magra had once or twice before this in their drunken frolicks cut off his clothes and had been heard to say (as I was told) that if it was not for the Law he would Murder him, these things consider'd induce'd me to think that Magra was not altogether innocent. I therefore, for the present dismiss'd him from the quarter deck and susspended him from doing any duty in the Ship, he being one of those gentlemen, frequently found on board the Kings Ships, that can be very well spared, or to speake more planer good for nothing. Besides it was necessary in me to show my immediate resentment against the person on whome the suspicion fell least they should not have stoped here.

Cook was never convinced of Jim Magra's guilt and later, in Batavia, raised the issue again. Almost immediately, another sailor, Patrick Saunders, deserted the ship and disappeared. However, all that was still to come; Cook, meanwhile, was still rooted in the events of the previous night and determined to find, then punish the guilty party. But what is more interesting is how he takes the whole affair as a personal slight:

I shall say nothing about it unless I hereafter discover the Offenders which I shall take every method in my power to do, for I look upon such proceedings as highly dangerous in such Voyages as this and the greatest insult that could be offer'd to my authority in this Ship, as I have always been ready to hear and redress every complaint that have been made against any Person in the Ship.

It's significant that this is the *final* draft of his journal – and he is clearly still fuming with what he saw as a gross injustice not only against Richard Orton but also himself. As well as reminding us what a brutal period Cook was sailing in – and just how drunk these sailors could get in spite of their daily rationed allowance – at the bottom of these voiced inner thoughts lie feelings of immense hurt and betrayal. Throughout Cook's life, he had exercised the most incredible self-control: he had studied hard, worked hard and always kept his eyes and his concentration on the road ahead. Yet commanding a ship full of rag-bag crew, some of whom were not even there by choice, coping with the vicissitudes of weather and currents and the variables that could destroy the voyage and their lives – all these conspired to shake his confidence for, though he might try, he could never completely control every critical component for success. And for Cook in particular, the stakes *were* high: he was someone who had had to work his way up through the ranks; not for him the automatic privilege of a gentleman officer; yet here he was, commanding his first big ship on a hugely important mission with almost a hundred lives in his hands and the eyes of the Navy and Royal Society on his every move. Little wonder that he reeled against his men's implied lack of respect.

It's easy to imagine him sitting in his cabin, stewing away, pen in hand, working out his thoughts – as much on the page as in his head. After all, he had been trying his best to be a different type of commander from the ones who stood on the deck barking orders and demanding spurious punishment. He had seen both good and bad commanders; Cook was determined to be the best: he would not let himself down, he would not let his men down – and he would not let his men let *him* down.

Thankfully, for everyone's sake, the needs of the ship soon took up his attention once more. Having spent the fateful night at anchor, the next morning Cook and others, including Banks, Tupia and the Gentlemen went ashore for the first time since Botany Bay. The landscape here was vastly different: tangles of mangrove fringed the sandy shore, while the occasional eucalyptus and birch punctuated the skyline. The climate was different, too: although it was winter and the day was cold, it was clearly warmer and more humid than further south. Again, there were signs of fire but not of the people who had made them. The Aborigines, it seemed, were not keen on contact.

Once ashore, Banks and Solander were like children in a sweetshop. In Botany Bay, they had found little they recognised, but here many of the plants were familiar from the East Indies, interspersed with yet more species new to northern eyes. The birds were similar in type to those further south – ducks, pelicans and large English-style bustards, one of which they shot and dressed for the table. According to reports, it tasted very good indeed and so the area was named Bustard Bay.

But despite the fresh meat and plentiful shellfish, there was not enough here to make Cook delay: they sailed again in the morning, then crawled through the gathering shoals. By now they were weaving through a maze of shallows, sandbanks and islands and often battling with ferocious tides. There was no time to fester over challenges to his authority; one man was swinging the lead almost continually to check the depth of the water which rose and fell like a jack-in-the-box. The rapid changes surprised and sometimes embarrassed Cook who eventually had to resort to using the smaller boats to scout the route ahead; more than once, Cook must have thanked the stars, the Navy or God for providing him with a sturdy and flat-bottomed ship. The pressure and concentration were continuous, tedious and deadly serious, even for a man who'd learned his trade on the sandbanks of England's North Sea coasts, then dodging the enemy on the St Lawrence River.

There was little to break the daily grind of routine. By now, both the ship and her crew were feeling the strain, so they anchored briefly at the mouth of an inlet which seemed to promise fresh water, a good look-out and a place to clean the bottom of the ship. Certainly, the last two could be fulfilled but there was not a drop of drinking water in sight. Cook ruefully named the place 'Thirsty Sound'. Nevertheless, he stayed here, despite some foul weather and even fouler mosquitoes, for two days of exploring, repairs and land-bearings while Banks and his men leapt at another chance to examine the strange new flora and fauna of the area, including the 'very singular phenomenon' of the mud-skipper fish, able to live both in and out of water. They also saw more smoke and the relics of human settlement but the people themselves stayed largely out of view.

As Cook set off again at an even more cautious pace, he must have wondered if he would ever get clear of the shoals that littered his path up the coast. He pushed on relentlessly – even sailing by night when the conditions allowed. More experienced sailors in better ships have foundered on these submerged dangers; Cook not only found a route through the hazardous maze, he did so whilst compiling the most astounding-quality charts: detailed and accurate as ever, they were as much works of art as of geography as he mapped the Whitsunday Islands, Cape Upstart, Magnetic Island (where his compass 'would not travis well') and the long sweep of coast past Rockingham Bay. To draw such masterpieces with such limited technology was impressive enough; to do so while sailing what was virtually an obstacle course was the mark of genius.

There were no more distractions of the human kind, either on or off the ship, save for a couple of Aboriginal men spotted on a beach with an outrigger canoe – the first they had seen in this strange land. At least the weather looked kindly upon them, with fair winds, reasonable sunshine and good visibility. They would soon need all the help they could get in these treacherous waters.

A brief foray was made by Banks, Solander and Hicks to explore some coconut-type trees on Palm Island (which turned out to be cabbage palms), but there was little in the way of respite from the long push north. On board the ship, the warmer temperatures and constant work had left water supplies again running low and it was not long before Cook was once more looking out for safe anchorage with a nearby river or stream. The coastline, however, had other ideas: thick mangroves buttressed the water's edge, blurring into dense jungle on vertical cliffs. Any thoughts of landing were futile. It was only when he rounded Cape Grafton that he at last found both shelter and fresh water in Mission Bay, to the east of modern-day Cairns. He must have thought that his luck was finally turning.

Cook had taken over three weeks to sail from Cape Moreton to Cape Grafton: I made the equivalent journey in one hundred and twenty minutes. Having seen the depressing view of modern-day Botany Bay I arrived in Cairns on the last plane in, much to the displeasure of my hotel receptionist who made it politely clear that she'd been waiting to go to bed. From what I could gather on the brief, neon-lit ride into town, Cairns was the centre of all tours to everywhere, and you could have those in English, German, French or Japanese. The tour I had in mind was a rather more individual affair and it would commence in a horribly short number of hours.

Sure enough, daybreak found me in a side-room at a small, commercial airfield along with two couples, both on their holidays, their small travel bags neatly packed with beachwear and sunscreen; I looked at my bag crammed full of notes, maps and photocopied articles and got the feeling that, somewhere down the track, I'd got the meaning of life badly wrong. The flight announcement came in the form of a large woman in shorts, sticking her head around the door saying, 'That's your plane ready!' We stepped out onto the sunbaked airstrip.

The plane itself was a little propeller affair with eight seats that had clearly done the rounds for a good many years. As we climbed on board, a member of staff shouted 'Smile!' and took a photo, to be made into a certificate and presented to us at the location. I felt like an impostor on someone else's honeymoon but latched on vicariously to the jolly holiday mood; after all, it wasn't every day you caught your own private plane to work.

The noise of the engines grew to a roar as we headed along the runway then up into the clouds. As we soared through the swirling mists of vapour, my heart sank that we'd see nothing on our trek north except blue sky above and grey wadding below but a few minutes later, the cloud thinned and finally broke apart, exposing the aqua, buff and black of the Great Barrier Reef. I had always thought that the reef would be a long, unbroken line far away from the coast, but some smaller sections looked as if they were just a few metres off the shore, cutting through the clear blue water and spitting up white foamy surf. Tantalising though these glimpses were, I tried not to worry that the view below came and went as we sliced through the clouds – the reef would be the main character in the story of the next few days, during which I would get to know it intimately, in all its beauty and danger.

At last, the plane landed on a short grassy strip in a field of cows. It had taken just forty-five minutes to fly a distance that had taken the *Endeavour* two days to achieve; two days that took both the ship and its crew inching towards their apocalypse.

On 10 June, 1770, Cook reached a point to the northeast of modern-day Cairns, which he named 'Cape Grafton'. He was hopeful of finding fresh water here to replenish the dwindling supplies – and indeed there was good water but it wasn't accessible and so, after the rest of the day exploring, they weighed anchor at midnight and pushed on up with a bright moon lighting their path. As dawn was breaking on that Trinity Sunday, they journeyed slowly up the flat coastline until Cook saw a small indentation and named it 'Trinity Bay'; the gently bulging cape at its north end he later named 'Cape Tribulation', for as he himself admitted, 'here begun all our troubles'.

Unbeknown to Cook, lurking under the now-sunlit water lay the world's greatest reef system. It stretches over twelve hundred miles up the east coast of Australia in a clumpy line of coral reefs, shoals and islets. At its southern end, unwitting boats sail into the mouth of a giant, deadly funnel as the shore and reef grow ever closer. Refined over the last five million years, it's one of the most challenging environments a sailor can face – and that is with a map and modern technology. But Cook had no map, no sounding equipment save the lead weights, no power but the fickle wind – and all too soon the tropical sun was dipping over the horizon. He was then sailing blind in treacherous waters.

At first things went well: there were near-perfect conditions with a calm sea, a 'fine breeze of wind and clear moonlit night'. To any sailor, such a night is manna from heaven; the water appears to glow, the breeze caresses your face and the rolling surf murmurs gently in your ears. Shortening the sails, Cook continued his way up the coast, hauling off-shore to avoid two small wooded islands that raised their heads above the waterline. These were easily seen and presented no danger; in fact, everything seemed under control so, with one man continually swinging the lead to test the depth of the water, he steadily sailed on into the night.

The first indication that something was wrong came just after 9 o'clock: for the past three hours, they had been in around fourteen to twenty-one fathoms of water, then 'all at once we fell into 12, 10 and 8 fathom'. Cook immediately raised the alarm.

I had every body at their stations to put about and come to an anchor but in this I was not so fortunate for meeting again with deep water I thought there could be no danger in standing on.

Emergency over, the mood returned to normal: assuming all was well, Cook and the Gentlemen resumed their dinner and then retired to bed. On deck, the crew relaxed as the water deepened but the serenity was not to last for long.

Before 10 o'clock we had 20 and 21 fathom and continued in that depth untill a few Minutes before 11 when we had 17 and before the man at the lead could heave another cast, the Ship Struck and stuck fast.

The *Endeavour* had hit a reef that seemed to have come from nowhere. They were now pinned on the jagged coral, in a holed ship, over twenty miles from the shore; the next twenty-four hours would prove a test of Cook's seamanship and of the *Endeavour* herself: if either failed, the result would be death. Banks gave a typically dramatic account of the crash:

Scarce were we warm in our beds when we were called up with the alarming news of the ship being fast ashore upon a rock which she in a few moments convinced us by beating very violently against the rocks. Our situation now became greatly alarming ... we were little less than certain that we were upon sunken coral rocks, the most dreadful of all others on account of their sharp points and grinding quality, which cut through a ship's bottom almost immediately.

One can only imagine what ice ran through Cook's body on hearing the roar of the smash: here he was, commanding his first ship, carrying the hopes of the Navy and responsible for the lives of almost a hundred men. Losing a ship was a court-martial offence – assuming you didn't drown in the process – and remarkable though it may seem for a man who lived his life at sea and thrived on being in control, James Cook had never learned to swim. Outwardly, though, he gave no sign of fear and within minutes the *Endeavour* was jumping with slick activity: the sails were taken in, anchors put out and boats lowered to assess the damage and take soundings around the ship.

The news when it came back was not good – she was lying in as little as three or four feet of water, at high tide, on the edge of the reef. In fact, the situation could hardly be worse for soon the tide would turn leaving her even more exposed and any chance of refloating the ship would be dashed for the next twelve hours – possibly along with the ship and its crew.

Cook's first course of action was to try to haul her off the reef with the smaller boats and anchors, but to no avail; she was wedged firmly on the coral. As the ominous creaks and grinding grew worse, Cook knew that desperate measures were called for. Anything superfluous or heavy went overboard – six cannons at over half a ton each, iron and stone ballast, oil jars, ruined stores and all their water; nothing was spared that could be lost. In all, around fifty tons went over the side – but *still* she would not float.

For the next twelve, long hours, more supplies went overboard, but again, the *Endeavour* remained stuck fast. It was now high tide once more – one more chance, perhaps the last, to float her off the reef – so another attempt was made to heave her off with cables, blocks and tackle. She barely budged an inch. And then, just when things looked like they couldn't get any worse, she heeled to one side and the water gushed in through a newly-gaping hole. At this point, even Cook must have felt dread rushing into his heart. He ordered two pumps immediately into position but they were useless against the power of the sea: in less than an hour, it was clear that the flood-waters were winning. The final two pumps were then brought out but one had rotted away and was totally useless. On deck, the crew now worked in an eerie, focussed silence. There was nothing to say – only actions or miracles would now save their souls. By five o'clock, eighteen hours after the crash, the water was rising and the weary men were battling for their lives.

As the situation grew ever more desperate, even the Gentlemen joined the call of all hands to the pumps. The work was backbreaking and relentless; one fifteen-minute shift was all the teams could manage at a time, and yet the officers remained calm and not a single oath was heard from the men. The entire crew was concentrated, orderly and giving it their all. But still that was not enough. Twenty-two hours had passed since the ship had hit the reef: twenty-two hours of non-stop work for every single man on the ship, and the water was flooding in faster than ever. By now, even Cook's belief in deliverance was fraying at the edges, but he knew there was nothing to be gained by despair. His account shows something of his resolve:

At 9 o'clock the ship righted and the leak gaind upon the pumps considerably. This was an alarming and I may say terrible Circumstance and threatened immidiate destruction to us as soon as the Ship was afloat. However I resolved to risk all and heave her off in case it was practical and accordingly turned as many hands to the Capstan and windlass as could be spared from the Pumps.

In truth, he had no choice: the longer she was pinned to the reef, the more her hull was being gouged away and the less likely she was to survive. As for the men, they would have to try their best to reach land in the smaller boats, without supplies and with no chance of rescue. Even if she were eventually to float free, the ship would soon be so badly holed that she'd probably sink before making the twenty or so miles to the shore. Desperate situations required desperate measures: they made one last attempt to heave her off the coral into deep water – and this time, twenty-three hours after striking the reef, she floated.

The feelings of relief were almost overwhelming but, if anyone thought they were out of danger, they were wrong. There were already more than three-and-a-half feet of water in the hold and as the *Endeavour* moved away from the reef, yet more gushed in through her riven beams. Every hand was set to the pumps except for the sick and the two men measuring the rising tide inside the ship. When they were swapping over, one of these men gave his first reading as eighteen inches deeper than his companion's. The news was enough to strike fear into the hearts of every man on the ship, and that included Cook, but this time luck was on their side: a second reading proved that he had measured the depth from the wrong mark, but the effect was electric: the men redoubled their efforts and the floodwaters finally began to sink. The anchors were brought in, the sails set, and *Endeavour* once more was under way.

At last Cook had time to review his options: if they were sinking too fast to make the shore, the wooded islands spotted two days before might give some temporary refuge. Accordingly, these were given the name of 'Hope Islands' but Cook had reckoned without the inspiration of his crew. A brilliant idea by the surgeon's brother, Jonathan Monkhouse, meant that, thankfully, those islands were never needed. The midshipman had once sailed on a merchant ship that had been badly holed and he had witnessed a radical technique known as 'fothering' to give a temporary repair. He explained his plan to Cook who at once put him in charge and set the men to work. Quick as they could, an old sail was covered with a mixture of rope fibre, wool and dung, then hauled with ropes under the ship's bottom to cap the leak, like a bandage over a wound. The results were amazing: where three pumps had struggled to control the rising waters, just one was now needed to keep the flood at bay – and Monkhouse earned the rare compliment in Cook's journal that he had directed and executed the whole process 'very much to my satisfaction'. As for his entire crew, Cook noted they could not have done better. They sailed on like this for almost a week until, on 18 June, seven days after the ship was holed, they landed in one of the most perfect harbours on the northeastern coast.

The low, grey sky warned of a forthcoming cyclone as I made my way out past Hope Islands. We'd been watching and waiting for several days now, but at last, at breakfast the captain had given the go-ahead to make our way out to the reef. Even though we were under motor, the journey seemed to take forever as we were buffeted by the steely waves and slapped by the wind. I looked at the array of radar, flashing lights and buttons at the helm: *Big Mama* would have no problem keeping out of danger. At least, I hoped so: there were some experiences I *wasn't* keen to relive.

I lay back on the deck of this sixty-foot yacht, trying in vain to capture the mood. Steel hulls, engines and satellite navigation – not quite what Cook had been dealing with, but at least the reef should be the same. The crew pointed out a line of blue and white in the distance: that was Pickersgill Reef which had given Cook his first adrenaline burst, and beyond was Endeavour Reef, the cause of its namesake's near nemesis. I zipped up my wetsuit, climbed over the rail and flopped down into a fizz-boat with about as much elegance as a beached seal. It was time to explore.

Despite the cool wind, the water was like a Jacuzzi: warm, frothy, promising fun but carrying a potential health risk, in this case, being pushed onto the poisonous, jaggy coral or being eaten by a shark. I remembered my environmental training ('take only photos, leave only bubbles – and steer clear of anything that'll kill you') and kept a respectful distance from all sources of danger. Being underwater was an experience that few of Cook's men would have had: like him, most never learned how to swim, preferring to die quickly than have a lingering death. For them, the sea was like a god with the power to cradle life in its hands or snatch it away in an instant. And, just as you were powerless against the gods, the sailors knew they were powerless against the force of the briny water.

Diving down, the silent architecture of the reef was from another world: cathedrals of coral rose up from the inky depths, sheer walls on the one side, flying buttresses and ledges on the other, etched out in rainbow filigree. Pausing for a while, I floated in reverence at its deadly beauty. This reef could so easily have marked the end of Cook's first voyage and the end of British hopes for colonising this real Southern Continent. How many other ships had met their fate off this shoreline – before and after Cook? And how much secret knowledge was locked in this watery tomb?

In January 1969, a team of divers had uncovered the *Endeavour's* ejected load of cannons, jars and ballast, lying close to a small 'bornie' that jutted upwards just in front of the main reef. The haul was cleaned up and distributed to museums around the world, while a lump of iron ballast found a home on the *Endeavour Replica* ship and has since circumnavigated the world. In the end, though, humans have got their revenge: careless tourism and global warming are slowly but surely killing the giant structure that has lain here since bear-dogs and sabre-toothed cats roamed the earth and the first whales swam in the oceans. I doubted that much would be left to explore in another two hundred and fifty years' time: in exchange for saving Cook's life, the coral had given its own.

As for the site itself, a steel peg had been hammered into the rock, marking the spot of this all-too-close encounter with the Great Barrier Reef. As I turned to swim back to the boat, I paid my last respects to this mighty living organism. In return, the purple polyps just slowly nodded and waved.

19

'A CALAMITOUS SITUATION'

James Cook 1770

HERE WERE ONLY two colours in the broad harbour into which slid a weary, limping *Endeavour*: the flat, dull green of the vegetation and the steely grey of the water and sky, pricked up by the gales that now assailed the battered ship and crew. The weather did not matter – they were lucky to be alive and they knew it. Cook immediately set up tents for the sick and also for the surviving stores, then set about organising parties to fetch fresh water and food. The eight or nine sick included the astronomer, Green, 'in a very poor way' according to Banks, and Tupia 'whose bad gums were very soon followd by livid spots on his legs & every symptom of inveterate scurvy notwithstanding acid, bark & every medecine our Surgeon could give him'.

As was his custom, Cook climbed the tallest hill nearby to see the lie of the land: he was not impressed – there was little but salty mangrove on the lowlands, then barren and stony highlands. The ship lay at the mouth of a large river that snaked its way inland but he knew he was fortunate to have made it here at all: the spot provided a safe, sheltered anchorage in which to make the necessary repairs to his ailing ship. She was in desperate shape, with seawater swilling around the hold and a large hole in her bottom on the starboard side that took even Cook's breath away:

The manner these planks were damaged or cut out as I may say is hardly credible, scarce a splinter was to be seen but the whole was cut away as if it had been done by the hands of Man with a blunt edge tool. Fortunately for us the timbers in this place were very close, other ways it would have been impossible to have saved the ship and even as it was it appear'd very extraordinary that she made no more water than what she did. A large piece

The Endeavour *being careened, an engraving after Sydney Parkinson*

of Coral rock as large as a Mans fist was sticking in one hole and several pieces of the fothering, small stones, sand &ca had made its way in and lodged between the timbers which had stoped the water from forceing its way in great quantities.

They were indeed lucky to be alive; had the coral not partly plugged the gap, the ship would have gone under. Nevertheless, the damage was extensive:

Part of the Sheathing was gone from under the larboard bow, part of the false keel was gone and the remainder in such a shatter'd condition that we should be much better of, was it gone also.

The carpenter and smiths were immediately set to work. Meanwhile, the Gentlemen took full advantage of the landing to explore the region and the botanical treasures that were on offer. As usual, the tell-tale signs of scurvy soon receded as they feasted on pigeon, fish, plantains and palm cabbages; the one-handed ship's cook was doing a fine job, though the crew balked at the acrid taro which Cook almost alone was able to stomach. Another source of potential food was harder to track down.

One of the men saw an animal something less than a grey hound, it was of a Mouse Colour very slender made and swift of foot.

Shortly afterwards, Cook saw one himself:

It was of a light Mouse colour and the full size of a grey hound and shaped in every respect like one, with a long tail which it carried like a grey hound, in short I should have taken it for a wild dog, but for its walking or runing in which it jumped like a Hare or a deer.

What was this strange creature that seemed like it was made from God's leftovers? Gore set out with his gun and a hunger for bagging one that easily matched Banks' rather more scientific motivation.

Mr Green was by now sufficiently recovered to help the captain observe the reappearance of Jupiter's first satellite, by which they were able to establish a reliable longitude – 145°17'30"E – just over two minutes out from the true position and a remarkable achievement given the conditions. However, the reading was a stark reminder that both Greenwich and home were a long way away: here they were, on the other side of the world with a ship that would barely stay afloat. At least there was plenty of wood for the repairs and for the smelting fires. Some of the damage was irreparable – they could get her as far as the dockyards of the Indies but then she would need a serious overhaul; Cook could do nothing but listen to Mr Satterly, the much-respected carpenter, take his advice and try not worry.

June rolled into July; by now, the men were well-fed with fresh supplies and the harbour reverberated to the sound of the smiths' hammers and carpenter's saw. Cook knew he had to make best use of the available time: he had seen from the surveys of the harbour and beyond that the route ahead was strewn with an insane labyrinth of shoals – there would be weeks of difficult sailing ahead, if indeed there was any way through the deadly maze that stretched beyond the horizon.

Some relief came in the form of contact with the local Gogo-Yimidir people who, nervous at first, were finally enticed into taking small gifts, though the nakedness of the women caused Cook no small discomfort. A few days later, Lieutenant Gore finally bagged 'one of the Animals' he had made his target – a Great Grey Kangaroo, bearing 'no sort of resemblance to any European Animal I ever saw', though it made 'excellent food'.

Relations with the Gogo-Yimidir continued to improve as the locals grew bolder and the men of the *Endeavour* developed an almost tender affection for these softly-spoken, painted people, with their sing-song language and broad smiles. There was one slight hiccup when the 'Indians' tried to take a turtle from the deck, were stopped by the crew and, in a fit of pique, went ashore and set fire to the few supplies that lay on the ground including a piglet that was scorched to death. However, the fracas did not last for long and soon the two parties were sat together on the floor, exchanging names and 'unintelligible conversation' once more. The Gentlemen asked the name of that strange jumping creature they had caught, to which the reply came, 'Kanguru'. The men excitedly wrote the word down, repeating it over and over – that was the animal which had so long evaded them. Ironically, there is a now a body of thought alleging that 'kangaroo' was not the name of the animal but Gogo-Yimidir for 'I don't know', but once written down, it was unquestioned and accepted as fact.

July wore on. They had been on land for seven weeks; the repairs were finished, the supplies restocked – even the Gentlemen had finished with their botanising. Everyone was impatient to go but now it was the weather's turn to cause delays. The winds grew, then fell calm, then grew again into August but Cook knew it was time to make his move. He ordered the last of the supplies to be stowed below and the ship made ready to sail into the maze that lay before them. He realised it would be difficult – there was no obvious route through the shoals, so he would have to edge forward by guesswork, good judgement and, he hoped, luck. The latter was not to be on his side: at his first attempt to leave the river-mouth, he was penned in by a sand bar stretching across his path; there was nothing for it but to wait for the high tide. Then, early on the morning of 4 August, he rode the bar and sailed out to sea, leaving the river he now named 'Endeavour'.

He did not get far. Within a few hours, he was anchored yet again while he climbed up the mast to take a clear view of the options that lay ahead. Proximity didn't help. Should he go southwards round the shoals? Or eastwards? Or northwards? All were equally difficult; all were equally dangerous. The usually confident captain craned his neck and looked out in despair. The best he could do was aim towards the northeast which looked the clearest passage and then, if need be, turn back.

Within a few hours, he was at anchor once more while he scoured the passage ahead and the boats went out fishing for clams, shark and rays. They returned fully laden but the captain was having less success. Everywhere was strewn with shoals – and then the winds turned to gales. A desperate Cook knew he was scuppered.

> After having well View'd our situation from the mast head I saw that we were surrounded on every side with Shoals and no such thing as a passage to Sea but through the winding channels between them, dangerous to the highest degree in so much that I was quite at a loss which way to steer when the weather would permit us to get under sail; for to beat back to the SE the way we came as the Master would have had me done would be an endless peice of work, as the winds blow now constantly strong from that quarter without hardly any intermission – on the other hand if we do not find a passage to the northd we shall have to come [back] at last.

He could do little but sit and wait for the weather to improve his chances of making it through the maze and hope that his anchors held. In all, he was stuck fast for three days before he could again set sail, this time to the north and hugging the coast. By 10 August, he was therefore edging inside the reef, sounding constantly and with everyone on keen look-out for the slightest sign of shoals. After a watery slalom through some offshore islands and a headland, it looked like they were safely through to open water

> but this we soon found otherwise and occasiond my calling the headland abovementioned Cape Flattery (Latde 14°55'S, Longd 214°43'W).

A lesser man might have panicked or fallen into despair; not so Lieutenant Cook: in all the confusion over which way to go, he never lost his calm and never once stopped taking co-ordinates for his beloved surveys.

It was growing crowded up the masthead as the officers pitched in with their analyses of the situation; in the end, Cook made for the coast, anchored yet again, and climbed yet another hill to peer through the haze. By now, he was racking his brain and straining his eyes: there must be a way through, no matter how tortuous, but his only conclusion was that he needed to climb a higher hill. He found a suitable candidate a thousand feet up on the offshore Lizard Island where he stayed all evening and then throughout the night as well, scouring the horizon for a way through the 'insane labyrinth' of shoals that to his 'mortification' seemed to surround him. At last he noticed gaps between the breaking waves – a channel, perhaps? The breakers were certainly big enough to indicate that this could be the boundary between ocean and shoal. It was enough to convince him and, anyway, there was no other choice: time was running out; they had barely three months of provisions left so to turn back now into the shoals that had plagued their journey would not only threaten them with almost-certain disaster, it was simply inconceivable.

He sent the men out in boats to sound and at last there came good news: there was a channel to the east, a narrow one, but a channel all the same. Cook put the dilemma to his officers and all were agreed: they would forge ahead as soon as conditions allowed. At dawn on 13 August, the *Endeavour* sailed to Lizard Island then inched its way cautiously through the deep crevasse in the coral. The roaring crash of breakers assailed them from either side; one false move and they would be crushed to matchsticks. Everyone held their breath; everyone waited; everyone placed their faith in the skill of their commander – and then, a flurry of faster water lifted them up and took them out to sea. They were through.

Even his leaking ship could not dampen Cook's spirits – a single pump could keep that water at bay. After what they had just been through, it was little more than a trifle: they had escaped from the shoals, for the first time in almost three months. The only thing he had lost was the chance to continue his survey of the coast as he was now too far out to see the shore; it would take another two attempts and fifty years for navigators to fill in his dotted stretch between Cape Melville and Cape Direction. Meanwhile, Cook had miraculously sniffed out perhaps the best passage that existed through the reef – a mile long and three-quarters of a mile wide – and a short sail to freedom.

While everyone else let out a collective sigh of relief, Cook steadied his nerves his own way: by considering the broader question of the voyage itself. He knew that, along with the myth of the Great Southern Continent, there was one other major mystery that needed clearing up: whether or not New Holland was joined with New Guinea, or if a strait did indeed exist, as Torres and his historic maps suggested. His present course would risk overshooting the region in which the Strait would lie – so he steered northwest again in an attempt to pick up the coast once more. The trouble was that meant getting back through the very reef he had just managed to escape. His obsession with the truth was about to make him a pawn in a deadly game of chance. He changed his direction – and headed in to shore. A few days later, on 14 August, he heard the familiar roar of breakers on the reef; next thing he knew, they stretched right across the horizon. It was too deep to anchor, the wind disappeared and the waves were taking them straight towards certain death.

> In this distressed situation we had nothing but Providence and the small Assistance our boats could give us to trust to.

The boats were lowered – if nothing else they would delay the moment *Endeavour* was smashed to smithereens against the sheer wall of the reef. Three hundred yards became two hundred, each crash of the breakers sounding their drumbeat to the gallows. Like a convict chewing his final meal, Green went on deck to take a lunar observation while Cook maintained the surreal sense of calm.

> It was 6 oClock and we were not above 80 or 100 Yards from the breakers, the same Sea that washed the sides of the Ship rose in a breaker prodigiously high the very next time it did rise so that between us and distruction was only a dismal Vally the breadth of one wave and ever now no ground could be felt with 120 fathoms. The Pinnace by this time was patched up and hoisted out and sent ahead to tow; still we had hardly any hopes of saving the Ship and full as little our lives as we were full 10 Leagues from the nearest land and the boats not sufficient to carry the whole of us, yet in this terrible situation not one man ceased to do his utmost and that with as much calmness as if no danger had been near. All the dangers we had escaped were little in comparison of being thrown upon this Reef where the Ship must be dashed to peices in a Moment.

And then – just when death seemed inevitable – a breath of wind escaped from the heavens, blew the ship two hundred yards from the reef and then died. It blew again and faded but by now the ship was a quarter of a mile from what looked like a gap in the waves. In the silent corridor, the men in the boats rowed for all their worth, knowing that at any second, fate could smash them against the coral. They rode the ebb tide like a water-slide, racing through the cut to spill out into safety and a big, flat sea. There was only one name for the passage: Providential Channel.

The tension that had kept him strong now buckled in relief as never before and his feelings splurged over the pages of his journal in a rare and poignant moment of emotional transparency – perhaps the most significant he ever wrote. In this early draft, he was writing for himself: the Admiralty, his colleagues or the general public were for once a distant irrelevancy. This is raw Cook – and, as his biographer, John Beaglehole, wrote nearly thirty years ago – it would be 'wrong not to quote him at length'.

'It is but a few days ago that I rejoiced at having got without the Reef, but that joy was nothing when Compared to what I now felt at being safe at an Anchor within it, such is the Visissitudes attending this kind of Service & must always attend and unknown Navigation where one steers wholly in the dark without any manner of Guide whatever. Was it not for the Pleasure which Naturly results to a man from his being the first discoverer even when it was nothing more than Sand or Shoals this kind of Service would be insupportable especially in far distant parts like this, Short of Provisions & almost every other necessary. People will hardly admit of an excuse for a man leaving a Coast unexplored he had once discover'd, if dangers are his excuse he is then charged with Timerousness & want of Perseverance, & at once pronounced the most unfit man in the world to be emply'd as a discoverer, if on the other hand he boldly encounters all the dangers & Obstacles he meets & is unfortunate enough not to succeed he is then Charged with Temerity & perhaps want of Conduct, the former of these Aspersions I am confident can never be laid to my Charge, & if I am fortunate to Surmount all the Dangers we meet with the latter will never be brot in Question, altho' I must own that I have engaged more among the Islands & Shoals upon this Coast than Perhaps in prudence I ought to have done with a single Ship, & every other thing considered, but if I had not I should not have been able to give any better account of the one half of it, than if I had never seen it, at best I should not have been able to say wether it was Main land or Islands & as to its produce, that we should have been totally ignorant of as being inseparable with the other & in this case it would have been far more satisfaction to me never to have discover'd it, but it is time I should have done with this Subject wch at best is but disagreeable & which I was lead into on reflecting on our late Danger.'

There is one final poignancy about the event and about this early draft of
his journal: in his entry for 16 August – that dreadful day of judgement –
he at first gives thanks to God for that saviour breath of wind. By the later
drafts, God is edited out and Chance is made responsible. In times of
danger and uncertainty, he keeps his world safe by keeping it rational;
belief is a private matter for him alone – and on that, he is inscrutable.

By 17 August, he was at anchor in the smooth sea inside the reef, his
new plan to hug the coast until he found the strait that was rumoured to
lie between New Holland and New Guinea. There was still danger from
the ever-present shoals, but if he took his time and proceeded with
caution, he would soon be on his way to the East Indies and home.

The air of normality quickly regained its hold: the exhausted men
feasted on 240 pounds of meat from the giant cockles brought in by the
boats, some shells requiring two men to lift them on board, while Banks
went exploring on a nearby island. The breezes were gentle and the
sunshine warm. Soon it was business as normal: coasting, surveying,
sounding and charting, just as they had done for the last four months; as
for the labyrinth that still strew their path,

> so much does great danger Swallow up lesser ones that those once so
> dreaded Shoals were now looked at with less concern.

As the land trended northwest, he knew he was reaching the final stages
of New Holland's eastern coast. Sailing by the broad Newcastle Bay and
'York Cape', he saw a passage between the mainland and an island; sailing
through, the mainland veered sharply west before falling away to the
south. He had rounded the northernmost tip of the uncharted coast;
further north and west lay only islands. On 22 August, he rowed across to
one of them where he climbed a low hill and looked into the open water
that lay before him: he had reached the top of New Holland and the
entrance to the legendary Torres Strait – and, unlike the Great Southern
Continent, it certainly did exist. The sight marked the end of debate and
the end of his New Holland journey. Hoisting the English Colours, he
then took possession of the whole of the eastern coast in the name of King
George III, and renamed it New South Wales.'

In his satisfaction, Cook now began to draw a line under his antipodean
experiences. There was nothing more to discover – he was now amongst
lands charted by the Dutch, Spanish and Portuguese before him. His
work was done and he was glad. He now busied himself by laying down
his final conclusions on the coasts, seas, flora and fauna of the land he
styled New South Wales. As to the people, he departed from his usual

scientific air of detachment to try out some cod-philosophy – perhaps to counter the miserable write-up they were given by William Dampier, the Englishman who had ventured around the west coast of New Holland around seventy years before, or perhaps he had been reading up on the Romantic notions of the 'Noble Savage' that were becoming increasingly popular at the time, or perhaps he was making a bizarre attempt to ape the high-brow language of Mr Banks; the two men had, after all, been cheek-by-jowl for two years now and Cook could not fail to be impressed by his erudite assertions. However, the elevated style was too obviously not his own and it leaps out from his journal like a riddling court-jester:

> From what I have said of the Natives of New-Holland they may appear to some to be the most wretched people on Earth, but in reality they are far more happier than we Europeans; being wholy unacquainted not only with the superfluous but the necessary Conveniences so much sought after in Europe, they are happy in not knowing the use of them. They live in a Tranquillity which is not disturb'd by the Inequality of Condition: The Earth and sea of their own accord furnishes them with all things necessary for life, they covet not Magnificent Houses, Household-stuff &ca, they live in a warm and fine Climate and enjoy a very wholsome Air, so that they have very little need of Clothing and this they seem to be fully sencible of, for many to whome we gave Cloth &ca to, left it carlessly upon the Sea beach and in the woods as a thing they had no manner of use for. In short they seem'd to set no Value upon any thing we gave them, nor would they ever part with any thing of their own for any one article we could offer them; this in my opinion argues that they think themselves provided with all the necessarys of Life and that they have no superfluities.

It is a relief when he goes back to discussing the 'Currents and Tides' and the familiar Cook – sure in reason and straight as a die – takes over once more. However, over-blown romanticism was the order of the day on board the weary *Endeavour* as both crew and Gentlemen succumbed to homesickness. Even Banks marvelled at the change in mood, with nearly three-quarters of the men experiencing 'Nostalgia':

> Indeed I can find hardly any body in the ship clear of its effects but the Captn Dr Solander and myself.

But before they made for home, they badly needed repairs and supplies – and they were best located in Batavia, around five weeks away by sail. They made a brief stop on the southern coast of New Guinea where they

were repelled by some belligerent locals; two weeks later, they were
coasting the Dutch colony at Timor, then Savu, where they tried to take
on fresh food amidst much politicking and hassle from the extortive
Dutch Factor and the region's King. It was a tedious welcome back to
European so-called civilisation – they were cheated, delayed and
deprived of the naturally easy relations they had developed with the
Savuans, but at last managed to obtain some basic provisions, enough to
send them on their way. On 21 September, a relieved crew set sail, their
decks heaving with animals for slaughter, the famous goat still doing her
duty but just one of Banks' much-loved dogs, the other regrettably having
been promised to the King in a drunken, grandiloquent gesture and no
doubt eaten soon after.

Batavia's position in the Indian Ocean was unassailable. Founded in 1619
by the Dutch on the ruins of Jakarta, this fortified city had quickly
become the most important port in the region and the centre of Dutch
power in Asia. Its layout was Dutch, the houses were Dutch and the canal
system certainly was: in all, it was a little piece of the Netherlands
transplanted into the dense heat of the steamy tropics, all under the vice-
like grip of the ruthlessly mercantile Dutch East India Company, or VOC,
who made the city their headquarters. They had a strict monopoly over
employment, works and goods: nothing could be done without their say-
so, but this had its efficiencies and the city was famous with mariners the
world over; here captains would repair and replenish *en route* around the
globe.

The Batavia that Cook crawled into at the beginning of October 1770
was almost smelt before it was seen. The standing water of the canals
oozed green with slime and sewage and clouds of deadly mosquitoes rose
off the surface. The stench pervaded their nostrils and tied their stomachs
in knots; were it not for the promise of docks and skilled workers, they
would have avoided the port like the plague, but the *Endeavour* that now
limped in was falling to bits about the seamen's ears and badly needed
attention. When they finally anchored, Banks received a grisly warning of
the state of their refuge in the guise of the officer sent out to meet them.

> Both himself & his people were almost as Spectres, no good omen of the
> healthyness of the country we were arrived at; our people however who
> truly might be called rosy and plump, for we had not a sick man among us,
> Jeerd & flouted much at their brother sea mens white faces.

They laughed too soon, but wasted no time in gleaning the first shreds of news from home, though they were forbidden from mentioning where they had been themselves and Cook had gone as far as confiscating all the journals he could find to keep the results of the voyage a secret from the inquisitive Dutch. When he was asked to give details of his passage, all he would give was the ship's name, nationality and port of origin. Discretion was essential: having come this far, he was not about to throw away his discoveries to a competitor.

Meanwhile, there was the very serious matter of the *Endeavour*'s condition. The officers were all agreed – she would not make it back to Britain in her current state without being taken into dry dock for a full overhaul. Cook ordered a list of defects from Mr Satterly, the carpenter: it made grim reading. Despite his excellent work at Endeavour River, she was leaking up to twelve inches of water an hour, her main and false keels were badly damaged, she was punctured from the reef and, along with other sundry damages, the pumps were also in dire need of repair. Cook immediately petitioned the port authorities for permission that the work be carried out and that meanwhile he should be allowed to purchase whatever provisions they needed. Permission granted, he set to securing some greens and fresh food for his men.

Three days after they arrived, he heard of a Dutch ship leaving for home and quickly scribbled a note to Philip Stephens, the Admiralty Secretary, saying where he was. Ten days later, he entrusted a precious copy of his journal in a package sent with a Dutch fleet heading back to Europe. This was dated 23 October, containing letters to the Admiralty and Royal Society, and charts of the 'South Sea', New Zealand and New South Wales. The letter to the Admiralty distilled the entire voyage to date into just six hundred and fifty words; it also distills the mood of the captain, with its mixture of pride and humility, achievement and apology.

> Altho' the discoveries made in this Voyage are not very great, yet I flatter my self that they are such as may merit the attention of their Lordhips, and altho' I have faild in discovering the so much talk'd of southern Continent (which perhaps do not exist) and which I myself had much at heart, yet I am confident that no part of the failure of such discovery Can be laid to my Charge ... Had we been so fortunate not to have run a shore much more would have been done in the latter part of the Voyage than what was, but, as it is I presume this Voyage will be found as Compleat as any before made to the South Seas, on the same account.

The package would electrify the Admiralty – even Cook's modesty had to admit that; more was the pity he was not there to watch them open it.

Banks, meanwhile, had headed ashore to find lodgings with Solander, Tupia and Taiata. They returned to the *Endeavour* with news of more than just accommodation: it seemed that the 'Spanish' ships that had been in Tahiti just before their arrival were in fact French ships under the command of Bougainville. The wisp of news intrigued Cook, who kept himself alert for other tales of South Sea exploration, concerned in case his discoveries had been pre-empted.

Meanwhile, Banks was tantalised by the thought of the new foods on offer in this cosmopolitan city, particularly monkey, which he had resolved to try along with Cook and Solander,

> but on the morning of our intended feast I happened to cross the yard of the House in which we resided and observed half a dozen of those poor little Devils with their arms tied upon cross sticks laying on their backs preparatory to their being killed, Now as I love all sorts of Animals I walked up to them and in consequence of their plaintive chattering and piteous looks I could not resist cutting the Strings by which they were bound and they immediately scampered off so that we lost our Monkey dinner.

This act of animal liberation may have saved the lives of the 'poor little Devils', but not Banks, nor even Mr Monkhouse the surgeon could prevent the slaughter that happened next: there was no human agent to be held responsible, just a small winged insect – the anopheles mosquito – playing the role of the angel of doom. Cook called it 'fever'; it is better known today as malaria.

Tupia and Taiata were among the first to succumb, followed by Banks, his servants, Solander and even the surgeon Mr Monkhouse himself. The sailors went down like skittles, and then dysentery set in and people started dying. First Taiata, then a heartbroken Tupia, then even Monkhouse himself; every day became a catalogue of those who had 'departed this life'. Just a fortnight before, Cook had written to the Admiralty that he had not lost a man through sickness; the pervasive disease of this sickly port had now proved those words a lie. Banks withdrew to the country; a sickly Cook stuck by his ship.

In a cruel parody of the tragedy playing out amongst his men, he now discovered that *Endeavour* was even more stricken than they had guessed. Worms had devoured the planking on her bottom while elsewhere just an eighth of an inch of wood had separated his men from a hungry sea. Going against his usual desire to pursue the truth, he concluded that – with all the other dangers they had had to contend with and particularly when hitherto there had been no chance to put them right – some things were better left unknown. Thankfully, however, the Dutch were now doing a fine job of cleaning, repairing and resealing her ailing timbers; his own men were too weak to do anything but lamely look on.

By now, Cook was seven men down – not helped by the desertion of Patrick Saunders who was chief suspect in the loss of Richard Orton's ears – but as the ship was restocked, it at last looked like they would soon be under sail for the final leg of the voyage. Christmas Day was spent putting together the finishing touches and, on 26 December, a restocked and repaired *Endeavour* finally weighed anchor with her sickly crew. Everyone had been ill; many still were; everyone, Cook remarked, except for John Ravenhill, the ancient sail-maker, who seemed to have kept disease at bay by remaining permanently drunk. That might have been the best strategy; it was certainly not doing his men any good to drink the highly dubious water that the Dutch sold them, water in which Solander observed the mosquitoes breeding. Cook could do little other than take his leave as swiftly as he could from the foul and stinking city of Batavia. His Dutch counterparts congratulated him on not losing more of his men to disease but that was small comfort: despite taking on board nineteen new recruits, he was now in command of nothing less than a 'Hospital Ship'. The Cape of Good Hope and Britain seemed a very long way away.

Christmas 1770 and New Years Day 1771 past unnoticed. He stopped briefly at Princes Island to get some more water and fresh food to sustain his ailing men; in fact, it made them worse: within weeks of departing, yet more of his crew lay 'dangerously ill of Fevers and fluxes', poisoned by the bacteria that infested the supplies. Violent dysentery now swept through the men already weakened by malaria. Within six weeks, this captain who cared so much for his men had lost another twenty-three on top of the seven already dead in Batavia. The grim roll-call broke his heart: John Truslove, his 'much esteem'd' corporal of marines, the super-talented Herman Spöring, the gentle Sydney Parkinson – even John Ravenhill whom the drink could no longer protect. The death of the astronomer, Charles Green, marked a wave of those who 'departed this life' until their names take up more room in his journal than details of the winds, co-ordinates and distance sailed. By the end of January, they had barely enough men to man the ship,

a Melancholy proff of the Calamitous Situation we are at present in.

And this from the measured pen of a man of understatement. Nothing he could do could stop the dysentery draining away the spirit of his men. On

6 February, in the middle of the Indian Ocean *en route* to Africa, Jonathan Monkhouse, whose fothering technique had saved their lives, finally lost his own. Cook retreated in despair to his astronomical observations, wishing they showed that he was closer to home. Six days later, John Satterly, the masterly carpenter, died, leaving only two of his team barely alive. Such was the general depression on board the ship that even those who had stayed well began to suffer hallucinations that they had been gripped by the 'bloody flux'. One unnamed sailor had been tending the sick when

> one morning coming upon deck he found himself a little griped and immidiatly began to stamp with his feet and exclaim I have got the Gripes, I have got the Gripes, I shall died, I shall die! – in this manner he continued untill he threw himself into a fit and was carried off the deck in a manner dead.

The man, however, recovered but was in the dire minority: of those badly affected, only Banks and one other man survived. Illness, madness and the interminable list of the dead began to take their toll on the captain. His weariness even permeated his journal which degenerated to brief facts and scant sentences – 'Nothing remarkable' or 'Saw an Albatross' replaced the news of the day. Everyone felt the length of the journey; everyone longed for home.

At last, on 5 March, 1771, the east coast of Africa rose up on the horizon, with Port St Johns just discernible through the haze. Cook now stood in towards the coast and hugged the reassuring form around its southerly point to Cape Town. Despite the gales that now impeded their progress into the harbour, there was no trace of frustration; just a relief to have ended the dark episode of death that they had endured. It seemed their luck had turned: after a welcome salute from the guns of Table Bay, the presiding governor assured the men they could have everything they wanted, whereby Cook quickly took the twenty-eight sick ashore and found them lodgings where they spent the next month being tended for the fair sum of two shillings each per day. Comparing notes with the other captains in the bay, it seemed his men had indeed got off lightly in terms of numbers of deaths; certainly, more Batavia horror stories abounded but he hoped that the Java nightmare would soon become a distant memory in the face of Cape Town's clean air, pure water and the promise of home.

Home. The concept seemed suddenly overwhelming, the sudden reality almost threatening. There was no way he could creep silently into an English port – the voyage was too well-publicised. In many ways, this was the limelight, the recognition he had secretly wanted, but staring him in the face was now a darker probability. At sea, he was in control; on land, he would be at the mercy of 'every News paper' that would give its own version of events, versions that would be grossly exaggerated or worse still, total fabrication,

> for such are the disposission of men in general in these Voyages that they are seldom content with the hardships and dangers which will naturaly occur, but they must add others which hardly ever had existence but in their imaginations, by magnifying the most trifling accidents and Circumstances to the greatest hardships, and unsurmountable dangers without the imidiate interposion of Providence, as if the whole Merit of the Voyage consisted in the dangers and hardships they underwent, or that real ones did not happen often enough to give the mind sufficient anxiety; thus posterity are taught to look upon these Voyages as hazardous to the highest degree.

This strange rant in his journal still takes the reader by surprise. It is as if he were paranoid that the near-wrecks on the reef and now this decimation of his crew through illness would outweigh the achievements he had made – a sign perhaps that his confidence was as shaken as his heart was broken by the tragedy of losing so many men. He had, after all, set out on this voyage to be a good commander, a commander who looked after his men. In return, his men had served him well and some had become close friends in the way only time and adversity can shape a close friendship. He had now lost around a third of his complement on the last leg of his voyage – a disaster that stripped off some of the gloss both personally and professionally – and whereas he had been able to maintain an astounding equilibrium thus far, the strain of the last three years was now beginning to show.

The mood, if deep and dark, was short-lived. The next day the sun shone fine and clear in the sky and he busied himself overhauling his ship. He gathered more news about Bougainville's voyage and picked up the news from home – more war on the cards against Spain – gave the men their on-shore leave and tried to fret no more. Two weeks later, he recruited ten more men, recovered his sick and set sail for England. As Table Mountain grew smaller behind them, Robert Molyneux, his good but intemperate Master, gave out his last breath.

The seas were fair and the winds on the whole benevolent so that by 29 April, Cook was crossing the Greenwich Meridian and completing his first circumnavigation of the globe. For him, it marked a rite of passage;

for his sea-faring goat it was just another feather in her cap. Two days later, Saint Helena rose up from the horizon along with a fleet of thirteen English ships. Was there a war? His first supposition was contradicted by Captain Elliot of the *Portland*, who reassured him there was nothing of the kind. The two men struck an instant rapport and Cook resolved to sail with the convoy back to England, meaning the briefest of stays on St Helena. The island had been a British colony since 1673, the current governor being none other than John Skottowe, son of Thomas Skottowe, Cook's staunch ally in Great Ayton, but there is no mention that Cook met up with his childhood friend in the three days they spent at anchor, restocking the stores, repairing the sails and mending the rigging; meanwhile, a newly slimline and irrepressible Banks caught up with some last-minute botanising, which was just as well because after this the next stop was home.

They sailed with the fleet on 4 May, passing Ascension Island six days later. Here, Cook signalled for Captain Elliot to come on board and gave him another packet for the Admiralty containing logs, letters, and copies of the journals as an insurance policy against disaster while ensuring, presuming the faster *Portland* got home first, that their results were known as soon as possible. For Cook, there was little now to do but keep the ship sailing. On 15 May, he observed an eclipse of the sun, 'merely for the sake of Observing' and four days later, hoisted out one of the small boats to bring aboard a surgeon from the fleet to look over the consumptive Lieutenant Hicks, who had somehow managed to cling thus far to life; nothing could be gained – Batavia had done for him as well – and, a week later, the body of this quiet, helpful man was committed to the sea with full honours.

The next few weeks rolled by with little action. There were promotions – the jovial and talented Clerke to Lieutenant and Isaac Smith to Master's Mate – the usual gales, some floating turtles and the chance meeting with some other ships, from which they picked up the latest news, namely that Britain was at peace, at least for the time being. The crew were kept busy holding together the exhausted fabric of the *Endeavour* where every day 'some thing or another is giving way'; however, to Cook's great surprise, they stayed in contact with the thirteen ships of the fleet until 23 June when they disappeared over the horizon.

A sense of isolation once more pervaded the crew. The *Endeavour* sailed in an empty ocean, with only birds for company. Banks had lost nearly all his entourage – his secretary, his servants, his precious artists – and now, in the final stretch, he lost his beloved 'bitch Lady'. Her death plunged him into deep grief.

On 7 July, a passing ship came into view and Cook was alarmed to hear that neither of his packages, nor his original letter sent from Batavia five months before, had been received by the Admiralty. The shock of the meeting cut both ways – the other captain was astounded to see Cook at all, let alone this close to home; all clever money had been on the *Endeavour* being lost at sea, a rumour that was even peddled in the newspapers. One story had them being sunk with all hands 'by order of a jealous court'! However, not only was *Endeavour* still afloat, by 10 July the eagle eyes of Nick Young on watch up the masthead spotted Land's End in the distance. Cook noted the event without emotion in his journal, though it would have taken a harder heart than his own not to have rejoiced at the occasion: he was back in familiar waters, coasting past Portland Bill, Beachy Head and then Dover.

On Saturday, 13 July, there was one final journal entry for the voyage of the *Endeavour* – an entry that remained as controlled and inscrutable as the man himself:

At 3 oClock in the PM Anchor'd in the Downs, & soon after I landed in order to repair to London.

After almost three years, Lieutenant James Cook was home.

Plate XXVII

J. Parkinson del.   J. Chambers Sc.

Two of the Natives of New Holland, Advancing to Combat.

New South Wales Aborigines by Sydney Parkinson

20

'THE IMMORTAL BANKS'

England 1771

N HIS LONG post-chaise ride from the Downs to Piccadilly on 13 July, 1771, James looked around him at this strange, familiar land. Farmers tended their burgeoning crops, people beetled about the villages while towns and gas lamps twinkled as the sun went down. Everything was so normal; it was he who had changed. He had spent the last three years with every sinew on edge, every sense on full alert. It was hard now to relax and cede control to the soporific bounce of the carriage. Accompanying him on the journey to London were Joseph Banks and Daniel Solander, men with whom he had shared the same hells and paradises, but now they were back on land, the differences between them rose up like prison walls. They had been on an adventure; Cook had been doing his job. After three years of forced intimacy, their lives would suddenly diverge into the natural order of their inescapable social status.

In the three years he had been away, San Francisco Bay had been discovered, Britain had fallen out and then fallen back in with America, the English impresario, Philip Astley, had started the first modern circus, James Watt had patented his condensing steam engine and Richard Arkwright had patented his first spinning machine. The world was changing and he was part of that change – but bumping along that rocky road to London, he had no idea just how great his influence would be.

The carriage reached its destination in the early hours of Sunday morning, the day after they had arrived in the Downs. Bidding their uneasy goodbyes, Banks and his friend retired to his house in New Burlington Street while Cook made the short journey to the Admiralty. He was under orders to repair there immediately he landed and, as ever, he took the orders literally. Like a schoolboy fidgeting outside the headmaster's office, he waited for Philip Stephens, the Admiralty Secretary, to come into work. He need not have worried: although Stephens knew Cook's reputation better than the man himself, he had already marked him out years before as someone worth watching and the recent arrival of the precious advance copies of the Lieutenant's discoveries had confirmed the faith that he had placed in him. The meeting was warm and welcoming; the Admiralty knew that in Cook they had their own prized discovery – not only a man of 'genius' and 'capacity' but one who could be relied upon to consistently deliver results beyond even their wildest dreams. Quite simply, the man was breathtaking.

Another group who knew his worth was the household at No 7, Assembly Row in Mile End. As soon as he had finished with officialdom, he raced across town to his waiting family. One can only imagine the scene that played itself out that 14 July in the small, end-terraced house next door to the gin distillery, but along with the happiness at seeing Elizabeth and the boys, he learned the shocking news that not only had his fourth child, Joseph – the baby he never got to see – died soon after birth, his precious little Elizabeth, just four years old, had died just three months ago when he was leaving Cape Town on his way back to Britain. Half his children were now cold in the grave, children he had barely got to know. But there was scant time to reel with grief: James junior and Nathaniel were ecstatic at the return of their father and wanted his full attention. By now, they were proper little boys – rising eight and seven, educated and well-mannered but bursting with excitement and already showing signs of their dad's impressive height and frame; officially, of course, they had been with him on the voyage, albeit only on the muster role; in reality, however, no amount of hugs could make up for the missed years of their childhood – or bring his other two children back.

Whatever his private thoughts, he had little time to relax in the comforts of home. Almost immediately he was busy with the seemingly endless paperwork from the voyage – reports to the Admiralty and Royal Society on everything, from his men and his equipment to collected 'curiosities' and the healing powers of 'Sour Kraut'. If he thought that he could bury his grief for his dead children this way, he was soon mistaken: death was very firmly on the priority list as he wrote to the families of those who had died in his care: Forby Sutherland's relatives in Orkney, the loved ones of Mr Green – and George Monkhouse of Cumberland who had entrusted his two sons with Cook only to now be told that both had perished.

While he conducted his grim affairs, a bizarre scene of hero-worship was being played out in parallel in the press, the scientific community and

London's social circuit. The subject of this adoration was not the man who had discovered forty new islands to add to the world map, the man who had cleared up centuries of geographical speculation and raised more questions about the earth; the fêted icon was a tall, by now rather fleshy man in his twenties – ebullient, confident and basking in the limelight. The public wanted a dashing hero – and Joseph Banks proffered himself for the role.

The Joseph Banks that returned was a million miles from Lieutenant James Cook: the old camaraderie of their lives onboard the ship now faded into the polite nod of acknowledgement across the walls of class and social milieu. While Cook buried himself in his work, like a butterfly emerging from a timber and sailcloth cocoon, Joseph Banks unfurled his brilliant wings and plumped himself up for display. If England wanted a hero, it would surely be churlish of Banks to refuse. The papers went mad: this flamboyant creature was a gift to them and the nation at large.

The day after they arrived in London, *Bingley's Journal* reported:

On Saturday last an express arrived at the Admiralty with the agreeable news of the arrival at the Downs of The *Endeavour*, Captain Cook, from the East Indes. This ship sailed in August 1768 with Mr Banks, Dr Solander, Mr Green, and other ingenious Gentlemen on board, for the South Seas, to observe the Transit of Venus; they have since made a voyage round the world, and touched at every coast and island, where it is possible to get on shore to collect every species of plants and other rare productions in nature.

A short time later in the *Westminster Gazette*:

The honour of [Banks] frequently waiting on His Majesty at Richmond.

Royal summons, illustrious dinners, grand speaking engagements – Banks accepted them all and played no small part in engineering their occurrence in the first place. This man, who had so failed in his studies at Oxford, was now welcomed back to receive an honorary doctorate. Everyone wanted to know about his adventures, everyone wanted to see his treasured collection. Linnaeus himself, the world's foremost botanist and cool man of science, proclaimed that New South Wales should be renamed *Banksia* and that there should be a statue raised to the 'immortal Banks'.

Just over a month after their return, the papers were already exalting Banks as the leader of another voyage of discovery – this time with two ships – back into the Southern Seas, and starting as early as next March; meanwhile, there was one young lady who certainly would not mourn his departure. Miss Harriet Blosset, fiancée to the immortal Banks, had seen precious little of her intended since he had returned. Her joy on hearing the news of his arrival had long since evaporated into angry despair at the silence that now stretched between them. Whether or not his comments about the beauties encountered on his travels had yet met her ears, or whether it was the fact that since he had stepped back on these shores he had shown her an ominous disregard, she now realised she had waited those three years for her betrothed in vain. While the rarefied scientists discussed his findings, those seeking gossip of a more personal nature found exactly what they were looking for in his personal conduct with Miss Blosset: there was some nastiness, much emotion and, according to his friends, a 'settlement' of £500. Miss Blosset could do little but accept the money and considerable social embarrassment, while Banks, now unencumbered, was free to enjoy every attention showered upon him to the full.

Beyond that first notice of the ship's arrival, James Cook barely received a mention in the press, though his name was uttered throughout the Admiralty in the revered and hushed tones reserved for the truly remarkable. His life offered nothing to the gossips and he was not the type for grand dinners and parties or for courting press attention. He sat at his desk at home or in the Admiralty offices – or even in Will's Coffee Shop at Charing Cross – conducting his affairs through courteous letters and an as-ever measured pen. There are no records of his reaction to the news that Banks was to lead another expedition: it may have riled a little, but he knew that if anyone was going to command those ships, it would be him and, once on ship, he was boss. A letter from Philip Stephens confirmed his good standing:

> I have pleasure to acquaint you that their Lordships extremely well approve of the whole of your proceedings and that they have great satisfaction in the account you have given them of the good behaviour of your Officers and Men and of the chearfulness and alertness with which they went through the fatigues and dangers of their late voyage.

Then, around the middle of August, he received his promotion, ironically being first informed of the news by Banks himself, who had got the information from his close friend, the Earl of Sandwich, now First Lord of the Admiralty. On his way home from work, Cook sat in his favourite coffee shop to collect his thoughts, and then penned this reply:

Your very obliging letter was the first Messenger that conveyed to me Lord Sandwich's intentions. Promotion unsolicited to a man of my station in life must convey a satisfaction to the mind that is better conceived than described – I had this morning the honour to wait upon his Lordship who renewed his promises to me, and in so obliging and polite a manner as convinced me that he approved of the Voyage. The reputation I may have acquired on this account by which I shall receive promotion calls to mind the very great assistance I received therein from you, which will ever be remembered with most gratefull Acknowledgements …

Banks may have got the public glory, but Cook had received what he most desired: the respect of his profession and status as a commander. Final proof of this new standing came when, on 14 August, Lord Sandwich introduced him to King George III so that he could explain at first hand the voyage and his discoveries. George III was no match for the medieval sponsor, Prince Henry the Navigator, but his interest in science and exploration was genuine and unshakeable. They spent a full hour in conversation; in return, the King showered Cook with praise and handed him his commission. It was a magnificent day.

Three days later, he shared his good fortune with his friend and former boss, John Walker, and here the official humility can be dropped in favour of raw pride and excitement. One line stands out for its honest appraisal of the facts:

I however have made no very great Discoveries yet I have exploar'd more of the Great South Sea than all that have gone before me so much that little remains now to be done to have a thorough knowledge of that part of the Globe.

A longer letter followed, in which he shared with his friend the details of his course and discoveries – and the rumours bubbling up all over London:

Another Voyage is thought of, with two Ships which if it takes place I believe the command will be confer'd upon me.

It was enough to set Whitby on fire. He may have been eschewed by the London media but in that small, coastal town, no amount of Bankses were valued as highly as Yorkshire's own son.

Both men had got what they were looking for; now both men got something they did not want nor seek. For Banks it was the unsavoury argument with Sydney Parkinson's brother over his personal and professional effects. This ended badly, with his opponent getting a pay-off and nervous breakdown; as for Cook, he was the focus for Matthew Cox's legal action over the discipline meted out in New Zealand when Cox and his associates robbed a Maori sweet potato plantation. The matter was taken up by the Admiralty and then quietly disappeared.

Another disappearing trick was done by the *Endeavour*. After the men had bade her farewell, Cook's ship – 'a better ship for such a Service I never would wish' – was docked and refitted at Woolwich then sent out almost immediately to the Falklands, which Britain was handing over to Spain. This tired old lady of the seas was pensioned off from the Navy in 1775 for £645. No sentiment allowed, she became a collier once more, reportedly even sailing under French colours, and delivering oil to a firm in Newport, Rhode Island. From there, her journey seems to have been all too short as today's explorations by the Rhode Island Marine Archaeology Project attest. There is no conclusive evidence but it appears that in 1778, *Endeavour* was scuttled by the English in the harbour mouth, part of a fleet sharing the same fate. Archaeologists are still trying to find her remains.

The subject of a second voyage now took centre stage. Banks wanted it, Cook wanted it, and Lord Sandwich was convinced of the need for it. Speculation filled the chatterings of scientific and social circles while poor Elizabeth quietly despaired of ever having her husband to herself. She had coped alone with the grief of losing first her baby then her four-year-old girl. How much more would she have to endure? She was caught in the limbo land of having James at home but working so hard she barely saw him. They were, however, both strong characters, both survivors, and in his scant spare time, he showered his wife and his children with affection, knowing only too well that their time together would be brief.

Little by little, the voyage was becoming a reality: words and ideas were backed up towards the end of September by an Admiralty instruction to purchase two ships for distant service – two ships that the Navy Board asked Captain James Cook to buy. Everything was going his way, and he knew exactly what kind of vessels he wanted. Although her advantages were lost on Banks, the snub-bowed *Endeavour*, with her flat bottom and solid waist, was perfect for the purpose of discovery. She could carry years' worth of supplies with ease, be sailed close to shore with small risk of grounding and cope well with the 'prodigious high' seas that they would inevitably meet *en route*.

While *Endeavour* was herself on the way to the Falklands, she was the inspiration for the choice of three Whitby cats that Cook suggested to the Navy Board, from which they selected two: the 462-ton *Marquis of Granby* and the slightly smaller *Marquis of Rockingham*. Within the month, they were registered as sloops and renamed *Drake* and *Raleigh* – however, they were not the only names issued: as proof that the Admiralty had been planning a second voyage almost as soon as the first one landed in the Downs, the principal officers for the rapid return were listed as Captain James Cook, a new recruit in the form of Robert Palliser Cooper as his First Lieutenant, and joining them on the *Drake*, his *Endeavour* Comrades, Charles Clerke and Dick Pickersgill. Commanding the *Raleigh* would be Tobias Furneaux, with Joseph Shank as his First Lieutenant.

So the plans were set in stone; Cook's desire – and Elizabeth's dread – had come true. The purpose of the voyage was simple: to go in search of the Great Southern Continent … again. The route was something he had mulled over night after night in his cabin and around the captain's table while the thought was as familiar to him as the sound of the waves against *Endeavour*'s bow. He was not a believer like Banks, Dalrymple and a good many other educated and intelligent people; whereas Dalrymple supported his grand assertions with historic maps and fabled sightings indistinguishable from cloud, Cook knew by the swell of the ocean and the trend of the currents that the Great Southern Continent was just a myth; if it existed at all, it would be so far south as to make it nothing more than a land of ice. But Britain was stretching her imperial arms and clawing new lands in with her fingers: if anyone was going to discover the Continent, it was going to be her, and if no such land existed, her favoured commander could do no better than securing some staging posts for his country in the deep blue waters of the Southern Seas.

As to why a known sceptic should be sent to find something he did not believe in, Cook gives his own answer:

> I think it would be a great pitty that this thing which at times has been the object of many ages and Nations should not now be wholy clear'd up, which might very easily be done in one Voyage without either much trouble or danger or fear of miscarrying as the Navigator would know where to go to look for it.

Along with the laying aside of doubt, Cook then let slip a more revealing motive behind his obsession: by using Tahiti as a base, where they were known and provisions were readily available, he could make his discoveries 'more perfect and compleat'. More perfect and complete:

these are the words of an obsessive. It is easy to see how discoveries can be made more complete – but more perfect? Like the scientist who sees perfection in a simple formula or the structure of a molecule, these are the words of a man for whom discovery is not a job, but a passion. As for his achievements, even perfect isn't good enough if he can make it more so. And, whether or not Cook was ready to leave his home and family to risk all once more, he could not ignore the haunting call of the sirens.

The intention was to sail as soon as possible, with the likely date being just four months away in March the following year. It was taken as read that among his complement would be the grandiose figure of Joseph Banks, though no one expected him to be responsible for the serious delay that afforded Elizabeth some precious extra time with her beloved husband.

Christmas 1771 was a special time for the Cooks. On 14 December, James had applied for three weeks' special leave to visit his aged father in Yorkshire. It was not quite a family holiday – the boys were to be left behind in London – but it would be a rare opportunity for Elizabeth to spend some time alone with James and also provide the first opportunity to meet his family. His mother had died six years before and his father now lived with his sister, Margaret Fleck, in Redcar, just up the road from Staithes and Whitby. They took the stagecoach to York, a journey of three days, with Elizabeth marvelling at the changing countryside: she had rarely left London, let alone come this far north. Although the bumpy road onwards to the North Yorkshire coast was not without risk for Mrs Cook, now newly-pregnant, they didn't hurry and arrived easily in time for the Christmas festivities; a few days later, when James decided to fulfil his promise and visit the Walkers in Whitby, he suggested Elizabeth stay behind and being a poor traveller, she reluctantly agreed.

On New Year's Eve 1771, he went on horseback across the moors to his former home, accompanied solely by the wind, the seagulls and the sound of crashing waves. Whitby itself was as familiar as ever, still smelling of the sea with the harbour crammed full of fishing boats and colliers. At the edge of the moors he spied a group in the distance – his friends, come to meet him and escort him to the coast. His spirits lifted above the wintry grey skies: it was good to be back.

The next few days were spent catching up with friends and exchanging news of ships and sailors. Despite his impressive rank, this local celebrity had stayed close to his roots as ever and there is little doubt that the spontaneity of Mary Prowd, the Walker's housekeeper, who forgot to call him 'sir' and instead threw her arms about him exclaiming, 'Oh honey James! How glad I is to see thee!', caused more laughter than offence.

Whitby was one of the few places on land where he could slough off the mantle of sober responsibility: perhaps it was the proximity of the sea, perhaps it was mixing with people of his own background and class, but here in this busy coastal town, he was truly at home.

While he was away, the Admiralty were busy plotting the voyage and swithering over the names of the appointed ships. *Drake* and *Raleigh* may have been proudly British, but the men hadn't exactly been popular with their Spanish counterparts and the names would cause offence at foreign ports. Thus, while others were tucking into their Christmas goose, the Earl of Sandwich was mulling over some alternatives: *Aurora*? *Hispera*? Nothing seemed to hit the mark. Then it came to him: the names would fit their commander and Gentlemen explorers – the ships would be called *Resolution* and *Adventure*.

Cook was told of the change by letter and confessed to a friend that he thought these names 'much properer!'

Early in January, he and Elizabeth were back with the boys in London, all thoughts of holidays over. Cook immediately went along to the Dockyards at Deptford where *Resolution* was being fitted out. There was much to do and no time to waste; in her dock at Woolwich, the *Adventure* was even further behind. Both ships needed modifications, supplies, extra protection from the waves and the worm that would beset them in the Southern Seas – and this time Cook knew exactly what he wanted.

Trouble was, Mr Joseph Banks had his own ideas about what the voyage needed – fifteen people, excluding their servants, comprising botanists, physicians, artists, draughtsmen, even a pair of hornplayers to keep the men entertained on the long ocean passages. Each profession had its needs, each its own baggage until the ship would have had no room for its crew. In the months since their return, Banks had been fêted and praised, pampered and indulged – all of which did nothing to mute his natural flaws of conceit and childishness. What Banks wanted, Banks usually got, and if he was unhappy, everybody knew about it.

When he went to look at the new ship – *his* ship as he saw it – he was astounded: there was barely enough room for his luggage, let alone his entourage. Marching straight to Hugh Palliser, now head of the Navy Board and in charge of its hardware, he demanded a larger ship or, at the very least, further modifications. Palliser gently held his ground: the ship was the best for the job and, as such, she would stay. Not content, Banks then went higher up the ladder, to his friend, Lord Sandwich, and issued an ultimatum: either make the changes to accommodate his demands or Banks would leave the voyage before they had even set sail. Sandwich considered the embarrassment and uproar if the Navy was seen to be standing in the way of this celebrated voyager, and acquiesced. The alterations would go ahead, and immediately.

The months rolled on. *Resolution* had her waist raised, a new deck added and new quarters built for Cook as the entourage would take over not only his cabin, but the entire Great Cabin. Her captain looked on bemused as little by little his sea-going vessel became a new stage for Banks's private dramas. Meanwhile, the Admiralty had its own designs on the voyage: the trip would provide the perfect testing-ground for new theories, techniques and products, particularly in the prevention of scurvy but also for everything from sweetening bad water to concentrated beer. Then, of course, there were Cook's instruments, improved both in quantity and quality from the first voyage and now including one very special piece of equipment that, at first, he was not at all convinced by. A carpenter by the name of John Harrison had invented a mechanical device which he alleged could keep time at sea and thus be used to determine longitude without the use of star-gazing and those complex astronomical tables; it had already been used by the astronomer Maskelyne with grudging but remarkable effect on his trip to Barbados and now an exact copy made by watchmaker Larcum Kendall had been given to Cook to try out on his voyage. It was, of course, the chronometer that would change the face of navigation – only Cook did not know it just yet. Three other chronometers were to be tested alongside Harrison's model. In all, there was as much to be done in terms of experimentation as there was discovery on this second voyage around the world.

Spring turned into summer, and at last Banks's changes were complete. *Resolution* was ordered to sail to the Downs, to test out how she handled. She never got there: even in the sheltered waters of the Thames, the pilot gave up sailing her, fearing she would capsize. She was condemned as 'an exceeding dangerous and unsafe ship'. Even Banks's friends recoiled in horror, Charles Clerke penning the damning words:

> By God, I'll go to sea in a grog-tub, if required, or in the *Resolution* as soon as you please, but must say I think her by far the most unsafe ship I ever saw or heard of!

The Navy Board was not to be made a fool of: *Resolution* was immediately ordered to Sheerness to have the modifications removed and the army of workmen once again climbed on board. Rather than smirk on the sidelines, Cook berated himself for not speaking out louder: he had known by instinct that the ship would not sit well – she was top heavy and unbalanced. He should have taken control; now he had wasted more months while watching the work and then the re-work to be carried out, and lost some of his own respect in the process.

As for Banks, when he heard of the verdict on his designs, he raced to Sheerness to see the re-re-modified *Resolution* – and was incandescent. A young midshipman, John Elliot, captured the scene in his memoirs:

> Mr Banks came to Sheerness and when he saw the ship, and the Alterations that were made, He swore and stamp'd upon the Warfe, like a Mad Man; and instantly order'd his servants, and all his things, out of the Ship.

The tantrums were impressive and long-winded, fuelled in part by fury and in part by the enormous loss of face: to him and the public at least, this had always been *his* voyage; it was inconceivable that it should not happen on his terms. He wrote at length to Lord Sandwich, unwisely treading on naval toes and sniping at Cook's role in the fiasco. The press took up his cause – there were even questions in the Commons – until at last Sandwich rose up against his friend and sent him a crushing rejoinder: no one had the right to demand Navy men to be sent to sea in an unfit ship, least of all a gentleman adventurer. The matter was over: if Banks was unhappy, Banks could take his custom elsewhere, at which point Banks did. Gathering up his entourage, he charted his own fully-manned ship and sailed to Iceland in an almighty huff.

Cook waited quietly for the *brouhaha* to die down; three years sailing with the gentleman concerned had taught him not to get involved. He summed up the affair in typical style:

> Mr Banks unfortunate for himself set out upon too large a Plan a Plan that was incompatible with a Scheme of discovery at the Antipode; had he confined himself to the same plan as he set out upon last Voyage, attended only to his own persutes and not interfered with the choice, equipmint and even Direction of the Ships things that he was not a competent judge of, he would have found every one concerned in the expedition ever ready to oblige him, for I myself can declare it: instead of finding fault with the Ship he ought to have considered that the Endeavour Bark was just such another, whose good qualities … gave him an oppertunity to acquire that reputation the Publick has so liberally and with great justice bestowed upon him.

Meanwhile, the much-slighted *Resolution* would get its revenge on Banks by proving her worth and becoming one of the most famous ships in British maritime history.

The two months swallowed up by Banks's tantrum meant Cook was running seriously behind schedule. More than half the *Resolution's* crew had deserted since they were first enrolled and at times he must have despaired of ever leaving British waters. The days were long and tiresome for the forty-three-year-old captain as he hurried to finish his paperwork and charts from the first voyage in preparation for the second. There was another reason for his haste: his French rival, Louis Antoine de Bougainville, had mirrored his career from the fighting in the St Lawrence to the exploring in the Pacific; he now heard the full report of his travels and was anxious to get his journal published as soon as possible to validate British sovereignty over his discoveries. It was impossible for him to write the book himself in the limited time remaining, so the Admiralty commissioned Dr John Hawkesworth, a journalist well known to the London social and scientific scene, to do the work for him. It was an offer no writer could refuse: Hawkesworth became the envy of the literary world with a commission that was guaranteed by its very nature to become a best seller, a fact reflected by his advance when he tendered the book to the publishing world. A bidding war ensued, the writer was granted an astronomical £6,000, around £365,000 today. Given Cook's views about the wanton hyperbole of the press, he was more than a little uneasy with how his journal would be treated but there was nothing he could do – he had to cede control.

There was also writing of another kind – a tribute to a sailor *par excellence*, a sailor with four-legs and a bountiful udder: the circum-navigatory goat. Having twice circled the world, the Admiralty ruled that her days on board were finally over. She had served them well: in more than a thousand days of sailing on the *Endeavour*, she had never failed to provide the officers with milk and, in return, the Admiralty signed a warrant admitting her as a pensioner to Greenwich Hospital. She was meantime showered with love and affection: Cook took her home with him to join the household at Mile End where she pastured in his back garden; meanwhile, Banks was so taken with this benevolent creature that he implored Dr Johnson, that famous eighteenth-century man of letters, to pen a distich for a silver collar to go around her neck. Next morning, a letter appeared at Banks's house in New Burlington Street, with Samuel Johnson's response:

> Perpetui, ambità bis terrà, praema lactis
> Haec habet, altrici Capra secunda Jovis.
> [The globe twice circled, this the Goat,
> the second to the nurse of Jove,
> is thus rewarded for her never-failing milk.]

This most famous goat in all the world was now a celebrity in her own right but she was not to enjoy her Greenwich retirement: a month after receiving her tribute, perhaps missing treading the boards of the deck of the *Endeavour*, she gave her last milk and died. Her death was reported in the *General Evening Post* and a nation sighed in sadness.

No goat, no Banks, no uniformed hornplayers: this second voyage would be strange indeed. Cook now faced having to receive on board the second, replacement, retinue of crew and gentlemen scientists to cover for those who had deserted, died – or stormed off. In all, the *Resolution* mustered 112 men including officers, with the *Adventure* numbering 81. Even without the hornplayers, this would be a musical voyage with bag-piping marines and a drummer who could also play the violin. Among the marines and promoted to corporal was the Tahitian deserter, Samuel Gibson; he had learned from his experiences and was now one of Cook's most devoted followers – a talented Polynesian linguist and a success for the captain's theories on discipline.

As for the *Resolution's* officers and men, next in command to Cook was his First Lieutenant, Robert Palliser Cooper. He was a relative of Hugh Palliser, the Comptroller of the Navy Board, but had served his time in Newfoundland and was to prove a staunch – albeit rather colourless – support for his captain. Under him was the jovial Charles Clerke – still as entertaining as ever but now with the maturity and experience of two circumnavigations transforming him into a well-rounded and excellent seaman. Shortly after his prima-donna episode, Banks had tried to lure Clerke away, as he had already done with Lieutenant Gore, but he declined the offer, having 'put too far on this tack to think of putting about with any kind of credit'. Banks's loss was the *Resolution's* gain.

Dick Pickersgill, that man of many charts from the first voyage, was again recruited for the second. As Third Lieutenant – and still with the same predilection for 'Grog' – he was by now a competent surveyor and astronomer and would prove his worth on the voyage. Of the other men on board, young Isaac Smith would continue to shine; although he was Cook's cousin by marriage, he had won his place on merit; twenty-one-year-old James Burney would be one of the highlights of the crew – brother of the novelist, Fanny Burney, he was erudite, witty and had a keen eye for detail. He had been appointed at the request of his father, Dr Charles Burney, an associate of Cook from the Royal Society, and the whole family was as excited as he was. After three years, his reputation would be larger than life, his epithet – 'clever and eccentric!'

One final name of a man to watch was George Vancouver – then 'about 13', a 'Quiet inoffensive young man', who would prove an eager pupil in the art of surveying and would later win fame and immortality exploring the Pacific coast of North America, where he would also leave his name. Cook's voyages were a breeding ground for the next generation of heroes, instilled with their captain's values and his passion for navigation; that even-handed meritocracy shaped the motley assortment of gentlemen, rogues and salt of the earth into some of the finest sailors the Navy would ever see.

The *Adventure* under the steady guidance of Tobias Furneaux, seems to have had fewer 'characters' than Cook's *Resolution*. Furneaux himself was in his late thirties and had earned his respect by effectively taking command of Wallis's voyage when both the Captain and First Lieutenant fell ill. He was well-liked, responsible and sympathetic to the native peoples he met on his travels, but he lacked the instinct of an explorer and was less effective when out of sight of Cook. One imagines that his ship was immediately enlivened when James Burney transferred from the *Resolution* to the *Adventure* at the Cape.

And then there was the new team of scientists, from whom comes much of the tension and drama of the voyage. Most infamous was the replacement botanist, John Reinhold Forster, a prickly man of learning or, as Beaglehole described him, 'dogmatic, humourless, suspicious, censorious, pretentious, contentious, demanding'. He was certainly well-educated, well-informed and an asset to the science of the voyage, but his utility was strictly professional – as a fellow-voyager, he was little short of infuriating. Hated by the men, he lived under the threat of being thrown overboard, was ejected from Cook's cabin, threatened with arrest by Charles Clerke and even punched to the floor by the Master's Mate. Would he have come on board were it not for the £4,000 already promised as a fee? Unlikely – although his temperament had lost him most of his jobs elsewhere. His son, George, therefore, must have taken after his mother: passionate about natural history, the seventeen-year-old had spent his childhood being dragged across much of Europe by his unemployable father. He was brilliant at most things he turned his hand to – a talented artist, a natural scientist and a skilled linguist who had translated Bougainville's voyage journal: he would make up for the sins of the father.

Each ship had its astronomer, and each man had the task of observing longitudes and latitudes from the heavens and comparing them with those of the 'sea clock' that would soon make them all redundant. The super-erudite William Wales, famous for his mathematical puzzles in the *Ladie's Diary*, was appointed to the *Resolution*, William Bayly went to the *Adventure*. Both men had observed the Transit of Venus – Wales at

Hudson Bay and Bayly at Norway's North Cape. Finally, in the footsteps of Sydney Parkinson, William Hodges was belatedly added to the list of supernumeraries. Prodigious landscape artist and all-round amiable companion, he was to prove immensely popular on board, even though he drew people to look like stiff wooden puppets.

At last the ships and crew were ready for the voyage. The final supplies were loaded on board, adding to a bizarre assortment that included 30 gallons of anti-scorbutic carrot marmalade, 20,000 pounds of sauerkraut, 19 tons of beer, 642 gallons of wine and 1,400 gallons of spirits. The men prepared to say goodbye to their families and the captain to his Elizabeth and the boys – now three in number with baby George. The Cooks had spent just under a year together – one year out of the last four. Their final farewell came on 21 June, 1772, the longest day of the year, and so it must have felt for Elizabeth, alone once more. That day, in Antarctica, the sun failed to rise.

James Cook travelled with William Wales to Sheerness where he joined the ship that was to be his home. A few days later, he received his formal instructions – to make further discoveries towards the South Pole in search of the Great Southern Continent, or at least, unknown lands. His last action on English soil was to post a letter to his friend, John Walker, and then collect the chronometers that were then started by the astronomers. As he turned back towards his ship, the words to his friend sped north to the one place on land he felt truly at home:

> Having nothing new to communicate I should hardly have troubled you with a letter was it not customary for men to take leave of their friends before they go out into the world, for I can hardly think myself in it so long as I am deprived from having any connections with the civilized part of it, and this will soon be my case for two years at least. When I think of the inhospitable parts I am going to, I think the voyage dangerous. I however enter upon it with great cheerfulness, providence has been very kind to me on many occasions, and I trust in the continuation of the divine protection.

As dawn broke through the clouds on 13 July, a year to the day since he had stepped off the *Endeavour*, the *Resolution* and *Adventure* slowly edged their way out to the English Channel. As he stood on deck, face into the wind, Dick Pickersgill took out his journal and in large, inky letters wrote the literary sigh, 'Farewell Old England'. He then drew a box around it and laid down his pen.

George Collingridge

21

THE DIEPPE MAPS

George Collingridge 1883

HE MAPS THAT George Collingridge was now poring over were not only sixteenth-century originals but, far from being isolated individuals, it soon emerged that they were part of a much larger series of maps and charts. These were drawn by the skilled cartographers from the short-lived but world-renowned school of map-makers in northern France's Dieppe, which gave the series its name as the Dieppe Maps. What makes them stand apart is that all of them show a vast, strange continent lying between the Pacific and Indian Oceans – the place where Australia should be.

By the 1500s, Dieppe was France's gateway to the Atlantic. A thriving port on a deep, safe estuary (the name itself is Anglo-Saxon for 'deep'), it bustled with the activity of sailors, shipbuilders, traders and maritime entrepreneurs. Most pilots and sailors would have plied their trade reliant on their own experience of the local waters or by keeping within sight of the coast but those heading further afield needed sea charts, and it was this demand that spawned the growing industry of cartography. However, since the Pope had divided the new world discoveries between Spain and Portugal, France had little incentive to send out its own voyages of discovery. But a few enterprising men left those shores regardless, pursuing their passion for exploration. No doubt they were spurred on by the tales of rich lands and exotic peoples filtering back from Africa, the Indies and South America, and there was still the elusive holy grail of Terra Australis – the Great Southern Continent; while Spain carved up the Americas and Portugal the Indies, why should that famous land not go to a Frenchman?

The only real French contender for discovering Jave la Grande was Jean Binot Paulmier de Gonneville. Around 1503–05, he had journeyed south via Africa's Cape of Good Hope into the Indian Ocean. Although his narrative survives, it contains no readings of latitude or longitude so it is hard to work out his course; his only key is his statement that he was on the 'true course to the East Indes' when he fell foul to savage winds which drove him to the south where, desperately short of water, he came across a large country, rich in every desirable resource. He named this land of plenty 'Terre Australle' and its people, 'Australians'.

On his way back to France with the amazing news, he met instead with disaster: he was shipwrecked and although he managed to survive and eventually make it home, the precious charts of his incredible voyage were lost to the depths of the sea. However, one piece of evidence did survive from that strange land – a piece of evidence that eventually made it home with him to France: Essomericq, a native of the exotic country he had explored, whom he later adopted as his son. Could he have found Jave la Grande? It is far more likely he found Madagascar. de Gonneville's journey was not the origin of the maps of Jave la Grande and it seemed there was no other great mariner who ventured into those waters in time to guide the cartographers' hands on the series of Dieppe Maps. But if there was no French voyage of discovery, then where on earth did Jave la Grande appear from?

In every other part of the world laid down on their *mappa mundi*, the Dieppe cartographers have used the most up-to-date information they could get their hands on; in fact, some of the coastlines are astounding in their detail – evidence that, if nothing else, these cartographers were some of the finest of their time. Elsewhere, they have been careful to separate fact from fiction; it seems unlikely they would have thrown caution to the wind in the case of Jave la Grande.

Perhaps the most talented of all their school was the geographer and sailor John Rotz. He was the first cartographer to think of representing the world as two hemispheres, drawn as two complementary circles, and it was his charts that George now pored over in the Sydney Public Library. Part-Scottish, part-French, he worked in Dieppe and may have even sailed to the Spice Islands before defecting to the court of Henry VIII. Here, in 1542, he presented the King with his *Boke of Idrography* – a magnificent maritime atlas containing a *mappa mundi* with eleven regional charts, bound into a single volume. In his dedicatory letter to the King, he claims:

All this I have set down exactly and truly as possible, drawing as much from my own experience as from the certain experience of my friends and fellow navigators.

Rotz is no cheat and he is certainly not a liar. Arguably one of the greatest cartographers in history, his work stands up to close scrutiny even today. So why would he and his Dieppe contemporaries draw in a continent that did not exist? And if they did believe such a land existed, from where – or whom – did they get the information that so convinced them? After all, it would take another fifty years before the Dutch officially 'discovered' the country that now occupies that position on the map, and another two hundred years to chart its coastlines with the detail provided by those of the mysterious Jave la Grande. There must have been another voyage of discovery, more probably a series of voyages to supply all the twists and turns of that vast land. But if they weren't sponsored by the French, then whose voyages were they?

As he stared down at these maps, working along the coastline of the strange continent, George had a growing sense that something was not quite right. Looking again, he retraced the list of place names that bordered the sea; the French words in the legends swam around in front of him, he blinked and looked once more. And then it clicked.

Unusually for the time – and particularly unusual for someone in the new colony – George was fluent in six languages (he later added a seventh, Esperanto, to the mix). For most of his life he had spoken in French, while picking up other European languages along the way. One of these was Portuguese and it was this that provided the break he needed: just offshore from the northern coast of the continent were two islands next to the words, 'Anda ne Barcha'. At first sight, this looked like the islands' names but when he looked more closely he recognised them as a Portuguese sentence, meaning 'No Boats go here!' Another perusal revealed that the islands were located in the shoal-strewn waters of the Timor and Arafura Seas, well-known for their treacherous navigation. But why would a warning on a French map be in Portuguese?

Over the following weeks and months, the question smouldered and burned itself into his mind; he went back to the maps and looked again. He then examined every single place name on all three maps for traces of linguistic confusion – and to his surprise found that there were other words that were barely French at all. He drew up tables comparing the place names on all the Dieppe Maps and noticed a pattern of irregularity in spelling. By now, the flames of curiosity were consuming his brain, hungry for answers. He asked around but no one else had noticed the anomaly; it seemed he was on his own but, not willing to give up, he made contact with geographical experts in Britain and then France and soon the whole of Europe. But, even so, the help they offered was piecemeal and limited: he needed more information.

To finance his growing library on the subject of the maps, he began to write articles for magazines and newspapers, discussing his findings and the questions these raised in turn. The workload expanded along with his interest; soon every spare penny was being invested into his growing passion for the maps and the truth that lay behind them. Then gradually, little by little, a picture began to emerge – a picture that would turn convention on its head and his world upside down: the maps may have been drawn in France but – for George, at least – the 'discovery' itself was Portuguese!

At last it made sense to him: the French cartographers had been copying a Portuguese original when they had come across the words 'Anda ne Barcha'. Not realising that the words were, in fact, a warning, they assumed they were the names of a small group of islands, lying off the modern-day Gulf of Carpentaria, on Australia's northern coast. From there, all the incongruencies began to slot into place: chaos became order and George had the key to unlocking the maps. All he had to do now was look back into time – to the beginning of the 1500s when the Portuguese first broke through into the waters of the Indian Ocean. But these voyagers were not looking for the Great Southern Continent, still less that land named Jave la Grande: they were looking for the Spice Islands.

Since time immemorial, Eastern nations such as China, India, Malaysia and Indonesia had used and traded the spices that sweetened the air, preserved their foods and made them palatable. Over the centuries, the traders spread their reach, eager to find the lucrative new markets. Wise Men from the East brought Frankincense and Myrrh to baby Jesus – but why stop there? The whole of Europe was desperate for the aromatic barks, seeds and resins that became as precious as gold. When, in 1501, the first Portuguese ships returned from the Indies laden with cinnamon, ginger, turmeric and other precious goods, Portugal became the envy of every nation in the world.

From then on, Portuguese ships ruled the southern seas, plying their route from the Cape of Good Hope then heading north to India, Sri Lanka and the Spice Islands. Gradually they charted the whole region; they bought, stole or captured Arab maps, befriended the locals and used their knowledge until their hegemony was complete. But while they could control the trade, they could not control the weather and they could not perfectly control their ships. Mistakes were made, ships were blown or sailed off course, other ships sailed on secret voyages of trade and discovery to avoid paying royalties to the crown – and some of those ships ended up on the western and northern shores of a dry, barren land that lay just to the south of the islands of Bali, Timor and the Moluccas that gave them their invaluable cargo – a land that was known to the trepang-fishermen of the region who would come here each year to fish. That land was Jave la Grande.

George looked at the continent that now filled the southern ocean, his mind already digging deeper into the mystery of the maps. Every question answered raised still more about its history: if it was indeed inspired by Portuguese voyages of discovery, who was it who had navigated its shores? And why should a nation of expert cartographers get the shape so badly wrong? These teasing riddles became the focus of George's life – and fired the compulsion that now sent him through the oceans of world history.

22

'FURTHER THAN ANY OTHER MAN'

James Cook 1772

T IS HARD TO comprehend the scope of Cook's achievements in his second voyage. In just over three years he scoured the waters of the Pacific and South Atlantic to prove that in terms of the Great Southern Continent, there was no discovery to make. He plunged time after time into the Antarctic Circle, taking his crew into uncharted waters and into terrifying seas of ice; there was no scent to follow like a foxhound, nothing beyond the vaguest sightings of his predecessors, nothing to lead him with certainty on a specific path. That is the whole point of the second voyage – he was the first to make systematic sweeps just to prove a negative. Absence of proof is not proof of absence, at least not for a man like James Cook; he wanted fact, with precise longitude and latitude laid down on the world map. In this sense, what he *didn't* discover was more important than what he *did*, as it laid to rest the myth that had fuelled the fantasy of nations for over a millennium. What is astounding is just how he went about it.

His plan was straightforward enough: he had already trawled the waters of the globe at around 40° South, proving that no Continent existed there or to the north, which had been criss-crossed by the discoverers of the last three hundred years. Now it was time to extinguish the flame of that belief in an undiscovered land by sailing further to the south – down to 60°S and beyond if he were able. The Antarctic Circle lies at 66°30'S. Beyond that lies the only Southern Continent that man will ever find: Antarctica or, for the eighteenth-century sailor, hell frozen over. Its summer temperatures range from an average of 0° on the coast to around minus 35°C in the interior; winter temperatures are the lowest on the planet – down to a record minus 89.2°C and probably much lower if you

The Resolution *in the Marquesas, by William Hodges*

could survive long enough to take the reading.

But it was not just the temperatures that made exploration exhausting: fierce winds characterise the region, cascading towards the coast from the frozen highlands, often laden with blinding snow scooped up from the ground and hurled into the air. It almost never rains in Antarctica. There may be water everywhere – in the seas and in the ice – but it is perversely classified as a desert; the extreme cold means that the air carries little water vapour for rain or snow, making it one of the driest places on earth. The irony was felt by Cook, desperately low on water, until he realised he could melt and drink it from the bergs.

The environment is not one to be taken lightly, particularly in the days before radar, sonar and even basics like waterproofs and central heating. So what fuelled his guiding flame to spend three years dipping into the Antarctic Circle? His motivation was clear:

> Ambition leads me not only farther than any other man has been before me, but as far as I think it is possible for a man to go.

That is what he achieved in this voyage – his ambition. He made more discoveries along the way, new islands to add to the growing map of the Pacific, discoveries of empty ocean where other lands should have been; he also fixed with certitude the positions of other navigators' discoveries. Like an accountant trawling through a company's records, he noted every credit and debit to the map of the world, validating the history of discovery like no one had ever done before. He bravely held his heroes and fellow navigators to account: Quiros, Tasman, Bouvet, Mendaña – men who had fired his imagination with their journals and charts and tales of adventure; he now set out to pluck bare fact from fiction. History was what could be verified; nothing else mattered.

One hundred years on, George Collingridge would be doing just that in his own attempt to set the historical record straight over the 'discovery' of Australia; two hundred years on, it would be my turn to meet accepted history head-on as I set out to discover the men who lay behind these two discoverers. Meantime, Cook was there first, blazing a trail of obsession across the oceans of the world in pursuit of the truth. He would prove the spur to both our quests and our unfolding stories – and this, his second voyage, was the key to his mind and soul.

Those three years in the southern hemisphere marked the apogee of his contribution to his profession and to the world at large. In terms of goal, execution and results, the plan was more than masterful – it was geographically beautiful. Yes, the men still suffered privations of food and water, and bitter cold; yes, they sailed for months without ever seeing land. They even broke the sailor's taboo about shooting the albatrosses that offered a chance of escape from their dwindling rations, but there is room for sentiment when facing death amongst the ice. It is now becoming widely accepted that Samuel Taylor Coleridge's epic poem, *The Ancient Mariner*, was inspired by that voyage: his tutor was William Wales, the *Resolution*'s astronomer and true man of genius, whose friendship with Cook was marked by profound respect from both sides; the legend of Cook, kindled by the success of the second voyage and the grief that marked the third, certainly dovetailed with the growing demand for romantic heroes at the end of the eighteenth century.

But behind this heroic figure, something happened to Cook on his second voyage. This was meant to be the voyage he had designed as the apotheosis of all his passions, but he grew tired, tired of the monotony of icy seas, the relentless crash of waves on bergs, tired of stripping his nerves raw with ambition. Physically and mentally, cracks emerged in the smooth, shiny gloss that surrounded this perfect naval icon, cracks that exposed the true cost of his obsession – cracks that would ultimately lead to his death.

This is the human story of the second voyage, the story of flawed beauty.

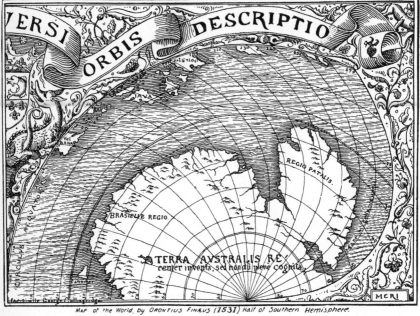

Map of the World by ORONTIUS FINÆUS (1531) Half of Southern Hemisphere.
(Reduced from Nordenskiöld's Atlas)

THE "MAPPEMONDE" OF "ORONTIUS FINÆUS" OF 1531—SCHÖNER'S WEIMAR GLOBE OF 1533—G. MERCATOR'S DOUBLE CORDIFORM MAPPAMUNDI OF 1538—HERNANDO DE GRIJALVA'S EXPEDITION TO THE SPICE ISLANDS.

Map of the Southern Hemisphere by Orontius Finaeus

23

THE END OF THE GREAT SOUTHERN CONTINENT

James Cook 1772

 CE WAS EVERYWHERE: huge bergs rose up two hundred feet high, catching the ships in their deadly shadow. The sails had frozen rock-solid and the rigging was so encrusted that climbing was becoming impossible – and all the time, the gale-force winds blasted super-cooled spray into the sailors' faces. These were dangerous waters; few of the men had seen anything like it.

They had sailed down via Madeira, the Cape Verde Islands and the Cape of Good Hope before heading almost 2,400 kilometres due south down towards the Antarctic. Somewhere in the empty waters was the land that the French explorer, Jean-Baptiste-Charles Bouvet de Lozier had gained a tantalising glimpse of in 1739. Bouvet had gone in search of the Continent reportedly found by his countryman, de Gonneville, in his voyage of 1503. Over two hundred years later, there was still the belief that seawater could not freeze, so when Bouvet came across the pervading fog, snow and ice, he assumed he was nearing land. And then he saw the icy cliffs ahead of him: was this the famed land of his forebear? He named the point, 'Cape Circumcision' as it was the Catholic Day of Circumcision (1 January), but was driven back by fog, leaving his discovery as just a teasing scrap of coastline on his chart. It was to this coastline that Cook now set his bows.

The land was nowhere to be seen and, after making several sweeps across, above and below the area, Cook doubted that it even existed. He had no way of knowing that Bouvet had misplaced it on the chart, plotting its longitude too far east. More remarkable was that the Frenchman had even found it at all: tiny Bouvet Island, as it turned out to be, is just five miles by three and one of the loneliest places in the world with over a thousand miles in any direction to the nearest scrap of land. Little wonder it was to take until 1898 before its position was accurately charted at 54°26'S and 3°24'E.

The journey down had passed without significant event for the expedition's commander; he had gained amusement from hearing of the 'gentleman' who had secretly arranged with Banks to join the ship at Madeira – a 'gentleman' who turned out to be Banks's mistress. The audacious botanist was thus with them in spirit, if not with them – and his mistress – in person. Sadly the mistress then disappears from the records. Cook was less amused with the cleanliness of his crew, who were ordered to wash their clothes at least once a week, air their bedding, scrub the decks with vinegar and fumigate their quarters with smoke bombs; he was even less impressed when some of the men's pet monkeys covered the deck with their faeces and, in stark contrast to Banks's sympathy for the beasts in Batavia and much to the horror and protestations of the Forsters, he immediately ordered the pets to be put over the side to drown. Later on, he would even organise inspections of his crew to check the cleanliness of their hands, punishing those who had failed to wash. Hygiene had always been one of his passions but to a shocked crew it was revolutionary, and not at all welcome. The eighteenth-century sailor did not like change – and this change was brutal. Refusal to clean was tantamount to 'mutiny' and would be punished by cutting the ration of grog, or lashes at the mast. For the men, there was no escape; for Cook, this obsessional cleanliness points as much to a desire for order in his mind as for the welfare of his men.

The weather grew colder as they trekked further south; protective 'fearnought' clothing was issued to the men who could feel the freezing wind chilling their bones. If nothing else, Cook's aim was daring – to circumnavigate the world at 40-60°S, proving once and for all that no Continent existed and that all reported sightings were islands, ice, or nothing more than fantasy. New Year 1773 brought gales and fog and more treacherous ice that mesmerised the men with its awful beauty; more practically, Cook used the opportunity for his own scientific experiments and discovered to everyone's amazement and relief that the water in the bergs was pure enough for drinking; he immediately sent out more boats to harvest it from those floating islands – a dangerous occupation as great shards of ice sheared off around them, falling like drawbridges into the sea. Just over two weeks later, on 17 January, the captain noted triumphantly:

At about 14 past 11 o'clock, we crossed the Antarctic Circle for at noon we were by observations four and a half miles south of it and are undoubtedly the first and only ship that ever crossed that line.

It is no slip that he forgets about his cohort – this was *his* dream, *his* passion; the *Adventure* was just an appendage to that dream.

They pushed through the ice as far as 67°15'S – almost ten degrees closer to the Pole than Cape Horn – before they were forced back by the ever-present bergs. Was there land here? If there was, its frozen wastes would be uninhabitable. Unknown to Cook, they had sailed within 75 miles of the Antarctic coast, the only southern continent that ever really existed and one that was a million miles from the legendary land of plenty that had fuelled the philosophers' dreams for more than a thousand years.

There was nothing else to do but head north again, in search of the land discovered by France's Kerguelen, but as they did so, they swapped one threat for another, in the form of a thick shroud of fog. Here, on 8 February, 1773, the *Resolution* and the *Adventure* parted company. Three days were spent searching through the white, soupy air; three days sounding the guns and listening out for any slight reply. Nothing could be done. With his usual impeccable planning, Cook had already arranged a rendezvous with Furneaux in New Zealand's Queen Charlotte Sound; the *Adventure* headed there immediately; Cook made one more swoop southwards to make sure the Continent was not lurking in high latitudes before setting his course for New Zealand.

When the two men met again in Queen Charlotte Sound, their different experiences were a portrait of their differing characters. Furneaux had done his duty: he had obeyed his orders, waited in the *Resolution*'s last-known position for three days and nights and then headed east along Tasman's track to Van Diemen's Land then north to the bay or strait that separated it from New Holland. He had hoped to clear up whether Van Diemen's Land was an island or joined to the mainland but soon turned back, for fear of the shoals that were strewn across his path. He left New Holland's waters for New Zealand, believing there was no strait – but not staying long enough to prove himself wrong.

Cook, meanwhile, had gone far beyond his orders, making a detour on his way to Queen Charlotte Sound. By now, his men were showing signs of scurvy; antiscorbutics were issued and Cook redoubled his obsession with cleanliness and order, even ordering the men to take up needle and thread to repair their tattered clothes. Realising his men were in a poor state and that Furneaux would almost certainly be heading north, he had continued his Continent-hunting in a more southerly track towards New Zealand.

By the time the South Island's Dusky Bay loomed on the horizon, they had sailed eleven thousand miles in 122 days without ever seeing land. For the last three years, the memory of being previously forced past the bay by bad weather had preyed on Cook's mind – it would now provide the perfect opportunity to explore, while restocking with fresh greens and supplies. He surveyed the fantastic coastline with its bountiful wood and rushing water, then met and befriended a native family, before continuing up the west coast and into the Sound to rendezvous with Furneaux. He makes no mention of the 'fever and violent pain in the groin, which terminated in a rheumatic swelling of the right foot'; that record is left to one of the kinder comments by J. R. Forster. We begin to see the first signs that all was not well with the health of the captain, despite the pains he went to in order to look after the health of his men.

His meeting with Furneaux might have come as a relief in terms of their safety but it was also a cause for anxiety and tension. The first point of friction was over the state of health amongst Furneaux's men: that captain had clearly not been following Cook's guidelines to make sure they consumed the antiscorbutic sauerkraut and salted cabbage, and the crew were 'much inflicted' with the disease. It was not only lazy behaviour by the *Adventure*'s captain, it was dangerous to the long-term success of the voyage and frustrating to its commander. All Cook could do was reiterate his orders on hygiene and diet in the most forceful terms – the captain must look after his own men.

The second point of irritation was entirely his own doing. He had become increasingly aware of a discrepancy between the co-ordinates he had given for New Zealand in the first voyage and the longitudes that William Wales was now providing from the stars and from the Kendall chronometer. On comparing further with the *Adventurer*'s astronomer, William Bayly, the master of precision had the growing suspicion that he and the dearly departed Mr Green may have made a mistake. For anyone else, this would have been an irritation; for Cook it was nothing short of a 'capital error', even though that error amounted to just over half a degree too far East. He could not, however, quite believe his eyes or his own fallibility and he took the rest of the voyage to be reconciled with having made the mistake.

Meanwhile, his second-in-command was clearly expecting to over-winter in Ship Cove but Cook had other ideas: he was not about to waste the winter months achieving nothing; instead, he gave the shocking orders that they were to prepare to sail immediately to the east and then, if they didn't meet land, were to head north to Tahiti where they would resupply and continue their discoveries in the northern Pacific.

The two ships left their anchorage at Queen Charlotte Sound at the beginning of June 1773, sailing eastwards through Cook Strait and then down into the southern reaches of the Pacific. If a Continent lay in these waters, he would surely find it as he made his way east across the ocean. Cook was now starting a giant anticlockwise loop of the Pacific Ocean that would take him almost halfway to Cape Horn, then north to Pitcairn Island, then westwards to Tahiti and the Society Islands, through the Cook Islands to Tonga, then almost due south again to New Zealand by the end of October. It was to prove a remarkable piece of navigation.

Furneaux was still frustrated: a month and a half after leaving Queen Charlotte Sound, he had one man dead of scurvy and twenty-six more ill from the disease and the added complication of the 'flux'. Cook did what he could by sending a replacement member of crew and orders to use the antiscorbutics, which the *Adventure*'s captain belatedly now employed. The men recovered but Cook was exasperated with his number two: when would he ever learn? The fatal deficiency was to become an almost permanent and totally unnecessary accompaniment to life on the *Adventure*.

As to the existence of the Continent, it would not have pleased Alexander Dalrymple, that passionate supporter of *Terrra Incognita*, that

> Circumstances seem to point out to us that there is none but this is too important a point to be left to conjector, facts must determine it.

And those facts he would establish with quiet satisfaction, inch by inch, mile by mile, across the empty ocean. It was not merely a matter of geography: Dalrymple never missed an opportunity to sneer at Cook or cast doubt on his integrity as an explorer; Cook now had the chance to expunge fantasy from the record and hopefully silence once and for all his troublesome rival.

The two boats reached Tahiti by the middle of August, its familiar mountains rising up from the sea, though by now the *Adventure*'s crew was so sickly, they needed to borrow some of the *Resolution*'s men to bring their ship to shore. The commander had little time to stew: a mistake by his helmsman overnight had taken both ships dangerously close to the reef. Once again, he was faced with being smashed to his death on the coral; once again, he is saved by a breath of favourable wind and the sterling efforts of his crew. There is no mention of the guilty party, nor less the words used by Cook towards the guilty man. Instead, there is a report by Mr Sparrman, a botanist brought on board at Cape Town by the Forsters. Like Dr Solander before him, he was a Swede; unlike the

good doctor, he was easily shocked by the events before him – not so
much by the thought of death but by the stream of 'Goddams' that
spewed from the officers' lips,

> And particularly the Captain, who, whilst the danger lasted, stamped about
> on the deck and grew horse with shouting.

This is the first clear mention of what his men would call Cook's 'heivas',
the frenzied jumping and stamping that became characteristic of his
growing furies. The expression was first used in humour – the foot-
stamping reminded them of a rather energetic Tahitian dance by the
same name – but soon the rages would become too insidious for joking.
This mild-mannered captain was showing worrying signs of strain; his
previous cool calm was now little more than a veneer on a seething pot of
rage. He could still do his job – and was still superb in a crisis – but the
atmosphere on board was beginning to ripple with tension. Something
was happening to their beloved commander and it left his men confused.
This was more than just bad temper, though it was not until later that
Sparrman gave the beginnings of an explanation for his irascible
behaviour.

> As soon as the ship was once more afloat, I went down to the ward room
> with Captain Cook who, although he had from the beginning been perfectly
> alert and able, was suffering so greatly from his stomach that he was in a
> great sweat and could scarcely stand. It was, indeed, hardly remarkable that,
> after so great a responsibility and so prodigious a strain on both his mental
> and physical capacities, he should be completely exhausted.

Sparrman administered the traditional Swedish remedy of a large dose of
brandy whereupon 'His aches vanished immediately'. Cook does not even
refer to the incident in his journal, as if denying that there is anything
wrong at all. Of course, the Admiralty was not interested in his digestive
problems but even if they were, it is unlikely he would highlight anything
that could be construed as weakness, whether caused by a medical
problem or triggered by stress. Meanwhile, the more personal journals of
his colleagues are peppered with references to their captain's failing
health and humour as the gripping pains and fraying temper become a
common – and worrying – theme of the voyage.

Since their previous visit, Tahiti had been badly shaken by civil war and
the old-timers were shocked at the much-reduced supply of refreshments

on the island. There was also a new hierarchy of chiefs to get to grips with, though some took this more literally than others. Poor Lieutenant Edgcumbe, a great friend of the captain, met with a reception from the wife of one new dignitary that left him reeling:

> This lady wanted neither youth nor beauty, nor was she wanting in using those charms which nature had given her to the most advantage. She bestowed her caresses on me with the most profusion, and before I could get clear of her I was obliged to satisfy all her demands, after which both she and her husband went away and I was never troubled with either the one or the other afterwards.

Though he might protest too much, it was a far cry from the behaviour of five men from the *Adventure* and *Resolution* who absented themselves from duty, 'quarrelled with the natives' and made 'too free with the women', later interpreted as attempted rape. Cook was outraged and, ever keen to prove that he was as even-handed to those who broke the rules on his own side as he was the locals, he ordered the men to be lashed with the cat-o'-nine-tails. He had become increasingly concerned over the treatment of native women on the islands they had encountered – and particularly unsettled over the reaction by both the local men and his own men that any woman was there for trading. In New Zealand he had worried that visits by his ships had actually stimulated prostitution, let alone the spread of venereal disease; now he was concerned about the 'Great Injustice' that was being done to the women of Tahiti by assuming they could all be paid for sex. He noted, however, that the Tahitians did not seem to stigmatise those women who did turn to prostitution:

> The truth is, the women who become prostitutes do not seem in their opinion to have committed a crime of so deep a die as to exclude her from the esteem and society of the community in general.

And, whether prostitute or not, he insisted that all island women were treated with respect.

The attitude of Cook towards island women and sex is another point that marks him out from his contemporaries. The norm of European explorers was to let their men relax and satisfy their desires as they pleased. Sex with indigenous women was perceived as a 'reward' for landing equivalent to being taken off ship's rations – in fact, the lure of the warm embrace of tropical beauties free of the straightened morals of their own countryfolk was one of the attractions of making the dangerous voyages to the South Seas in the first place. For Cook, however, it was inhumane to infect the locals with the sexually-transmitted diseases inevitably carried on board his ships and unjust to behave any differently towards native women than they would to women back home. Just because a female was 'foreign' did not mean that there should be any suspension in the accepted moral framework. However, from the journals of his officers and crew, it seems that not only were his ships almost alone in being commanded this way, he was pretty much in a minority of one in his views. Sailors were beasts of tradition – and Cook's ideas about chastity stuck in their throat as much as their diet of sauerkraut: both might do you good, but they can never be enjoyed.

While the behaviour of his men may have caused him extreme anxiety, the seemingly 'loose' behaviour of the islanders did have a wider benefit. When the reports of the South Sea islands began to filter back home through conversations, journals and the growing popularity of the new breed of travel books, they spawned much debate on the nature of 'civilisation', and bolstered the rise of the idea of the 'Noble Savage'. In turn, the different cultural attitudes towards sex in these islands – which included nakedness, polygamy and even routine infanticide – provided a useful counterpoint to eighteenth-century sexual mores, shoring up Europe's idea of what was right and proper – and what was dangerously libidinous. Just as Jesus needed Satan to test and affirm his faith during those forty long days in the wilderness, the dark pleasures of hedonism tested the structures of Georgian polite society: they were analysed, questioned and rebuilt even stronger. No one realised that Polynesian Society was just as complex as their own – that the women who seemed to offer sex freely were actually bound by their own rigid set of rules. The Great Men of Science used their flawed understanding to interpret a society that made sense to them, and the myth of sexual freedom in these paradise islands was embedded into the map of the Pacific.

Despite the pleasures the island offered his men, Cook did not want to tarry long: the leeward islands of Huahine and Raiatea were in sight, and soon they departed once more. Their reception at Huahine was almost overwhelming as 'brave old Chief' Ori was reunited with his beloved Cook. This was no matter of international diplomacy: there were the usual ceremonies but the depth of feeling between the two men was apparent to all who watched. Ori embraced Cook: 'the tears which trinckled plentifully down his Cheeks sufficiently spoke the feelings of his heart'. The feelings were returned, 'for I regarded this old man as a father'.

This was no empty rhetoric: in contrast to his increasing furies with his men, the second voyage had been marked by a growing tenderness in

Cook towards the people he encountered on his journey; gone was the wry amusement at the Gentlemen's interest in the indigenous people of the Pacific, here was a genuine and passionate interest – not as curios but as human beings. In New Zealand, he had impressed his men by fearlessly walking up to a Maori family in Dusky Bay and, unarmed, rubbing noses with the father as a sign of welcome, then later at Queen Charlotte Sound, he had mused over the real effects of contacts with the so-called 'civilised' world:

> Tell me what the Natives of the whole extent of America have gained by the commerce they have had with Europeans.

What his biographer, Beaglehole, dismissed as 'bursts of sentimental nonsense' seem more of an attempt to reconcile his strong feelings on fair treatment of humanity with the general view of the age that these people were little more than savages. Back home, the rationalist thinkers of the Enlightenment and non-conformist groups like the Quakers were becoming increasingly vocal in their view that slavery was morally untenable. This had raised a wider debate on what it meant to be civilised, a debate that clearly carries through into Cook's journal of the second voyage. Though influenced by conversations in the Great Cabin – and in particular with William Wales, in whom he had found a soul-mate – he had matured from the first voyage. His views are now his own, not Banks's, not Rousseau's; instead of criticising the manner of their delivery, it is more illuminating to put them in the context of a farm-labourer's son who had spent over half his life in rough living at sea. The very human view of the indigenous peoples he encountered – and the responsibilities he felt when making contact with them – may be clumsily expressed, but his education was coming from real life, not from the philosophical teachings of Oxford and Cambridge. He was never convinced that being 'discovered' was in the best interests of the indigenous peoples he encountered: he knew it put them at risk of disease, exploitation and cultural ruin and this uneasiness tugged at his conscience with increasing ferocity. His knowledge was both empirical and highly personal. More significantly, with the formal movement for the abolition of slavery not gearing up for another decade, these views were well ahead of his time.

When Cook bade his friend Ori farewell, his ship was weighed down with hogs, yams and breadfruit; Furneaux also had his fresh provisions but he left carrying a memento of these islands that would not perish on the long journey ahead. Among his ranks was now an extra person, a young refugee from Raiatea called Mae who had pleaded to be taken to

'Britania' and who, once there, would cause a sensation.

Meanwhile, the ships continued their work. Cook's plan had originally been to head back to New Zealand by the shortest route; that thought was now swept aside as a much grander scheme took over. Cook was about to team up with his arch-detractor, the man who had railed against him after the *Endeavour* voyage for not doing more to find the Great Southern Continent and the man whose jealousy of Cook would darken his writings for the rest of his life: Alexander Dalrymple. Cook had with him a copy of Dalrymple's *Historical Collection of the Several Voyages and Discoveries in the South Pacific Ocean*, published in two volumes in 1770–71; he now used that collection to work out his route back to New Zealand. Rather than head straight there, he would flex the muscles of his own imagination and travel back via the legendary isles of his discovering forebears, verifying the historical accounts of Pacific voyaging over the past two hundred and fifty years.

The next two months were spent chasing the scents of his heroes across the Pacific, fixing their discoveries with exactitude, finding others and expunging from the record those that proved themselves nothing more than myth. When they eventually learned of it, this astounding act of supererogation would amaze the Admiralty; that passion to go beyond his orders would also make him the toast of learned society, though perhaps only begrudgingly by Dalrymple himself.

Heading west to Tasman's Amsterdam – part of the islands of Tonga – Cook ticked or crossed off islands from the chart, surveying an extraordinary amount of the area and noting down comments on their people's lifestyles, and speculating about their possible common origin. At last, at the beginning of October 1773, he headed south to New Zealand.

By the end of October, he was back in the waters off Cook Strait, battling against the storms for access to the safety of Queen Charlotte Sound. Conditions deteriorated badly; soon the two ships were facing not only a 'furious gale but a mountainous Sea'. For the next ten days, they were gripped in the teeth of the most diabolical weather and the *Adventure* disappeared out of sight. Cook tacked up and down the coast, desperate to reach the sanctuary of the Sound, where he assumed Furneaux was already waiting; when he finally collapsed into Ship Cove on 3 November, his sails ripped to shreds by the savage wind, the *Adventure* was nowhere to be seen.

Cook's first job was to mend his battered ship and resupply his exhausted men and stores. He was at least in familiar surroundings with plentiful wood, water and fresh food for the taking. Charles Clerke amused himself by going one step further and securing a severed human head from one of the Maori, then offering a slice of its meat to one of the local bystanders: the man devoured it with relish, confirming beyond doubt his people's cannibalistic habit. Another slice was broiled and similarly devoured. By now a crowd had gathered on board, with Cook, Wales and Forster looking on in mortal curiosity. Down in the Great Cabin, the debate continued long after the flesh had been finished and the crowd dispersed, with Cook ruminating long and hard on how to reconcile the ghoulish events with his deep respect for the native New Zealanders.

> Few consider what a savage man is in his original state and even after he is in some degree civilised; the New Zealanders are certainly in a state of civilisation, their behaviour to us has been Manly and Mild, shewing always a readiness to oblige us; they have some arts among them which they execute with great judgement and unwearied patience; they are far less addicted to thieving than the other Islanders and I believe strictly honist among them-selves. This custom of eating their enimies slain in battle (for I firmly believe they eat the flesh of no others) has undoubtedly been handed down to them from the earliest times and we know that it is not an easy matter to break a nation of its ancient customs let them be ever so inhuman and savage, especially if that nation is void of all religious principles as I believe the new Zealanders in general are and like them without any settled form of government; as they become more united they will of concequence have fewer Enemies and become more civilised and then and not till then this custom may be forgot.

Had he known the fate that would befall the *Adventure*, he would have had even greater delvings into his conscience, but at that point he assumed she was either at anchor further up the coast, or already heading onwards to the Cape of Good Hope and home. Although they had been alone at Ship Cove for almost a month, he was not concerned for her safety in the slightest; in fact, the prospect of continuing on his voyage unencumbered was almost pleasing. However, in case she did arrive after he had gone, Cook left a message for Furneaux in a bottle, outlying his vague plans but not expecting – perhaps not even hoping – his second-in-command would attempt another rendezvous. Like Alice in Wonderland, he buried the bottle under a tree, into which were carved the words 'LOOK UNDERNEATH!' Next day, on 25 November, 1773, the solitary *Resolution* sailed once more from New Zealand.

Cook's plan was far from returning to the Cape. He now had in mind an audacious, giant second sweep of the Pacific that would take him firstly south and east – dipping twice more beyond the Antarctic Circle in search of the Continent. He would then turn northwards off the coast of Tierra del Fuego to Easter Island, sailing up as far as the Marquesas then back down anticlockwise to Tahiti, Tonga, south of Fiji and as far west as the New Hebrides. Here, he would turn south to New Caledonia, Norfolk Island and back to the west coast of New Zealand. To modern eyes, his track looks logical enough – but then, we are looking at the islands he plotted on the map; his own eyes looked only at empty charts and largely rumoured lands: he was sailing into a void of speculation.

Cook says his men were happy at the prospect of this great voyage of discovery and historical verification; certainly, the prospect of again returning to Tahiti cheered the men's hearts and whetted their appetites for the sun, food and women they would find there. Had they known that they would be sailing the Pacific for almost another year, they might have thought again, and they might well have reconsidered as they were driven within a ship's length of a terrifying iceberg – 'the most *Miraculous* escape from being every soul lost, that ever men had' according to their horror-stricken captain.

With their lives on a knife-edge, they ploughed on through the freezing waters, dense fog and vicious gales down to latitude 67°27'S – about ten degrees further south than the southernmost tip of South America and well inside the Antarctic Circle – until the sails froze as hard as iron, the rigging was encased in burning ice and the cold was 'so intense, it was hardly to be endured'. Their grisly presents, on Christmas Day, 1773, were more icebergs – 'these devilish Ice Isles' – some over two hundred feet tall and, according to Charles Clerke, almost numerous enough to have two each. Cook, meanwhile, watched the rise and fall of the ocean swell: there could be no Continent here. He headed north once more.

Their supplies of greens had long since run out and the men were back on their standard rations. Soon, however, even these were growing scarce and the men grew tired of the monotonous diet and the monotonous cold and wet. Once more, their minds turned to the thought of home – they were now in line with New Zealand, though far out to the east. The Cape was now just a short sail away.

It was not to be. With the men reduced to two-thirds rations and much to their 'very severe mortification' – the words are those of midshipman Elliot – on 11 January, 1774, Cook hauled southeast once more: they were heading back into the ice. Dejection spread through the crew like an agonising groan; the older Forster complained bitterly. Why were they turning south yet again? To the north lay refreshment and rest; to the south lay only hard sailing, bitter cold and danger. For the men, the choice was easy – but their captain had other ideas. His compulsion to explore overcame the discomforts of cold and hunger, and if he could stand it, so would they.

The incident raised the issue of Cook's lack of consultation: they all appreciated a commander who was willing to take control, but was there really a need to be this secretive? There was no doubt that Cook was 'his own man'; however, the prevailing mood in the ship was that a little more openness would go a long way to improving crew morale. Mr Forster noted with genuine surprise and some pique that he had not been consulted – though the thought that a naturalist should be consulted over the navigation of the ship says more about Mr Forster than his captain. Nevertheless, if there was a dictatorship, at least it was reasonably benign, which is more than could be said for the weather.

'Excessive hard gales' assailed the ship with sleet and snow stinging the men's eyes. This was hard sailing, but still Cook stood south. At last, on 26 January, the *Resolution* crossed the Antarctic Circle for the third time, still searching for signs of the Continent. For four more days she wove between bergs the size of cathedrals, creeping through the fog like a deadly game of blind man's buff. Then the weather cleared, the waves were pacified and an eerie silence descended around them. It was too good to be true: the skies now cleared to reveal a sea of blinding white ice. No one on board had ever seen anything like it – the floating ice became more and more compressed until it was one solid mass, reaching up into the sky like mountains. Even Cook conceded they could go no further.

> I will not say it was impossible anywhere to get in among this Ice, but I will assert that the bare attempting of it would be a very dangerous enterprise and what I believe no man in my situation would have thought of. I whose ambition leads me not only father than any other man has been before me, but as far as I think it is possible for a man to go, was not sorry at meeting with this interruption, as it in some measure relieved us from the dangers and hardships, inseparable with the Navigation of the Southern Polar regions. Sence therefore we could no proceed one Inch farther South, no other reason need be assigned for our Tacking and stretching back to the North.

He had spent a year and a half pursuing a Continent just to prove it did not exist – and proving to himself that he could stretch the limits of his own endurance. The weariness that permeates this entry in his journal spreads like a sigh across the page. He almost welcomes the ice taking control and making his decision for him: his searching in the frozen wastes of Antarctica was over; it was time to head to the sun and the possibility of real discoveries.

As the ship went about at 71 10', two men were guarding their own ambitions. George Vancouver and Mr Sparrman were each vying for the record of the man who had reached furthest south: Sparrman calculated that he had achieved this by retiring to his cabin in the stern, while the Young Vancouver showed some of the spirit that would become his trademark by sliding to the very end of the bowsprit, waving his hat and exclaiming, 'Ne Plus Ultra!' The only arbiter was the creaking ice field – and it kept its verdict to itself.

Cook's mind now focussed its attention to his personal agenda. The map of the Pacific was still clouded with myth and legend, if not with the Great Southern Continent itself. The sightings by the greatest navigators in history needed verification – and here he was, with a ship designed for discovery, a healthy if hungry crew, and a clean slate ahead of him. His men seemed eager to return to the warmth of the tropics so, with no impediment, he turned to his arch-enemy once more: Dalrymple and his *Historical Collection* would again become his adversary in the battle between fact and fiction.

In 1563, Juan Fernández had become famous as a 'brujo' or wizard by sailing from Peru to Chile in a third of the usual time. He followed up this feat with a series of voyages westwards into the Pacific, where he discovered a series of islands. These were laid down in Dalrymple's map as lying around 38 latitude, just south of Concepción in modern-day Chile – and they now became the beacon that guided Captain James Cook. The weather melted into mist and rain but three days' search yielded no fruit and he headed on to Easter Island, convinced that the isles were either tiny or did not exist at all.

In Cook's mind, all dangers had been left behind – the weather was fine, the icebergs long gone and he was sailing in open water. He had not accounted for his own fallibility. At the end of February 1774, he collapsed dangerously ill into bed. His own journal is brief: his illness a 'Billious colick ... so violent as to confine me to my bed'. George Forster, who had nursed him before, had watched him grow paler and his appetite wane; now James Patten, the surgeon, stepped in. Cook was in agony but nothing in Patten's repertoire would ease his pain. Finally, after a week and more hot baths and poultices, the gripes subsided and the Forsters' dog made the ultimate sacrifice to tempt him back to food.

When the Captain returned to the deck, he found his crew growing sick with scurvy. It was three months since they had their feet on the land;

food was basic rations – and some could not even bring themselves to eat that – but he resolutely kept to his plan. The next island in his sights was Easter Island, discovered by Jacob Roggeveen in 1722; this was found, fixed, surveyed and explored – though not by Cook who was still too weak to walk far. The men stared at the giant, ghostly statues from which they had identified the island, and met with the impoverished Polynesian inhabitants. They had little to offer in terms of food for the men, so four days later, the ship sailed on.

With the island fading into the wake, Cook again took violently ill though this time he recovered without dog broth. For three long weeks, short of water and low on food, the *Resolution* headed northwest to the islands laid down by çlvaro de Mendaña 1595, thinking them at first to be the Solomon Islands he had also discovered nearly thirty years before. On both occasions, his mission was to find and colonise the Great Southern Continent; on both occasions he had found only islands.

It was Mendaña's second discovery – the Marquesas – where Cook arrived on 6 April, 1774. Here, and by now as a matter of dire need, he secured fresh food and water for his men before completing his mission to verify the Spaniard's discovery and fix the islands' positions; he also discovered one more island to add to the group. However, much to his annoyance, any serious chance of resupplying was ruined when one of his men traded a quantity of red feathers for a pig – after that, no other currency would do. Cook realised it was now futile to remain in the islands; there was nothing else to do but move on to his next piece of historical substantiation: the Tuamotus.

Little by little, Dalrymple's map was being redrawn. Cook negotiated the tricky shoals of the Tuamotu Archipelago, fixing and charting as he went with both observations and 'the watch' but by now his main goal was to reach the familiar welcome of Tahiti, the next major island *en route*. He arrived in the welcome arms of Matavai Bay on 22 April, almost five months after leaving New Zealand. Remarkably, all signs of scurvy had vanished and, although the visit provided a welcome opportunity to resupply with food, wood and water, the main reason for stopping was so that William Wales could do his own piece of verification on the chronometer. As for Cook, he used the opportunity to reflect on his relationship with the native Tahitians after he was again plagued by their thievery:

> Three things made them our fast friends. Their own good Natured and
> benevolent disposition, gentle treatment on our part, and the dread of our
> fire Arms; by our ceasing to observe the Second the first would have wore
> off of Course, and the too frequent use of the latter would have excited a

spirit of revenge and perhaps have taught them that fire Arms were not such terrible things as they had imagined, they are very sencible of the superiority they have over us in numbers and no one knows what an enraged multitude might do.

It is with a sense of tragedy that we now read these words of fatal prescience, knowing only too well the events of Valentine's Day, February 1779. He knew the theory; if only he had remembered these words in practice.

Three weeks after arriving, he left Tahiti for the last time in the voyage. After brief visits to neighbouring Huahine and Raiatea, he sailed on for more than a fortnight, passing more small islands before catching sight of his goal: the land of Tasman – Rotterdam, or Nomuka, in the Tongan Archipelago. Here, he was put in the embarrassing predicament of being offered a beautiful young lady by a fearsome, elderly woman. Cook was mortified – not only was he the strongest opponent of sexual contact with the islanders, he was no doubt being watched enviously by his comrades. They would have enjoyed the spectacle: their usually cool commander was totally stymied.

> I soon made them sencible of my Poverty and thought by that means to have come off with flying Colours but I was mistaken, for I was made to understand I might retire with her on credit, this not suteing me niether the old Lady began first to argue with me and when that fail'd she abused me, I understood very little of what she said, but her actions were expressive enough and shew'd that her words were to this effect, Sneering in my face and saying, what sort of a man are you thus to refuse the embraces of so fine a young Woman, for the girl certainly did not [want] beauty which I could however withstand, but the abuse of the old Woman I could not and therefore hastened into the Boat, they then would needs have me take the girl on board with me, but this could not be done as I had come to a Resolution not to suffer a Woman to come on board the Ship on any pretence what ever and had given strict orders to the officers to that purpose.

Thankfully for Cook, it was not only the young woman's charms that were bountiful: having extricated himself from the awkward situation, they were able to resupply with as much fresh food and water as they desired then, unsurprisingly, the captain resolved to leave what he had decided to call the 'Friendly Archipelago' in honour of their 'Courtesy to Strangers'. No irony was intended.

As June slipped into July, the *Resolution* continued its passage westwards in search of the lands discovered by the great Spanish navigator, Pedro Fernández de Quirós. In 1606, he had gone in search of the Great Southern Continent to bring it Christianity; a hundred and sixty-eight years later, Cook went in search of accuracy. Passing through the lower reaches of Fiji, he sailed on to the northwest to look for 'Quiros's Isles' – Austrialia del Espíritu Santo – Bougainville's Great Cyclades – now known as Vanuatu.

Cook knew he was not going to 'Quiros's Isles' to make discoveries, merely to set down as cartographic fact what had for too long been geographical confusion. What resulted was nothing short of perfection. In around a month, he charted the profusion of islands with astounding precision, especially given that most of his surveying was done from a moving ship. However, in contrast to all the scientific certainty, one fact rankled in the captain's mind: the behaviour of some of the islanders when they stopped for wood and water had been decidedly odd; they did not want to trade, they did not want to come close – in fact, they just seemed to want him and his men to go away. What Cook could never know was that to the Melanesian people he was now encountering, his white skin was proof that he and his men were ghosts.

Having surveyed the long string of islands, he spent the last fortnight on one he called Tanna. When asking its name from the locals, his men had pointed to the ground: the locals told him the word for what the men were pointing at – 'tanna' or 'ground' – and the name was then mistakenly given to this beautiful, volcanic island because only travellers need to have names for places. The Melanesians on Tanna were also convinced these strange white visitors were ghosts and did their best to keep out of the men's way. Cook was bemused by this strange reception but as they were allowed to go about their business unimpeded, he thought things were going well. He ruminated on their relationship with their hosts with a maturity that is breathtaking when compared with his comments from his first voyage – then it was the locals who were the objects under scrutiny – now it is the visitors themselves:

> We found these people Civil and good Natured when not prompted by jealousy to a contrary conduct, a conduct one cannot blame them for when one considers the light in which they must look upon us in, its impossible for them to know our real design, we enter their Ports without their daring to make opposition, we attempt to land in a peaceable manner, if this succeeds its well, if not we land nevertheless and mentain the footing we thus got by the Superiority of our fire arms, in what other light can they

than at first look upon us but as invaders of their Country; time and some acquaintance with us can only convince them of their mistake.

Then, on their last day on the island, disaster struck. The men were loading wood onto the ship, watched as ever by a crowd of villagers. One of these raised his bow and arrow – Cook thought in display – but one of the sentries raised his musket and shot the man dead. The captain could barely have been more furious. Wasn't this precisely the kind of situation he had ordered his men to avoid? The sentry was flung into irons and ordered to be flogged. The officers, however, took the sentry's side and a ferocious argument ensued in which Cook finally relented over the flogging but was condemned by his Midshipman, Elliot, for losing sight 'both of justice, and Humanity'. As for the sentry, he would soon lose his own life by falling overboard when drunk.

Cook's last major task in these islands was to find and explore the famous bay in which Quirós had landed. Like retracing the steps of a hero, Cook left his offering of latitudes and longitudes on the paper altarcloth of his chart of the Pacific and, on 1 September, left the land of 'that great Navigator' disappearing into the distance, having called the island by the Navigator's name, *Tierra Del Esp'ritu Santo*, the only remains of Quiros's Continent'. To the whole island group he gave his own name, seeing that he had added more islands to those 'Great Cyclades' laid down by his arch-rival, Bougainville. It would be called 'New Hebrides'.

The last of Dalrymple's historical curios had now been resolved: Cook's work in the Pacific was nearly over. All that remained was to head south to New Zealand and replenish his supplies before abandoning the ocean that had been his home for the last three years. But he was not yet thinking of home; instead, in his mind he was formulating one last 'Southern Cruise'.

Four days later, where should have been open sea, he sighted a low, unknown island, long and thin and flanked to the north and east by perilous reefs. It was the fourth largest island in the Pacific and he spent the rest of September attempting to circumnavigate it and commit it to the rigours of the chart. The land was inhabited by poor but friendly people who spoke a language that was totally unrecognisable and, most shockingly of all for the sailors, by women who were not interested in trading their bodies for anything they could offer. On 12 September 1774, Cook annexed 'New Caledonia' in the name of the King, then sailed the next morning to continue his survey.

Just off the southern end of the island, adjoining some more shoals, was a smaller island containing some bizarre structures like tall colonnades.

After much discussion, some argument and more investigation, they turned out to be a new kind of giant tree and the island was accordingly christened the 'Isle of Pines'. What followed was a strange episode that pointed to the changes in Cook since he had set off on his first voyage five years before. Then, he had laughed at the botanising obsession of Mr Banks and his Gentlemen; now, he was about to jeopardise the voyage just to get a closer look at those trees. Once again, the problem was shoals. In a grisly replica of his experiences on the Great Barrier Reef, he had unwittingly sailed into a large funnel of deadly reefs – at sunset and in gale-force winds. All night they tacked to and fro between the lethal banks of coral, serenaded by the crashing breakers that would mean certain death, with the men lining the deck and looking out. It was the longest of nights, and when daylight came, their commander made a surprise decision:

> I was now almost tired of a Coast I could no longer explore but as the risk of loosing the ship and ruining the whole voyage, but I was determined not to leave it till I was satisfied what sort of trees those were which had been the subject of our speculation. With this view we stood to the north.

He was deliberately sailing into the neck of the funnel – just to look at trees. It was bizarre, obsessive behaviour that the officers and men found hard to understand. Meanwhile, he found an anchorage near the shore and, taking the Forsters, went to explore. The infernal trees turned out to be a kind of spruce; ultimately, they became known as 'Cook Pines'.

With the captain away, his Master had taken to the masthead to search for a route around New Caledonia to explore its western side but at last Cook saw the light and agreed that the route ahead was just too risky and that a shipwreck would waste all their efforts thus far. But they were still left with the problem of escaping the labyrinth of shoals in which they were currently trapped. Once more, they were rescued by a change in the wind and, seizing the opportunity, they sailed southeast leaving the island in the distance.

The passage back to New Zealand was straightforward enough, even with the discovery of Norfolk Island due south of New Caledonia. They arrived back at the entrance to Queen Charlotte Sound on 18 October to evidence – both from the Maori and from the shore – that the *Adventure* had indeed returned, though by now she was long gone and Furneaux had failed to leave a note for his commander. Cook was not unduly worried: they set up camp, harvested the usual greens, and the locals 'embraced us over and over and skiped about like Mad men'. There was, however, clearly some nervousness on behalf of the Maori – nervousness, and much talk of killing – but they assured Cook that the *Adventure* had got away safely and he could do nothing but believe them.

His last few days in that favourite land were spent swallowing the painful truth about the error in his longitudes when drawing that very first chart of the country and also testing out the accuracy of the Harrison-Kendall chronometer. Although it had an accumulated error of just over 19 minutes, 31 seconds in just less than a year, this was deemed be an excellent result: Cook was now a convert to the mechanical method of determining longitude and would never again sail without this new and most trusted of friends.

On 10 November, restocked and ready for the final haul homewards, the *Resolution* finally left the waters of the Sound, headed through Cook Strait and then steered southeast towards the Horn. This time there was no last-minute turning: on 30 December, 1774, they rounded the tip of South America and sailed through the Strait of Le Maire, to the west of Staten Island. Cook had meantime pondered on his work in the Pacific:

> I … flatter my self that no one will think that I have left it unexplor'd.

But his work was not over yet: there was one final search to make for the Great Southern Continent. On his 1769 *Chart of the ocean between South America and Africa*, Dalrymple had located some alleged snatches of Continental coastline that lay in the Atlantic. Of these, the most significant were the Gulf of St Sebastian, just to the east of Staten Island and the Falklands, and Bouvet's Cape Circumcision, which Cook had searched for upon leaving the Cape at the start of the voyage in 1772. These now became his mission.

Cook already doubted that the large protrusion of the Gulf of St Sebastian existed but, this time, proving that it did not exist was relatively easy: heading eastwards from Staten Island, he sailed straight over what should have been land if Dalrymple's map was correct. Once again, it seemed, his old rival was peddling nothing but fiction. And then, on 14 January, as the winds grew colder, they brought sleet, snow, petrels and penguins – then, rising up in ghostly whiteness through the blizzard was the undeniable sight of land. At first, it looked like it could have been another berg but then the rocky mountains broke through the filter of the snowclouds, revealing slopes that led down to bays and headlands filled with ice. Was this the infamous Continent? If it was, it was hardly worth discovering, thought Cook. Further investigations revealed cliffs of sheer ice that split and went crashing into the sea and a coastline that eventually went around in a circle: it was just another island. The only inhabitants here were the seals, penguins and sea-birds; the only vegetation tussock grass and a few meagre plants. The land was generally 'savage and horrible'. The name was given by J. R. Forster – 'South Georgia'.

They left the barren isle on 20 January, 1775, sailing through shrouds of sleet and snow, keeping to the unexplored waters of the far south in search of signs of land, on little more than an inglorious mopping-up exercise – hardly inspiring after the discoveries and warmer climes of the tropics. Cook made a rare admission:

> I was now tired of these high Southern Latitudes where nothing was to be found but ice and thick fogs.

More sparse, broken land appeared on the horizon through the gaps in the thick fog that now fell round them like a cloak. A series of small islands stretched out in front of them,. If nothing else, it was a chance to flatter his men by conferring their names – Freezland Peak, Forster's Bay, Forster's Passage – a dubious honour, considering their captain described the land as 'the most horrible Coast in the world'. At least they were in good company: collectively he would call it 'Sandwich Land' after his supportive boss and mentor.

As to how far Sandwich land extended to the south – and whether it turned into the continuous land of a continent – that was really of little importance now. Any land that did exist was largely within the polar circle – no 'golden land' at all but one of blinding white ice:

> I can be bold to say, that no man will ever venture farther than I have done and that the lands which may lie to the South will never be explored. Thick fogs, Snow storms, Intense cold … the inexpressable horrid aspect of the Country, a Country doomed by Nature never once to feel the warmth of the Suns rays, but to lie for ever buried under everlasting snow and ice.

Dalrymple's dream was frozen into grim reality. Just one last land haunted him – Bouvet's Cape Circumcision. He now stretched east towards the southern tip of Africa.

They crossed the Greenwich Meridian on Valentine's Day 1775, still in the same latitude as Sandwich Land, surviving icebergs, gales and the 'prodigious high sea' that came from the south. Bouvet's land was nowhere to be seen, but then he was looking for it in the wrong place, led astray by inaccurate charts based on faulty co-ordinates. However, with the southern swell so great, Cook reasoned that if it did exist at all, it was certainly no great tranche of land. At best it was an island, and a small one at that. His reasoning was sound; the island lay northwest of his wake. As for Cook, he would leave it at that.

As he stood north for Cape Town, he knew his voyage of discovery was now complete.

> I had now made the circuit of the Southern Ocean in a high Latitude and traversed it in such a manner as to leave not the least room for the Possibility of their being a continent, unless near the Pole and out of the reach of Navigation; by twice visiting the Pacific Tropical Sea, I had not only settled the situation of some old discoveries but made there many new ones and left, I conceive, very little more to be done in that part. Thus I flatter my self that the intention of the Voyage has in every respect been fully Answered, the Southern Hemisphere sufficiently explored and a final end put to the searching after a Southern Continent, which has at times ingrossed the attention of some of the Maritime Powers for near two Centuries past and the Geographers of all ages.

He had also broken the tyranny of the idea that seawater could not freeze and therefore that any ice that floated in the sea had come from rivers and thus from land. He had proved that no rivers could flow in the extreme cold of Antarctica and therefore 'the Sea will freeze over'. Ever the scientist, he had eagerly taken part in experiments to measure the temperature of the Antarctic waters and found them to be below freezing point even in summer, a fact he put down to the 'Salts' it contained and the 'agitation' of the surface. Although baffled at times by the strange ocean currents, he had measured and logged them, arguably becoming the founding father of Antarctic oceanography; he was certainly the first to take such a rigorous approach to the study of those waters and his spirit of enquiry was, in turn, to stimulate much debate on his return by those Philosophick Gentlemen of the Royal Society, though not in time to dispel the idea of an ice-free sea at the North Pole, which would be a main driving force for his final, fatal voyage.

But all that was in the future: meanwhile, the weather grew warmer and the winds softened to a breeze. On 16 March, 1775, the watch spotted two ships on the horizon – the first they had seen since losing the *Adventure*. Two days later, the ships came alongside but, instead of general news of the world over the last few years, came some shocking news of his lost cohort, chilling his blood as much as any Antarctic ice: Furneaux had arrived at the Cape a year ago, safe and reasonably well, but with his crew badly depleted. When he was still in New Zealand, a boatload of his men had been viciously attacked and then eaten by the Maori.

So, the mumblings of killings from Queen Charlotte Sound were true. Cook was now numb: he felt passionately about the New Zealanders – they had been his welcoming hosts and had become his friends over the past six years. He knew of their habits, had written of them and excused them; now those habits had been turned on his own men. Had he really got the people so wrong? There must be a reason – and until he knew the facts, he was not prepared to comment further.

> I shall make no reflections on this Melancholy affair until I hear more about it. I shall only observe, in favour of these people, that I have found them no wickeder than other Men.

Other ships, including one British vessel, came into view and confirmed the *Adventure*'s story. To the *True Briton* he gave a note for the Admiralty giving their position and their state of health before sailing on north in an increasing wind. He told no one of the state of his own mind which was now doing somersaults to reconcile the stories with his own beliefs and experiences.

Two days later, at the end of March, he anchored in Cape Town's Table Bay which provided a salve, or at least a plug, to his worries. The men may have been in reasonable condition but the *Resolution* was in a pathetic state of repair: after 60,000 nautical miles, her sails were torn to shreds, her rudder damaged, her sides leaking. She would be five weeks in port being restored to health.

It was time for that botanising Mr Sparrman to take his leave of the Forsters and the ship, and continue his studies at the Cape; meanwhile, the men stretched out and enjoyed the hedonistic delights of so-called civilisation. Cook let them have their heads – there was a time for work and a time for rest; anyway, he was busy overseeing the works and tidying up his papers. For his men, he had nothing but praise; for the Harrison-Kendall chronometer, a damascene conversion to the joys of mechanical methods of determining longitude. The watch had 'exceeded the expectations of its most Zealous advocate' – high praise indeed from that measured pen. And then there was Furneaux's letter which awaited him, giving grisly details of the loss of eleven men and a boat in New Zealand, and then his route home. He had made no more discoveries on the way.

It was also at the Cape that he met Julien Marie Crozet, Captain of a French Indiaman that was anchored nearby. The two men were like-minded and quickly became close companions, comparing notes, maps and stories from their travels. He heard the tale of the voyage of Marion du Fresne, with whom Crozet had sailed to New Zealand; once there,

Marion du Fresne and yet more sailors were murdered by the Maori – making Furneaux's experiences part of a pattern. But even more gripping than the story of the Frenchmen was the chart he now showed Cook of their discoveries and sightings in the Pacific, which triggered in Cook's mind a new plan that could be launched when he returned home:

> All the discoveries, both Ancient and Modern [should be] laid down in a Chart and then an explanatory Memoir will be necessary and such a Chart I intend to construct when I have the time and the necessary materials.

A far less pleasing meeting was with a copy of 'his' journal, as rewritten by the official journalist, Dr John Hawkesworth. It was bad enough that it bulged with sycophantic references towards Joseph Banks – or sections that were really Banks's but attributed to the captain – but making matters worse still was the claim that Cook had allegedly read and even approved the edition – all news to him – particularly as it was littered with appalling mistakes. For a perfectionist such as Cook, this was mortifying in the extreme but there was little he could do: the journal by now was a *fait accompli* though it sealed his views about journalists and the press in general – and the need to keep strict control of his journals from the current voyage.

After five weeks in Cape Town, the works on the *Resolution* were finally complete; she was reloaded, resupplied and ready for the off. The port had delivered all that it had promised, with none of Batavia's deadly bacterial cargo. As before, her captain would not be leaving alone – an English East Indiaman, the *Dutton*, would be her escort and together they sailed out of the bay, to the serenade of a Danish band and a gunfire salute, on 27 April. Two weeks later, they arrived at St Helena.

The island's Governor was still his Great Ayton associate, John Skottowe, son of Thomas Skottowe, his childhood benefactor. This time the old acquaintances managed to meet up, although Skottowe's wife and friends were quick to tease him about the way his journal had portrayed their island. However, the joshing was not unkindly meant and they showered Cook with hospitality throughout his brief stay; he repaid them by writing a much more complimentary entry in his current journal.

The ships sailed again on 21 May, Cook to Ascension Island, the *Dutton* straight to home. The burdens of his mind and failing health seemed now to slip away into the familiar waters of the Atlantic and for the last few weeks of the voyage, Cook became the same captain of old: calm, focussed and almost boyish in his enthusiasm for discovery; for his crew, that meant that they, too, could finally relax – there would be no tantrumous heivas, rants or steely anger on this last leg of the journey.

After one last piece of obsessional legend-chasing when he headed northwest to fix the position of Fernando de Noronha off the coast of Brazil (it seemed a shame, Cook mused, to waste the opportunity for want of arriving home a week or so earlier), he at last set sail for the Azores and England. The waters grew familiar, the South England coastline unfurled with the welcome smile of a long-lost love. Then, on 30 July, 1775, he anchored at Spithead, having been away 'three years and eighteen days' on the greatest piece of exploration in the history of navigation.

24
TERRA AUSTRALIS COGNITA
George Collingridge 1885

Y THE TIME 1883 whistled to a close, George's curiosity had become a passion and soon the passion turned to obsession. He and his beloved wife, Lucy, had just lost their first child, stillborn on 17 October. The pain was acute. He headed into his study and he threw himself into his work.

His engraving kept him busy and earned the family a handsome income but like an itch that will not go away, he could not stop thinking about those maps. Gradually, he invested more and more time and energy into finding answers, pursuing his voyage of discovery with a commitment worthy of Cook himself – not through the unknown seas of the Southern Hemisphere, but through the uncharted territory of his continent's history, the continent he now called home: Australia, *Terra Australis Cognita* and perhaps, just perhaps, Jave la Grande.

His passage was slow and laborious. Few of the materials he needed were available locally or even in the colony so he would spend hours at night writing letters to the learned geographers of Europe and ordering materials and information; from 1882 there was a postal service in Berowra but he would still have to row the five or so miles down from his newly-discovered Collingridge Point to Berowra Waters, continuing on his way by horse or carriage just to mail the precious documents. But even that was not the end of the matter: there was just one postal service per week to Britain, leaving on a Thursday and then taking four to six weeks to reach Liverpool by boat (some boats being faster than others), and from there, a further day or two to reach the final destination.

By the 1880s, Britain was well-provisioned with railways; Europe was less fortunate and letters could easily spend a week or more getting to the

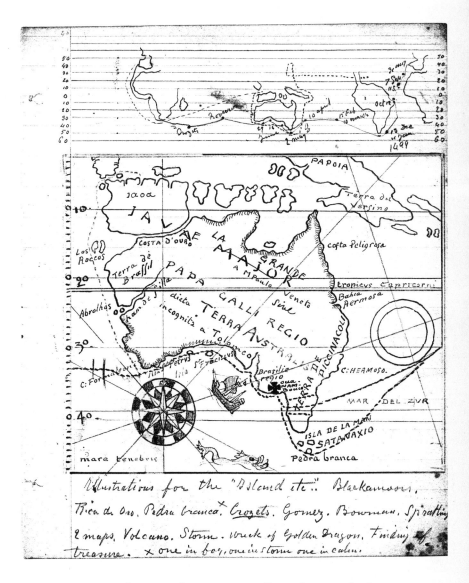

A working map from George Collingridge's notebook

relevant person or institution. The recipient would then need time to reply before the process was repeated, only this time in reverse. It is hard to imagine in these days of telephones, international couriers and email how much patience a researcher would need: a simple question might easily take four months to answer. And at least a letter could go by post: when George needed to go into Sydney for the Public Library, work or meetings of his historical society, he faced the five mile row to Berowra, followed by a three to four hours on horseback to Ryde, and then a ferry trip into the city.

Thankfully for this self-styled Hermit, his famous good humour and easy-going nature counterbalanced the extreme frustration he must so often have felt. Things were also going well at work: he was in demand for his engravings, busy with his campaigns to get road and rail access up to Berowra (he had already been active in the 1882 campaign for a postal service) and, on 6 January, 1885, Lucy gave birth to his first surviving child, a boy, whom they named Edward. Lucy now had her work cut out for her with her husband away in Sydney and a new baby in the middle of nowhere. Not much had changed for women in the previous 130 years since Elizabeth Cook had coped alone with her growing brood but, in some respects, Elizabeth was lucky: at least she could open her front door and see people, shops and transport – not for her the less-than-glamorous rowing-boat to civilisation from the house at Collingridge Point! However, there was no hint of complaint; Lucy was a mature woman of thirty-three when Edward was born, more than half-way through her life. Having been born and bred in Australia, she knew the hardships faced by rural settlers but, just like her adventurous émigré husband, the pioneering spirit flowed through her veins. She and George were an excellent match.

There is no doubt that George loved Berowra: he had gained enormous satisfaction in putting that extra five miles of shoreline, from Still Creek to Calabash Bay, literally on the map and the place offered him a soulful retreat from the mad pace of life in the colonial city; but still the flames of his geographical and historical researches burned within him. When another child, Catherine, was born in November 1887, their life in the bush became even more impractical, and a year later, the Hermit of Berowra had had enough: he put down a deposit on three acres of land in the outlying Sydney suburb of Hornsby and, after one false start, built a small stone cottage. There was only one name for this new family home – a name that enshrined his passion and proved that home was where his heart was. He called it 'Jave la Grande'.

The cottage still stands, with the name of his obsession resolutely mounted on the wall. Now a chapel in the grounds of the hospital at Hornsby, his granddaughters took me round one Saturday afternoon. Walking around the perimeter, they regaled me with stories of how George used to summon his children back from playing in the dense bush by standing at the doorway and blowing a silver bugle, just like the father in *The Sound of Music*. A true eccentric, it seemed George did everything with style. We borrowed the keys from the janitor and stepped inside.

Although the cottage had been partly remodelled, there were traces of George everywhere from his photo and landscapes in the antechapel to the original painted glass he had made for the windows. It felt strange seeing the rows of plastic chairs lined up for the congregation in what should have been his sitting room; it was even more bizarre to catch sight of a lectern, cross and church organ. George had spent the second half of his life preaching the Word on the discovery of Australia and now his sitting room was devoted to the other great belief of his life. As for me, I felt slightly uncomfortable coming to his house on a personal pilgrimage when people would normally flock here for religious observation. It was unnerving enough just talking out loud in the hushed half-light of the chapel-cum-museum; posing for photographs outside seemed distinctly sacrilegious. George himself was staunchly Catholic – would he see the irony in the visit? I suspected he would have been faintly pleased and hugely amused at the whole situation. We paid our respects and left.

By the turn of 1890, seven years after the birth of his obsession for uncovering his continent's past, George sat in his study at Jave la Grande looking at the story so far. The blank sheet of Pacific history was gradually filling in as each correspondence bore fruit; experts across Europe sent him generous replies, books, maps and papers and, little by little, an outline appeared. His grasp of languages had allowed him to spread his net far and wide and, within a few short months, although he was a lone voice in Australia, he now found a few key soulmates in Britain and France who were similarly intrigued by the mysterious set of maps.

One of these was Keeper of Maps in the British Museum: Richard Henry Major. He had written a paper as early as 1859 suggesting that the maps – though drawn by French cartographers – were based on Portuguese originals from Portuguese discoveries in the Pacific and Indian oceans. However, some of his evidence was uncertain, other arguments were overstretched to breaking point and he finally lost his nerve to uphold his ideas, switching the honour of discovery to the Provençal French – and losing much of his professional credibility along the way.

When George had first come across the Dieppe Maps in 1883, the arguments had been a mêlée of confusion consigned to the extreme fringes of geographical debate. By the time he made contact with Major, the Keeper had retired from the library, rather shaken by the rough treatment his theories had received. However, Major was still intrigued by the curious series of charts and the two men entered into a private geographical debate, sharing contacts and information, testing their ideas and evolving new ones to try to solve the riddle of the maps. Like children in a secret pact, they spurred each other on, not always agreeing but remaining respectful friends until Major's death in 1891. One of his last letters was to George and, inevitably, it concerned yet another possible line of enquiry.

George also became a close correspondent with Elisée Reclus, the great French geographer. In many ways, Reclus was a man after George's heart: a former Communard, he had taken part in daring ascents by balloon from the besieged Paris before being captured by the army and sentenced to death; his life was only saved by the outcry from his geographical colleagues who pleaded for clemency, and instead he was sent to live in exile in Switzerland. However, the friendship between George and Reclus is all the more remarkable given that it was the Communards who had wrecked George's Paris studio in May 1871. But he was too big a man to bear a grudge, and anyway, the greater battle was now for the truth. Through Reclus, he published two early articles in the *Bulletin* of the Neuchatel Société de Géographie which bolstered his confidence: Australia may have been resistant to his radical theories but this gained him some much-needed academic credibility abroad.

The fire of curiosity burned stronger with each passing year; the more he learned, the more it seemed there was to learn. With no language barriers to stand in his way, he scoured the whole of Europe for the slightest reference to early exploration and geographical thought, going back centuries and then millennia. So engrossed would he be in his work that he would write on anything that came to hand – the back of old pamphlets, tiny sheets a few inches tall, even bills from his book-buying – and, when he had used up the last inch of space in his notebook, he would turn the book round ninety-degrees and continue writing his train of thought at right angles to his original lines. The result would be almost impenetrable to anyone trying to decipher his work.

Australia's National Library still holds his archives: a mountain of old school jotters or ones that were home-made from scraps of browning folded paper, lapsing from one language into another as if he barely noticed. The thick black inky writing jags up and down like an excited needle on a seismograph, the lines getting closer and closer as space becomes at a premium, until they are almost illegible. One thing is clear: they are the work of a man of passion – sewn up with gold and scarlet silken threads the way a child might bind a treasured story as a gift – a work of passion *and* torment. The puzzle of the maps ate away at him until every spare moment was spent in his researches and writings. The faded pages of his notebooks still bubble with embroidered inky doodles of caravels half-drowned by stormy waves while ghostly sea-monsters snake through the foaming waters with eerie sirens' calls. Over one hundred years on, they still cannot be silenced.

Lord Sandwich. Engraving by Valentine Green,
after Johan Zoffany

<h1 style="text-align: center;">25</h1>

THE DINNER PARTY

James Cook 1775

OSEPH BANKS steered clear of London that summer of 1775. It suited him to be elsewhere, sailing down the Channel with his high-ranking friends. Over the past three years, he had matured enough to look ruefully at his pre-voyage histrionics with shame and embarrassment – and anyway, he could rest safe in the knowledge that his true and honest friend, Daniel Solander, would keep him abreast of the captain's return. Banks had long since mended fences with Lord Sandwich but Cook's lengthy absence had prevented any *rapprochement* with the *Resolution's* much-maligned commander. Luckily, Solander did not disappoint: his first letter on the subject came straight from the lion's den:

> Two o Clock Monday [31 August, 1775]
> ... this moment Capt Cook is arrived. I have not yet had an oportunity of conversing with him, as he is still in the board-room – giving an account of himself & Co. He looks as well as ever. By and by, I shall be able to say a little more ...

The Captain had just arrived at the Admiralty by post-chaise from Portsmouth with the Forsters, William Hodges, William Wales and the chronometer that was now his trusty friend. Philip Stephens, the Admiralty Secretary, was ready and waiting, having already received the bundles of papers and charts that Cook had sent ahead. He was not disappointed in what he had read – far from it; even knowing Cook as well as he did, the voyage notes and charts had taken his breath away. Last time he had returned, it was Banks that got the glory; this time, it would be the captain himself.

His bosses did not keep him long, knowing that he was anxious to be in Mile End with his family. He gave a brief account of the last three years, praised his men and was then released from the boardroom. Solander was waiting outside. The two men greeted each other with the genuine warmth of old and respected friends. Cook passed on his very best wishes to Banks, as did Charles Clerke who gave Solander an effusive letter to enclose with his own. Compared with the miserable, complaining and tetchy John Forster, even Banks' worst tantrums were now forgivable.

There is no record of the meeting at Mile End between James and Elizabeth Cook, though we know from Solander's letter that he raced home to see her; the fact that Elizabeth was pregnant again within weeks of his return suggests the reunion was a happy one but it wasn't all smiles: in a macabre rerun of his return home in 1771, he learned the tragic news of his baby son's death. George had lived for just four months before dying with his father still *en route* to Antarctica in October 1772. As for his surviving boys, James was now a healthy and active twelve-year-old, studying at the Naval Academy in Portsmouth and his brother Nathaniel would soon be following in his footsteps. In itself, that was a sign of Cook's growing esteem – you could only get your sons into the Naval Academy if you had a reputation or connections and, by now, Cook was growing in both. His children had little need of a benefactor like Thomas Skottowe.

Less pleased with news of the captain's return was his old adversary, Alexander Dalrymple. The dreams and schemes of this thirty-eight-year-old would-be discoverer of the Great Southern Continent were laid to waste in an instant: there was no *terra australis incognita*, no great land of wealth and beauty, no chance for Dalrymple to be fêted as its champion until the end of time. The seed of desire that had lodged in his brain and been nurtured for almost two decades had now been crushed. The Continent was nothing but geographical fantasy – and Dalrymple looked a fool. However, Cook had not only scuppered his private plans; in 1775, Dalrymple had published his *Collection of Voyages, chiefly in the Southern Atlantick Ocean*, which had not only printed charts of the sections of 'Continent' that had been discovered, it also laid bare his offer to go there at his own expense to start colonising it for Britain. As the nation reeled at press reports that no such Continent existed, Dalrymple boiled with rage that, once again, Cook had usurped his glory.

It was not just Dalrymple who was shocked that no Continent had been found: the newspapers seemed almost unsure how to report this voyage of discovery whose biggest find was of the *non-existence* of a land that had been written, sung and spoken about for more than a thousand years. The myth had pervaded every stratum of society, from Kings, Queens and the erudite men of the Royal Society, to the lowest rank of mariner, who staked their lives in pursuit of the dream. Now, struggling to find something more newsworthy to write about, the papers contrived to hype-up the discoveries of new islands, with fertile soils and civilised peoples, but the reports all fell flat. It was as if Apollo 11 had failed to find the moon.

Thankfully, in its place British society had already found another star to worship. Captain Furneaux had returned from the voyage a year earlier with the young Tahitian man called Mae, and – if society wanted exotica – it found it in him. Mae had been called 'Jack' by his shipmates, and later became known under his adoptive name of 'Omai'. To a Britain already enthralled with the magic of the South Seas, Omai was a wondrous spectacle. Just as his name had been refashioned to suit his hosts, upon his arrival into London Society Omai was transformed from a middle-ranking refugee of a defeated nation to nothing less than the very embodiment of the Noble Savage. Banks, of course, swooped on him – where Tupia had died, here at last were his lions and tigers and curios all rolled into one. He dressed him in the finest clothes, introduced him to the finest of his friends and instilled him with the finest manners – he even famously was introduced to the King and Queen, and reportedly greeted the monarch with the words, 'How do, King Tosh'! Within weeks, the 'wild Indian' of the early press coverage of 1774 was a 'private Gentleman of a small fortune', courtesy of an allowance from King Tosh himself. His portrait was painted by Sir Joshua Reynolds, Nathaniel Dance and William Parry, he was entertained by Dr Johnson, Lord Sandwich and the Burneys. Britain was swept up in Omai fever and the impressionable, twenty-something, young man loved every single second of it.

Upon their return, the Forsters (of course) were appalled: Omai should be learning useful skills to benefit Tahiti on his return, not which knife and fork to use at dinner; but to the wider intelligentsia, he was an intriguing specimen of a primitive society, unsullied by the corrupting influences of so-called 'civilisation'. Here was man in the raw, with his innate goodness and a background in the Arcadian paradise of the South Seas. The magic of those islands had been spread first by Wallis and then unwittingly stimulated by Cook, who had written in his *Endeavour* journal how the people seemed to live almost effortlessly off the fruits of nature without any of the toil of their European counterparts. Here, then, was a land of bountiful food, glorious sunshine and sexual freedom; Bougainville had even called the islands Nouvelle Cythere, after the Greek island famous for its cult of Aphrodite, goddess of beauty and sexual love. Omai was thus conceived as a child of nature from a society suspended in time. A measuring stick for the eager philosophers, he was the key to understanding our own fall from grace. He was the trophy of the Enlightenment and living proof of everything Europeans had lost – and for those less interested in such highbrow ideas, he was also the main subject of intrigue in every form of literature from poetry to pantomime and also in pornography.

Meanwhile, the 'civilisation' of Omai was on line for his destruction. Praised by Fanny Burney and James Boswell for his impeccable manners, his head swelled with the sense of his own importance; he demanded toys and European clothes and learned to gamble like a professional. Few could anticipate how this painted doll who tantalised both science and entertainment would smash on the sands of his native land. Civilisation was rarely kind to its guests – and so it would prove with Omai.

Once again, Cook's return had been overshadowed by a media-darling but soon he noticed a sea-change in his own reputation. Things started coolly enough, with the usual press reports of his return and the disappointing news that the famed Southern Continent did not exist, but soon the official gloss began to shine through into the upper echelons of eighteenth-century London. His voyage was the subject of passionate interest in the rarefied circles of the Royal Society and, on 9 August, 1775, he had a personal audience with the King where he was officially promoted to full post-captain. For the first time in his life, ahead stretched a life of ease: a residence at Greenwich Hospital with a fine pension of £230 per annum, free fuel and an allowance of over a shilling a day. He replied, graciously accepting the post, though laying out one condition:

> If I am fortunate enough to merit their Lordships approbation, they will allow me to quit it when either the call of my Country for more active Service, or that my endeavours in any shape can be essential to the publick; as I would on no account be understood to withdraw from that line of service which their Lordships goodness has raised me to, knowing myself Capable of ingaging in any duty which they may be pleased to commit to my charge.

The Admiralty agreed to this demand and meanwhile set about confirming the promotions suggested by Cook for his men, most significant of which was the promotion of Charles Clerke to captain of the *Resolution*, which would be repaired and sent straight back to Tahiti to take that country's celebrity visitor home.

As before, a truer expression of Cook's own feelings was communicated to his Whitby friend, John Walker, a week after his royal appointment. After thanking him for his letters and 'kind enquiryes', he continues:

> My fate drives me from one extream to an other. A few Months ago the whole Southern hemisphere was hardly big enough for me and now I am going to be confined within the limits of Greenwich Hospital, which are far too small for an active mind like mine, I must however confess it is a fine retreat and a pretty income, but whether I can bring my self to like ease and retirement, time will shew ...

Less than a month later, on 14 September, he wrote again to his friend:

> I did expect and was in hopes that I had put an end to all Voyages of this kind to the Pacific Ocean ... but Sending home Omai will occasion another voyage which I expect will soon be undertaken.

Cook was slowly acknowledging that he was tired – tired of his endless days and nights of uncertainty, of unrelenting pressure to perform and of the sheer volume of work that discoveries entailed. He was nearly forty-seven, with a fraying temper, a capricious digestive system, a possibly diseased gall-bladder and a weary heart. He now sat at his desk with a mountain of papers and charts to prepare, a newly-pregnant wife next door and two boys he had scarcely seen all their lives. An easy future beckoned – if only he could escape the siren's call of the sea.

For the remainder of 1775, he was busy enough to bury the dilemma. Two uncomfortable meetings were avoided – with Furneaux, who had been sent overseas within days of his return, and with Dr Hawkesworth, who had published Cook's account of his first voyage. The journalist who had so 'mortified' Cook with his rendition of the journals had gone to print, collected his astounding £6,000 fee and even seeing his work reprinted within two months. And then the critics started their attack. Dalrymple launched in, furious that Cook had not done more to chase after his beloved Continent; reviewers panned his style, his opinions and amateur theorising. It was Hawkesworth's turn to be mortified. This was meant to have been his big break as a writer; instead, Hawkesworth's nerves frayed beyond repair and within six months of the June release he was dead.

The consequences for Cook were significant and very much to his approval: the Admiralty decreed that this time the captain would write up his own journal, with a little help, when needed, from his friends. It was a conclusion one suspects that Cook had already decided upon – his second journal is full of revisions, theorising, attempts to make sense of the world he was encountering, not only for himself but for a wider audience. He is no longer writing as 'just' a captain but as a confident and highly competent commentator. The only unfortunate matter was in the Admiralty's choice of friend – John Reinhold Forster.

Unlike Omai, Forster needed no one else to bolster his sense of importance. He was convinced that Cook and the Admiralty needed him – and not only that, but that he would write the story of the voyage and claim the vast financial and social rewards that it would bring. What followed was a travesty of human pomposity: Forster's sample chapter was rejected, there were tantrums worthy of Banks himself, accusations of vanity and intractability, counter-accusations that Cook wrote with 'inaccuracies and vulgar expressions' and finally, when he refused to have his work corrected, the inevitable acrimony of Forster's divorce from the Admiralty. He blamed everyone except himself. One mediator described him as 'certainly out of his senses'; Cook described him as deceitful and an 'undeserving man'. His presence would not be missed.

Throughout the animosity, the captain had kept as far from the flying letters and venom as he could; not only was he uninterested in becoming embroiled in a vicious slanging-match, he was racing against time to edit his journals for publication. With editorial help from the Rev. John Douglas, the canon of Windsor, he finished the journals just in time – not for publication, but for his own departure – and the voyage now in mind was somewhat longer than the road from Mile End to the Greenwich Hospital.

Upon his return from the South Seas, the Admiralty had informed him that the *Resolution* was to be immediately overhauled and sent once more to the Pacific to return Omai to Tahiti – at least, that would be the official story. Once again, under the guise of a simpler mission lay an audacious plan that would burn its way into the history books, but this time it was not the *South* Pacific that formed the area of enquiry: this time, they were planning a voyage to the North Pacific, in search of the Northwest Passage.

Along with the Great Southern Continent, the Northwest Passage formed the other great geographical conundrum of the age; both marked the union of scientific and trade interests, both linked the Navy with the Royal Society. But whereas the Continent would have brought the discovering nation new lands to colonise and trade with, the Northwest Passage represented a new route to the old established trading nations of Asia. When Pope Alexander VI had divided the undiscovered world into two between Spain and Portugal then France, the Netherlands and

England, who also had discovering and trading aspirations of their own, were left without a sea route to the lucrative lands of Asia either via Africa or South America. This was the significance of the Northwest Passage: if politics prevented you getting to Asia by a southern route, there must be a passage to the north of America, or via a northeast passage to the north of Russia that would not be barred by Papal decree – the only perceived difficulty was finding it.

The assumption that a passage must exist was based on faulty science. Even as late as the eighteenth century, it was generally believed amongst the learned that sea water did not freeze – and therefore all so-called 'sea ice' must come from freshwater streams and rivers on the land. Cook himself had been surprised to find that the icebergs of Antarctica had yielded fresh water and it had given him much pause for thought over their origins. His scientific discoveries were not yet published and his verbal accounts had yet to be absorbed and verified; meantime, the belief persisted that without land and its freshwater rivers, the sea would be clear of ice and thus also clear of any impediment to sailing through the Passage over the Pole to the prized trading-grounds of Asia. All that it needed was luck, daring and skilled navigation.

The first recorded British attempt had been made in 1497, when Henry VII sent John Cabot in search of a northerly route to the Orient. Over the next two hundred and fifty years, this was followed by around fifty more goes at finding the entrance to the passage by probing tempting rivers such as the St Lawrence or Hudson's Bay or the Davis Strait. All had met with failure; many had not returned at all. The main difference between the Great Southern Continent and this other geographical challenge was that the Northwest Passage does, of course, exist – the only problem is that it lies five hundred miles inside the Arctic Circle, extending for nine hundred miles through Canada's Arctic Islands and the route is littered with thousands of giant icebergs fringing the outlying edges of the polar ice cap. From Cabot's voyage to the first successful non-stop transit of the Passage at the end of World War II would take almost four hundred and fifty years – and many more lives.

By the time Cook returned home in 1775, plans were already underway to send a voyage of discovery in search of the sea route to Asia. Behind the scenes, lawyers and Admiralty Lords had been beavering away to get an extension of the 1745 Act that granted a massive £20,000 in prize money for whoever discovered the Passage; in monetary terms, it was the equivalent of solving the longitude problem; commercially, in the long run, discovery of the Passage was even more valuable. In December 1775, after almost a year spent going through the House, the new Act became law and the riches were laid on the table, ready for the taking.

The Admiralty's hopes were vested in the *Resolution* under the command of Charles Clerke – and, as the most experienced navigator of Pacific and icy waters, Cook would be its consultant. He scoured the available literature for charts and maps and accounts of foreign voyages, placing alleged coastlines over alleged coastlines to see where any congruence lay, storing up knowledge of histories, explorations and ocean currents as if they were precious kegs of sauerkraut and pickled cabbage to be lodged in the holds of his mind. He amassed every shred of information on the region and then sat down to devise the best possible route – from the Cape to Tahiti, then up the west coast of America to Drake's New Albion, modern-day California, and beyond to the coasts and seas of Vitus Bering.

At the beginning of the eighteenth century, surprisingly little was known about the northern coasts of Europe – still less if Russia was joined to America or whether they were different continents. In 1728, the year of Cook's birth, Bering had signed up with the Russian Navy to lead an expedition to solve this question and search for any passage between the two landmasses. He went through the Strait that bears his name (it had previously been discovered by Semyon Dezhnyov but as so often happened, that knowledge had been lost) and although he could not see America because of the fog, he concluded that the two lands were indeed separate. He was not believed.

In 1741, he set off to the region once more with his former lieutenant, Alexei Chirikov, in search of what lay beyond Siberian shores but after only a fortnight, the two men were separated. Chirikov went on to discover some of the Aleutian Islands while Bering sailed into the Gulf of Alaska, surveying its southwest coast before moving on to the Alaska Peninsula and more of the Aleutian Islands. Within a few months, however, Bering's ship was so wracked with scurvy that it crashed on an island off the Kamchatka coast, killing most of the crew and also its captain. Chirikov had also glimpsed the American coastline but ran out of water and had to return to Kamchatka less than three months after they had set off.

Cook now managed to track down some translated accounts of the voyages and, best of all, a map – the Müller map – depicting the coastline of northern Asia including the Kamchatka peninsula, the Aleutian islands that had been sighted and even some sketchy outlines of the Alaskan and American coasts. However, this map gave little suggestion of a Northwest Passage; it barely had the west coast of America with any degree of certainty. He was also given an altogether different map, by a man called

Jacob von Stählin – secretary to the Academy of Sciences. This was based on Russian trading voyages across the Aleutian islands to Alaska and purported (by Stähliná himself) to be a 'very accurate little Map of the new discovered Northern Archipelago, which is drawn up from original accounts'. Unfortunately, the author had too high an opinion of his contributors' veracity: his 'Alaschka' was an island, some way off the American shore. Significantly, however, it also left a potential passageway open to the north of that continent.

As voyage consultant, Cook studied the maps and histories and journals, had discussions with the Admiralty and the learned gentlemen of the Royal Society, and gradually worked out a plan. The best route would be via the Cape of Good Hope, across the area where the French (according to his new friend, Crozet) had recently made their discoveries, then into the Pacific and to Tahiti where Omai would be returned. And from there? For Cook, the northern Pacific was an unknown quantity but, using Tahiti as a base for refreshment, it could be explored in a series of forays until the coastlines were surveyed and the potential passage explored.

Seventeen seventy-five rolled on with Cook busier than ever on his journals and preparations for what would probably be Captain Clerke's voyage. For the first time in four years, he spent Christmas with his family, and the new year could at last be faced with happiness by his long-suffering Elizabeth: she would give birth to her sixth child who would grow up knowing *both* his parents, they were now financially secure and, after thirteen years of marriage, she would finally have her beloved James at home by her side. Seventeen seventy-six, it seemed, was surely a year to celebrate.

For Cook, the dark days of January were spent in offices and boardrooms, meetings and maprooms, working out the details for the forthcoming voyage. It was hard to let go and accept that this was not *his* voyage: it was his conception, as much as the child in Elizabeth's belly. It was the object of his passion and inspiration; and his mind, that so feared containment, had a whole new ocean to consider – an ocean that held a geographical puzzle that had teased men for centuries, a puzzle with a £20,000 prize.

The pivotal moment was not officially documented, but twelve years later Andrew Kippis, his first biographer, wrote of the evening and his version is as likely as it is dramatic. Four gentlemen were at a dinner party – Hugh Palliser, Philip Stephens, James Cook and Lord Sandwich, who was hosting the event. Its purpose was simple: to decide the list of officers for the forthcoming voyage, a voyage of immense national, strategic, scientific and commercial importance. The three Admiralty men knew whom they really wanted to take command but they would never presume to ask. The man in question had spent too many years away from home and had contributed more than anyone could ever have hoped. His reward was to be retirement, not the pressure of refusing a command.

The evening progressed as the four went through the remit of the voyage, its importance for the country and the possible options for commander. As the wine flowed, so did the conversation and so did the passions. Who should command such a prestigious voyage? Charles Clerke was the obvious choice – experienced, sensible, but did he really have the *gravitas* to lead his men on a dangerous voyage into the unknown? There were few others suitable for such a task – John Gore was another capable pair of hands, but did he have the capacity for such leadership? One by one, the names were raised along with doubts and objections. And then he could bear it no more. Cook jumped up and announced to the room that he, himself, would command the voyage – if the Lords would agree to such a proposal. The Lords most certainly would.

It is said that a cheer went up from the remaining gentlemen – this is what they had dreamed of, but would never have presumed to ask. Any pressure from Sandwich, Philip Stephens and Palliser was tacitly expressed: of course everyone *wanted* Cook to command the voyage – he was really the only man for the job – but here he was at 47, with a comfortable retirement stretching out ahead of him and the opportunity to live out his days as a respected post-captain with a record that would stand for all eternity, and on top of that he finally had the chance to be with the wife and children he adored. So why on earth would he risk all that for a venture that would take him back to an ocean he had already admitted that he hoped to quit forever, and then into the menacing ice that had worn him down over the last three years?

Why indeed. There was no doubt at all that he *was* the best man for the job and that he knew this as well as his superiors. He was the most experienced at discovery, at negotiating unknown coasts and Pacific winds and waters. What is more, his 'capacity and genius' as a surveyor had been recognised for years. In short, he had all the skills required for the forthcoming voyage. But that doesn't explain why he volunteered.

Part of the reason was duty: his sense of duty to the Admiralty to do the best job he could was never in doubt. What surprised his bosses, and the public at large, was the level to which he went *beyond* his duty – two great sweeps of the Pacific in the last voyage alone – and to a large extent, he was going beyond his duty now. That was his mission as he perceived it. A month after his return home, he had written to a young Frenchman who hoped to make his name as a discoverer. How do you become a famous explorer? The key, Cook replied, was simple:

> Car je soutiens que celui qui ne fait qu'exécuter des orders ne fera jamais grandes figures dans le découvertes.
> [For I believe that he who learns only how to obey orders can never be a great explorer.]

A man would never achieve much in terms of discovery if he only stuck to his orders. But there was more. Throughout his voyages there was a need to prove himself: it is there in his apologia or explanations for his actions; it underpins his concern over what the Admiralty would think of his behaviour and it is the reason for him diverting halfway across the Atlantic on his way home after three years at sea to survey Fernando de Noronha *because it is there*. The North Pacific was also 'there' – and it called to him like a seductress. Without discovery, without a reputation, without work he did not exist, and this had driven his passion and his obsession for the last thirty years.

Other factors were less glorious, but they drove him just the same. The first was control – and this was much easier to achieve at sea where he was supreme commander than on land with its Dalrymples and Hawkesworths and gentlemen's committees. On land, he was at the mercy of other people's chaos; within the confines of the ship his world was orderly, disciplined and emotionally safe – his word was law, and his men obeyed.

The final factor in his decision to command a third voyage was status. He had designed and steered the course of the forthcoming voyage, lived with it and breathed it. Then, sat around that dinner table, came the crystallisation of reality: someone else could end up leading it, someone else could end up with the status and the honour that was rightfully his, while he collected his pension in his room in Greenwich Hospital. For Captain James Cook, that was not going to happen. At sea, in his ship, his own status was assured: he was the captain, even the Gentlemen looked to him – but all that changed as soon as he reached the land. It was evident in the tone of letters between him and Joseph Banks – polite, engaged but never without the barriers of class or with the warmth of genuine friendship that so marked his correspondence with John Walker in Whitby. The rigid hierarchy of the eighteenth century was beginning to loosen – the rising wealth from the Industrial Revolution and political turmoil was seeing to that – but you still needed money to uphold the lifestyle of a member of the social élite. He may not have been born to greatness like Joseph Banks or Lord Sandwich, but he had cleverly and capably worked his way up the social ladder to a position of respect. Trouble was, it was never quite enough to look a real gentleman in the eye. Respect was only half the entry-ticket: he also needed a personal fortune to become a man of substance, with all the ostentatious trappings of wealth that the times demanded. If he could now discover the Northwest Passage and win the lion's share of the £20,000 prize, his place in society would be assured. And, as ever, he had calculated well.

As soon as he volunteered himself as commander, Sandwich went to the King who instantly gave his approval. He was congratulated by the Royal Society and also the Navy and, suddenly, he had the makings of a hero. If Omai had monopolised the limelight from the last voyage, he was now a tiresome plaything compared with the new champion of the day: Captain James Cook – commander of the Navy's expedition to discover the Northwest Passage. What Elizabeth had to say about his sudden appointment was never documented.

Over the next few months, she was to see even less of her husband as he began a race against time to finish his book of the second voyage and get his ships ready for the third. On 14 February, 1776, he took time out to write to his old friend, John Walker, laying out his plans and hinting at his motives.

> I should have Answered your last favour sooner, but waited to know whether I should go to the Greenwich Hospital, or the South Sea. The latter is now fixed upon; I expect to be ready to sail about the latter end of Apl with my old ship the Resolution and the Discovery, the ship lately purchased off Mr Herbert. I know not what your opinion may be on this step I have taken. It is certain I have quited an easy retirement for an Active, and perhaps Dangerous Voyage. My present disposition is more favourable to the latter than the former, and I imbark on as fair a prospect as I can wish. If I am fortunate enough to get safe home, theres no doubt but it will be greatly to my advantage.

'Greatly to my advantage': as ever, he anticipated success in finding the Passage and winning his share of the £20,000. But it also sounds like he was expecting something more. A vast bounty from his journals and charts? Further promotion? A knighthood, perhaps? He made no other comment but here, at last, is the honest Cook: the Voyage was as much to benefit him as it was for the benefit of his country – and he seems to have forgotten his degenerating health and temper from the last time he was at sea.

Meanwhile, there were other matters that needed attending to: he was preparing a paper for the Transactions of the Royal Society on the health of his men at sea; he had legal wrangles over his brother-in-law who had been caught smuggling; and there was also the curious occurrence of him having his portrait painted. Admittedly, this was not his own idea – it had been organised and paid for by Joseph Banks – and although the artist was not Reynolds (as for Omai) but the second-string Nathaniel Dance, the portrait certainly bolstered Cook's social standing. He was flattered at this sudden aggrandisement and the likeness was remarked to be a good one.

As his status rose, so did the demands for his company. He mingled with the great and the good of the arts and science world at Young Slaughter's Coffee House in St Martin's Lane and Jack's Coffee House nearby. He met with James Boswell, the great diarist and friend of Samuel Johnson, who quickly became enraptured by the great circumnavigator, finding him

> a plain, sensible man with an uncommon attention to veracity. My metaphor was that he had a ballance in his mind for truth as nice as scales for weighing a guinea … He seemed to have no desire to make people stare, and being a man of good steady moral principles, as I thought, did not try to make theories out of what he had seen to confound virtue and vice.

Ever a man of passion, Boswell even resolved to accompany Cook to the South Seas – though he was quickly disabused of this rather fanciful notion. He did, however, meet his new hero soon after for dinner at the Royal Society Club where the President, Sir John Pringle, apologised for the quality of the food:

> 'I have had a feast,' said I, (pointing to the Captain;) 'I have had a good dinner, for I have had a good *Cook*.'

A few days after that, he visited Cook at home in Mile End and later presented him with a copy of his book, *An Account of Corsica*, in recognition of their friendship; together they had discussed the woes of editors, with Cook telling his friend of the sorry tale of Dr John Hawkesworth. Boswell had retorted, 'Why, Sir, Hawkesworth has used your narrative as a London Tavern-keeper does wine. He has brewed it!'

However, the meeting that gave Cook the most pleasure of all was on 7 March, 1776, when he was duly admitted as a Fellow of the Royal Society. He had been nominated shortly after his return by an incredible twenty-six Fellows including Banks and Solander, the Astronomer Royal, Nevil Maskelyne, and a host of dignitaries from the world of science; not only that, they lauded him with the humbling citation:

> Captain James Cook, of Mile-end a gentleman skilful in astronomy, & the successful conductor of two important voyages for the discovery of unknown countries, by which geography and natural history have been greatly advantaged & improved, being desirous of the honour of becoming a member of this Society, we whose names are underwritten, do, from our personal knowledge testify, that we believe him deserving of such honour, and that he will become a worthy and useful member.

The month afterwards, his famous paper on the health of seamen was published in the Society's *Philosophical Transactions* and he and Elizabeth – now heavily pregnant – were invited to dine at home with the President himself; then, a few months later, he joined Nevil Maskelyne in nominating his good friend and fellow scientist of the *Resolution*, William Wales, to become a Fellow, too. In short, if he wanted status and respect, he had won it: Captain James Cook was now a fully-fledged member of the intelligentsia of eighteenth-century London. But this was never going to be enough: on the table was the prize money and even greater respect – and he would, of course, go after that 'because it was there'.

In all the whirl of social gatherings and accolades, Cook had not forgotten the voyage that lay ahead of him. In many ways, he was lucky: had he stayed on active service it was possible that he would have been sent, like Furneaux, to the war in America, which had broken out in 1775. War was not Cook's style; his abhorrence of extreme force may well have aided his diversion into surveying during the French and Indian Wars.

For this most famous of navigators, his mission was rapidly taking shape: he would take two ships, the *Resolution* and a recent acquisition, the *Discovery*, to the Cape of Good Hope, then onwards in search of the lands reportedly discovered by Kerguelen and Marion du Fresne. After validating – or not – the French discoveries, he should head to New Zealand for refreshment if it were needed, then on to Tahiti where he would deposit Omai. By then, it would be the start of 1777 so, to make the most of the spring and summer season, he should head to Drake's New Albion on the American coast, sailing northwards from a latitude of around 45° (just south of modern-day Seattle) to 65° (just short of the Arctic Circle) 'or farther, if you are not obstructed by Lands or Ice'. If a Northwest Passage existed anywhere, the best available advice showed that it should be here, so Cook was to make a detailed investigation of 'such Rivers or Inlets as may appear to be of a considerable extent, and pointing towards Hudsons or Baffins Bay'. If he discovered the Passage, he should sail through it; if not, he was to spend the winter of 1777–78 at the Kamchatka Peninsula on the Russian side of the North Pacific, before trying again the following spring for either a Northwest or a Northeast Passage and returning home by the best available route 'for the improvement of Geography and Navigation'.

As ever, his scheduled departure was already slipping: April became May and May rolled into June. James and Elizabeth's sixth child was born – a boy named Hugh after James's good friend and mentor, Hugh Palliser. Meanwhile, the two ships the *Resolution* and *Discovery* were being fitted and supplied in the naval dockyards, under as watchful an eye as Cook could afford, given his journal and other demands on his time. Unfortunately for the voyage commander, his eye was not watchful enough. *Resolution* had spent six months in the yard and dock at Deptford. In those six months there should have been plenty of time to give her a thorough overhaul; instead, the work was shoddy and she would leak like a sieve giving nothing but problems from the moment she sailed.

The *Discovery*, however, was a fine ship – another collier in the Whitby style and one who would prove herself faster and more nimble than her famous companion. She would take 70 men to *Resolution*'s 112 and would be under the command of the universally popular Charles Clerke. By now, he was a renowned sailor in his own right – still only thirty-three, but with the approbation of the Admiralty as well as of Cook – and if there was any pique on being relegated to the second ship, Clerke certainly never showed it. 'A right good officer,' as a colleague described him; 'at drinking and whoring he is as good as the best of them, but Clerke had matured into a responsible and courageous mariner. He had sailed twice before with Cook and was his most loyal and devoted officer. The two men patently adored each other – a feeling as intense as the mutual respect they shared; unlike with Furneaux, the two men were perfectly in tune.

Under Cook in the *Resolution* was another old friend and three-times circumnavigator, the American, John Gore. He had missed the second voyage, and hence his main chance of promotion to Captain, by being away with Banks in Iceland, but Cook respected his abilities as well as his judgement; he was certainly not as entertaining as Clerke and somewhat less inspired, yet he was a good man and a good sailor and Cook was pleased to have him back under his command. However, Gore was not as straightforward as he might seem – there are references to 'Nancy', his 'Favourite Female Acquaintance' and to a 'Young one' whom Banks had promised to look after in the case of Gore's death, but any more references to his emotional life are kept tantalisingly out of reach.

A newcomer to the Cook voyages was the brilliant, gentle and studious James King. He was appointed underneath Gore as Second Lieutenant on the *Resolution* when just twenty-three years old, on the recommendation of Hugh Palliser and the astronomer, Thomas Hornsby. The son of the Dean of Raphoe and an heiress, he came from a high-achieving and well-connected family: his brother was Walker King who became Bishop of Rochester and married the daughter of King George's physician, while he himself had taken time out from the Navy (where, like Cook, he had served under Palliser in Newfoundland) to study science in Paris and then at Oxford. It was during his time at Oxford that he met Thomas Hornsby who took an interest in this extremely intelligent and capable young man. Under Hornsby's tutelage, he had become well-read and trained in astronomy to the extent that on the third voyage Cook had no need of a professional astronomer – James King could do everything required. He would also look after the precious chronometer, by now Cook's trusty friend and constant companion, as well as debate with Cook the leading geographical theories of the day. He was certainly one of the most useful men on board the *Resolution*, if not the whole voyage.

King was also unusual in that he was politically informed and highly astute. He and his brother were friends of the famous statesman and political theorist, Edmund Burke, with whom he continued to correspond mid-voyage when the occasion allowed. As a character, he was reflective and calm, sensitive and kind, much-loved by Cook and by most of his fellow-seamen. In many ways the perfect companion for his Captain, he would even be taken as his son by some of the islanders met *en route*, with the young midshipman, James Trevenen, remarking,

> In short, as one of the best, he is one of the politiest, genteelest, & best-bred men in the world.

Under James King was the Third Lieutenant, John Williamson – a bizarre misjudgement on the part of the Captain. He was the antithesis to King – gruff, moody, mean and almost universally detested. He was also prone to violence and was the kind of person whom you would do anything to avoid being stuck with on a long voyage. Another rather dark character on board was William Bligh, who would go on to achieve infamy in the mutiny on the *Bounty*. Unlike Williamson, though, it is clear why Cook selected him: personality aside, he was a gifted surveyor and talented seaman, and Cook had nothing but praise for him. This twenty-one-year-old Cornishman had been at sea since the age of seven, though had only officially served in the Navy since 1770; since then, his rise through the ranks had been nothing short of meteoric and he was brought onto the *Resolution* as its sailing master. As a personality, however, he seems to have had the proverbial chip on his shoulder: he hated James King as a 'pretentious poseur' and had harsh words for many of his colleagues after the voyage, although his relationship with Cook seems to have been based on the highest mutual respect.

There was not much respect to spare for the marines, and Cook must have rued the loss of the valiant John Edgcumbe. In his place was the inexperienced Lieutenant Molesworth Phillips, who had taken the advice of Banks to switch from the Navy to his current post; he would probably have been just as useless in either capacity, though the contacts brought him a wife: Susan, the sister of James Burney. By all accounts, he made a bad husband.

There was none of the usual retinue of 'Gentlemen' on the *Resolution*. This time the only supernumeraries were Omai and the voyage artist, John Webber. This twenty-four-year-old had been educated in Paris and Switzerland and was noticed by Solander when he exhibited a portrait at the Royal Academy in 1776. His appointment was rather last-minute but he was certainly no disappointment: he would prove himself a prolific and dedicated illustrator of all sides of the voyage. The lack of official scientists was a new departure for the Admiralty, particularly on this voyage to the unknown lands of American continent. One possible explanation comes from Cook's biographer, John Beaglehole. He came across a German edition of Lieutenant John Rickman's journal from the *Resolution*, to which John Reinhold Forster had written the introduction. According to Forster, when James King was appointed and called on Cook to pay his respects, he commented that it was a shame that no scientists were on the voyage, to which Cook allegedly erupted in a fury and shouted words to the effect of:

Curse all the scientists and all science into the bargain!

It seems unlikely that Cook would curse science itself but his experience with Banks and more grossly with John Reinhold Forster would certainly leave him wondering about the nature of its apostles. As for King, it was a salient early warning of the temper of his commander.

On board the *Discovery*, there were a few more familiar faces, though on the whole the officers were less colourful: Captain Clerke would be assisted by James Burney, now First Lieutenant – on his own merit this time rather than through the favours of Cook and Sandwich. He had heard of the proposed voyage when fighting in America and had done all he could to make sure he was included. A great fan of Cook's, he would become a useful officer to Clerke once he learned not to talk out of turn.

Also joining the ranks of the *Discovery* was William Bayly, again on board as the ship's astronomer, and he shared the lower decks with the Cambridge-educated surgeon's mate, William Ellis, friend of Banks and a keen artist. David Nelson was one of Banks's more direct appointees: he worked at the Royal Botanical Gardens at Kew and was under orders to collect what specimens he could from the discoveries *en route*, though he mostly kept himself to himself.

The midshipmen of both ships were to provide much of the recorded humour and humanity of the voyage. As a band, they stuck together despite being apportioned between the two ships. The *Resolution* had the hyperbolising James Trevenen, perhaps Cook's greatest fan of all if one ignores his reference to him at one point as being a despot. He did not get on well with Lieutenant Gore, but wrote to his mother of 'the sublime and soaring genius of Cook'. Like Bligh, he was a Cornishman. Unlike Bligh, he had had a prestigious training at the Royal Naval Academy at Portsmouth and was generally regarded as a warm-hearted, genial and sensitive member of the crew. He was to die tragically young when fighting for the Russians at Vibourg. Another talented midshipman who would die before his time was Edward Riou in the *Discovery*. He had the reputation as the perfect naval officer, much-loved, especially by his peers, and was talented enough to rise to become one of Nelson's captains in the 1801 Battle of Copenhagen. George Vancouver, midshipman from the second voyage, would become almost as famous as his beloved commander, and certainly would rank alongside him as a surveyor of the lands in North America he would shortly visit for the first time.

There were a record six surgeons and mates on this third voyage, including Banks's friend, William Ellis, and most of these became as well-known for their extra-curricular activities as their medicine. Ellis had his painting, William Anderson was a brilliant natural historian and linguist. Intellectually, he was a good match for Cook and could also rank alongside him as a scientist. The two men had become esteemed colleagues on the previous voyage; this next one was to cement their relationship into friendship, rudely ended by the travesty of his death from tuberculosis over which even his skills were impotent. Under him was an altogether different character – the bawdy, ebullient and irreverent Welshman, David Samwell. He had inherited none of the piety of his religious father and could rival Clerke in his love of wine, women and song, but that was off-duty; when at work, he was diligent and sober and rivalled Trevenen for the role of Cook's most adoring fan. It was Samwell who later looked back with nostalgia on his days with Captain Cook and the men of that fateful voyage:

> We are perhaps somewhat partial to one another, for it is an article of Faith with every one of us that there was never such a Collection of fine Lads take us for all in all, got together as there was in the Resolution and Discovery.

Among the 'fine lads' of the lower deck were a few old-timers, one of whom even followed Cook out of retirement. William Watman had been granted a place at Greenwich Hospital at the behest of his former captain but gave it all up just to sail with him again; then there was that deserting marine from the first voyage, Samuel Gibson, who was one of a half-dozen to make it a hat-trick of Cook voyages. The absence of men like Pickersgill was felt strongly, particularly as he would have been far preferable a shipmate to John Williamson; at least he got his deserved promotion but was sent, instead, to Baffin Bay on a bizarre Admiralty scheme that involved traversing the Northwest Passage from the other end and meeting up with Cook halfway. The expedition was a spectacular failure and he drank his way out of the Navy. In all, however, there was the usual mixture of experience and rawness, extroverts and introverts, troublemakers and heroes; in that respect, it was just like any other voyage of Captain James Cook.

As the summer of 1776 rolled on, and the final supplies were loaded on board, Cook was enjoying his new standing as a member of the British Establishment. He dined at the House of Commons, he dined with his co-Fellows of the Royal Society, he even entertained Lord Sandwich and fellow dignitaries with a magnificent feast on his ship. When he could, he took Elizabeth with him and, in those rarefied surroundings, that 'grave, steady man, and his wife, a decent, plump Englishwoman', whom Boswell reported, must have made a touchingly human sight. As if he knew his fate, he began to worry how she and the children would cope without him. His letters of the period make constant reference to the hazards and dangers he was about to face as he sailed back into the infernal ice that so plagued his previous voyage and left him weary. More than ever, he refers to Elizabeth in his letters to friends and officialdom: her wishes and needs were paramount in his mind – and, on 24 June, 1776, when finally came the time to say goodbye, their parting was as painful as ever.

He travelled down to Plymouth with the child-like Omai, pristinely dressed and as uncertain about leaving Britain as Cook was himself. At Plymouth, he settled to write his last remaining letters. To Banks he sent news of another accolade that made him burst with pride, the Royal Society's Copley Medal, received in recognition of the best paper contributed to the Society's *Transactions*; from the health of his men to the ministering of his discoveries, he was, by now, a very rounded scientific navigator. He was also, as ever, a very protective husband. His last letters of all were to Lord Sandwich and his friend and fellow Yorkshireman, Dr Richard Kaye, FRS. To Dr Kaye he writes:

> I cannot leave England without answering your very obliging favor of the 12th of last Month, and thanking you for the kind tender of your service to Mrs Cook in my absence. I shall certainly make an acknowledgement the way you wish, if it please God to spare me till I reach the place for Discoveries.

The 'acknowledgement' seems to have been the naming of part of the American coast after the good doctor – a small price to pay for the care of his wife. The last letter to Sandwich underlines Elizabeth's worth to her loving husband:

> My Lord, I cannot leave England without taking some method to thank your Lordship for the many favours confered upon me, and in particular for the Very liberal allowance made to Mrs Cook during my absence. This, by enabling my family to live at ease and removing them from every fear of indigency, has set my heart at rest and filled it with gratitude to my Noble benefactor. If faithfull discharge of that duty which your Lordship has intrusted to my care be any return, it shall be my first and principal object …

The next day, Captain James Cook set sail for the last time from British waters. With him was the normal motley crew of men and a veritable ark of animals – a present from 'Farmer George', the King himself. He had personally donated his own menagerie to join the usual beasts on board, and the decks were now littered with goats, sheep, rabbits, pigs, poultry, a bull and two cows with calves and even a peacock and its hen, all for providing fresh meat *en route* and for 'enhancing' the native wildlife of Tahiti and the Pacific. It was, after all, two hundred years before environmental concern over 'introduced' species – and for the King at least, he was doing his dominions a favour.

Other baggage on board the *Resolution* included all of Omai's essential possessions – the suit of armour, the jack-in-the-box, the velvet clothes and the furniture, a hand-organ for music, the Bible and globe for direction. The goods spewed out of every available space on the lower decks and almost drove the Captain mad.

There was all the usual paraphernalia for astronomy and scientific navigation for the use of Cook and King and, once more, this included Cook's Harrison-Kendall chronometer, without which he would not dare sail. He had his charts and books and maps of the North Pacific; he also had with him his Admiralty instructions – secret to the public who knew nothing beyond the returning home of their celebrity Tahitian. He had almost everything, and more, that you could think of. The one thing he didn't have with him when he sailed on 12 July, 1776, was his second-in-command.

Lieutenant James Burney had sailed the *Discovery* down the Thames and onwards to Plymouth, much to the delight of his family; for the Burneys, it was a mark of distinction; for Cook it was a concern, for there she sat waiting for her Captain to arrive. Captain Charles Clerke failed to show up at the eleventh – and twelfth – hour before departure, for instead of having his moment of glory, he was rotting in a debtors' gaol in London's St George's Fields. For weeks, this jovial soul had languished in its filth and mire, his humour slipping away from him as readily as his health; what made it worse was that the debt was one of honour and the moneys owed that had brought him there were not even his at all. He had loyally stood as surety for his elder brother, Sir John Clerke, who had repaid his brother's kindness by sailing off to the West Indies leaving both creditors and his brother exposed. Everyone now tried to get him out of prison – the Navy, Banks, Lord Sandwich himself, even the Speaker of the House of Commons – but still the King's Bench refused to budge. He wrote, distraught, to Banks: 'There's a fatality attends my every undertaking.'

It took until the end of July before he escaped to Plymouth and onto the deck of his waiting ship. It was an ignoble start to his noble captaincy but he swept that aside as he took up his orders:

Follow me to the Cape of Good Hope without loss of time,

his commander had written. Three weeks after Cook's departure, his friend now obeyed and without delay: 'Huzza my boys, heave away ... I shall get hold of him, I fear not,' he was said to have shouted as the ship picked up speed and sailed into the Channel. Buoyed up with adrenaline, he scanned the horizon that was now calling out to him. He had good men, he had his command – and he had escaped the paraphernalia of King Tosh and Omai; little did he know he carried something far more weighty: the fatal spores of tuberculosis.

The first recorded picture of a kangaroo? Frontispiece from the de Jodes'
Speculum Orbis Terrae, 1597

26

CLOSING THE LOOP

F COOK'S FIRST voyage had put Australia on the map and the second had blazed a trail for correcting history, this last voyage would prove a lesson in the fatal end to obsession. It was a pattern that would be repeated just a century later by George Collingridge in his researches into the Great Whodunit of who 'discovered' Australia. By now, I had followed both men around the globe, unearthing fragments of their lives, hoping the pieces would eventually form a whole. However, instead of finding harmony or completeness with each new discovery, the more the fragments slotted together, the darker the picture emerged of what happens when your obsession becomes stronger than your link to reality.

As for myself, I had spent months trawling through map-rooms and libraries, retracing their footsteps or trawling the internet in pursuit of my quest to explore these two explorers. Just as lands were discovered and then lost again through errors in cartography or the shipwreck of the news-bearer, my own understanding of Cook and Collingridge ebbed and flowed as I struggled to make sense of each new fact in relation to what I already knew or believed: two steps forward, one step back – the dance of a tango for three.

My salvation came with total immersion. I had had enough of words; it was time for a change in tack. Two hundred and thirty one years after Cook had sailed to Australia on board the *Endeavour*, I signed up as a crew member for the voyage of a modern replica bark which was circumnavigating the continent. It is one thing to read of life on board his ship; it is quite another to live it. I had chosen to sail the waters where Cook's reputation as an explorer had taken a beating: round Tasmania via the Bass Strait to Melbourne. On his second voyage, he'd been disgusted that Furneaux had left the area without settling whether Tasmania – then

Van Diemen's Land – was joined to the mainland; on his final voyage, he would also leave the matter unresolved. It had therefore seemed poignant to make this journey now to the place where Cook's legendary curiosity had come apart at the seams.

Working in three dimensions on the tiny deck and forty metres up in the rigging, seeing the tangerine sunrise and amber sunset, feeling the crew meld into a single community, I at last began to understand the call of the sea on his final, fatal voyage. This was life in the raw, bathing in the elements of sun, wind and water. Here, also, was order: the captain is a king who needs no crown: his position is unassailable; his word is law. For Cook who was a no one on land, he could rule his own world at sea.

Ironically, however, the moment of clarity came not on the deck, or even in the rigging but in the middle of the Bass Strait with nothing but emptiness on the horizon. On a perfect day, with someone on sharkwatch, we had leapt over the side to go for a swim.

The freezing water snatched my breath: the roar of contact exploded in my ears before dissolving into a fizz of tiny bursting bubbles. I opened my eyes and stared through the blue. For just a few moments, I was caught in silent, suspended animation as the opposing forces of gravity and buoyancy wrestled for control of my body, before propelling me to the surface. I broke the water like a new-born child, blinded by the brightness, senses screaming and gulping for lungfuls of air. As I trod water, waiting for my turn to scramble up the rope ladder and back into the ship, I took the chance to sink back into the swell, letting its powerful arms lift me and lower me, letting myself feel the vulnerability of being alone in the water, out of sight of land, just me, the sky, the sea and some substantial planks of wood.

I stared up at the ship: she was dwarfed by the expanse of ocean that surrounded us but this tiny floating island had become the centre of our universe. In a few short weeks, its thick wooden fingers had fed our ambition, our achievements and our desire for adventure, transforming a motley assortment of people into a fully-functioning crew. We felt invincible, self-sufficient; it was easy to forget that we were floating in miles of nothingness. And so it had been for Cook. Sometimes you have to leave security to appreciate what you've left – and sometimes, like Cook, you have to leave your home before that home appreciates you.

He was not to know he would be leaving his home forever, but it suited Britannia well: she liked her heroes dead – it made them easier to control.

My immersion into George was just as explosive. I had met him in the library at Oxford, followed him to Australia and now dived into the maps that had proved to be his nemesis. Even on land, you can still make a splash: the obsession that wrapped him up and left him steeped in controversy left a paper trail that stretched from the Sydney public library to the government of New South Wales. How dare this French-speaking Catholic undermine the legend of a true-blue hero like Captain Cook? Cook was synonymous with all that had made the empire great, yet the ripples of an amateur historian would spread out ten thousand miles, until they lapped Britannia's shores. And you can no more wash away the stains of history than you can stop the tide from rolling in.

Take one Cook and two Collingridges and it's a recipe for tension. In our own ways, all three of us had been explorers, though with marked differences in time, space and scale. What had finally united this disparate trio was not geography or even history, but the friction of being outsiders in someone else's system of beliefs. Cook had swum against the tide of acceptance of the Great Southern Continent and now the Northwest Passage, George against blind acceptance of the Greatness of Captain Cook; as for me, I'd come up against the fashions of acceptable history. 'Discovery' is about the meeting of two different cultures, with all their baggage and beliefs. Both sides must attempt to make sense of the new world order: it doesn't really matter where or even when those cultures are: you either fit in, or you clash.

Three people, three stories, three hundred years on, where is the wisdom that you can't escape your fate?

27

THE FINAL VOYAGE

James Cook 1776

HEN THE Cape Town skyline finally punctured the horizon on the 10 November, Captain Clerke was in fine spirits: his ship had sailed like a dream, while the atmosphere had been one of hard work and equally hard play. Even the traditionally drunken festivities on crossing the equator had not slowed their progress – in fact they had beaten Cook's passage to the Cape by a whole ten days. The two captains greeted each other with the warmth of old friends; as for the crews, they celebrated the ships' reunion in typical style with drinking, whoring and holidaying under the lazy gaze of the South African sun.

Cook had arrived in Table Bay on 17 October with his own reasons for being glad to anchor: within days of leaving Plymouth, it was apparent that the naval dockyard at Deptford had done a shoddy job on the *Resolution*; she was leaking badly and had to be put in immediately for repairs. There was also the matter of a near-miss on the rocks at Boa Vista, one of the Cape Verde Islands off the coast of West Africa, though it is unclear whether the reckless navigating was down to Cook or his humourless sailing master, William Bligh. It had not exactly been an auspicious start to the voyage but at least Cape Town held little in the way of surprises, and most of those were pleasant ones. By now, Cook was well-known in the area and was treated with huge respect and courtesy by the town's Establishment – there were dinners, royal salutes and flattering toasts in his name. While his men relaxed, the revered captain could be certain that his every need was attended to and worries sloughed off his shoulders like a shed skin.

England, with its journals and Forsters and pressures, was now over five thousand miles away and Cook settled down to tidy the last few ends

Captain Charles Clerke by Nathaniel Dance, 1776

of British business and write forests of letters to his friends and associates. His good mood was evident in a buoyant communiqué to Banks:

> We are now ready to proceed on our Voyage, and nothing is wanting but a few females of our own species to make the Resolution a compleate ark for I have added considerably to the Number of Animals I took onboard in England.

He may have been making a rare joke about the 'ark' but there was no hyperbole whatsoever when it came to the animals: on top of the King's bequest, he had added two bulls, two heifers, two mares and horses (stabled in Omai's cabin), two rams, several ewes, goats, rabbits and poultry – all without, it seems, too much thought about the Antarctic weather, the burdens of fodder and water and the prodigious amount of manure the menagerie would create. For someone with an obsession about cleanliness and order, this was an early indication of his progressively erratic behaviour, which would soon become a worrying feature of the voyage.

When the two ships sailed together out of Table Bay on 1 December, 1776, they headed southeast in the direction of the lands reported by Captain Crozet, Cook's acquaintance from his last visit to the Cape. In his hands was the chart that Crozet had given him of the islands discovered by Marion du Fresne – islands which took him ever-closer to the frozen edge of Antarctica. As the ships went further and further south, the weather deteriorated and the animals started dying in droves. The first of the islands were spotted and quickly left and then came the long, miserable sail through the familiar fogs that threatened to conceal even the largest islands. King grew concerned; Cook merely stretched out confidently for the 'tedious and dangerous' passage until, on Christmas Eve, they sighted land, exactly where it should have been.

Kerguelen's land was no great find: it lay before them like a smashed snowball in the freezing waters of the southern Indian Ocean with nothing but mountains and glaciers to add interest to what was once believed to be the Great Southern Continent. Having dispensed with that myth already, there was little here to detain him: he made a running survey of any coastline not cloaked in fog and then headed onwards, safe in the knowledge that the charts had been verified and the positions fixed in the rare instance of anyone caring about the desolate scraps of land. The celebrations for Christmas Day, 1776, made the most of the limited opportunities on offer – at least there was land to rest upon, penguins for dinner and fresh water to drink in the unusual event of the crew shirking their grog. Anderson did his botanising and one of the men even found a gift in the form of a message in a bottle from Kerguelen's voyage itself, to which Cook added a record of their own visit and a silver tuppence before leaving the bottle mounted within a cairn under a rather dejected British flag, flapping in the cold, dank breeze of what Cook styled the 'Island of Desolation'.

As 1776 blurred through the suffocating fog in to New Year, 1777, the two ships sailed eastwards, careful to avoid separation in what seemed like perpetual darkness. The conditions on board were grim – the animals were running out of fodder, the men could barely see beyond the bows and then a heavy squall snapped two of the *Resolution*'s masts. Mindful of his separation in these waters from Furneaux, Cook had arranged a similar rendezvous at Queen Charlotte Sound but, despite already being a month behind schedule, he suddenly now changed course and diverted both ships to Tasman's Van Diemen's Land for rest, fodder and repairs.

The decision was not based on need alone – New Zealand was just a matter of days away; however, the gales had driven Cook north of this land on his first voyage, Furneaux had done his cursory exploring on the second, and this, Cook knew, would be his last chance to visit this strange appendage to the vast continent of New Holland. Moreover, the question still remained: was Van Diemen's Land part of the mainland or a separate island? Even though the voyage was already hopelessly behind schedule, for Cook the niggling question overweighed the need to make up lost time and on 24 January, 1777, they sighted the coast of Tasmania.

The broad, curvaceous sweep of Adventure Bay was a welcome sight after weeks of little but sea and fog and they anchored here two days later. Shore parties were despatched for wood, water and grass under the watchful eye of the Tasmanian Aborigines with whom Omai and the men tried unsuccessfully to communicate. They had no luck with the Aboriginal women, either, who much to the sailors' chagrin were quickly ushered by their menfolk back into the forest. While the sailors went about their usual antics, Cook's behaviour was becoming stranger than ever. Almost as soon as the two ships had anchored, before Bayly had even finished putting up his observatory, he seemed to regret diverting here at all: he announced that they should make ready to sail once more and was only prevented from doing so by a capricious wind that dropped away to the force of a baby's sigh. The men may have been confused about their commander's changing whims but they were not disappointed at having to stay: they made good use of their days resupplying the hold and trying unsuccessfully once more to tempt the women, while Anderson conducted a more scientific relationship with the Aborigines and Bligh surveyed the harbour that Furneaux had named Adventure Bay.

However, it was clear that Cook was edgy to leave so, as soon as the wind picked up on 30 January, they weighed anchor and left the beautiful bay behind them. By now, the mood on the ships was growing tense: the officers were only too aware that they were hopelessly behind schedule – according to their instructions, they should have been leaving the Society Islands to find the Northwest Passage before the polar ice made exploring impossible; instead, they were at the other extreme of the Pacific Ocean, with little realistic chance of making up the time. So why had they made the unscheduled stop at Adventure Bay? Cook's normal rationale would have been to use it as a base for clearing up, once and for all, the debate over Van Diemen's Land – whether it was an island or part of New Holland. This was precisely the question that Furneaux had failed to clear up when he had anchored here four years previously. Now, when they were within a few days' sail and with little to lose from a schedule that was already blown apart, Cook could have settled the matter once and for all. The old Cook would almost certainly have done so – here was a challenge, here was an open question begging for an answer. But here, also, was a tired man, a man who has lost the lust for discovery, a man whose obsession had tipped over into irrationality. His mind was made up: he sailed out of the Bay and straight for New Zealand. For someone whose entire career was spent going beyond orders in extreme supererogation, the lack of curiosity was as ominous as it was bizarre.

It took a mere ten days before the familiar sight of the New Zealand shoreline rose up from the horizon and, by 12 February, 1777, both ships were anchored in the comfort of Ship Cove. Everything he needed to refresh his complement of men and beasts was within easy reach, and within reach, too, was the true story of what had happened to Furneaux's men at nearby Grass Cove. His old friends among the Maori were strangely wary as the men spilled out of the boats – and Cook, in turn, was equally wary, making sure that his men were well-supported by guns or marines every time they left the safety of the ships. The captain took his time to extract the story of what had happened, and when it came, the awful travesty of trust between visitor and host was only too apparent.

One of Cook's closest Maori friends related the tale as a suddenly-sober Omai translated: Rowe and his small party of men had landed their boat to eat lunch on the shore, guarded by Furneaux's black servant and with just two or three guns. As usual, they were soon joined by locals and there inevitably had been much drinking. It was well-known that Rowe disliked the 'Indians', regarding them as little more than ignorant savages, so what came next was less than surprising. There was some jostling and thieving that turned first into a quarrel and then into a fight. Rowe shot two Maori men but before they had time to reload their guns, they were overpowered by the dead men's friends, who swooped down on the party and clubbed them to death. The rest of the story was already known only too well by James Burney who had led the search party when the men had failed to return. He arrived at Grass Cove into what he described as 'Such a shocking scene of Carnage and Barbarity as can never be mentioned or thought of, but with horror': large rush-baskets of cooked human flesh were strewn along the shore amidst scraps of clothing and discarded body-parts – Rowe's hand, the servant's head, an unknown hand – the relics of the crew's last supper and the victorious Maori battle; meanwhile, further inland, the warriors had lit enormous fires which glowed in the dwindling light to the sounds of rejoicing. Burney had realised that little could be achieved by revenge – it would only risk more lives from an already under-manned ship. There was nothing to do but burn a few canoes to make themselves feel better, and then retreat.

Omai and Burney now heard the Maori story with heavy hearts, but none were as heavy as their commander's: this meaningless slaughter was precisely what Cook had always strived to avoid and its murmur now vibrated in their every dealings with the people who had become their friends. There was nothing to gain from belated punishment, even when he met the man who claimed to have murdered Rowe; Cook knew that the sailors had played their own part in the tragedy. Publicly, he announced that he had always been a friend to the Maori and a friend he would remain unless events proved otherwise; privately, he felt bitterly betrayed by both sides and the feeling slowly rotted away at his soul. The Maoris were astounded at his lack of vengeance, which was accepted and even expected from those who had been slighted; as for his men, they were learning that anger and forgiveness were increasingly doled-out according to the captain's whim.

Cook had the truth, he had his fodder and provisions – he even had some extra supernumeraries in the form of two Maori boys who had pleaded to come with them as Omai's companions. What he did not have when he finally left Ship Cove for Tahiti was time. The schedule for discovery had been unrealistic from the start: in his letter to John Walker, he had hoped to be away in April but the normal delays of Deptford Docks had put paid to a timely departure. The rush around Marion du Fresne and Kerguelen's lands had been pointless; more pointless still was the hasty retreat from Van Diemen's Land. The game was over before they even left England – they had missed the summer season for their polar explorations and left a stream of partly-surveyed islands in their wake.

It could have been the teasing winds or the pressure of time that brought him low, it could even have been the frustration of facing failure for the first time on a voyage, but on leaving New Zealand at the end of February, the mood on board the *Resolution* degenerated into anger and malcontent. Within weeks, relations between the upper and lower decks had reached rock-bottom. As ever, the immediate cause was simple enough – there had been some petty theft and when no one came forward, Cook cut the whole crew's rations of meat for a day in punishment. However, the aggrieved crew retaliated by refusing to take any meat at all, saying that innocent men should not be punished, at which point their furious captain threw a fit and declared their behaviour 'mutinous'. The stand-off did no one any good and it marked the start of a growing distance between this previously-beloved commander and his men.

Meanwhile, their passage to the Society Islands was tediously slow and the ships were soon running perilously low on both water and fodder. It was now six weeks since they had left New Zealand to become the play-things of a contrary wind; Cook had already killed his sheep to ease a little of the pressure on food but his concerns over shortages were for the long-term, as well. Reconciling himself to having missed the season for exploring in the North Pacific, his voyage would now have to be extended for another year and his meagre resources thus stretched even thinner. In this light, the need to resupply became more urgent than ever.

At the end of March 1777, on what should have been a stretch of empty water, there rose up the certain shape of an island – Mangaia – teeming with wood and lush vegetation. It seemed the answer to his prayers but for two things: it was surrounded by an impenetrable reef and had some decidedly unwelcoming inhabitants. There was nothing for it but to sail on and two days later another island appeared. Here, at Atiu, in what became known as the Cook Islands, they received a friendlier reception and were soon embroiled in efforts to trade and the usual battle against thievery; neither was successful and, again, Cook pushed on. A deserted island yielded scurvy grass for the men and fodder for the animals but there was little in the way of fresh meat and water on this or any of the islands. He had to make a decision – Tahiti and the Society Islands were just a few degrees to the north and east but the winds were against him; to the west lay Tonga and the Friendly Islands where he knew he could get everything he needed; meantime, they were critically low on water and the animals would soon start dying. He chose to go with the wind to Tonga.

As he sailed from the Cook Islands, he left behind a series of undiscovered islands, some large, like Rarotonga, and laden with supplies that could have weighed both ships down with everything they needed and more. On this occasion, the omission could perhaps be explained away by the captain's dire and immediate need for a reliable source of food and water, which he knew he could find in Tonga. But at their next destination, Cook's lack of his usual geographical curiosity was nothing less than shocking.

The last days of April 1777, brought the welcome sight of the Friendly Islands where they were to remain for the next eleven weeks, gaining little except rest and recuperation and some worrying insights into the decaying mind of their commander. To begin with, the characteristic Cook was in charge: the normal restrictions on trade were in place until the holds were once more brimming with stores and the usual change had been made to a healthy land-based diet of fresh meat, fruit and vegetables, washed down by the inevitable grog or home-brewed beer. From the locals, there was also the usual thieving, which Cook took as seriously as he did the thefts amongst his own men, even when it involved one of the local chiefs. He received a flogging for his efforts before being held to ransom for a hog and, though it meant they were no longer troubled by upper-class thieves, the *Resolution's* surgeon, William Anderson, was outraged by the level of punishment, convinced it outweighed the crime. Unlike Charles Clerke who, with characteristic humour, merely humiliated offenders by shaving half their hair off and then throwing them overboard, under James Cook the floggings became more and more severe until they reached a terrible sixty lashes. Cook noted little of the punishments in his journal but his officers expressed in their own private writing their shock and horror at the increasing brutality. Even his normally loyal supporters, like midshipman George Gilbert, grew increasingly uneasy at their commander's savage behaviour:

> Captain Cook punished in a manner rather unbecoming of a European, viz by cutting off their ears, firing at them with small shot, or ball, as they were swimming or paddling to the shore; and suffering the people as he rowed after them to beat them with the oars, and stick the boat hook into them.

Floggings, ear-cuttings and even crosses slashed into the offenders arms – all were meted out to those who incurred the captain's wrath. Clerke was merely bemused as to why they were staying here for so long at all when they now had everything they needed. Bligh was busy with his surveys, Anderson was busy with his observations of humankind and nature, Bayly could content himself with his astronomical observations, aided by the useful King – as for everyone else, they were doing little but twiddling their thumbs. Two and a half months would have provided plenty of time to check out the reports of the other islands that lay close by, the largest being Fiji and Samoa, just a few days' sail away, but Cook seemed happier to rant and rage over the thieving in his role as the mighty commander than pursue his usual passion for exploration and discovery. No one dared ask him why they were there and not *en route* to Tahiti; no one dared challenge this secretive, changeable man that stood before them in place of the fair-minded Captain Cook. Any questions were kept strictly to the privacy of personal journals. The Tongans merely looked on in confused amazement at the ball of fury in stockings, jacket and bright-white breeches who one day threw fits and the next day threw parties.

At last, on 17 July, the ships weighed anchor and left the paradise Friendly Islands for the familiar land of Tahiti. Cook wrote up his journal with no mention of his rage; no mention was made, either, of a secret plot by the chiefs on one of the islands to kill the entire voyage crew and plunder their riches; that was learned of years later when other visitors sailed to the islands and found Cook revered by some and hated by others for his barbarity. The captain, himself, was unaware of all of this – his own world was becoming more and more detached, if not from reality then from the humane values and restraint that had underpinned his every action on his previous forays into the Pacific. The tiredness seeps through his journal as well as his actions: he now did his job but nothing more – and even that is done with a weariness. If he was aware of the changes in himself, he certainly gave them no mention.

28

THE SECRETS OF THE MAPS

George Collingridge 1895

AVE LA GRANDE: that mis-shapen continent, filling the southern seas under a jumble of Spice Islands – why did it look so strange? A leading Sydney newspaper had already claimed the bizarre continent on the Dieppe Maps bore no relation to Australia and George now realised this was a major stumbling block to the public's acceptance of his theories; not only that, it puzzled him, too. Portuguese maps had been renowned for their accuracy – but if Jave la Grande was indeed Australia, parts of its coastline were barely recognisable. How could a nation with some of the best cartographers in the world get the shape so badly wrong? The answer, he found, lay buried in the murky waters of international rivalry and skulduggery that would define European history from the end of the Middle Ages to the time of Cook himself.

While Portugal enjoyed its supremacy as a global super-power, Spain boiled with rage and the two nations sparred like jealous siblings in the New World of the Atlantic. When the Pope finally split them up with his Line of Demarcation, he might have thought that was the end of the matter. But he was sorely mistaken. When the survivors of Magellan's fleet arrived home in Spain in 1522, they brought with them proof that the world was a globe and that it was feasible to reach the precious Spice Islands by sailing not east like the Portuguese but west around South America. Until then, Portugal had had the Indian and Pacific Oceans exclusively to itself and it was not in the least happy to share its bounty with its enemy.

Whereas the issue of who-owned-what had been straightened out in the Atlantic by the Papal Line, by the time that Line had to be extended around to the other side of the world, it was almost impossible to

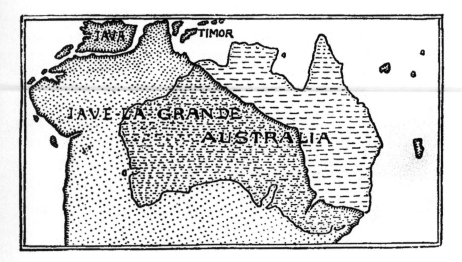

Australia and Jave la Grande compared, from
The Discovery of Australia and New Guinea, *1906*

determine its correct position. Fixing longitude was still hopelessly inaccurate without clear skies and endless computations – and the average navigator was not overly-learned in mathematics. Both the Spanish and the Portuguese knew that the line must run through the heart of the spice trade – the question was, who had the lion's share of the centres of supply? The Portuguese arrived in the Spice Islands from the west, the Spanish from the Pacific Ocean to the East: where the two nations met, both claimed sovereignty over the treasure-trove islands. Here, on the other side of the world, a geopolitical struggle was breaking into warfare and the weapons of choice were its maps.

When the Spanish ships returned home from their trade-routes and voyages of discovery in the Pacific, their charts were given to the authorities and turned into maps. Some of these maps, guessed George, would have also shown the east coast of a vast, strange land to the south of New Guinea where they had been blown by strange winds or steered by poor navigation. Once known, the land would have been a magnet to those looking for their own El Dorado, and little by little, the coast would have been explored and Spanish names assigned to the twists and turns of the coastline. And, just to make sure that they were not transgressing over the Papal Line, the coast would have been laid down a little too far to the east to make sure that it lay in Spanish waters. Likewise, these maps would show the Spice Islands on the Spanish side of the world; however, the Portuguese were also busy gerrymandering their maps to ensure that all valuable lands were firmly on *their* side of the Line – and, best of all, until the Line could be accurately determined, the spices were effectively up for grabs.

With the stakes so high, the spice-producing lands danced to and fro across the two nations' sides of the Line, adding to the distortion already caused by the problems in fixing longitude. But the longitudes on the Dieppe Maps showed Jave la Grande too far to the west and it was this fact that now added weight to the argument that they were from Portuguese sources. On top of this, to finally muddy the waters, it also seemed as though the original cartographers had exaggerated the size of the continent so that it would block the Indian Ocean off from the Pacific, leaving just a few thin passages that could be easily defended with a series of forts. It may have sounded far-fetched but George found plenty of evidence that supported his developing theory of deliberate distortion.

Foremost amongst the witnesses was a Spice Islands pilot called Juan Gaetan. Although he was Spanish, like many of his counterparts, he sailed ships to the north of Australia for the Portuguese and had some harsh words for his employers' veracity:

I saw and knew all their charts. They were cunningly falsified, with longitudes and latitudes distorted, and land-features drawn in at places and stretched out at others to suit their purposes, etc, etc, and when they found out that I understood their little pranks they made strenuous efforts to get me to enlist in their service, and made me advantageous offered, which, however, I scorned to accept.

Other evidence was on the Dieppe Maps themselves. As he was staring at the coast of Jave la Grande, George noticed that there were a series of little islands that did not seem to match up with any known lands. Try as he might, he could not reconcile fiction with fact. It was only when he compared them with a modern map of the world that he made a startling discovery: the islands picked out the real position and shape of the Australia, correct in both latitude and longitude! It seemed that the original cartographers *had* got it right after all – but they had chosen to keep the true shape and position hidden to all but those in the know. Far from being genuine islands, these small blobs of land were none other than 'land marks' on an otherwise falsified Portuguese map.

Other details needed no cover-up. On the east coast of Queensland, roughly in the place where Lieutenant James Cook was almost shipwrecked in the *Endeavour*, lay the name 'coste dangereuse': the cartographers were warning of the Great Barrier Reef – just as Burney and Dalrymple had noticed other 'correspondencies' with the names on Cook's own map. At last, the strange brew of fact and fiction began to make sense. George was convinced that Jave la Grande was indeed a cunning representation of the island continent of Australia.

It was well-known amongst historians that as well as distorting their maps, Portugal, Spain and all the major European powers also operated a formal Policy of Secrecy. Despite its position in the main Atlantic highway, the Portuguese had kept the discovery of St Helena secret for nearly a century! The British Policy of Secrecy was the reason why Cook's orders to search for the Great Southern Continent were officially designated 'sealed orders' – for the captain's eyes only, and also why all the journals written by officers and crew had to be handed over to the Admiralty as soon as the ships returned. Cook had taken the precautionary measures of collecting in journals himself on their disastrous visit to Dutch Batavia – and before that had frustrated the Governor at Rio by refusing to give full details of his intended voyage. Secrecy was not only a matter of pride, it was an essential policy to protect colonial interests, particularly when those interests lay in an area far away and one contested by the Spanish according to the rules of the Pope.

There was nothing to be gained by handing accurate charts over to your enemy: falsifying maps and official silence was thus a deliberate strategy in geopolitical subterfuge.

But if the Policy of Secrecy was so strictly enforced, how come such precious information on Portuguese, and even Spanish, discoveries ended up in the hands of the Dieppe cartographers? The answer to that was as straightforward as the Jave-la-Grande coastline had been confusing: throughout Europe: knowledge was power – and knowledge about the New World held the keys to unlock its enormous wealth. It was therefore only a matter of finding the right person to bribe or someone with a grievance against their country – and then settling on the right price. Beneath the heroics of famous voyages lay a dark and persistent layer of geographical skulduggery, with secret agents, double agents, traitors and clueless innocents, that spawned a lucrative underworld in cartographic espionage and illicit trade. Even Portugal's punishment of death for handing over maps to an enemy could not deter those offered irresistibly large sums of money.

Evidence abounds of cartographic crime, particularly after Spain won its foothold in the Spice Islands: around 1535, one of Portugal's secret maps of the East Indies was stolen by Konrad Peutinger; about the same time, the Portuguese mapmaker, Gaspar Viegas, defected with his maps to Spain, while it seems a spy smuggled a copy of the Carta Anonima Portuguesa (c.1533) out of Portugal where it was traded with her enemies. Perhaps most famously of all, Frederick Houtman took stolen Portuguese maps with him on the first Dutch voyage to the East Indies.

Some of this treachery was understandable enough – the politics of both Spain and Portugal were notoriously unstable, making loyalty and favour more difficult to guarantee; furthermore, the crown exacted large royalties on its subjects' voyages of discovery, so there was a large incentive not to advertise your intentions to the authorities – and then sell your results to the highest bidder; and some of it was not treachery at all but resulted from foreign nationals employed on the ships of a rival nation – like the Spanish Juan Gaetan who sailed with the Portuguese or even the disaffected Portuguese explorer, Ferdinand Magellan, who defected to Spain. Even James Cook's crew managed to smuggle out a few secret journals which would then be published anonymously if the price was right. You could make more money from selling your secrets than you could in three years of sailing – and for many sailors, that offer was too good to refuse.

As for the Dieppe Maps, would they give up their secrets, too? George now looked at the evidence in front of him: the maps themselves were

undoubtedly genuine, gifted to Kings and other great men in the
sixteenth century. He was convinced that the land of Jave la Grande
represented Australia and that it resulted from Portuguese, and later
Spanish, voyages of discovery and of trade with the Spice Islands to the
north. The information had then made its way by nefarious means to the
Dieppe School of Cartographers who used it to make offerings to French
Princes and English Kings. But one question remained – who were the
first Europeans to step on the shores of Jave la Grande? The Portuguese
had explored those waters first so George firmly believed that they were
the lead contenders – but who was that captain that had first brought
home the news of more land to the south of the Spice Islands? That was
now the hardest question of all. His research convinced him that the
Portuguese had arrived sometime after 1511 and charted all but the
southern coast by 1530 – but as to who held the smoking gun, he could get
no further. Portugal's secret maps had been kept under lock and key in the
archives in Lisbon but in 1755, the city with all its buildings and secrets
was destroyed by a violent earthquake. All that remained of Portugal's
magnificent collection of charts and voyage journals were the usually-
stolen foreign copies or scant references in letters and chronicles. The
puzzle over who had made those original voyages of discovery now
taunted George's mind.

More articles, papers and speeches continued, picking up in volume by
the early 1890s. By now, it was almost a decade since he had first become
interested in the subject of Australia's discovery by Europe but, while his
research was going well, in terms of paid work as an engraver, things were
getting desperate. By his own estimates, his obsession with uncovering
this secret history had cost him around £900 on books and materials –
almost £50,000 at today's rates – no mean figure for a self-employed artist;
at the same time, he was witnessing the twilight years of professional
engraving: photo-processing was taking over from his own laborious
profession and though, ironically, it meant it was easier to get copies of his
precious maps, it now sucked the life-blood from engravers like George.
Far from being just a chronicler of Australia's history, he now became part
of the history of art. With mounting horror, he watched his fees plummet
from the £1-an-inch he had earned on his arrival in Sydney to a pathetic
two shillings per square inch ten years later. He could still make money
from his teaching and from the sale of his paintings but, from now on, the
Collingridges were feeling the pinch.

There is no record of what Lucy thought of their dwindling incomes
and increasing expenditures; George's letters of 1891–92 hint that the

household was facing financial difficulties, with attempts at securing a loan or selling some of his assets, yet at the same time, he was ordering books from London which today would amount to well over £800. Like a man possessed, nothing seemed to matter except his beloved history of Australia – but then, what price was the truth about who had first stepped on its shores? George was no religious extremist, but he was staunch. He had staked his life against Garibaldi to defend his faith – money was a mere materialist detail; the crux of the matter now was setting history right. In the meantime, the trouble was that there was always one more fact, one more book to order, one more paper to read until his study groaned under the weight of the continent's past.

By 1895, his researches had connected him with every relevant expert in the field, he had examined every document or map on the region's history and could honestly claim to have read every single book ever published on the subject. His growing fame as an expert on European discoveries in the region, on the maps themselves and Australia's history, now brought him to the attention of a firm of Sydney publishers. Hayes Brothers knew that many people in the developing colonies of Australia were just as curious about the history of their adoptive homeland, and the press coverage on the bizarre French maps had done nothing to dent their interest. The prevailing belief was that Australia's modern history began with James Cook – that heroic Englishman and role model for all the citizens of the glorious British Empire. He not only embodied the spirit of the mother country, he stood at the grand altar of British Achievement. Now an artist-turned-historian was daring to suggest that Australia's pioneer hadn't been British at all. The Hayes Brothers knew they had a scoop on their hands.

29
ALASKA
James Cook 1777

T WAS A four-week sail through both storms and calms to Cook's second home of Tahiti, where he arrived on 12 August. For Omai, this was the end of an international adventure that had started as a child when he and his mother, already refugees, had stood quaking under Captain Wallis's cannonfire on Tahiti's One-Tree Hill and, from there, had taken him thousands of miles across the world's major oceans to Britain and now back home. He was excited to be back, gleeful at the chance to show off but sad to be leaving his new friends. For their part, the crew tolerated him as they would a kid-brother – sometimes amusing, sometimes endearing, but generally annoying. Cook had advised against him being taken in the first place. Unlike Tupia, he was not clever or skilled at navigation and he proved himself of limited use as a translator. During his time in Britain, he had learned the manners of the aristocracy but these were of little effect in the crowded camaraderie of a ship. Now, as the moment of their arrival drew near, Cook entertained his vanities like a parent plays along with a child, and warned him to be wise with his possessions. Inevitably, the advice evaporated into the warm, Tahitian breeze.

He was welcomed by his sister and ignored by everyone else until they discovered his trove of precious red feathers and exotic paraphernalia. Pathologically naïve, Omai failed to notice that his countrymen were more interested in the goods than they were in him. Meanwhile, Cook caught up with the news since his last visit. There had been more fighting, more deaths of those he knew and another change in the hierarchy. There was also much talk of Spaniards who had visited their shores, treating them well and leaving hogs and cattle and other goods behind them. Just

Captain James Cook by John Webber, 1780

as Cook's heart was sinking that his own menagerie had been brought in vain, he learned that much of the talk was exaggeration – there was one scraggy bullock and a few Spanish pigs: his beasts would be welcome after all. He then asserted himself and his King by stamping his mark on the cross the Spaniards had inscribed. Their 'CHRISTUS VINCIT CAROLUS III IMPERAT 1774' was firmly appended, 'GEORGIUS TERTIUS REX ANNIS 1767, 69, 73, 74 & 77'. This was a British discovery – and God had nothing to do with it; as for the Tahitians, they were as disinterested in the Spanish Friars' religion as they were of dire Spanish warnings about Cook and were as welcoming to the British as ever.

After the strident assertion over the claim to the island, he then did something he had never done before in all his years of discovery: he called his men together, brought them into his confidence and really sought their advice. He told them that they had missed the season for exploring the Northwest Passage (which most would have guessed already) and explained what this meant in terms of their schedule, and most importantly, their supplies of grog. The choice was clear – drink now and have nothing in the cold reaches of the North Pacific, or conserve their stocks now so they could benefit from its warm glow over the coming months. Showing unusual restraint, the men chose the latter. For Cook, however, this was even more unusual; perhaps this was a belated placatory response to their 'mutinous behaviour' over the beef rations, but it was becoming harder and harder for any member of the ship's company to second-guess their increasingly erratic captain.

He then relieved himself and his ships of the 'very heavy burden' of his ark: the turkeys, geese, ducks and sheep, the bull and cows, the horse and mare – not forgetting the peacock and hen – were all deposited around the island to go forth and multiply, or, more likely, be eaten by the locals. It was not a sad farewell, however ingenuous the justification may have been:

> The trouble and vexation that attended the bringing these Animals thus far is hardly to be conceived. But the satisfaction I felt in having been so fortunate as to fulfil His Majestys design in sending such useful Animals to two worthy Nations sufficiently recompenced me for the many anxious hours I had on their account.

Meanwhile, Omai continued his descent from his own perceived glory. Despite Cook's own vain hopes that he would marry well and build on his position, Omai squandered his precious objects and preferred to mix with the island's scoundrels who flattered him in exchange for presents. The men did their best but there was no telling him: his future was inevitably one of decline. He threw lavish dinners but then ignored the invited king and chiefs; he joined Clerke and Cook on their rides along the sandy beaches, but kept sliding off his horse to the sniggers of the crowds; he paraded around in his suits and dresses like a one-man buffoonish pantomime, and instead of respect, he drew nothing but derision. He gaily paddled his new *Royal George* war canoe wearing the full suit of armour, at which point even Cook had to smile and shake his head. And, when all the surprises and presents had been given away, he was simply ignored.

When the ships set off to explore the neighbouring island of Moorea, which Cook had strangely never visited before, he could not bring himself to leave Omai behind, although more for the young man's protection than out of a sense of loss. Moorea itself was well worth the wait – a volcanic paradise of hills and valleys, pure streams and rich vegetation. He anchored so close to shore that he could tie the ships to the hibiscus trees that fringed the perfect bay. Whereas Tahiti was gifted with farm animals, Moorea, it was hoped, would become home for the rats that had infested the ships after the Tongans had stolen some of their cats. The men constructed a rat-bridge from ship to shore but, despite its promise, few took advantage of their potential new home.

The human population of Moorea were equally cautious: all was not well between them and the Tahitians; there was a history of skirmishes and much talk of war but gradually Cook won their trade and their confidence – or so it seemed. Inevitably, the cause of the start of the trouble was theft: a sailor had stolen from a Moorean who had retaliated by stealing one of their goats. Cook sent out the usual threats and the goat was returned and with a plausible explanation. However, just as that matter was being cleared up, another goat was stolen and Cook now flew into a monstrous fury, sending two men in pursuit to the other side of the island. Too late, he realised his mistake:

> I was now very sorry I had proceeded so far, as I could not retreat with any tolerable credet, and without giving incouragement to the people of the other islands we had yet to visit to rob us with impunity.

Once again, he was wracked by indecision over the right course of action, seeking advice from the Moorean elders and even from Omai. Thankfully, he ignored their suggestion to go out with a party of men and shoot every soul he met, but in its place came something almost as terrible: he was about to commit an act that would shake to the very core his belief in himself, and the belief his men had vested in him.

Like a man possessed, he took an armed band of men and marched across the island, sending the locals fleeing into the forests as he torched canoes, houses and anything of value to the Mooreans until the flames grew taller than the trees; Williamson was sent by sea to the other side of the island with three heavily-armed boats; next day he sent a message to the king warning that if the goat was not delivered, he would burn every canoe on the island and 'continue destroying' until the goat was returned. Then, as if to demonstrate that the threat was real, he smashed the nearby canoes to pieces before progressing to the next harbour where he wrought even more destruction. As if this fed some violent lust, Omai and his men joined in with vicious delight, plundering and destroying whatever came in sight – canoes, houses and their precious crops, everything went up in sparkling pyres of smoke and flames that lit up the sky well into the night. When at last they returned to base, exhausted from their frenzy, there stood the goat grazing lazily on the shore. It brought Cook some belated pause for thought:

> Thus the troublesome, and rather unfortunate affair ended, which could not be more regreted on the part of the Natives that it was on mine.

Regretful he might have been, but some of the officers were decidedly uncomfortable. They noted something new in this ruthless, vengeful Cook, something out of control and terrifying; but even those who disapproved dared not publicly question their captain's actions for fear that the rage would be turned on them. Even as trade and relations slowly got back to normal, James King noted poignantly:

> In future they may fear, but never love us.

It was a muted crew who left soon after, heading for the island of Huahine where the sailors' Tahitian lovers – by now a permanent fixture on board both ships – told the gruesome tale of the last few days to the appalled inhabitants. If nothing else, mused Cook, it might make them think twice about stealing. It was now nearing the middle of October: they had disposed of their animals, gathered everything they needed, and all that was left was to find a home for Omai and his two New Zealand servants. Omai's preference was to go back to his father's land on the island of Raiatea and, with guns blazing, drive out the Boraborans who had taken it from his family, killed his father and forced him and his mother to flee as refugees to Tahiti. Ironically, it was now Cook who preached peace and restraint; he was becoming more unpredictable with each new island.

Instead, Cook asked the Huahine chiefs if he could have some land on which to build Omai a permanent residence; this was duly given and the ships' carpenters were set to work building an English-style house and gardens, complete with locking door and engraved name. During this time, one of the ships' sextants was stolen and Cook erupted with cold fury: did the people not believe what had happened on Moorea? He now threatened even worse if the equipment was not returned unharmed; the thief was delivered up, a confession extracted by a gleeful Omai and the sextant found intact. As for the thief, he was not unharmed or left intact: his head was shaved and both his ears were cut off, on the express orders of a cold-blooded captain. When the thief turned his vengeance against Omai, Cook had him once again flung in irons but this time he escaped while the sentry was asleep and was not seen again; the unfortunate watchcrew received the punishment instead – three dozen lashes, demotion and banishment from his ship.

By the end of October, Omai's house and gardens had been repaired and he spent his days holding court to the small group of retainers that had joined him. Cook looked at the house and the childlike man and knew that, whatever the future held for the young Tahitian, his job at least was done. As a farewell gift, he left Omai the horse and mare, a goat, a boar and sows and, reluctantly, some powder for his firearms. He had no great hopes for his continued success, although he wished him well.

> Whatever faults this Indian had they were more than over ballanced by his great good Nature and docile disposition, during the whole time he was with me I very seldom had reason to find fault with his conduct. His gratifull heart always retained the highest sence of the favours he received in England nor will he ever forget those who honoured him with their protection and friendship during his stay there.

The parting, when it finally came, was heartfelt on all sides; Omai had his strange mixture of souvenirs – scars from Wallis's cannonfire in 1767, presents from good King Tosh himself and now his 'British' house; for Cook, relief mixed with genuine sense of sad finality, particularly for the two New Zealand boys who desperately regretted leaving their homeland. As the *Resolution* sailed out of the harbour, Omai clung to the officers, bedecked in his finery and trying his hardest not to cry. One by one, he said goodbye to the men and the officers who had become his friends. And then he came to Cook:

He sustained himself with manly resolution until he came to me.

Omai could bear it no more: he flung his arms around the Captain's neck
and broke down into tears. It was left to the compassionate James King to
gently lead the sobbing young man down into the boat that waited on the
water below. He then climbed into the *Royal George*, awash with tears
from the locals and the two Maori boys. The sounds of their crying floated
over the waves to the departing ships. Cook looked over the stern at the
retreating scene to which he would never return: the island was etched
against the setting sun and there stood Omai, a tiny figure at the bow of
his canoe, standing tall, his arms outstretched and his head raised to the
heartfelt moan of the breeze.

The mood on both ships was reflective: the decks were strangely
vacant, silent of the cacophony of animal grunts and calls that had
serenaded their passage and clear of the heavy smell of fur and feathers,
hide and dung that had clung to their nostrils for the past fifteen months.
Also gone were the familiar sing-song sounds of Polynesian from Omai,
the boys and their own Tahitian lovers. They were not to go without the
last for long: Cook now gave the unexpected command to steer for
Raiatea, leaving his officers more confused than ever as they had all the
supplies they needed and could gain nothing at all from the extra stopover
on their journey north except the loss of precious time.

Another loss their captain never anticipated was that of the men, now
thoroughly homesick and less than eager to trade the kindly embrace of
the 'fine Girls' of the Society Islands for the frozen seas of the Arctic. A
wave of melancholy had swept through the crew throughout their recent
travels; talk of desertion was everywhere. Clerke's tuberculosis had
worsened and now William Anderson was showing the same symptoms
and the two even considered a formal request to live out the rest of their
foreshortened lives in the relative comfort of the tropics. They were wise
and realistic enough to know that they would go north to their deaths; the
others just fancied life with their lovers. One man did try, was caught and
duly punished, though Cook himself was always understanding of
deserters. He gave a grave speech on the fate of any more who might try,
which quelled the action if not the desire of the men on the *Resolution*; as
for the *Discovery*, it lost two men – a midshipman and the Gunner's Mate
– to the lure of the ladies, and they proved more troublesome to recover.
Threats were made, hostages were taken and eventually the deserters
were recovered on a far-flung islet by the chief himself, before being
lashed and flung in irons for their troubles.

The women were again removed from the ships and the two sloops sailed on to Bora-bora – an island well-known to Cook by repute but previously unvisited by any of his ships. The official reason for the detour was slim: the recovery of one of Bougainville's anchors for the use of its iron; more likely, it was a useful excuse to visit a new island. The old and curious Cook was back again but before the men had time to get used to it, he changed his mind once more and gave the urgent order to sail north. He had already lost one season and was suddenly anxious not to waste a second. He had no idea that the order left two of his closest friends on a knife-edge. Clerke and Anderson were still contemplating staying, wrestling with their conscience, balancing life against experience and searching their souls. As the ships weighed anchor, the two men remained stoically on board, unwilling to abandon their duty, their commander and their friend – and knowing they had signed their death sentence.

There was nothing on the horizon but air and water and the rise and fall of the great ocean swell to gently soothe Cook's fretful mind. Here, at last, was the purpose of the voyage – they were heading north through empty seas towards unknown lands and endless opportunities; the only certainties were danger and the disabling cold. The charts before him showed nothing but open water between the islands they had just left and the coast of Drake's New Albion, and from there, Captain James Cook was charged with filling in the gaps; what was more, if he was to arrive on schedule at 65° North, albeit a year late, he had just six months to travel around six thousand miles. It was achievable, but there was little room for manoeuvre.

Christmas Eve, 1777, brought with it an early present, wrapped up in the glow of dawn: it was a large island, a coral atoll, with a hundred miles of coastline and a barren interior. A deadly reef surrounded the vast coral interior and it took almost an entire day to find a route suitable even for the small boats to pass through, and even then their problems were not over. If the prospects of getting through a passage were not daunting enough, the young midshipman, James Trevenen, noted even more cause for concern:

> The service was rather a perilous one, as we had to pull into the lagoon over a very high sea (which, however, never broke) through a narrow passage with which we were little acquainted, and where we could see the bottom the whole way; had any sunken rocks projected higher than the rest, we would have been destroyed, but luckily we never encountered any. On every side of us swam sharks innumerable, and so voracious that they bit our oars and rudder, and I actually stuck my hangar into the back of one while he had the rudder in his teeth.

Once on shore, the atoll did not offer much except good fish, the possibility of turtle and the opportunity to observe a solar eclipse on 30 December. Clerke was too ill to take part in any of the activities; Anderson was suffering, too. The science was left to Cook, Bayly and King, with Cook's observations being embarrassingly awry. Once again, he had lost his usual finesse.

The only other event of note on this sun-baked, wind-blasted, almost treeless island was the loss of two men for up to two days – not through desertion but from a genuine loss of direction. Unpredictably, Cook remained sanguine at this almost heroic level of failure:

> Considering what a strange set of beings, the generality of seamen are when on shore, instead of being surprised at these men lossing themselves we ought rather to have been surprised there were not more of them.

They quit what would become Christmas – or Kiritimati – Atoll on 2 January with the hold packed full with three hundred green turtles. Four days later, Cook gave out the fearnoughts and Clerke rationed the water: both captains were expecting a long and landless haul north; both captains were wrong. On 18 January, the rising sun revealed land rising up from the skyline where should have been only ocean – first one island, then two, then three. They had reached a new series of fertile, volcanic islands, the Sandwich Islands, modern-day Hawaii.

The eight major islands are strung out in a line running northwest to southeast, starting with Niihauand Kauai and ending with the 'Big Island' of Hawaii itself. As the world's most isolated archipelago, almost right in the middle of the Pacific Ocean, it is hardly surprising that they had lain undiscovered by Europeans for so long. When Cook had enquired of the Raiateans if they had heard of any more land to the north, not even these famed seafarers were aware of their existence. He knew that he had stumbled upon a major discovery.

The ships skirted the southern coast of Kauai, in the shadow of the central volcano that rose over five thousand feet into the cloud. The island was cloaked in rich vegetation, dense forests occupied the valleys and water gushed from mountain streams. Soon, the inhabitants took to their canoes and came to investigate the strange giant floating islands that had come close to their shores; the astonishment was on both sides, for when James Burney asked in Polynesian what their island was called, these people answered immediately in what sounded like Tahitian! Once again, Cook mused over this incredible race of people who had scattered so far and wide across the Pacific. As for the locals, they soon built up the confidence to come up on to the ships, whereupon Cook was more convinced than ever that they were the first Europeans that these people had ever seen; they looked around in awe at every detail on board, showing caution and much respect but total fascination.

With the inhabitants friendly enough, Cook started to look for a suitable harbour which he soon found in Waimea on the southwest coast of the island. As usual, he gave his orders controlling trade and relations with the women; as usual, he forbade anyone with venereal disease from leaving the ship – and, as usual, the orders fell on deaf ears. His men were already eyeing up the 'fine girls' whom Samwell wasted no time in closely researching.

Meanwhile, Williamson was sent out with the boats to search for water. He was a poor choice of ambassador; his humour had not improved over the course of the past year and he did not think much of 'Indians' of any islands. Most worryingly of all, this unlikeable man was quick to act and slow to think – and then quick to defend his actions. Now, growing scared of the hoards of Hawaiians who crowded around his boat, he fired his gun and killed outright a handsome, chief-like man. Williamson almost gloated over his actions, though he was canny enough to keep the matter quiet from Cook. When the captain eventually found out, he flew into one of his almighty rages that made the volcanoes shudder in terror.

However, Cook had concerns of his own. When he stepped ashore for the first time in Waimea Bay, the beach was also crowded with curious on-lookers, but rather than surge forward, what came next quite simply took his breath away. As he climbed ashore, the people fell flat on their faces; shocked, he gestured them to stand, whereupon they showered him with offerings of pigs and plantain fronds, all very curious indeed. Unbeknown to Cook, he was assumed to be a divine being, a kind of Hawaiian demigod. For the meantime, however, it suited him not to understand.

Watering should have been easy: they found an endless supply of pure, sweet streams and started refilling their holds as quickly as they could; more of a problem were the winds that kept them tacking for days off the Waimea coast, during which the captain almost lost that deserter-turned-admirer and Polynesian translator, Sergeant Gibson, who rolled overboard when drunk but was thankfully rescued. When their ship was blown towards the neighbouring island of Niihau, John Gore was put ashore with twenty men to finish gathering water but so bad were the storms that he was stranded there for the next two nights. When Cook was finally able to collect his party, he was met by the same strange response from the locals, who flocked towards him and prostrated themselves on the ground. Bizarre though this was, there was no time to discover the reason – the weather had made him impatient to sail and at the start of February 1778, the *Resolution* and *Discovery* once again headed north, leaving the newly-named Sandwich Islands as mere pin-pricks in the distance.

The decision to sail highlighted an unusual flaw in Cook's normally rigorous organisation. In the five weeks they had spent in the islands, they had failed to finish their watering despite the valleys being awash with rivers, ponds and streams. Nevertheless, they had restocked with fruit and vegetables and knew that New Albion was only a matter of weeks away, assuming all went well.

As the days wore on and the temperature dropped, Clerke was not the only one to feel the cold. The chill wind whistled around the decks and slapped the cheeks of those who faced up to it. The warmth of the Sandwich Islands soon became a sliver of memory and, were it not for the exotic produce in the stores, they could have seemed nothing more than a snatch of imagination. Not many of his men shared Cook's lust for northing, least of all the sickly Clerke.

> We have been so long Inhabitants of the torrid Zone, that we are all shaking with the Cold here with the Thermometer at 60. I depend on the assistance of a few good N:Westers to give us a hearty rattling and bring us to our natural feelings a little, or the Lord knows how we shall make ourselves acquainted with the frozen secrets of the Artic.

Their latitude steadily increased to the designated 45° of Cook's instructions; the first signs of land began to appear in the form of seals and birds and then, on the morning of 7 March, New Albion lifted its head in welcome. There was nothing much to commend it – just wooded slopes and indifferent hills; Tahiti or Hawaii it certainly was not, as the weather now proved by throwing wind, rain, fog and even snow into their eyes. Clerke tried to remain buoyant; Anderson grew quiet.

Their respective ships did what they could to coast northwards up the New Albion shoreline, balancing the chance of a close-enough view for a survey with the risk of being blown to their death on the rocks. As far as they were aware, they were probably the first Europeans to chart much of this part of the world. They knew nothing of the Spanish voyages sent to reconnoitre the lands to the north of Mexico: the Spaniards had reached as far as Alaska but they knew how to keep their secrets; knowledge was power and British New Albion was almost impossible to defend.

With the foul weather plaguing their every move, there was little sighting of the coast for surveys; the best they could do was creep north keeping their wits about them. When they reached the area of the famed Strait of Juan de Fuca, Cook poured scorn on the mythmakers, little knowing that he had passed the broad inlet under cover of darkness but would soon be finding shelter within its reach, nestling in the shelter of today's Vancouver Island.

By the time land came once more clearly into view, the landscape had changed from boreal slopes to white-topped mountains. Coming in to land, they heard the melodious singing of the locals who quickly gathered around the ships, clothed in animal skins and smeared with paint – unkempt but eager enough to trade. They found an anchorage in what Cook called King George's Sound but the Admiralty renamed Nootka Sound, on the western side of Vancouver island, and the next month was spent in repairing the ships and resupplying their empty casks of water and food. While the ships were re-rigged and masted, King and Bayly set up their observatory, Bligh and Edgar went sounding and surveying and any spare men were set to brewing spruce beer to eke out their dwindling rations of essential alcohol. There was plenty to see for the natural historians – Anderson gloried in the profusion of birds that flocked around the land while James Burney tried to note down both the songs of the bird and those of the local population.

Cook's obsessional hygiene had by now rubbed off on his crew: few of the men were interested in trading for sex with the local women who were deemed too caked in grease and dirt, though according to the redoubtable Samwell, some hardier and more persistent souls found that if they were first scrubbed clean with soap and hot water, they provided most satisfactory love interest. Just as he had got his men to follow his lead on cleanliness, he gave up his equally strict efforts to control thieving through use of punishment, deciding to accept the inevitable losses; it was almost as if the dark days of the Moorean carnage were finally troubling his conscience. As for Clerke, he had long resolved not to bother with disciplining thieves if the visit would only be a short one, viewing that the bad will it engendered was too heavy a price to pay for the theft of 'trifles'; anyway, as his health declined, he had little energy to waste on losing battles with the locals.

Cook's more relaxed stance again showed itself towards the end of their stay when he took time out to row (or rather be rowed) around the sound with his midshipmen. For thirty miles, they surveyed the shoreline of the sound and what Cook named 'Bligh Island' before returning exhausted but content to the ships. James Trevenen recorded the event in his journal:

We were fond of such excursions, altho' the labour of them was very great as, not only this kind of duty, was more agreeable than the humdrum routine on board the ships, but as it gave us an opportunity of viewing the different people & countries, and as another very principal consideration we were sure of having plenty to eat and drink, which was not always the case on board the Ship on our usual allowance. Capt. Cooke also on these occasions, would sometimes relax from his almost constant severity of disposition, & condescend now and then, to converse familiarly with us. But it was only for the time, as soon as we entered the ships, he became again the despot.

The midshipman certainly had cause to consider Cook a despot: the captain was as firm with his young trainee officers as he was with the seamen but as the romantic young man scribbled in lines of poetry (using Cook's Tahitian name of 'Toote'):

Yet not now I'll remember thy wholesome severity,
Or remember 'twas meant but to give me dexterity:
No! rather I'll think on that happier season,
When turned into they Boat's crew without rhyme or reason ...
Sometimes more substantial tokens of favour
Than mere empty praises reward our endeavour,
And hunger excites us to use every effort,
While good beef and pudding more solidly pay for't.
Oh, Nookta, thy shores can our labour attest
(For 30 long miles in a day are no jest)
When with Sol's earliest beams we launched forth in thy sound,
Nor till he was setting had we compass'd round.
Oh Day of hard labour! Oh Day of good living!
When Toote was seized with the humour of giving!
When he cloathd in good nature his looks of authority,
And shook from his eye brows their stern superiority.

Their constructive adventures in Nootka Sound were brought to a close on 26 April when the ships sailed out, serenaded by the Nootka Indians. Their melodies were soon drowned out by the growing howl of the wind and the blunt slap of their bows on the mounting waves: they had left behind the calm of their anchorage and sailed into the jaws of a five-day hurricane. The *Resolution* sprang a leak that even had Cook 'not a little' alarmed, though it seemed worse than it was and quickly subsided with the use of a pump. More worrying was the fact that they had lost sight of the land – and thus any potential entrance to the Northwest Passage that was now their primary goal.

For his men, it seemed that the old Cook was back with them, the steely navigator who believed nothing but what he saw with his own eyes. As the hurricane subsided, he headed straight back towards the coast in an effort to lay to rest another geographical fantasy: 'the pretended strait of Admiral de Fonte'.

> For my own part, I give no credit to such vague and improbable stories, that carry their own confutation along with them nevertheless I was very desirous of keeping the Coast aboard in order to clear up this point beyond dispute.

He was too far north when land again came into view on 1 May but the indented shoreline did not look promising; in fact, it did not look inviting at all. Cook decided not to explore – a calculated risk but one that paid off: there is no Northwest Passage here, just thousands of tiny islands, channels and craggy rocks. The violent storms had taken their toll on Anderson who withdrew to his cabin to contemplate his fate; Clerke, however, was apparently re-energised and keen to push up into the waters traversed by Bering and Chirikov almost forty years before.

For the next ten days, the two ships crawled in teasing airs along the rugged coast while the men scoured its line for any sign of a passage and their share of the £20,000 reward. Cook compared the shore with the Müller map and the account of Bering's voyage but it was hard to reconcile these with the confusion of points and islands that now stretched north into the distance. Every shred of his attention was fixed on the coast: like a hawk hungry for prey, he lived through his eyes; nothing else counted; the old obsession was back and he was on form.

With anticipation building as they approached the zone of discovery, Cook took another bold decision and deviated from his Admiralty orders: they had commanded him to ignore any river or inlet until 65°N so as not to waste any time – yet here he was in the Gulf of Alaska, at 61°N, taking up his precious days in exploring an opening into a vast, indented bay that seemed to penetrate deep inland. 'We are kept in constant suspense,' records King, 'expecting every opening to the Nward will afford us an opportunity to separate the Continent.' Instead of open water, they met what Clerke called the 'fine jolly full fac'd Fellows' with tattoos and bones piercing their lips, noses and ears, who paddled out to inspect them. Although no one could decide if they were 'Indian' or Eskimo, they were friendly enough and seemed totally ignorant of fire-arms; Cook was just thankful that they remained so even at the end of their visit, in spite of the blatant thieving.

Still, this was as good a place as any to repair the leaky ship, particularly as another storm was brewing out to sea; moreover, the stopover also meant Gore and Bligh could take out the boats to make their own assessment on whether they were in an inlet or the longed-for Passage itself. Bligh returned dismissive, believing he had seen the end of the sound; Gore held out more hope; Cook settled the matter by deciding to set sail and leave the inlet altogether, believing a Passage 'not only doubtful but improbable'. His instinct was right once again, and he called the place Prince William Sound.

It was now 20 May, just eleven days before their June deadline by which time they should be at 65°N to begin their serious exploration for the Passage, and instead of the coastline taking them north, it was forcing them back down to the south towards some kind of headland: could this be the entrance to the Passage at 59°N? Cook and King scoured both Müller and Stählin's maps for clues, comparing them with the icy land that tempted them into a broad expanse of water between what looked like two capes. As the tension built, Cook's strength of mind at last began to fail him: he swung between hope and despair, the indecision of whether to stay and explore, or just sail on, eating away at his soul. For that experienced commander, the lie of the land tipped his mind into near-certainty that they were chasing nothing but dreams but there was stiff opposition from his officers. Once again, Gore had high hopes of a Passage and his arguments finally persuaded Cook to abandon his scepticism. With his resolve deserting him, on 25 May, he ordered the ships to sail inside the channel.

> This land was every where covered with Snow from the summits of the hills down to the very sea beach, and had every other appearence of being part of a great Continent, so that I was fully persuaded that we should find no passage by this inlet and my persevering in it was more to satisfy other people than to confirm my own opinion.

His loss of self-belief now cost the voyage sixteen days, which lead to nothing but dead ends and dreadful weather. Gore was resolute, naming one stretch of shore they surveyed, 'Nancy's Foreland' after his 'Favourite Female Acquaintance' but even he had to bow to the mounting evidence: they were in Cook Inlet in the Gulf of Alaska; there was no Passage here, not even the mighty river that Cook believed led inland. Impatient to press on, he stopped short of gaining the evidence to prove the river existed; had he done so, had he spent just one more day exploring, he would have proved that there was not even the slightest possibility a Passage could exist – the inlet was a dead-end. It was a strange lack of rigour on the part of this previously most rigorous navigator – but now he had greater concerns on his mind:

> The season was advancing apace, we knew not how far we might have to proceed to the South and we were now convinced that the Continent extended farther to the west than from the Modern Charts we had reason to expect and made a passage into Baffin or Hudson bays far less probably, or at least made it of greater extent. But if I had not examined this place it would have been concluded, nay asserted that it communicated with the Sea to the North, or with one of these bays to the east.

Almost twenty years later, the remarkable midshipman, George Vancouver, would return to the Gulf and quell the Passage dreamers once and for all, changing the Admiralty's name from 'Cook's River' to Cook Inlet.

It was now the beginning of June and the beginning of the end for the valiant Anderson; he was now too weak to continue writing up his journal and sat wretched and shivering in his cabin. The mood was sombre as they retraced their route, emerging once again into open sea and back where they had started. Their captain cursed the 'late pretended Discoveries of the Russians' – all talk of a known entrance to the Passage was nothing more than the geographical fantasy that had left him chasing around the world for the last ten years. The captain began to consider that there was no Passage, there would be no £20,000, and that on his last great voyage he had been tilting at windmills.

His immediate concern, however, was tracking the coastline that, far from taking him north to the Arctic, now forced him southwest down the sweeping arm of the Gulf of Alaska. He was travelling in completely the opposite direction to his Admiralty instructions – once again, belief and reality were not matching up. The landscape, when he could see it through the dense fog, rain and snow, stretched out for miles descending from snowcapped hills and mountains into the beautiful, dreadful monotony of the low craggy shoreline. For days he could not be certain of his position as the sun was blanked out from the sky. Navigation was painstaking, the winds capricious and the shoals deadly and yet he was sailing against the clock, anxious to increase his latitude and to find or dismiss the Passage once and for all. A weary tension enveloped the ships and even the ebullient Clerke:

> I hope and trust Providence will favour us with a little clear Weather: never had a set of fellows more needed of it, here's such a Labyrinth of rocks and

Isles, that without a tolerable distinct vision, they will puzzle our accounts, confoundedly.

By now, Cook and Clerke were sailing blind along a coastline that even today, ships are warned to steer clear of; the reefs and shoals are still poorly surveyed but, in testament to the judgement and skill of that great navigator, they made it through unscathed and then coolly fished for halibut in the waters at the far side, under the icy shadow of a giant, smoking volcano. Unbeknown to Cook, this surreal landscape was the last finger of continent in the outstretched arm of the Alaskan Gulf – ahead lay the start of the thousand-mile chain of Aleutian Islands that swept across the ocean to Asia. His mind was now flitting between confidence and caution. His maps were of little use and the weather, once again, was his tormentor – but all these cannot explain his loss of purpose: quite simply, he dithered and by doing so, missed the ten-mile-wide passage off Unimak Island into the Bering Sea. The next day, he switched from indecision to a rampant gung-ho attitude, running with the wind at full speed in visibility so poor they could barely see the length of the ship; Bligh was appalled, the officers horrified but, like a man possessed with a death-wish, Cook charged forth into the fog.

They heard the danger before they saw it: the malevolent smash of sea on rock, suddenly all around them. Quick as a flash, he hauled the ship to and dropped anchor, signalling *Discovery* to do the same. The coast lay less than a mile in front of them – they had been ploughing directly into its jaws, miraculously sailing between two jagged rocks that could have smashed the ships to toothpicks. They had rarely come so close to disaster and Cook alone was responsible.

Providence had conducted us through between these rocks where I should not have ventured in a clear day and to such an anchoring place I could not have chosen better.

Clerke was more forthright:

Very nice pilotage, considering our perfect Ignorance of our situation.

They stayed at the eastern end of Unalaska Island for the next few days, collecting water, greens and a surprisingly large amount of information about the Eskimos they encountered. The Russians had been here before them, though in trade rather than discovery, and signs of their visit were everywhere, from the tobacco smoked by the Eskimos to their canny understanding of trade. The enterprising Samwell combined the two to procure his women, professing himself highly satisfied with the 'very comely' results; the surgeons were less satisfied with the rampant gonorrhoea that swept through the crew. King, meanwhile, had desires of a more aesthetic nature and climbed a snowy hill to gauge the lie of the land but failed to spot a nearby crevasse that almost provided an icy grave. In all, however, the visit was a success and before they pushed north into the Bering Sea, they left a note with their hosts containing details of their visit for future visitors.

All July, they skirted the far side of the Alaskan Peninsula, heading north-east along the mainland coast and playing cat and mouse through the fog. On the sixteenth, Williamson was sent ashore to assess the land and try to get bearings; he took possession of the barren, icy land and called the headland Cape Newenham, after a friend. The land, once again, was teasing them, directing them south when they wanted to go north – but when they at last rounded the Cape, they sailed into a deadly maze of shoals that confounded their every move for the next five days and even to Clerke it became a 'damn'd unhappy part of the World'.

Standing out to sea, they edged slowly north in the suffocating fog until the sun briefly pierced through on 29 July and they were at last able to take a fixing: 59°55'N– still more than five degrees short of the golden latitude for discovery. Like swimming against the tide, this was tedious going and did nothing to improve the mood of the commander. According to Müller's map, they were sailing over land; Stählin had them jostling between islands. Instead, they were in open water in the middle of the Bering Sea. He silently cursed his comrade chartmakers.

St Matthew's Island loomed up through the mist, a silent ghost that departed as ethereally as it had appeared. Then, on 3 August, departed the soul of William Anderson – esteemed surgeon, acute observer of natural history and by now a close friend of all. Cook's mood could barely get any lower as he struggled to write the obituary to this 'agreeable companion, well skilld in his profession': his loss would be gravely felt though Cook hoped his name would live on in Anderson's Island. King rated their comrade's value second only to their great commander's; as for Clerke, the death of this 'much esteemed Member of our little Society' was the knell to his own.

At last, on 9 August, the fog cleared, the sun broke through the hazy skies and the men could finally look about them. They had reached the target 65°N: ahead was the vast jutting headland of Cape Prince of Wales and then open water; Cook could not see the fifty miles across the Bering Strait to Asia and, when he eventually sailed across, was uncertain whether or not he had actually reached the eastern limits of Siberia or was merely on Stählin's island of 'Alaschka'. He anchored, confused, in Lawrence Bay on Siberia's Chukotskiy Peninsula and spent a few hours talking and trading with the Mongoloid Chukchi people, his spirits lifted by the clearing weather and the sight to the north of open water. Two days later, they passed through the Bering Strait and into the Arctic Ocean.

The dreams that had sustained them – of a Passage, of home, of that £20,000 – now buoyed them through whatever gales the region could muster. King was busy calculating the distance to Baffin Bay; ahead was open water and so it must surely remain, as the best scientists in Europe had assured them that the sea could not freeze.

68°, 69° and, on 17 August, 70° North. But the noon-day sun brought with it the awful glint well-known to Cook from Antarctica: the ominous glow of ice. Within hours, it filled the horizon, rising up in sheer cliffs from the sea in front of them and dashing their hopes for a Passage home to glory. They could go no further.

The silence of the empty sea and fog was now skewered by the violent groans of ice against ice and the haunting bellows of the walrus that littered the floating platform. These creatures were huge, cumbersome and slow – easy prey for the parties of men who now turned the ice red. The bleeding beasts were hauled onto the decks to be butchered by hungry sailors, desperate for fresh meat to vary the monotony of their diet. It was small compensation for the icy blockade but Cook resolved to stop all normal rations of dried food except their biscuit. At first, the men were happy but the novelty was short-lived. The meat was disgusting and tasted like rank oil; it was good for lamps but not for men. Dissent rumbled and then increased to a roar: on one side the furious Cook, spitting with rage and cursing the 'damned mutinous scoundrels' – they would eat walrus or starve; on the other side were the sailors, bound by tradition, unable to stomach the 'disgustful' taste and angry enough to go on hunger strike.

Within days of the stand-off, the famished crew were ready to collapse; Cook had no option but to soften his stance. The officers were bemused and highly concerned: what on earth had happened to their genial commander? Was this the same man who had so successfully got his men to demand sauerkraut on the first voyage through leading by example? Where he once used guile, he now used punishment and the effects drove a wedge between the captain and his men. That previously cool, calm commander was now losing his grip of reality and the unassailable trust of his men. His crew may have been confused by his decaying temper but – to the man who set so much store in controlling his environment – losing control of himself must have been terrifying. In near-paranoid delusions, he now saw insolence not incomprehension in the hollow faces of the mariners and not even his officers dared to broach the subject in his presence. He makes no mention of his own inner thoughts on the matter in his journal – a journal that he knew would be the object of public scrutiny; instead, he blamed everyone but himself for the near-mutiny.

Over the next few days, the men's concern grew even deeper. To everyone except Cook, it was clear that their journey north was over: at times, the ice was advancing at over a mile an hour; there was really no option but to turn back. But Cook refused to accept what he took as failure in the face of an old and hated enemy. Like a fly at a window, he smashed his head against the ice, first the north and then to the west, trying to find a route through or around it. If the Northwest Passage was blocked, he would try the Northeast, over the top of Siberia and back home to Britain. He would find a good harbour; he would fight his way through. With the fixation of a madman, he fought both the encroaching ice and wind until he stood on deck exhausted and utterly defeated, cursing the 'Closet studdying Philosiphers' who had their theories so badly wrong. His frozen foe came not from rivers at all but was formed, here, in the sea where it rose up against him, mightier than all the armies in Europe. After a year's planning and over two years' sailing, he had spent just three weeks in the Arctic Ocean and a mere eight days in sight of the American continent. Calling his officers in front of him, he announced their retreat south to overwinter and restock for a second attempt to discover the Passage the following year.

On 27 October 1778, Captain James Cook celebrated his fiftieth birthday in characteristic silence at sea off Unalaska. He had corrected the 'erroneous' Russian maps, resupplied with wood, water and food at Unalaska Island, met with inhabitants, fur traders and even some friendly Russian officials but a plan had been forming in his mind that would take them far from these freezing reaches. Why waste time, he mused, in wintering at Kamchatka when the months could be better much spent in exploring the new-found Sandwich Islands that seemed to overflow with everything they required? Unlike Mr Stählin, who had not 'the least regard to truth' when it came to his maps, Cook resolved to fix these islands on a definitive chart thus aiding both geography and navigation.

Before he had left Unalaska, he had given the Russians a letter for the Admiralty in London, his first since leaving the Cape of Good Hope. In it he outlined his efforts so far, the battle with the ice, and his plans to retreat to Hawaii for the winter before returning north next year for a continued assault. And, as if preparing the ground for his failure, he also expressed his doubts at ever succeeding in his mission to find a Passage in that 'far from ... open Sea'.

Kealakekua Bay, Hawaii

30

OBSESSION AND BETRAYAL

James Cook 1779

T TOOK JUST a month of sailing for the two ships to see land striking up from the horizon. The weather was hot, the winds had been generally kind and, despite the setbacks in their hunt for a Passage, their spirits were raised by the prospect of fine food, women and recuperation on the sun-baked shores of terra firma. Cook had been steering for Kauai but instead the island of Maui was first to rise up and greet them. This land was new even to their charts – another island of similar mould to the others with its central volcano poking its head ten thousand feet into the clouds, while the folds of its cloak fell in cascades around its girth. Although they continued sailing clockwise around the coast, the people seemed as friendly as before and soon took to their canoes to come and investigate this strange incursion.

The captain issued his usual directives on trade and added two more of a specific nature:

> And whereas it has frequently happened that by Officers and others travelling in the Country with Fire-Arms and other Weapons, in order to obtain which, the Natives have committed thefts and outrages, they otherwise would not have attempted; it is therefore Ordered that no Officer or other person (not sent on duty) shall carry with him out of the Ships, or into the Country, any fire Arms whatever, and great care is to be taken to keep the Natives ignorant of the method of charging such as we may be under a necessity to make use of.

The other command was just as typical: at Unalaska, he had noted the increase in the cases of venereal disease – the other great scourge upon the inhabitants of new-found lands. As such, there were to be no women at all on board the ships, anyone with the disease was to stay on board at all times and if any were found having sex with local women, they would be severely punished. He reiterated that these rules were to

> prevent as much as possible the communicating this fatal disease to a set of innocent people.

However laudable his intentions, his behaviour shows that he had once more lost touch with reality – albeit a reality he vehemently despised. His efforts at keeping the two sexes apart were now as much scorned by the local women as they were his own men; when the potential 'girlfriends' were turned away from the ships, they hurled abuse that, though not easily translated, was entirely understood. Moreover, Cook should have been honest enough to admit that he could not prevent contact altogether: as soon as the men came into land, the women were more successful in their efforts, procuring nails and scraps of iron in steamy exchange.

As the two ships sailed clockwise around the Maui coast, the locals made no attempts at stealing and even rescued the *Discovery*'s cat that had fallen overboard into the water. All was amiable, all was dignified – even the hoisting aboard of a chief, wobbly from drinking kava, encrusted with scabs with watery, red eyes, who despite his appearance was of seeming importance. He said his name was Terreeoboo and presented Cook with a stunning feathered cap and cloak. But although they were beautiful, something else had caught the captain's eye – another island in the distance, much larger than the others, with tall mountains clothed in rich vegetation, with snow-capped summits and streams glinting silver in the afternoon light. The chief's men called it 'O'why'he' and he immediately resolved to go and investigate.

They arrived on 1 December but if the weary sailors thought they were about to land, they were in for a shock. For some strange reason unknown to all but Cook, he stood off the coast and refused to anchor for the next month and a half; the men were beside themselves, so near to heaven but with it just beyond their grasp; even his officers could not comprehend the bizarre strategy when the men were so exhausted from their mammoth Arctic trek. They all knew that their captain was very much his own man – there had long been complaints that he rarely discussed his plans with others – but now it seemed as though he forgot the needs of everyone but himself. Resentment was building amongst his men while the officers beat down their incomprehension about the purpose of the tacking. Each time they plied to and from the shore, working clockwise down the coast, the wedge that had been planted between Cook and the crew was driven a few inches deeper.

By now, the only predictable side to their commander was his unpredictability: just when the men were cursing his stubborn selfishness, he ordered more beer to be brewed from local sugar cane. Despite the officers' reports of its excellent drinking, his

> mutinous turbulent crew refused even so much as to taste it and demanded their grog … I took no step either to oblige, or perswaid them to drink it; for as we had plenty of other vegetable there was no danger of the Scurvey.

The crew were certainly mutinous – they had been told it was cane beer or nothing; what was more, they were still on short rations while zig-zagging round an island that could have given them every comfort they desired if only their despotic captain could have seen beyond his nose. A 'very mutinous letter' followed their stand against the beer, with pointed comments about the rations, which Cook seemed surprised to hear. The captain of the last two voyages would never have forgotten to feed his crew well but the captain of the last two voyages had also rarely heard a mutinous whisper. Once he realised his mistake, full rations were immediately resumed but on the matter of the beer, he would not budge an inch: if they did not drink the beer, they would not get the grog.

Eventually, however, the two sides relaxed – and relaxed, too, with women on board. The sailors' world suddenly looked rosier with their food, drink and girlfriends, even though they were still plying to and from the shore; Cook, meanwhile, had merely transplanted his fury through his journal and to the Navy Board, which was blamed for all the ills of the voyage and for the regard it paid to its voyagers. There was no denying that he had suffered from leaking ships, tattered sails and worn-out rigging from almost the start of the voyage but he now spat his disgust at the work of the naval dockyards as though they were beneath contempt.

There was fury, too, when he and the *Discovery* were separated by a storm and, when they were reunited after thirteen long days, Clerke thought his friend looked more tired than ever and grew concerned to hear about the increasing fits of rage. To everyone on board, it seemed as though the cool, calm commander of old had disappeared; in his place stood a vexed and prickly tyrant, lashing out at anyone who had the misfortune to hit a nerve; in turn, the vexed and prickly tyrant was worried about his second-in-command – behind the mask of humour the tragedy of tuberculosis was playing out before their eyes: Clerke's chest was wracked with agonising coughs and the colour drained from sallow cheeks on a gaunt face.

By January 1779, with tensions rising and both ships leaking badly, Cook realised he could no longer have everything his own way: they needed a harbour, and needed one quickly, but the landscape was now scrubby and bereft of supplies. At last, on 15 January, the sun rose to a magnificent sight – the coast was green with lush vegetation while the water teemed with locals paddling out to greet them. What's more, the vague outline of a bay stretched out like the corners of a smile three leagues away in the distance. Bligh was immediately sent out to investigate while in the meantime unfolded a grand opera of dramatic proportions that left the most seasoned of travellers rooted to the decks.

A thousand canoes, laden, were paddling through the waves towards them, laden with vast quantities of food that could feed them all for months. Littering the sea – both in and out of the water – were ten thousand people, unarmed but screaming with adrenaline. The spectacle continued throughout the time Bligh was away, watched over by the bemused crews who were already salting down their new provisions or trading for keepsakes and sex. With Bligh's return came the news they hardly dared hoped for: this bay of plenty was about to become their home. On 17 January, 1779, the ships dropped their anchors and prepared for land.

Kealakekua Bay – 'the path of the Gods' – has been a perfect spot for people and boats for more than a thousand years. Just over a mile wide, it is large enough to be enticing and small enough to be sheltered from all but a south-westerly wind. Two broad, crusty arms of solid black magma descend from the slopes of Mauna Loa to hold the bay in a deadly embrace; every three and a half years, the gaping mouth of this active volcano still spits out its wrath, while the lava-flows nestle in the crook of its elbow and long fingers claw at the earth.

In January 1779, these arms also enclosed thriving settlements and well-tended vegetation, all dug-in to the brittle, bony dirt, and it was from these settlements that the people now flocked to the anchored ships. If the size of the welcome was bizarre enough, stranger still was the manner of the visitors. Far from being shy of contact, they clambered on board until the decks had barely an inch of space, the ships were pushed low into the water and *Discovery* had developed a list. The ships soon became a pressure cooker of all the usual activities of the Pacific islands – the noise and energy of trading, stealing and seduction grew to a frenetic crescendo at which point Cook could stand it no more. He implored two local chiefs called Parea and Kanina to get their people under control, which they did with remarkable speed and efficiency by literally throwing some of their subjects over the rails and down into the water. Meanwhile, a priest came to the fore – a scabby, red-eyed diminutive old man called Koa, who had clearly sought God through copious amounts of alcoholic kava. Despite his appearance, he was deeply revered and communed with Cook with high ceremony and a grossly-long prayer. The captain began to realise that this was no ordinary welcome.

Matters became more perplexing still when they came to land: as soon as he stepped from the boat, he was aware of a hush that descended over the bay. Far from thronging towards them in welcome or defence, the people fell flat on their faces and prostrated themselves in his path. The very last words he wrote in his journal stand in stark contrast to the melodrama that was unfurling:

> In the after noon I went ashore to view the place, accompanied by Touahah [Koa], Parea, Mr King and others; as soon as we landed Touahah took me by the hand and conducted me to a large Morai, the other gentlemen with Parea and four or five more of the Natives followed.

His journal makes no mention of the only word to escape from mouths of the prostrate Polynesians: 'Orono', repeated over and over again. The small party were led up the slope to a tall, sacred stone *heiau* surrounded by a fence emblazoned with around twenty human heads on the posts. At one end was a tower with an altar laden with sacrificial pig and fruits, at the other two huts and some carved, grinning deities. Cook and King were taken inside, then the captain was led hand-in-hand with the priestly Koa to the tower where prayers were sung before the altar and Cook was draped in a strip of sacred red cloth. The priest then prostrated himself before a small, covered deity and bade his guest to do the same – which he calmly did. More incantations followed and still that same word: 'Orono, Orono!'; then the protracted ceremony ended with a feast, in honour of the captain. Throughout the kava-laden proceedings, Cook remained politely attentive, only baulking when he was handed some fetid pork, which Koa even more politely then chewed and handed back to him.

The men were relieved finally to escape down to the water and the waiting boats, unsure what to make of their strange reception. The pageantry was clearly deeply felt – but this was no normal welcome ceremony and, rather than being something to celebrate, the small party felt decidedly unsettled. Over the days that followed, the ships underwent their repairs amidst an orgy of love-making and thieving, with the locals patently believing that both were morally acceptable, but each time it came for the captain to step ashore, there was the same hushed reverence and prostration. To Cook and the officers, it was almost as if he was considered a supernatural being – at the very least some powerful king – but as they planned to stay such a short length of time, it seemed easier to tolerate the strange behaviour than risk losing respect or causing offence. Cook therefore endured the obsequious flattery; only Clerke found the gestures genuinely intolerable: he 'disliked exceedingly putting so many people to such a confounded inconvenience' and immediately insisted that the locals stand up and behave normally.

Meanwhile, on shore, the watering parties were doing their best, David Nelson was in heaven with his botanising and King and Bayly were busy with their astronomy. Their encampment was attended only by priests and seemed to have taken on the religious aura of their captain; the effects of this sacrosanct *tapu* were unerring but it kept the camp empty of on-lookers and saved them from the trials of constant thievery. However, the mood on these islands was decidedly odd: whenever Cook came to visit them, exactly the same pattern of events would unfold – he would be greeted on the shore by priests while the people fell away from his path like the Red Sea parting for Moses.

On 24 January, the atmosphere became even more surreal when the people, women and provisions evaporated after a strict *tapu* was extended across the bay. Almost two days later came the reason – a visit from the King of all the Hawaiian islands – the same red-eyed, crusty-skinned, shaking figure of old Terreeoboo, from their previous stop at Maui. He arrived, looking magnificent in a brightly-coloured cloak and head-dress, in a regal-looking catamaran, and yet seemed chastened to be in the presence of Cook. After yet another welcome ceremony – though this time thankfully brief – in the astronomer's tented encampment, the king went back to his village for the night and, in his place, reappeared the women, much to the men's relief.

The king's arrival marked a noticeable change in the way the men were received; it was as if this last ceremony had marked the end to all the high drama and pageantry of their short stay in Kealakekua Bay. Little by little, the trade dried up and the thieving again began. Life was getting back to usual, and it seemed that the locals were hoping the ships would soon be gone.

Cook was also hoping to quit this earthly paradise as soon as he could to finish watering at Kauai and make a thorough survey of the islands. One man, though, would never leave these shores, albeit not by design: William Watman, the old sailor who had followed Cook out of retirement at Greenwich Hospital and whose health had been causing his captain much concern, suddenly had a stroke and died. After getting agreement from the chiefs, he was buried on land on 1 February with the full Christian ritual followed by three days and nights of Hawaiian ceremony with much singing and wailing and sacrificing of pigs. It was a tragic loss of a well-loved companion and Cook rued the day he had allowed him to leave his wife and home to accompany him on this final journey around the world.

By now, the locals were making it patently clear that the ships had outstayed their welcome. Blunt comments and actions left the officers under no illusion whatsoever that their hosts would be pleased to see them leave – that is, all of them except one. The courteous James King may not have received the deification of his commander but the people had taken him to their hearts. They now pleaded with him to stay, saying he would become a great chief – and when he refused, they even sought permission from Cook himself! In a final effort not to offend his most generous hosts, he havered and suggested that perhaps it might happen the following year ... King was last on board as the two ships made their final preparations to sail, having been embarrassingly detained by his heartbroken followers.

At last, on 4 February, the *Resolution* and *Discovery* left Kealakekua Bay, weighed down not with visitors but with every kind of food imaginable. The stay had been at times weird and even disconcerting, but all that was in the past: they were now *en route* to collect water at Kauai before eventually heading back north in their search for the great Northwest Passage. Once more, the men looked on in sorrow as the land of their lovers grew smaller and smaller until it was nothing more than a smudge on the horizon.

Cook was relieved to get back to the straightforward business of navigation, unencumbered by ceremony and endless diplomacy. Little did he know that his hosts were in turn equally pleased to be seeing off a god whose season had come to a rather protracted end. 'Orono', the name they had been intoning, was the divine spirit of light and peace, of the earth and its harvest and it was the personification of him that had sailed into Kealakekua Bay. The timing was perfect: Orono, or Lono, had a season from October to February, when hard work and war would both be temporarily forgotten and the people would circle the island collecting the fruits of his harvest. The symbol of this ritual was a square of *tapa* cloth attached to a wooden pole and cross-beam, a symbol not unlike the sail of a ship that had also circled the island, collecting 'tributes'. Clerke had guessed right when he thought that the respect shown to Cook was the respect for a god – and King was now right to worry about the effect it would have if that respect wore thin. What was more, with the death of William Watman, the Hawaiians were left in no doubt whatsoever of the mortal status of Orono's followers: far from being untouchable divine beings, they were just as vulnerable as themselves.

As the ships sailed north up the coast of Hawaii, the vacuum of the departing Orono was filled by a change in religious personnel: Orono's opposite was 'Ku' – equally mighty but this time the god of war and human sacrifice. He, too, had his season, and it was just around the corner. In the meantime, Orono still had a large retinue of followers alongside him – islanders, the priests, King Terreeoboo and the ever-present women, paying their last respects to this departing god.

At noon on 6 February, the weather turned gusty, then squally, then stormy. They had almost reached the northernmost tip of the island where a vast bay gaped like a basking shark and High Priest Koa went off with Bligh to search for water and shelter: Bligh came back alone. Changing his name to High Priest Bretanee was clearly enough of a goodbye from the withered, shaking man – his devotion did not extend to staying on board the ship in a raging gale and monstrous sea.

The tropical paradise was now showing its teeth. As the ships pitched in the foaming waters, the women became quiet, then green and then sick. A handful of locals, rescued when their canoes overturned, sat huddled limply on the lower decks, assailed by the noise of the raging wind, the slam of the waves and then the sound of splintering wood. One glance at the weatherdeck was enough to show the reason: the *Resolution* had sprung its foremast and, what was more, the damage was so bad that the whole structure would have to be taken out for urgent repairs – and that could only be done on shore. Cook was now faced with a dilemma: should he go north to find a suitable spot with the wood and water they desperately needed – or risk a cool welcome back at Kealakekua? Lieutenant King captured the mood, little realising the men's prescience:

At 10 we bore away for Karakakooa, all hands much chagrin'd & damning the Foremast.

On 11 February, still beset by storms, the ships anchored at the north end of Kealakekua. Despite their politeness, it was clear that the locals were damning the foremast, too. Relations were cordial but decidedly cool. The bay itself was eerily empty of people and provisions and although trade did continue, this time the price for goods was high: the only objects that the Hawaiians seemed to want in exchange were iron daggers. The blacksmith had been busy, forging the long, metal spikes from the scrap metal collected for the purpose – Bougainville's anchor from the Society Islands, hammered into shape at Nootka Sound.

The men were meantime busy on the repairs – within two days, the old mast was heaved out and sent ashore, under the authority of Lieutenant King. On land, all seemed cautiously harmonious; on the ships, things were beginning to go awry. A light-fingered islander had already stolen a set of tongs from the *Discovery's* blacksmith, had been caught, severely punished with forty lashes and held prisoner until the tongs were returned; Clerke now worried about the rising level of theft from his ship and made everyone leave, except for the priests: King had been right – the former respect was now wearing thin.

He saw the effects himself when called to deal with some trouble with the watering party. A group of locals had turned mischievous, throwing stones and abuse at the sailors and their paid local helpers to such an extent that the quartermaster fled to Lt. King to ask for marines. King and an armed marine went over the stream and demanded that the chiefs control their people; the trouble stopped and the watering party could get on with their work. What was more curious was Cook's reaction when he heard the news:

> On the first appearance of throwing stones or behaving insolently ... fire ball at the offenders.

Fire ball? Cook had always insisted that small shot was used in warning first, that loss of life should be avoided at all costs, but here he was suggesting that anyone who even vaguely stepped out of line should be killed. King could do nothing. He passed on the captain's orders to the corporal of marines.

Meanwhile, on the *Discovery*, a grim pantomime of mischief was into its second act. While Clerke was in his cabin entertaining one of the chiefs, one of his subjects raced across the deck and stole the armourer's tongs and chisel before paddling off in the chief's canoe. Edgar and Vancouver gave chase in a boat but were no match for the speed of the nimble locals. By the time the sailors reached the shore, the thief had absconded, leaving behind the tongs and chisel which were immediately handed over.

Cook and King – onshore with the mast repairs – had heard the firing and seen the chase. They did not know its cause but, assuming it serious, they immediately gave chase to the fleeing thief. Now Cook chased the thief, followed by a jeering mob who purposefully misdirected the furious captain miles in the wrong direction. What made matters worse was when the armed marine accompanying Cook threatened to fire his musket but, instead of being scared of the gun, the mob just laughed in his face.

The pantomime now descended into grisly farce: while Cook was chasing the thief and the mob was chasing Cook, Edgar and Vancouver captured and confiscated a Hawaiian canoe which they thought contained the thief but was instead the canoe of a by now very angry chief. In the ensuing struggle to seize the vessel, the chief was hit by one of the men's oars at which point the crowd onshore went berserk and grabbed stones from the beach, hurling them at Edgar and his men before falling on the boat and plundering anything they could steal. In the end it was the chief himself who halted the fighting and returned the boat to the wounded and shaken men, along with as many of the stolen goods as he could recover.

When Cook heard of the proceedings, he flew into another rage – both at his officers and the locals. An anxious King quietly watched his mood darken with the night sky as he realised the balance of power had shifted irretrievably. Any more trouble would be met by force. The lines were being drawn between visitor and host: obeisance he could cope with, insurgency he could not. The people who had treated Cook as a superior being were now laughing in his face.

It took all night for Cook's fury to subside. This man, with his obsession for order and decency, was all too aware he was being mocked by the very people he insisted his own men respect. Confused and angry, he retired to bed, his mind clouded by rage and weariness. Had he not always tried to treat the locals with all imaginable humanity? This voyage had seen that humanity spat upon by increasing numbers of indigenous peoples as the relationship broke down and descended into violence. He lay in the darkness stewing over the terminal decline of what had seemed to be a friendship: they had not only betrayed his genuine offer of amity – they had now betrayed his trust. He never once thought that it is hard to stay friends with a living volcano whom you cannot predict and, even less, understand; he never once thought that the sense of betrayal can cut both ways.

The breaking dawn brought more disaster: the *Discovery*'s cutter – its only large boat – had been stolen in the night right under the noses of the crew on watch. In the half-light of dawn, Clerke rowed over to give Cook the solemn news and the two men immediately drew up a plan of action: they would blockade the bay and hold the canoes as hostage until the boat was returned. Clerke's men led by Rickman went to the south of the bay,

Cook's men under Lanyon, the Master's Mate, to the north. However, by the time Lieutenant King came on board after finishing his shore-watch, Cook had already changed his plans, unbeknown to his second-in-command. Not only was he arming himself and his double-barrelled gun – one barrel with shot, one with ball – he was planning to go ashore. By the time Clerke had rowed back to give his orders and then back to the *Resolution*, Cook was gone. It was not yet seven o'clock.

With the small boats playing cat-and-mouse with the native canoes, the ships fired their cannons in warning to the shore. King was alarmed at the threatening mood so went immediately to Koa to explain the situation and ask for peace. Meanwhile, Cook landed at Kaawaloa village at the north end of the bay with Lieutenant Molesworth Phillips, nine armed marines and his musket loaded with shot and ball. In his mind was his oft-used plan to take one of the chiefs hostage until the cutter was returned, but this time, he went one better: this time he was after the King himself. By now, Cook knew Terreeoboo and his two sons well and intended them no harm. That so, he was armed with marines and had two boats under the trigger-happy Williamson and the more cautious Roberts waiting in the shallow water of the shore, in amongst the tongues of lava.

Marching up the beach, the party arrived at the house where Terreeoboo was still sleeping. Phillips was sent inside to rouse the king who came out to greet the impatient captain. Cook explained the loss, immediately accepted Terreeoboo's total innocence and asked if he would come on board the *Resolution* until the matter was sorted – to which the king agreed. They started walking towards the beach, with the sons running happily ahead towards the boats. Then, just as they reached the water's edge, things began to go badly wrong.

As he was about to climb into the boat, Terreeoboo's wife pleaded with him to stay. There were tears, there was anguish – and the poor king seemed totally confused. He sat down on the beach looking dejected and frightened. A crowd was now building around them as people came to investigate the source of the trouble; they, too, urged the old man to stay or else be killed by his alien captors. Meanwhile, Cook was pressing him to climb into the boat to join his son who was already waiting. All the time, the two sides got louder and angrier and the argument more heated. The marines looked around, growing edgy; the Hawaiians began to pick up stones and flash their daggers in the morning sun. A priest started wailing and making offerings to the gods. All around was the dreadful hum of danger.

Cook realised the situation was getting out of hand. Turning to Lieutenant Phillips he said they could not think of compelling Terreeoboo to go aboard without killing a number of the crowd which he was loath to do – but he failed to recognise that he was already powerless. Instead, he slowly began walking towards the shore, ambling, almost dragging his heels, and in no hurry whatsoever. The boats were waiting, he was seconds from the shore. He had no idea what had happened on the other side of the bay.

Rickman had positioned the launch to seal off the south end of the bay when a canoe tried to break through the blockade. Shots were fired and someone slumped into the bottom of the canoe. The dead man was Kalimu, a high-ranking chief well-known to Cook's men. His friends now paddled directly to the ships to protest vehemently at his killing, and then at full speed, took the dreadful news to the crowd waiting on the shore, who exploded with violent anger. A tidal wave of emotion swept northwards along the shoreline, racing towards the spot where Cook with his marines was slowly walking to the water. The wave broke as it reached him: a local warrior lifted his arm. In his hand was a dagger. Cook fired his musket but the small-shot just bounced of the warrior's armour. For a split second, there was silence – and then the crowd erupted with the roar of their guardian volcano. A chief lunged his iron dagger at Phillips and a shower of stones flew through the air, knocking down one of his marines. Cook now fired ball and a man fell dead. Phillips then fired and the crowd surged towards them in a frenzied passion for blood.

In the water, the king's son leapt terrified from the boat as the men began to fire at the crowd, joining the marines who were already shooting at random. Cook was astonished and waved at the boats to cease firing and come to collect them. But it was already too late: stones and daggers lashed the air; Corporal Thomas fell to the ground. Phillips somehow managed to reload his musket and heard Cook shout 'Take to the boats' before he was himself hit by a lump of stone. As he stumbled and fell, he was stabbed in the shoulder by a man with a dagger but somehow managed to shoot his opponent at point-blank range before scrambling into the waiting pinnace. Phillips barely had time to recover his breath before he saw Jackson – blood streaming from the spearhole in his face – lurch through the water, half-drowned and desperate, struggling to reach the boat; in a supreme gesture of bravery, he dived out to rescue the ailing man and gave him his own place in the pinnace before swimming out to Lanyon's cutter. In all the pandemonium, he had lost sight of Cook.

On the shore was a blood-lust like they had never seen: Private Harrison, hacked to pieces; Thomas Fatchett's skull smashed by a stone; Theo Hinks, dead from frenzied stabbing. The men in the boats watched in frozen horror as their colleagues were buried in the flailing ball of hatred.

In the launch, Lieutenant Williamson saw Cook waving for the boats; he said later that he had understood it as the sign to retreat so commanded his men to row away from the shore, by now foaming red. His men refused, apoplectic with rage at abandoning their comrades; Williamson was furious and threatened to shoot them if they did not row away; from that moment on, he was treated as a villainous and cowardly outcast.

Accounts of what happened next are confused and contradictory. Those still on shore were fighting for their lives; all was chaos; all was panic. One of the best views was from those still aboard the two ships, with the *Discovery* being closer in to land. As the ship's bell rang out the alarm and the cannons fired at the shore, they craned their necks and strained their eyes towards the tumult at the water's edge. Every man was on deck; every man beside himself with worry, jostling for the telescope to get a better view of the terrible drama on shore.

They saw Cook fire his gun at the warrior, they saw the warrior fall – and they saw with utter helplessness the terrible events that followed. Walking down to the water's edge, Cook waved the boats to come in. With his back turned he had no way of seeing the warrior behind him raise his arm; no way of knowing it held a club until it came crashing into his head. Bent over, he staggered forward a few dazed steps into the water, pursued by the crowd. Another man drew out one of the very iron daggers the sailors had exchanged in trade. He now surged forward and plunged it into the captain's neck, sending him face-down into the waves before the warrior himself was shot dead. A curdling scream rose up from the crowd who lunged down onto Cook's flailing body; blows rained down on him from the warriors' clubs while shiny, new daggers pinned him to the seabed. Seconds later, at just after 8 a.m., to the bellowing sound of cannon-fire from the ships, he disappeared forever in the pink foam of the surf.

Nothing moved. Broken bodies lay crumpled on the beach like discarded puppets in the sun. At the same time, a little out to sea on the hushed decks of the ships, the empty cannon stood open-mouthed and frozen in shock. An oppressive silence smothered the bay.

And then, in the safety of their respective communities, both sides numbly began to count their dead. The grim tally took on human form: seventeen Hawaiians, four marines, one Captain Cook. Many could not believe he was gone forever; everyone was stunned. Tears were followed by anger and calls for revenge but Clerke was resolute: there was nothing to be gained by vengeance but more bloodshed; hadn't there been enough of that already?

Looking for a villain on whom to pile their grief, many of the sailors wished Williamson's body was among the dead; they despised him for his cowardice and held him responsible for the death of their beloved captain, though in reality there was little he or anyone could have done. Clerke was almost numb with horror; he then slowly and purposefully took up the mantle of voyage commander with all the authority of his dead friend and colleague, and began pulling together the piecemeal accounts of Cook's final moments. How to make sense of it all? Who was to blame? One thing was clear: the catastrophe had not been premeditated but was the result of an 'unfortunate string of circumstances tending to the same unlucky point'. Captain Clerke now had it in his power to define the official version of events, the version that would define the role Cook played in the appalling tragedy – the version that would set the seal on Cook's death as accepted history and also be the linchpin to the future relations between two peoples who both felt utterly and devastatingly betrayed.

> Upon the whole I firmly believe matters would not have been carried to the extremities they were had not Capt Cook attempted to chastise a man in the midst of this multitude.

Where the master had failed, the pupil now took up the challenge of finding balance in a world turned upside-down.

The immediate priorities were to strike camp ashore, retrieve the precious chronometers, recover the bodies of the dead and refit the *Resolution*'s foremast before leaving this place of death as quickly as possible. The mast was brought on board and laid out on the deck so the men could finish their work; as for the bodies, that was a more delicate matter. King and Burney were deemed the most suitable to plead for the corpses' return and so they rowed to shore under a flag of truce. They did not get very far – halfway to the beach they were met by High Priest Koa who was swimming out to see them. When they explained what they wanted, Koa looked concerned: the marines' bodies had already been distributed amongst the villages and could never be recovered; as for Cook, his body had also been sent inland to important chiefs around the island. It would be hard to recover the parts, but he would try and would speak to them in the morning.

It was no comfort that night to see the fires burning in the darkness and hear the sounds of celebration, and it was the following night when a young frightened priest arrived at the ships with a slice from Cook's thigh: he had risked his life to bring it. He described how the rest of the body had been burned and distributed around the island, with Terreeoboo keeping hold of the bones. The mariners felt sick to their stomachs and it was all Clerke could do to summon up the strength to reassert to the priest that he wanted Cook's remains back. It was hard to keep a lid on the cold anger that now seethed up like bile among the men; it was made harder still after reports that some locals had been taunting them by spinning Cook's hat on a pole, waving the tattered uniforms of the dead marines and brandishing their bare buttocks at the men on the ships. Bligh went on the rampage on one trip to shore, shooting everyone in sight despite the protests of a mortified Bayly; meanwhile, when a watering party led by Rickman was ambushed and stoned by other locals in the bay, they turned their wrath against the villagers by shooting and decapitating anyone they saw, putting the severed heads on poles to jeer and taunt at their enemies.

And then, just when the hatred was hardest to contain, two warriors swam out to the ships, sang a fifteen-minute lament for the death of their sacred Orono before presenting their spears in heart-felt atonement and diving back into the water. The astounded men watched, open-mouthed: these were strange, unpredictable people indeed.

At last, on 20 February, Clerke had his wish when Cook's broken body was brought back to his ship. A peaceful procession of villagers and priests made its way down the beach to the waterfront, solemnly carrying a well-wrapped package to the sound of incantations and beating drums. Clerke accepted the package graciously before retreating to the privacy of his cabin with the grim offering. Once inside, he carefully peeled open the black and white feathered cape and examined the contents: there lay the scalp, the skull minus the jawbone, all the long bones, thighs, legs and arms. There were no ribs or spine or feet but his hands – identifiable from the Newfoundland powderhorn scar – still had the flesh attached which had been slashed and stuffed with salt for preserving.

Next morning, another package arrived containing Cook's missing jawbone, feet, shoes and battered musket. These were put with his other remains in a coffin, weighted down and, as the sun dipped towards the horizon on 21 February, 1779, Captain James Cook was buried at sea. Grief was universal among officers, marines and men: the hour-long ceremony was conducted amidst silence from the mourners who stood, heads bowed, upon the deck; flags flew at half-mast, the yards were crossed and half-minute guns rang out across Kealakekua Bay. By 6 p.m., it was over.

With nothing left to detain them, the ships made ready to sail. The mast that had provoked the tragedy was hoisted into place and re-rigged, and the officers slipped into their newly promoted positions: Gore went as captain to the *Discovery*, much to the relief of Bligh who had never much liked the American; King had been prevailed upon to stay on the island as the new 'Orono' but chose instead to become Clerke's First Lieutenant on the *Resolution* with the detested Williamson as his Second Lieutenant, solely by dint of his seniority. No one was in the mood to celebrate their advancement; all passion had evaporated from this voyage of discovery. They knew that they were sailing back into the ice with little hope of success in finding the Passage. As for Clerke, his lungs were now so weak that he knew would never last the journey. Even now he had to leave the navigation to William Bligh, with orders to explore the remaining Sandwich Isles before once again heading north. The heart had been ripped out of their exploring; were it not for their combined sense of duty, all would willingly have sailed home. Instead, in the evening of the 22 February, on the merest breath of a breeze, the two ships sailed out of Kealakekua Bay for the very last time.

31

KEALAKEKUA BAY, 2001

WO HUNDRED and twenty-two years after the death of James Cook, his legacy of 'discovery' is embedded in the very fabric of the lands that now belong to America. With all his fears for the indigenous peoples following contact with the so-called civilised world, he must be spinning in his watery grave to see the 'Sandwich Islands' today.

The island of Hawaii is a famous holiday destination, with multi-national hotels, shopping malls and thousands of tourists. The radio blares the strange syncretism of hula and rock, the vast American cars languish in the sun-baked parking lots while the tourists roast themselves to cinders on the beach. Outside of the brash resorts at Kona, the pace settles down to a gentle hipsway as the long stretch of empty highway takes you out and around the island and back into the land where nature exerts its grasp.

The small, modern townstead of Captain Cook lies directly on Highway 11. There's barely a sign to announce its existence, let alone its provenance: it's just *there*. I arrived at nine o'clock at night when the restaurants had closed and the hotel nightman was preparing to leave my key on a hook out the back. Captain Cook seemed more of a transit town than home to a community – guarded and quiet but with a restless soul and its eyes looking out along the highway. There was no pizzazz to announce itself, just an assured nod that I'd found the right place to search for a legend; it was, though, perfectly in keeping: the town embodied his spirit, if not his status. The only expectation that hung in the thick night air was felt by me: tomorrow, I would end my quest to follow in the footsteps of the great explorer, sitting in quiet contemplation in the place where Cook had died; yet tonight the cars sped past regardless: two ages, united in history, divided by culture; one brutal, one numb, both polarised in pace.

Elizabeth Cook (courtesy of the National Library of Australia)

I was woken by the light nudging the window to my veranda. I'd left the blinds open on purpose: having ordered a room with a view, the first thing I saw when I opened my eyes was the broad sweep of Kealakekua Bay but, now, instead of rising, I lay there for a while, surveying it cautiously like a foundling at last introduced to its mother.

I packed my backpack for the long hike down to the shore: the food for my Last Supper – cameras, film, video, notepad – then, leaving the car at a nearby gas station, I set off down the road. The passing cars drove deeper my sense of isolation: I was an outsider, a walker in a land of drivers; a searcher in a town of tourists. As they sped past, the drivers looked at me like some strange creature from outer space, dressed in walking boots, shorts and bikini-top with a pack on my back and a mission in mind. From the outside, it must have seemed bizarre as I hiked down the side of the highway; inside, I pushed down the emotions, set my face to the breeze and took a large breath.

After a few hundred metres, I found the track off the road. There was no sign, other than some rather foreboding 'Private!' ones for the neighbouring properties, which got progressively stronger as I left the road behind ('No Trespassing!', 'Keep Out!', 'Electric Fence!', 'Impending Death!'). The traffic noise grew faint as the bordering vegetation grew higher; gardens gave way to trees, which gave way to elephant grass two metres tall while, underfoot, the loose chips dwindled to dusty outcrops of volcanic rock and sand. And all the time, the sun beat down as the cicadas sang louder and louder. It was hot and heavy going; I wished I'd brought more water.

After half an hour or so, the track emerged from a relic boundary line, turned a corner and descended sharply. I traded the ghostly rustle of the tall grasses for the voodoo rattle of dense, thorny scrub. I suddenly felt not only very alone but very vulnerable. The only weapons that I could use in self-defence were the heavy black rocks of magma that were strewn along the path – the same rocks that had bludgeoned Cook and his marines to death and now lay in wait for my feckless ankles.

I was so busy watching where I placed my feet, it took me a while to notice the big, blue curve of ocean that licked across the horizon. I stopped and took a long, quiet look at the scene before me, slowly unscrewing the lid of my water bottle and taking a large draft of the by-now warm liquid in an attempt to mask my embarrassing emotional reaction to anyone who just happened to be watching: so, this was it: Kealakekua Bay, Cook's last journey.

Frustratingly, although I could see it, it took another hour of thirsty hiking (and occasional body-surfing) down the solidified spewings of magma before I finally reached the flat of the coastline. As the path levelled out, the trees grew dense again, but this time sprouted from the black stone walls of what looked like some ruined sheep-fank. It was only when the broken lines mapped out a village that I realised where I was: these were the homes that Cook had walked through on that last, fateful morning of 14 February. The ghosts of the villagers were all around me in the dappled light, watching my every move through the eyes of the mongoose that stood stock still before scuttling into the leaf-litter. The houses crowded in on me; the branches scratched my face. I passed through this tunnel of trees and then out into the blinding light of the beach.

The scene was at first shockingly intimate. Lumps of white coral lay like bleached bones along the shoreline; flabby black tongues of magma lapped at the murmuring water – and then, pricked out from this monochrome scene, lay the scattered red and yellow plastic canoes of a party of visiting snorkellers. They had paddled here to explore the waters famous for the sealife that swam among the coral. That is the reason why most people come to the area; few hike their way down the tortuous rocky path and even fewer come to see the death-place of Captain Cook, or his memorial that lies under the water a few feet out to sea. Set back from the shoreline is an obelisk to his memory, ringed by a chainlink fence. On one side is the inscription, 'Whites go home', daubed onto the bright white surface, then blotted out itself by a thin layer of white paint. You can still read it clearly, despite the efforts of the authorities. They need not have bothered; the whole bay shrugs its shoulders at the mention of his death. The world has moved on; Captain Cook is just another name of another rambling town.

As for the snorkellers, any reverence to dead sailors is at best an afterthought – an interesting curio to join the strangely-coloured fish. They had slipped out of their canoes and were seal-diving about in playful discovery; still more lay like reptiles, sunning themselves on the hot black stone. I found a spot in the shade of a tree and hid there, like an uninvited guest at someone else's party.

It wasn't meant to be like this: I should have been alone in a tranquil bay suffused with quiet memories of significant events. I had come to pay my last respects and let the waves of painful experience from both sides of the story flood into my mind. Instead, modernity had pierced the soft skin of the past and drained its blood into the water. There was nothing left but the infrastructure of stone and water. Brightly-coloured plastic kayaks lay like husks upon the beach yet, for me, Kealakekua Bay was empty.

32

THE END OF AMBITION

England 1780

N 11 JANUARY, 1780, an announcement appeared in the *London Gazette*:

> Captain Clerke of His Majesty's Sloop *Resolution*, in a letter to Mr Stephens, dated 8th of June 1779, in the Harbour of St Peter and St Paul, Kampschatka, which was received yesterday, gives the melancholy account of the celebrated Captain Cook, late commander of that Sloop, with four of his private Marines having been killed on 14th of February last at the island of O'Why'he, one of a group of new discovered Islands in the 22nd Degree of North Latitude, in an affray with a numerous and tumultuous Body of Natives.

It had taken eleven months for the news to reach London, overland from Kamchatka and across the vast landmass of Russia to Berlin and finally England. Now all the nation joined in mourning this great navigator. The same newspaper carried his obituary:

> This untimely and ever to be lamented Fate of so intrepid, so able, and so intelligent a Sea-Officer, may justly be considered as an irreparable Loss to the Public, as well as to his Family, for in him were united every successful and amiable quality that could adorn his Profession; nor was his singular Modesty less conspicuous than his other Virtues. His successful Experiments to preserve the Healths of his Crews are well known, and his Discoveries will be an everlasting Honour to his Country.

Clerke's letter had arrived at the Admiralty the day before: Mr Stephens

*The coat of arms that was granted by
George III to Cook's widow Elizabeth*

would have guessed from the writing that the package was not from his friend Captain Cook, nor less from Captain Clerke who was already dead from his consumption and interred to the frozen Kamchatkan soil when Gore made up the Admiralty packages. Stephens would then have known that bad news was inside. A flurry of letters followed the shock of its reading – from Sandwich to Banks:

> Dear Sir: what is uppermost in our mind allways must come out first, poor Captain Cooke is no more …

from Banks to his friends, and from there out to the glitterati of London and beyond.

There is no record of how Elizabeth heard of her husband's death, though one presumes a messenger was sent from the Admiralty. After all she had endured, it is hard not to hope that Stephens, Palliser or Sandwich might have gone to Mile End personally to help break the devastating news. It was now three and a half years since she had bade her husband farewell; baby Hugh was a young boy and both James and Nathaniel were rising up the Navy ladder having finished their training at the Academy in Portsmouth. Did they grieve for their father? They had only known him for a few brief months at a time between voyages, though the intimate way he wrote of his family cuts through much of the distance. As for Elizabeth, she had lived all her married life knowing that James might not return but the shock still ripped her world apart. She was still only thirty-eight years old.

From the day she learned of his death, she dressed only in black, a locket of his hair encased in the ring on her finger. He had given her some *tapa* cloth from his last voyage to the Pacific and she had spent her days and nights cutting, sewing and shaping it into a waistcoat to surprise him on his return. She fancied that he could wear it for his audience with the King and embroidered the elegant side panels with garlands of flowers – tiny stitches in coloured silken threads, with silver for the stems and for the detail on the pockets. The waistcoat was folded and put away unworn. This time, there would be no audience.

For his part, the King was greatly moved and did not forget Elizabeth either, as *The Gazette* again reported:

> His Majesty who had already the highest opinion of Captain Cook, shed tears, when Lord Sandwich informed him of his death, and immediately ordered a pension of £300 per annum for his widow.

But pensions, annuities and the alleged £12,000 that would come from his journals were small compensation for the losses she had borne. In more than sixteen years of marriage, she had lost three of her children and had her husband at home with her for just four years. And more grief was on its way. Later that year, on 3 October, Nathaniel's ship went down with all hands in a Jamaican hurricane; the next day, her husband's returning ships anchored in the Thames without him.

In 1784, Elizabeth wrote to Banks:

> My greatest pleasure now remaining is in my sons, who, I hope, will ever strive to copy after so good an example, and, animated by the honours bestowed on their Father's memory, be ambitious of attaining by their own merits your notice and approbation.

But the years that followed would bring more tears for this woman who had endured so much. Young Hugh would not go to sea: he was destined for the clergy and, in 1793, went to study at Christ's College, Cambridge. Within months, he was stricken with a violent fever and died on her wedding anniversary on 2 December the same year. A month later, James – her oldest and last surviving child – caught an open boat at Portsmouth to join the *Spitfire* sloop of war as a newly-promoted commander. He never arrived. His body was found on an Isle of Wight beach, a blow to his head and his pockets empty. No member of the crew was ever seen again. He was thirty-one years old.

When she heard the news, Elizabeth's strength finally broke down. Totally overcome, she took to her bed, refused to eat and suffered a series of terrible fits. At fifty-two she was utterly alone. She spent the last forty-two years of her life with her Bible and her four annual days of mourning for her husband and three sons; her only close family was her cousin, Isaac Smith – the young boy who had been the first to step on the shores of Botany Bay and was now a retired rear-admiral living in Clapham. She went to live with him, then, when he too died, she returned to her own house in Surrey where she lived as quietly as she had always done, guarding her privacy as tightly as her grief. Just before she breathed her last at the age of ninety-three, she burned all the personal letters between her husband and herself.

The qualities that attracted Cook to the young Elizabeth had stayed with her to the end: a strength of purpose, that clear, quick mind, a lack of pride or arrogance – and if anything she had grown more dignified with age. She was also unusually canny for an eighteenth-century woman, though her upbringing in the alehouse may have left her worldlier than most: she wrote confidently, though politely, to Lord Sandwich and Sir Joseph Banks and proved herself quite the businesswoman; certainly, it was thought so on her death: when her estate was added up, it amounted to almost £60,000 – the results of careful planning and clever investment. She left hundreds of curios and mementos collected over the years by her husband; her only regret was the portrait that made him look too severe – hers was the gentle James who loved his wife and adored his children, not the despot of the final voyage.

On 13 May, 1835, Elizabeth Cook departed this life. She lies buried under the floor in the aisle of St Andrew the Great Church in Cambridge, along with her beloved sons, Hugh and James. On the wall to their left is a cream marble plaque, ornate with embellishments and listing all the six children of that remarkable couple. She had outlived her husband by fifty-six years – over three times as long as they had been married; while her tomb still lies in that cold damp earth, the bones of her husband form part of the coral – refuge to brightly-coloured fish that hide from the tourists as they swim in warm Pacific waters, seven thousand miles away in time and space.

33
TROUBLESOME GEORGE COLLINGRIDGE AND THE IDEAS REVOLUTION

N AUGUST 1895, George Collingridge walked into a small bookshop on Elizabeth Street and saw a large book slumped lazily on the shelf. Picking it up, he carefully opened the ox-blood cover that creaked like an old man's bones. As its pages bathed in unaccustomed daylight, he traced the words on the inside leaf:

THE DISCOVERY OF AUSTRALIA

A Critical, Documentary and Historic Investigation Concerning the
Priority of Discovery in Australasia by Europeans before the arrival of
Lieut. James Cook, in the Endeavour, in the year 1770.
With Illustrations, Charts, Maps, Diagrams, &c. Copious Notes, References,
Geographical Index and Index to Names.

BY

GEORGE COLLINGRIDGE

MEMBER OF THE COUNCIL OF THE ROYAL GEOGRAPHICAL SOCIETY OF AUSTRALASIA, SYDNEY.

HON. CORRESP. MEMBER OF THE ROYAL GEOGRAPHICAL SOCIETY OF AUSTRALASIA, MELBOURNE.

HON. CORRESP. MEMBER OF THE NEUCHATELOISE GEOGRAPHICAL SOCIETY, NEUCHATEL, SWITZERLAND.

HON. CORRESP. MEMBER OF THE PORTUGUESE GEOGRAPHICAL SOCIETY, LISBON.

HON. CORRESP. MEMBER OF THE SPANISH GEOG. SOC., MADRID, &C, &C. FOUNDER AND

FIRST VICE-PRESIDENT OF THE ART SOCIETY OF NEW SOUTH WALES, SYDNEY.

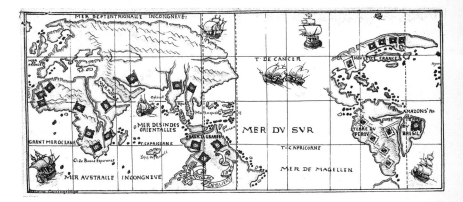

Facsimile of Nicholas Desliens' 1566 Dieppe map

The papers went wild. Captain Cook hadn't discovered Australia? How could he say such a thing? It was tantamount to heresy. But after the inevitable backlash, the groundswell of commentators and reviewers had to admit that George had conducted a most thorough piece of research – no one in Australia had read more books or knew more about the subject than the author, no one spoke all the necessary languages needed to contradict his evidence and no one else had cast their net as wide in gathering every shred of information to support their theory. More significantly, even the most cursory examination of conscience had to accept that the Dutch had certainly reached Australian shores at the start of the seventeenth century which led to the mapping of western Australia – and they were just occupying the lands previously held by the Portuguese. If the Dutch could explore the Great South Land/New Holland, why shouldn't other nations have explored their own Jave la Grande? The logic was incontrovertible but just as important in quelling a major storm were other factors of a more practical nature: relatively few people could afford to pay out the thirty shillings to purchase a copy of the book and even fewer would wade through the 376 dense pages of text, maps and quotations untranslated from their original Latin, Spanish, Portuguese and French. In essence, therefore, the book was critically acclaimed but languished unread on the shelves.

George, meanwhile, was unstoppable. While admitting that he had not made a penny from publishing the book, he continued with his studies and his papers and his talks, all in the name of the true history of Australia. Towards the end of the 1890s, however, a curious adversary to his ideas arose in the form of the Archbishop of Sydney, Cardinal Moran. Although they were both Catholics, the two men were vastly opposed in their beliefs as to who had 'discovered' Australia. Whereas George was more firmly convinced than ever that it was the Portuguese, shortly after their arrival in the region around 1511, Cardinal Moran was busy asserting his own claims that it was the Spanish explorer, Fernàndez de Quirós, who had landed in 1606 – not in the New Hebrides as was generally accepted, but at Gladstone, just north of Brisbane on the Queensland coast. By this reasoning, Moran cleverly asserted that Australia was therefore officially a Catholic country as its discoverers had claimed it in the name of God and their King, with mass being celebrated on its shores. Though his theories were preposterous, Cardinal Moran was an immensely powerful and charismatic man who had even stood as a candidate in the New South Wales elections for the Federal Convention. Although he had significant support from large sections of the Catholic community, he was by no means universally popular among those who shared his faith and was even less popular with the press. The *Sydney Morning Herald* detested him while the United Protestant Conference passed a resolution calling him 'the sworn soldier and servant of a foreign power'.

As a Catholic and a historian who dared to say that James Cook *hadn't* got there first, George found himself being tarred with the same disdain as Cardinal Moran. Whereas, until then, his critics had accused him of errors of judgement, he now stood accused of working to a hidden religious agenda. Frustrated and concerned, he immediately wrote an article for the *Australian Magazine* in which he issued a strong rejoinder to the Cardinal but it was already too late: he was caught in the patriotic backlash against any suggestion that Australia was not rightfully British.

The trickle of dissent over his theories soon gathered momentum as Australia moved towards Federation in 1901. With the new national pride, the public became more interested than ever in the history of 'their' continent, glorying in the 'official' line that James Cook had 'discovered' their shores. Even the Dutch – who had charted all but the east coast since 1606 – were edged out of the story, much to that Government's disgust, but it seemed that it would take more than one book and a ream of papers on the subject of Portuguese priority to challenge the hold of the British Empire: it had the power to define history, and its voice was louder than George's.

More than ever, he realised that convincing his countrymen was going to be an uphill struggle and, despite having passed his fiftieth birthday, his studies became more time-consuming than ever. To those around him, the research even seems to have overtaken his painting and particularly his engraving, which was becoming increasingly obsolete in the face of new technology. By 1900, he was earning no more than a sixpence per square inch of work – hardly enough to fund his postage bills, let alone support his family that had now grown to four boys and a girl. However, by expanding his teaching and taking on private pupils, he and Lucy somehow managed to survive – and to keep funding the never-ending researches into the discovery of Australia.

Then, in 1904, came a piece of good fortune that would not only earn him money but would finally confer the kudos and recognition he had been seeking. He was approached by the Under-Secretary for Public Instruction who asked him to turn his 'Discovery of Australia' into a school history book – taking out the more contentious theories but leaving in the history. Quite how the Under-Secretary imagined the book fitting into the syllabus for primary schools is unclear, and it certainly wasn't a concern for George: with renewed excitement, he worked quickly on the revised text which he completed and handed to the Government's appointed publisher, William Brooks & Company, by the end of the year.

The First Discovery of Australia and New Guinea began with a note from the publishers:

> Ten years ago, Mr George Collingridge published 'The Discovery of Australia' – a large quarto volume, bulky, erudite and expensive. It took its place as a valuable contribution to the literature of the country, and remains a world-accepted authority on the important and interesting subject with which it deals. But it was in nowise [sic] suited to the general reader-being designed more for the scholar than for the person who desired to conveniently possess himself of authentic information relating to the earliest annals of Australian discovery.
>
> To meet the requirements of the general reader, and to serve as a text book of Australian History, the present publication has been issued as a handy compendium of the original volume.
>
> From this book, all controversial matter has been omitted as irrelevant to a work intended as a handbook for either scholar or student.
>
> The valuable facsimiles of rare and ancient maps have been retained, many illustrations have been included in the text, and the story of the explorers has been dealt with at greater length by the author, whose patient antiquarian research, his knowledge of European and Oriental Languages, and his opportunities as a member of several Geographical Societies has given him unusual facilities for the compilation of a work which may confidently be expected to find its way into every scholastic, public and private library in the Commonwealth.

Both George and Brooks thought his moment had come: soon, his work would be in every school, shaping every child's understanding of the history of their continent. And then disaster struck: on the eve of the book going to the printers, the Under-Secretary for Public Instruction suddenly dropped dead – and as if that was not bad news enough, the first thing his replacement did was cancel the contract and scrap all plans for *The First Discovery* to be used in Australia's schools.

George was devastated: not only was it bad enough to suffer such an intellectual and public snubbing but financially it was a disaster. The pages lay still on the printing press waiting to bring truth to the nation's schoolchildren, but even more hurtful was the fact that after more than twenty years of pouring his heart, mind and soul into his researches, he had been rejected by the Establishment as irrelevant. Irrelevant or – perhaps more accurately – too threatening. Cook was Britannia's legitimacy for colonising a country that had been visited by the Dutch for over a hundred and fifty years – and to the new Under-Secretary, like most whites at the time, the history of Australia began with the British, regardless of who had been here before. If the Aborigines failed to figure in their claim for the continent, no one else stood a chance, least of all a tiny, insignificant squib of a country like Portugal. And they were certainly not going to have an artist-turned-amateur historian 'French' Catholic telling them differently!

Although it was never proved, it seemed that the new Under-Secretary had been warned to steer clear of George's controversial account of Australia by the country's rising historical establishment – an establishment that was beginning to flex its muscles in the new Australian Universities and historical societies that had become increasingly popular since the turn of the century. If anyone was going to teach the nation's children about the history of their county, it was going to be a recognised 'expert' teaching 'official' history, not some upstart artist with fancy and decidedly un-British ideas. The dismissal had been swift and catastrophic: George now found himself increasingly sidelined from mainstream opinion.

Determined not to be beaten, in 1906, he published his book regardless, though it languished in dusty warehouses before limping off the shelves. The academic fraternity dismissed the book as the curious work of a patent amateur who even stooped so low as to advertise his family's painting lessons on the back pages! The wounds cut deep. George was now facing prejudice as an amateur, a heretic and a catholic – and the harder he tried to change opinions, the harder they set against him. However, try as they might, the academics could not completely ignore George's theories. Arnold Wood, the Professor of History at the University of Sydney, managed to maintain a usually-polite, if condescending, relationship with his amateur rival, though he never lost an opportunity to remind George that his views were not popular. The surviving letters between the two men make for interesting reading in the art of the professional put-down:

> The exceedingly kindly way in which you received some rather savage criticism at the Society's meeting, make me sure that you will not resent the fact that in some respects I have ventured to differ from your opinions ...

Wood and his colleagues might not have approved or agreed with his conclusions – and there was certainly suspicion of his motives – but there was no denying that George knew more about early Australian history than they ever did, even though some would rather choke on their own bile than admit it. Until well after the Second World War, the 'Australian' history of schools and colleges was just standard British history taught in a warmer climate; only a small minority dared to venture into the political quagmire of early European contact and, if they did, it was often easier to use George's research without permission than to admit that they needed his help. Having already endured their disdain, he now had to suffer the added insult of seeing his precious maps reproduced without him being asked or their origin being acknowledged – or sometimes with his name very obviously rubbed out!

Somehow, throughout it all, George managed to retain his characteristic humour. When Wood wrote to George asking permission to use his maps for a lecture, George replied:

> Yes, certainly … I know that you won't cut out my name like Albert F. Calvert, Filch-it, the Dutch, Germans and others have done.

He struggled to remind himself that the politics of his work were mere ephemera: it was more important to find the truth than to stay inside the narrow conventions of the day through fear of rocking the Establishment's boat. The bitchiness and the theft of his ideas and charts may have been offensive in the extreme but he was wise enough to know he was up against a powerful adversary; instead of biting back, he hid the hurt that gnawed away inside him, and carried on as best he could.

The final and crushing blow to George's dream of acceptance came at a public meeting of the Royal Australian History Society, late in 1917, when Professor Wood delivered his violent demolition of the Portuguese theory. Taking the arguments one by one, the Professor ruthlessly attacked them. The style and confidence with which he launched his assault dealt a mortal wound to George's credibility as a historian; George had not been brought up in the ideas-jousting of academic life and was grossly unprepared to match fire with fire. It was David versus Goliath – only this time Goliath had won. His victim was left a broken man.

Looking back on that night over eighty years on, the tragedy is all the more acute since later research has proved that on the subject of early European discovery, Wood was basically wrong – and it must have only added to George's confusion that while he was being pilloried in his own land, he was being fêted overseas. By the time of that humiliating fall from favour, it was gratifying that he had been given the Portuguese Order of St James and the Sword and the Spanish Royal American Order of Isabela La Catolica; back home in the Sydney suburbs, he vowed that while he would continue to preach the same gospel about Australia's European past, he would never publish a book on the subject again.

There are reports of George in his final years, sitting in his favourite tea shop in Hornsby where he displayed his painted reproductions of the Dieppe Maps in the hope of making a sale. To anyone that would listen, he would explain his theories and the evidence he had gathered over the last forty years. As the old man talked, a fire would spark in his eyes with the passion of that thirty-year-old *émigré* who had first seen the glorious charts that were the Dieppe Maps – and then that fire would flicker and fade as his audience politely nodded and left the room.

On 1 June, 1931, George Alphonse Collingridge de Tourcey died, betrayed by his countrymen and by the tyranny of history. He was eighty-three years old and had never once given up his fight to teach Australians what he believed was the truth about their continent. A few days later, he was buried in the Catholic section of the Field of Mars Cemetery in Sydney where his dust joined the soil of a land almost four billion years old. Like the faded outline of the land of Jave la Grande, it knew how to keep its secrets.

The Dieppe Maps continue to incite passion – for and against their whispers of early voyages of discovery. In the absence of that final, definitive piece of evidence, the debate will continue for as long as the hot wind blows across the Australian earth. The key witnesses may have died and the maps faded but the stories live on – stories like George's – a tale of obsession with the truth and betrayal by the keyholders of a nation's history; they seem to have been more concerned with empire-building than uncovering the facts – even if it meant their empires were built with rotten wood on shallow foundations – and they used their power to gag debate. The high ideals of academia were exposed as a mockery, and knowledge was mired in the dirt of those who protected their ivory towers rather than defend the freedom of ideas and the pursuit of truth.

But regardless of what humans do on earth, and whatever name by which they choose to call it, the land itself remains. It survives to give succour to those with a passion and a spirit of adventure, those who know the difference between truth, fantasy and fraud – men like George Collingridge and Captain James Cook.

Dreaming painting by Mona Rockman – an Aboriginal map

34

HEROES, HERETICS AND THE GREAT WHODUNIT

F COURSE, the first *true* discoverers of Australia were the Aborigines – and no map or argument will ever prove otherwise. Fossil evidence from skeletons affectionately known as 'Mungo Man' and 'Mungo Woman' shows with certainty that their ancestors go back at least sixty thousand years and there are suggestions that they may go back even further. Elsewhere in Australia, brightly coloured cave paintings show ancient hunters fighting what we would class as prehistoric animals: giant mega-fauna, such as wombats the size of rhinos and birds as tall as elephants. The Aborigines migrated to the land we now call Australia over land-bridges from Indonesia, formed during the last great Ice Age when sea levels plummeted. At that time, Australia was also connected to Tasmania, but when sea levels rose again, the tribes were essentially cut off from their neighbours, evolving different patterns of culture and language even amongst themselves as they stretched across the vastness of their new land. With each ensuing millennium of isolation, the memory of these migratory people was gently erased as the seas closed in to protect the secret continent and its inhabitants.

Geographical secrets didn't come any bigger than the vast island continent of Australia. After Cook had exposed the Great Southern Continent as nothing but fantasy, Europeans were desperate for a land to take its place – and the 'discovery' of Australia by the myth-slayer fitted the bill nicely; in fact, it could hardly have been designed more perfectly: here was a man who had risked his life to serve his King, who had sailed to incredible lands of earthly paradise, made exciting discoveries for his country – and then died a hero's death. Less than a decade after Cook's dramatic demise, Australia had received its first British colonists at the encouragement of Joseph Banks and the former *Endeavour* midshipman, James Magra. And, as the continent itself was being talked-up, so was the man who had mapped its shores.

It is a truism to say that, in history, timing is everything but in the case of Australia, the time-line could not have been scripted better. 'New South Wales' appeared on our world map just at the moment when Britain was losing its stronghold in the Americas along with some of its glory back home. The end of the eighteenth century saw Britannia frantic for new colonies and new heroes. The cool, measured mood of the Age of Reason was melting into the bubbling passions of the Age of Romanticism; the new social commentators were not learned men of science but writers and poets such as Coleridge, Byron and Shelley – and, as New South Wales was elevated to the status of the New World, the man who had given it its name was elevated to the status of an icon. The irony is that the sea-faring champion of truth and fact had now become an object of romantic fantasy.

Whether that icon was also really taken as a Hawaiian god – or whether that was just a piece of cultural confusion and anglocentric storytelling – has recently been the subject of much debate, but regardless of what happened overseas, the British certainly took his deification to an artform. What had started in the *Resolution*'s Great Cabin with Charles Clerke's careful editing of the story of Cook's death, continued in the voyage journals completed by James King: as early as the afternoon of that tragic Valentine's Day, 1779, history was being shaped and managed. Cook had all the raw materials to be the superhero that the times demanded – and he also had the spin-doctors to work those pieces into perfection.

In the same way that Banks had promoted Australia, he now did the same with Cook. The slightly patronising air that had kept the men at a distance in life now worked to Cook's advantage as Banks effectively *became* his patron and managed his growing reputation. In a new era that worshipped the cult of the romantic individual, Banks wore the badge of Cook as proudly as he wore his Tahitian tattoo, and spun his tale to perfection. In death, Cook now grew more famous than he could ever have imagined, with all the accoutrements of a national celebrity, including poems, plays, monuments, celebratory cups and plates – even Captain Cook wallpaper! By the time the nineteenth century had got under way, Britannia was bathing in the reflected glory of this most heroic of heroes.

As for the colonies in Australia, it suited them to have their heroes, too – and who wore the laurels better than the man who had mapped their shores? No one seemed to notice the irony that Cook hadn't actually thought much of their country and never again visited the mainland after his departure at the end of August, 1770. Given the choice of base in the

South Pacific, he chose New Zealand every time – but such details are small barriers to the creation of a legend.

However, in another of his 'new found lands', the legend of Captain Cook was also taking shape and, while it may have included the same amount of convenient re-working, this time it resulted not in exaltation but in infamy. Hawaii might only have been five thousand miles away across the ocean but it was a million miles away in terms of how its people viewed the great navigator. According to their version of history, Cook was the scourge of the islands' history, bringing nothing but death, disease and destruction to their shores. Missionaries had arrived soon after the ships' departure, when there were still people alive who remembered the Captain's visits. The more they heard the Hawaiians' stories about Cook accepting such deification, the more they turned against him. How dare he allow himself to be treated like a god when only God Himself should be given that honour! The fault lay not in the Hawaiian people but the arrogance of a baptised Christian who elevated himself to the level of the Almighty. It merely added insult to terminal injury that he had also entered the locals' temple and worshipped and kissed their idols: by now, nothing was too bad to be believed. Once the seeds were sown, they soon bore more bitter fruit: stories grew up that Cook had bedded a young Princess, even though it later transpired she was only eight years old. The men had also brought with them mosquitoes that caused a plague of malaria and sexual diseases causing infertility and death. In effect, Cook had presided over the decimation of the Hawaiian population for years to come.

It didn't seem to matter that the stories were largely untrue – that Cook had never had sex with anyone on his travels and he had publicly and endlessly tried to stop his men from having 'relations'; moreover, while they undoubtedly did bring some gonorrhoea and syphilis to the islands, the locals' itchy rashes that pricked his conscience on his second visit to the islands was just as likely to be yaws – a contagious skin disease endemic to the Pacific – as disease from his men. As for the mosquitoes, they most probably came with the missionaries themselves! However, the point remains that Cook did allow himself to be treated as a superior being, though he seems to have accepted it as the natural respect given to any great chief, albeit somewhat over the top. As for him worshipping their statues, today one would call that religious respect.

Cook knew that cultural confusion was the inevitable outcome of a voyage of discovery, and he was also aware of the damage done by the 'corrupting' contact with 'civilisation'. But he knew it was his job to make that contact and better that it was made by someone sensitive to the indigenous populations than the more usually brutal captains of

European ships who would most often shoot first and talk later.

But the real key to Cook's appalling reputation in the Hawaiian Islands was not so much what he did or was supposed to have done – but who had the power to define history. The native Hawaiians had a fantastic oral history but no written language, so it was up to the missionaries and their students to collect the first-hand accounts of the sailors' visit and the manner of Cook's death then translate them onto paper. And in that translation was the inevitable influence of their own beliefs and values which placed Cook as a wanton idolater and wannabe god. Trouble was, once it was written down, it became 'fact', regardless of the original truth, and the facts formed the basis of Hawaiian history and teaching.

It has only been relatively recently that historians of those isles have gone back to check 'fact' from reality – and found that the two didn't match – but by then the story of the demonic Cook had rooted itself deep in the nation's psyche. Any change from that position over the last few years has been more to do with apathy: few people now care about his role in their islands at all.

Meanwhile, almost fifty years after the death of George Collingridge, Australia faced its own revolutions in the wheel of fame and fortune. In 1976, fed up with importing British rules for its language, Australia produced its first home-grown dictionary, with its own words and slang, expletives and expressions; looking back now, it is unbelievable it had taken so long, but around the same period, Australia also stopped importing its history. It could have been the profound mood of national reflection that came along with its 'bicentenary', it could have been the shame over its treatment of the Aborigines or it could just have been the usual signs of a new society reaching maturity, but it was suddenly acceptable to find answers from within its shores – and that meant challenging the hegemony of Captain Cook as the point zero of Australia's past.

Into the breach flooded a series of books, papers and articles exploring the history of European contact with the continent – and the vast majority of those concerned the period during the sixteenth century when the Portuguese and Spanish were making their discoveries in the region. Almost a century after he published his first paper on the subject of a Portuguese 'discovery' of Australia, George and his theories now hit centre stage – and this time, they were seriously listened to.

Whereas George had clashed with the mood of the moment, by the late 1970s and early 1980s, the timing was perfect. During the previous decades, on the other side of the world, a Portuguese scholar named Armando Cortesao had been trawling through his country's shambolic archives, unearthing and collecting together the curious references to its early voyages to the lands of the Indian and Pacific Oceans. Little by little, from the snatches of text in the dusty manuscripts, a picture began to emerge. Most of his evidence was in narrative form – poems, chronicles, reports and letters – and much of it was circumstantial, but it all pointed one way: to a series of organised voyages of discovery by the Portuguese of the sixteenth century. When the literature was added to the cartographic evidence, the case seemed almost cast-iron: the Portuguese had discovered, mapped and explored the large continent named Jave la Grande within the time frame (1511–c.1540) suggested by George. And not only that: the researchers shored up the belief of Portuguese priority with a name – Christopher Mendonça – a voyage, and a date of 1521–22. What had become known as 'The Great Whodunit', the subject to which George had devoted his life, was now one step closer to being solved.

The theory is plausible enough: Christopher Mendonça sailed with three ships in search of Magellan, whom the Portuguese knew was trying to find a Spanish route to the Spice Islands. Little realising that Magellan had come from South America and was heading *west* towards the Philippines, the Portuguese fleet crossed through the Torres Strait, around Cape York and then down an east coast riddled with shoals and the Great Barrier Reef (Coste Dangereuse) around Fraser Island, to the north of Brisbane, and past 'Coste des Harbiages' – the area around modern-day Botany Bay to the south of Australia, reaching possibly as far as Warrnambool to the west of contemporary Melbourne.

Could Mendonça's voyage have triggered the exploration of the land named Jave la Grande? There is little in the way of direct or hard evidence but what keeps the flame of curiosity burning are the fifty or so pieces of circumstantial evidence, some flimsy in the extreme but others more credible, the sheer volume of which add weight to the argument. From reported sightings of 'Mahogany' ships in the sand, to some early sixteenth-century cannons and original documentation of a shipwreck on the north coast in 1542, the trail of the Portuguese refuses to wither and die – and this time the pendulum has swung towards acceptance.

Other people – including the former Keeper of Maps at the British Library – have brought forward contemporary evidence suggesting the Dieppe Maps were the result of French discoveries. In 1529, the Parmentier brothers sailed from Dieppe to the South Seas in search of fame and fortune. Jean Parmentier was a true Renaissance Man – a poet as well as a navigator – and though his charts were probably destroyed when the English blew up Dieppe in 1692, they may well have formed the basis for some of the infamous maps. Today his poems are all that remain, painting just as vivid, if not as detailed, a picture:

> I often wonder why, for this odd fantasy
> I Europe leave, and why it lies to me
> To circle Africa so near around,
> Nor can I yet contented be
> Until the coasts of Asia shall be found,
> To such an effort am I tied;
> My head is fired, my spirit has not died.
> So, making ready, I am filled with joy,
> If questioning still the ends of my employ.
>
> translated by David Beers Quinn

Jean Parmentier and his brother made it to Portuguese Sumatra where they both died, leaving their ship to be sailed back by their pilot, Pierre Crignon, with reports and possibly local maps of a vast land to the south. Could Crignon, therefore, have been the source of information on Jave la Grande?

New Zealand, too, has been examining its pre-Cook and even pre-Tasman past. The oral histories of the Maori mention men in large ships calling at the islands, while early European helmets and coins have also been found, though there was never the same level of antagonism to those who dared to suggest another 'truth' as there was in neighbouring Australia. As far back as 1827, the British Admiralty chart of New Zealand showed a strangely-named bay on the west coast of the South Island, labelled 'The Gulf of the Portuguese, 1550'; the information was taken from a Frenchman – Monsieur D'Apres de Mannevillette – but the trail frustratingly appears to die with him.

It was against this background that I arrived in the Antipodes in a personal quest to explore the explorers that had spanned three centuries, three people and – if you count Hawaii as North America – three continents. Just as George caused a storm by talking about Portuguese discovery at a time when Cook was king, I had been warned when heading off to Australia not to mention Cook's name too heavily in certain academic circles – that *he* was now 'persona non grata' in the new 'open-minded' world; in fact, that world would rather not talk about discovery at all: it was too embarrassing a reminder of the dark ages of colonialism. How can you 'discover' a land that's been inhabited by other people for millennia? It's all so arrogant and crassly Eurocentric! Seemingly, the wheel of fame and fortune had made another turn; no one else seemed to see the irony that one tyrannical history was merely being replaced by a new one.

However, I quickly found that there are advantages to being on the outside of a culture. When Cook had arrived on Tanna and asked the name of the island, the locals didn't 'get' the question which – to them – seemed perfectly stupid. Why do you need to have a name for somewhere that no-one ever leaves? Over two hundred years later, it was my turn to roll up and ask the 'stupid' questions – and I found that more often than not, the reply was brutally revealing. Sometimes the simplest query can garner a wealth of information – intended *and* unintended. At first, no one wanted to talk about heroes and heretics – the words had no meaning in the new era of all-embracing inclusion: everyone was welcome, whatever their colour, creed or code of beliefs; but scratch beneath the surface and the old prejudices and rivalries remain.

The Portuguese protagonists claimed they had won the day; the non-believers said, 'Rubbish' and stuck with the Dutch discoveries; a vocal camp claimed that the Dieppe Maps' alleged land of Jave la Grande was nothing more than a misplaced Vietnam, blown up and part of it inverted 180°. The point is – unless stunning new evidence turns up in some dusty corner of a distant archive – the case can *never* be settled with certainty and so all groups can say that they are the ones who have got the story right.

Meanwhile, a paper has recently appeared in a leading academic journal discussing a European lead weight, scientifically dated to between AD1410 and 1630. It was found buried deep in the ancient sand on Queensland's Fraser Island – an island that correlates with one clearly drawn and shown in the correct latitudes on Jean Rotz's Dieppe Map. This time, however, the discovery could not be so easily dismissed as fake or fantasy: the discoverers were not amateurs – they were respected government scientists taking core-samples in the sand as part of an unrelated research project. They have since shown, without doubt, that the weight was buried in a sufficient depth of sand to prove that it had rested there for centuries – and yet it has taken twenty-three years to get the results of analyses into the date and origin of their remarkable discovery published in a reputable journal as their conclusions were not deemed 'appropriate' – that is, they did not 'fit' with the version of history that had been accepted as fact. It seems it can sometimes still be a difficult matter to win acceptance for suggesting that James Cook might *not* have got there first.

Also alive and well, even in these days of George's partial Renaissance, are the old attitudes and prejudices that helped destroy him. I purposefully didn't give my last name to one interviewee – a world-renowned historian of the Cook School of Australian discovery. When I asked him what he thought of George Collingridge and his theories, he replied, 'Now there's a good stick with which to beat the English Dog!'

Clearly, your background still counts as strongly as your ideas when it comes to challenging history.

Given the time, conditions and geographical isolation in which he was working, George Collingridge produced a remarkable piece of work. But more than that, subsequent research with the benefit of new evidence from Australia and the Portuguese themselves has tended, if anything, to strengthen his claims. He was eccentric and colourful and too given to whims of fancy and dreadful puns, but the bulk of his research is basically sound. As a geographer, I could respect him; as a relative, I'd grown to love him.

As for Cook, the tragedy behind the hero had at last made him real. Modern thought assigns his degenerating behaviour and judgement to a chronic gastrointestinal disease that left him deficient in the vitamins essential for controlling the nerves. The agonising colic and decaying mind are well-enough documented in the journals of his peers – but that story didn't fit with the Empire's need for a hero.

Heroes aren't allowed to have flaws, only humans do, but it is the *human* story of Cook, of how he rose and fell, then was used and abused by generations for their own purposes, that brings history alive. And so, too, does the story of George and the Dieppe Maps – the grit in the oyster, fly in the ointment and the little boy who dared to laugh at the emperor's new clothes. My own journey as an explorer through five hundred years of maps had left me more in awe than ever of their depiction of power and control: far from being value-free, their coastlines and oceans contain as vivid an expression of the beliefs and desires of their creators as you'll find in any official history. They can cheat, lie, proclaim fantasy or expose the truth but – though they're little more than freeze-frames in the game of politics – they cannot be rubbed out when the wheel of fortune turns.

Our maps today show no Great Southern Continent or strange land called Jave la Grande, but we cannot pretend they did not exist – even if they did so only in the minds of dreamers and kings. Shortly after George's death, the maritime historian, Dr James Williamson, published his own account of the Dieppe Maps and his conclusions are impossible to deny:

> It is a matter of weighing probabilities, and one can only conclude that if these maps were guesswork, they represent the most inspired guesswork ever recorded.

Rewriting history is a dangerous game; the map of the world is there for a reason – but sometimes, just sometimes, reality *can* overcome myth.

SELECT BIBLIOGRAPHY

FOUND A number of books particularly useful for my research and would recommend the works cited below anyone wishing to read more about the subject. For those without access to the world's libraries, the most comprehensive source of Cook journals, letters and related materials can be found in the five-volume collection by J.C. Beaglehole, while an essential companion would be John Robson's brilliant Cook story in maps.

Beaglehole, J.C. (ed) for the Hakluyt Society: *The Journals of Captain James Cook on his Voyages of Discovery*, Cambridge University Press, 1955–69 (four volumes)
Beaglehole, J.C.: *The Life of Captain James Cook*, Cambridge University Press, 1974
Robson, John: *Captain Cook's World – Maps of the Life and Voyages of James Cook R.N.*, Random House, 2000

Books:
Beaglehole, J.C.: *The Death of Captain Cook*, Limited Edition for Alexander Turnbull Library, 1979
Collingridge, George: *The Discovery of Australia – A critical, documentary and historic investigation concerning the priority of discovery in Australasia by Europeans before the arrival of Lieut. James Cook, in the "Endeavour", in the year 1770*, Hayes Brothers, Sydney, 1895
Collingridge, George: *The First Discovery of Australia and New Guinea*, William Brooks & Company, 1906 (reprinted as a facsimile version by Pan Books, 1982)
Edgell, Vice Admiral Sir John: *Sea Surveys – Britain's Contribution to Hydrography*, Longmans for The British Council, 1948
Estensen, Miriam: *Discovery – The Quest for the Great South Land*, Conway Maritime Press, 1999
Frost, Alan & Williams, Glendwr, (ed): *From Terra Australis to Australia*, O.U.P. Melbourne, 1988
Frost, Alan: *The Voyage of the Endeavour – Captain Cook and the Discovery of the Pacific*, Allen & Unwin, 1998
Grant, Joy: *Hethe-with-Adderbury – the story of a Catholic Parish in Oxfordshire*, Archdiocese of Birmingham Historical Commission, 2000
Hervé, Roger (Transl: Dunmore, John): *Chance Discovery of Australia and New Zealand by Portuguese and Spanish Navigators between 1521 and 1528*, Dunmore Press, 1983
Hough, Richard: *Captain James Cook – a Biography*, Coronet, 1995

Hunt, Julia: *From Whitby to Wapping – the Story of the early years of James Cook*, Authentica, 1991

Kamakau, Samuel L.: *Ruling Chiefs of Hawaii*, Revised Edition, Kamehameha Schools Press, Honolulu, 1992

McIntyre, Kenneth: *The Secret Discovery of Australia*, Souvenir Press, 1977

Nordyke, Eleanor C. & Mattison, James A.: *Pacific Images – Views from Captain Cook's Third Voyage*, Hawaiian Historical Society, 1999

O'Sullivan, Dan: *The Education of Captain Cook*, for the Captain Cook Schoolroom Museum, 2000

Price, A. Grenfell (ed): *The Explorations of Captain James Cook in the Pacific*, Dover Publications, 1971

Rae, Julia: *Captain James Cook Endeavours*, Stepney Historical Trust, 1997

Snowden, Keith: *The Adventurous Captain Cook – the Life and Voyages of James Cook, R.N., F.R.S.*, Castleden Publications, 1999

Spate, Oskar: *The Spanish Lake*, Croom Helm, 1979

Stamp, Tom and Cordelia: *James Cook, Marine Scientist*, Caedmon of Whitby Press, 1978

Whitfield, Peter: *The Image of the World – 20 Centuries of World Maps*, The British Library, 1994

Williamson, J: *The Observations of Sir Richard Hawkins*, Argonaut Press, 1937

Wiseman, Ross: *The Spanish Discovery of New Zealand in 1576*, Discovery Press, 1996

Wood, G. Arnold: *The Discovery of Australia*, Revised by Beaglehole, Macmillan, 1969

Articles & Papers:

Bushnell, O.A.: Aftermath: Britons' Responses to News of the Death of Captain James Cook, in *The Hawaiian Journal of History*, vol 25, 1991

Collingridge, George: Archives/Papers, held in the National Library of Australia and the Dixon Library, New South Wales, Australia.

Collingridge, Winsome: *Lecture notes on George Collingridge*, Ryde Historical Society, 1981 (personal communication)

Daws, Gavan: The Unlucky end of Lono, in *Orientations*, March 1976

Fisher, Susanna: The Organisation of Hydrographic Information for English Navigators – Five Hundred Years of Sailing Directions and Charts, in the *Journal of Navigation*, vol 54, no. 2, May 2001

Fogg, G.E.: The Royal Society and the South Seas, in *Notes and Records of the Royal Society*, vol 55, no. 1, January 2001

Kane, Herb Kawainui: *The Deification of Captain Cook*, pamphlet from Hawaiian Historical Society, © 10 Sept, 1994

Richards, Rhys: Rongotute, Stivers and "Other Visitors" to New Zealand "Before Captain Cook", in *The Journal of Polynesian Society*, vol 102, no. 1, March 1993

Spate, Oskar: Archives/Papers, held in the National Library of Australia

The Proceedings of the Third Annual Pacific Islands Studies of Conference: *Captain Cook and the Pacific Islands*, Pacific Islands Program, University of Hawaii, 1978: 3

Digital Resources:

CD-ROM: National Library of Australia/National Maritime Museum (Australia): *Endeavour – Captain Cook's Journal*, 1768–71

There is a vast array of websites I found useful. Along with the on-line catalogues of libraries, good starting points are:

Captain Cook Study Unit Website: *www.CaptainCookStudyUnit.com*

For Eighteenth Century Resources: *www.eserver.org/18th/*

Discoverers Web: *www.win.tue.nl/cs/fm/engels/discovery/*

History of Cartography: *www.ihr.sas.ac.uk/maps/*

INDEX

Aborigines 180
  attempts to contact 166
  Gwiyagal 165
  Tasmanian 293–4
  as true discoverers of
    Australia 361
Académie des Beaux-Arts, Paris
  24–5
Admiralty 119, 199
  Cook calls on after transit
    voyage 207–8
  reaction to St Lawrence
    surveys 51
Adventure 215, 254–5
  leaves on expedition 221
Age of Enlightenment 82
Aireyholme Farm 14, 15
Alaska 306–25
Alaska Peninsula 272, 323
Aleutian islands 272
Alfonso XII, Collingridge illustrations
  for marriage of 64–6
All Saints Church, Great Ayton
  15–16
Amherst, General Jeffrey 41, 43, 46
Ancient History of the Maori (White)
  151
Ancient Mariner 231
Anda na Barcha 225
Anderson, William (*Resolution*) 282,
  297, 312, 321, 323
Anson, Commodore 37, 96
Antarctica 86, 228–30
  aridity of 230
Antarctic Circle 228, 235
Antelope, HMS 63
Arnhem Land 101
Art Society of New South Wales *see*
  Royal Art Society
Ascension Island 204, 256
astrolabe 90, 94
astronomic tables 93–4
astronomy 73, 82–5, 109–10, 190
  see also eclipse; Transit of
    Venus
Atlantic Ocean 41
Australia
  British view of history of
    356–7
  circumnavigation of 100
  Cook's first landing in 165
  etymology of 99, 224
  first British colonists in 361–2
  idea of settling as colony 109
  reason for shape of on Dieppe
    maps 299
  see also Dieppe Maps; New
    Holland; Terra Australis
Australian Art 78
Australian Magazine 355

Baltic 29
Banks, Joseph
  awarded place on *Endeavour*
    112
  background 110–11
  encouraging emigration to
    Australia 361–2
  on *Endeavour* 98, 110, 114,
    115, 134, 139, 145, 157, 172
  hero-worship of 208–10
  journal 123
  leaves *Resolution* for Iceland
    expedition 217
  loss of Indian canoe 75
  mistress joins *Resolution* 234
  promoting Cook after his
    death 362
  relationship with Cook 275
  on *Resolution* 214:
    requirements for 215
  on return of Cook 265
  seasickness of 117
  on Tahiti 131–2
  team on *Endeavour* 112–13
Bark, definition of 105
Bass Strait 163
Batavia 98, 99, 100, 197–200
Bathurst engraving 78, 79
Batts, Elizabeth 61–3
  see also Cook, Elizabethatts,
    Mary 61
Batts, Samuel 61
Bay of Gaspé 45
'The Bay and Harbour of Gaspey'
  (Cook survey) 45
Bay of Inlets 174
Bay of Isles 174
Bayly, William 341
  on *Adventure* 220–1
  on *Discovery* 282
Bay of Success 124
Beaglehole, John 86, 93, 151, 195,
  281
Beauport 49
Bell Tavern, The 59
Bering, Vitus 272, 319
Berowra 79, 258
Bevis, Dr John 74
Bingley's Journal 209
von Bismark, Count Otto 52
Blackburn, John 61
Blaeu, Joan 101
Bligh, William 280–1, 290, 330, 341,
  342
Blosset, Harriet 210
Board of Longitude 85
Boke of Idrography 171, 224
Bolckow, Henry 15
Boscawen, Admiral 41, 43, 46
Boswell, James 277
Bootie, John 123

botany *see* natural history
Botany Bay 1, 109, 167
Bougainville, Louis-Antoine de 47,
  102, 129, 200, 218
Bouvet Island 234
Bouvet de Lozier, Jean-Baptiste-
  Charles 233
Break Sea Spit 177
Brewhouse Lane 59
Briscoe, Peter 127
British East India Company 39
British Museum 261
de Brosses, Charles 163
Buchan, Alexander (*Endeavour*) 113,
  132–3
Burgeo Islands 73
Burney, James 174
  on *Adventure* 220
  on *Discovery* 281
  on *Resolution* 219, 295
Byron, Commodore John 108, 111

Cabot, John 271
Campbell, Captain John 85
cannibalism *see* Maoris
Cape Bojador 89
Cape Breton Island 42
Cape Circumcision 233, 252, 253
Cape Direction 193
Cape of Good Hope 89–90, 99, 233
Cape Grafton 182
Cape Horn 102, 124, 125, 126
Cape Howe 164
Cape Kidnappers 149
Cape Lookout 177
Cape Maria van Dieman 153
Cape Melville 193
Cape Newenham 323
Cape Palliser 157
Cape Prince of Wales 323
Cape Town 202, 290
Cape Tribulation 182
Cape Turnagain 149, 157
Cape Upstart 180
Cape Verde 233
Captain Cook Birthplace Museum
  15
Carta Anonima Portuguesa 303
Carteret, Philip 102
cartography
  in Australia (New Holland)
    164–5
  crime in 303
  in New Zealand 155–6, 236: in
    Botany Bay 166
  in North America 44–7, 50–1,
    67–75
  in South America 125–6
  in South Seas 247
  in Tahiti 139
Catholic emancipation 23

Ceylon 99
Charlton, John (*Endeavour*)
Chirikov, Alexei 272
chronometer 85, 90
   Harrison's 110, 216, 221,
     236, 247, 252, 255, 262, 340
Chukotskiy Penisinsula 324
cleanliness on board 122
Clerke, Charles
   on *Endeavour* 108, 136, 204
   on *Discovery* 268, 272,
     273, 281, 290, 297, 312, 316 ,
     323, 329–30, 339, 340, 342
   on *Resolution* 213, 219,
     242–3: account of Cook's
     death 347–8, 362
   death of 349
Clive, Robert 38–9
clothing 114, 122
coal trade 62
Coleridge, Samuel Taylor 231
Collection of Voyages, chiefly in the
   Southern Atlantick Ocean
   (Dalrymple) 266
Collingridge, Alfred 33–4
Collingridge, Arthur 54, 57, 77
Collingridge, Catherine 260
Collingridge, Charles 57
Collingridge, Edward 260
Collingridge, George 1–2, 9, 11
   articles on Jave la Grande 226
   birthplace of 21
   in Britain 66
   Catholicism of 21–5
   character of 24
   current status of 368
   death of 359
   education of 24
   emigrates to Australia 77,
     168: artistic and social
     excursions in 170
   emigrates to France 24
   exhibiting internationally 79
   final years of 359
   finances of 304–5, 355
   fluency of 80
   with Garibaldi in Italy 25, 31
   in history text competition 171
   loss of child 258
   marriage of 80
   moves to London 23, 54
   moves to Sydney 260
   publications in Australia 78
   rejected by Establishment
     356–7
   religion of 261
   returns to artistic pursuits 58
   returns to Paris 34, 56–7
   'South Sea Shilling' episode 28
   in Spain 66
   wood engraving work of 25,
     54, 78, 355
   see also Discovery of Australia
Collingridge, Lucy 170, 258, 260
Collingridge, William 21
Collingridge Point 79–80
Colville, Lord 49, 50, 51, 69
Compleat System of Astronomy
   (Leadbetter) 73
Concepción 92
Concepción 246
Constable, John 61
Cook, Elizabeth 63
   accompanying Cook on social
     occasions 283
   after death of Cook 349–50

allowance to, during Cook's
   absence 284
births of: Elizabeth 75;
   George 221; James 69;
   Joseph 115; Nathaniel 72
concerns about Cook's South
   Seas voyage 107, 115, 212
death of 350–1
deaths of children: Elizabeth
   208; George 266; Hugh
   350; James 350; Joseph
   208; Nathaniel 350
with Isaac Smith 350
pension for, on death of Cook
   349
pregnancy of 63, 273
Cook, James
   ambition achieved on Great
     Southern Continent
     expedition 230
   apprenticeship as merchant
     sailor 28, 30
   assessment of significance
     of 361–8
   attitude to cannibalism 154,
     254–5
   aspirations of 37
   astronomy, interest in 73–4,
     109
   as Australian hero 362–3
   birth of 13–4: registration of
     15
   birthplace of 14–15
   British establishment, as
     member of 283
   burial of 341
   career as sailor, determines
     on 28
   character of 3–4, 16, 29, 155,
     275
   characteristics of 27–8, 29, 30
   death of 6, 339, 347–8
   at dinner party discussing
     Northwest Passage 273
   discipline of 72
   doubts over discovery of
     Australia 354–9
   early sailing of 29
   education 30
   fate of body of 340–1
   fighting at sea, witnessing 40
   friendship with John Walker
     29
   handwriting of 19
   Hawaii, Cook as scourge of
     363–4
   health of 236, 238, 269, 276
   health of seamen, paper for
     Royal Society on 277, 278,
     284
   ignored by press after
     Transit voyage 210
   injuries: to hand in
     Newfoundland 71–2
   instruments for *Resolution* 216
   introduced to King George
     III 211
   joins: *Freelove* 29; *Grenville*
     71; *Northumberland* 49;
     Pembroke 40; *Resolution*
     221; *Solbay* 40
   journal on Great Southern
     Continent voyage: sees
     Hawkesworth version of
     256; agrees to write own
     version 269

journal on Transit voyage:
   completion for publication of
   218; sent to Admiralty 199,
   204, 205
as King's Surveyor 63
legacy of 77–81
marriage to Elizabeth Batts
   61–3
Master examinations 39–40
in North America 41–51
objectivity of 155
portrait painted 277
promotion: to Master's Mate
   38; to Boatswain 39; to
   Lieutenant 96; to Captain
   210–11; to full post-Captain
   268
publishing Newfoundland
   surveys 73
at Quebec 47–51
reasons for joining Navy 35–7
reflections on completing
   survey of East coast 195
religious views 196
reputation of, growing 51
response to defeat of Banks
   217
Royal Society: admitted as
   member of 277–8; Copley
   Medal of 284
at school 18
skills of 4, 43: *see also*
   education
as Skottowe's son 18
sources for study of 4
suspicion of newspapers 203
temper of 238, 256, 276
Transit of Venus
   expedition: apprehension on
     return from 203; journey to
     London after 207; selected
     to command 95
treatment of native women
   and 239
use of earlier maps 174
views on Great Southern
   Continent 213
visiting family: after great
     Southern Continent voyage
     266; before Transit voyage
     106; after Transit voyage
     214–15
   and Walker household 28–9,
     30, 214–15
as white Anglo-Saxon hero of
   Australia 77–81
see also cartography; Cook,
   Elizabeth; *Endeavour*; Great
   Southern Continent; Northwest
   Passage; Transit of Venus
Cook, James (junior) 109, 208, 266,
   349
Cook, James (senior) 13, 15, 17
Cook, Nathaniel 109, 208, 266, 349
Cook Inlet (Gulf of Alaska) 320–1
Cook Strait 100, 157
Cooper, Robert Palliser (*Resolution*)
   213, 219
Copernicus, Nicolaus 84
Coral Sea 98
Coromandel Coast 99
Coromandel Peninsula 152
Corot, Jean 25
Cortesao, Armando 364–5
Counter Equatorial Current 120
Cox, Matthew 212

'crawfish' 123
Crozet, Captain Julien Marie 159,
    255–6, 292

Dalrymple, Alexander 44, 85–8, 94,
    98, 113, 142, 161, 173, 237, 246,
    266, 269
    refused command of the
        Transit of Venus expedition
        95
Dampier, William 11, 14, 171–2, 197
Dance, Nathaniel 277
Darling Harbour, Sydney 10
Dauphin Map 173
Davis Strait 271
dead reckoning 44, 74, 91
Defoe, Daniel 18
Delescluze, Charles 56
Deptford dockyards 215
Desceliers, Pierre 171
desertion 140
Dezhnyov, Semyon 272
Dias, Bartolomeu 89–90
van Diemen, Anthony 99
Dieppe 222
Dieppe maps 222–7, 258–63, 359,
    367, 368
    French sources for 365–6
    Portuguese sources for 261,
        301
    reasons for shape of Australia
        on 299–304
diet 113–14, 119, 200, 244, 297, 324,
    329
    see also scurvy
Discoveries made in the South Pacific
    (Dalrymple) 98, 113
Discovery
    chosen for Northwest
        Passage voyage 276, 278
    crew on 281–2
    theft of cutter at Kealakekua
        336
Discovery of Australia (Collingridge)
    352
    as school history book 355–6
Dolphin, HMS 102, 108, 131
Drake 213
'Draught of the River St Lawrence'
    (Cook, Holland, Simcoe) 50
Dunster, Thomas 119
D'Urville Island 159
Dutch East India Company 98–9,
    198
Dutton 256
Duyfken 99
dysentery 201–2

Eagle, HMS 38, 39, 41, 48
Eanes, Gil 89
Earl of Pembroke 105
    see also Endeavour
earth, proof that it is round 93
Easter Island 246, 247
East India Company 85, 87
East Indies 160, 179, 303
Elliot, Captain 204
Ellis, William (Discovery) 282
Endeavour 10
    cost of 106
    crew of 107–8
    damage to 188–90, 199, 200–1
    description of 105–6
    discovery of jettisoned cannons
        187
    fate of 212

goat on 218
handling of 122–3
journal of 267
officers of 107–8
refitting of 105–6, 114–15
repairs to (after shipwreck)
    185–6, 190–1
shipwreck of 183–5
Endeavour Reef 186
Endeavour Replica 187, 287–9
Endeavour River 192
English Channel 29
English Pilot, The 73
Esk, River 29
Eskimos 322–3
Espíritu Santo 98
Essay (on maritime surveying)
    (Dalrymple) 44
exercise 120

Fatchett, Thomas 338
'fearnought' clothing 122, 234
Feminist Club Rooms 79
Fernández, Juan 246
Fernando de Noronha 257, 275
Fijian Islands 100, 249
fireships 48–9
First Discovery of Australia and New
    Guinea (Collingridge) 356
Flower, Peter (Endeavour
    supernumerary) 107, 121
Form and Colour (Collingridge) 78
Formosa 99
Forster, George (Resolution) 220
Forster, John Reinhold (Resolution)
    220, 253, 267, 270, 281
France 87
Fraser Island 177
    discovery of lead weight on 367
Freelove 29
French Polynesia 129
French Second Empire 52
du Fresne, Marion 159, 292
Friendly Islands 297
Fuegians 124
Furneaux, Tobias (Adventure) 213,
    220, 254, 255, 267, 269, 294

Gaetan, Juan 301
Galileo Galilei 84
Gallions Reach 115
Garibaldi, Giuseppe 25, 31–2
George II, King 13, 50
Gibson, Samuel (Resolution) 140
Godington, Oxfordshire 21, 23:
    church 21–2
Gogo-Yimidir people 191
de Gonneville, Jean Binot Paulmier
    222, 233
Gore, John 274
    on Discovery 342
    on Endeavour 131, 136, 151
    on Resolution 219
Grand Banks 67
Grape Lane 28–9, 30
Graphic, The 54
Graves, John 16
Graves, Captain Thomas 69
Great Ayton 14, 15, 49, 62
Great Ayton school 18
Great Barrier Reef 181, 182, 192–3,
    302
Great Cyclades 250
Great Dividing Range 177
Great Southern Continent 1, 86–8,

94, 102, 156
    accidental discovery by
        Portuguese 227
    Admiralty Instructions on
        Transit voyage to search for
        142
    attractions to French 222–3
    beginning search for 143–5
    end of search for 233–57
    non-existence proved 266
    origins of idea of 224
    place names on maps of 225
    public response to non-
        existence 266–7
Great Southern Continent expedition
    211
    Admiralty visit by Cook on
        return 265–6
    Adventure crew attacked in
        New Zealand 254
    Antarctic exploration in 244–5
    cleanliness of crew on 234
    clothing of crew on 234
    Cook's health on 246, 247
    Cook's lack of consultation on
        245
    Cook 'tiring of Southern
        latitudes' 253
    crossing Antarctic Circle
        228–30, 245
    crossing Greenwich
        Meridian 253
    Easter Island exploration in
        247
    health of crew on Adventure
        236
    leaves New Zealand 237, 252
    loop of Pacific in 237, 243–4
    message left in bottle for
        Furneaux 243
    planning for 212, 230–1, 243
    proving absence of
        continent 228
    purchase of ships for 212–13
    renaming of ships for 215
    returns to Spithead 257
    ships lose each other 235, 242
    on Tahiti 237
    visits Ascension Island 256
    visits Cape Town 255
    visits Huahine 240–1
    visits St Helena 256
    visits Vanuatu 249–50
    see also diet; Endeavour;
    icebergs; Resolution; scurvy
Great South Land see Great
    Southern Continent
Green, Charles 109–10, 134, 201,
    208
Greenslade, William 127
Grenville 71, 72–3, 74, 75
Gulf of Alaska 272, 319–23
Gulf of Carpentaria 99, 101
Gulf of St Lawrence 42, 46–7
Gulf of San Sebastian 252
Gulliver's Travels 96

Halifax, Nova Scotia 42, 46, 50
Halley, Edmund 82, 84, 87, 93–4
Hamer, Captain 38, 39
Hardman, Thomas (Endeavour AB)
    107
Harleian map 171–2
Harrison, John 85, 90–1, 338
Hartog, Dirck 99
Hawaii today 343–6

see also Sandwich Islands
Hawke Bay 149
Hawkesbury River 79
Hawkesworth, Dr John 218, 256, 269, 277
  criticisms his version of Cook journal 269
Hayes Brothers 305
health of the crew 108
  see also diet; sickness; venereal disease
heights of Abraham 49
Henry the Navigator, Prince 89–90
Hicks, Zachary (*Endeavour*) 107–8, 136, 204
Hinks, Theo 338
Histoire de France (Michelet) 64
Historical Collection of the Several Voyages and Discoveries in the South Pacific Ocean (Dalrymple) 242
History of Cleveland (Graves) 16–17
Hodges, William (*Resolution*) 221
Holland, Lieutenant Samuel 43–4, 46, 69
homesickness 197
Howson, William (*Endeavour* AB) 107
Huahine 240, 248, 310
Hudson Bay 171
Hulme, Nathaniel 114

icebergs 244, 324
Illustrate Sydney News 78
L'Illustration 64
India 38–9
indigenous groups, attitudes towards 5
Industrial Revolution 50, 275
iron in trading, value of 102
Isle of Pines 251
Italy 31, 33

Jack's Coffee House 277
Jakarta *see* Batavia
Jansz, Willem 99
Java 99
Jave la Grande *see* Great Southern Continent
Jenolan Caves 79
Johnson, Samuel 35
Jupiter 190

Kamchatka Peninsula 272
kangaroo 108, 166
  Great Grey 190, 191
  origin of name 191
Kauai 315
Kaye, Dr Richard 284
Kealakeku Bay, Hawaii 6
  battle on beach 338
  bay blocked 338
  burial of Cook 341
  change of attitude of Polynesians at 333
  Clerke version events of 340
  Cook orders firing ball at residents 335
  counting the dead 339
  death of Chief Kalimu 338
  death of Cook 339
  hostages taken 337
  reception at 330–2
  revenge expedition by Cook 336–9
Kelly, John (*Endeavour*) 108

Kendall, Larcum 216
Kimberleys 101
King, James 280, 323, 337, 342
King George's Land *see* Tahiti
King George's Sound 317–18
King's Surveyor 63

Lane, Michael 74, 75
latitude, measuring 94
  see also longitude
Leadbetter, Charles 73
Le Mare, Jacob 124
Life of Captain James Cook (Beaglehole) 151
Lind, James 114
Line of Demarcation 90, 91, 299
Linnaeus, Carl 111, 112, 209
Lizard Island 193
London 29
London Illustrated News 54
longitude
  difficulties of measuring 94, 98, 301
  and latitude, tables of correction for 44
  lunar tables for 90
  see also chronometer; dead reckoning
Louisbourg 42–3
  siege of 43, 45
Louisiade Archipelago 98
Lusitania 168

Mackenzie, Murdoch 44
Madeira 119, 233
Mae 241–2, 267
  see also Omai
Magellan, Ferdinand 91–3, 131
Magnetic Island 180
Magra, James (*Endeavour*) 109, 178
  encouraging emigration to Australia 361–2
Maguire, Louisa 21, 23
Major, Richard Henry 261
Makinson, Lucy Monica 80
Malacca 99
malaria 200
Mangaia 296
Maoris 147–9
  cannibalism of 151–2, 154, 242, 243, 254, 294–5
  system of exchange 151
  wars of 151
mappa mundi purchase by Sydney libraries 171
mapping *see* cartography
maps, political nature of 70
Marco Polo 94
Maritime Museum, Sydney 10
Marquesas Islands 97, 247
Marquis of Granby 213
Marquis of Rockingham 213
Marton, Cleveland 13, 14–15
Marton Grange 14
Marton Hall 15
Maskelyne, Nevil 85, 93–4, 216, 278
Matavai Bay 129, 132, 247
Maui island 327
Mauritius 99
de Mendaña, çlvaro 97
Mendonça, Christopher, route of 365
Mercator, Gerardus 44
Mercator Projection 44
Mewburn's Farm 14
Middlesborough 14

Mile End Road, Cook's home in 70, 208, 262
Miquelon island 67, 69
Mission Bay 181
Molyneux, Robert (*Endeavour*) 108, 125, 203
Le Monde Illustre 64, 78
Monkhouse, Jonathan (*Endeavour*) 108, 185–6, 202, 208
Monkhouse, William (*Endeavour*) 108, 127, 136, 208
Montagu, John *see* Sandwich, Earl of
Montcalm, General 48, 49
Moran, Cardinal, Archbishop of Sydney 354–5
Mr Drummond's Educational Establishment 24
Müller map 319
Murderers' Bay 154, 159
Muslim merchants of North Africa 90

Napoleon III 52, 55
National Assembly (France) 55
National Library of Australia 262–3
natural history observations
  Bay of Success 124–5
  Madeira 119
  New Holland (Australia) 175–7, 180
  New Zealand 160
  South American coast 123
  Southern Ocean 145
  Tahiti 139–40
navigation, scientific 44
Nelson, David (*Discovery*) 282, 332
New Albion 316–17
New Caledonia 250–1
Newcastle Bay 196
Newfoundland 67–75
New Guinea 98, 100, 101, 163, 194, 197
New Hebrides 250
New Holland 101, 161–96, 293
  Cook 'takes possession' of East Coast 196
  see also Australia
New South Wales 77, 175, 196
Newton, Isaac 84
New World 96
New Zealand 146, 160, 294, 366
  North Island 156
  South Island 100, 150, 151, 156, 159, 236
Niger, HMS 111
Ningaloo 101
'Noble Savage' 197, 240
Nootka Sound *see* King George's Sound
Norfolk Island 251
North America 39, 40–1
  British strategy in 41
North Sea 29
Northumberland, HMS 49–51, 61
Northwest Passage 270–2
  description 271
  prize for discovery of 271, 273, 276
Northwest Passage expedition
  animals on 284, 292, 293, 308
  Cook accepts leadership of 273–4
  Cook blames Navy Board for problems 329
  Cook as consultant for 272, 273

Cook's death on 342
Cook's erratic behaviour on 290–78, 309, 325, 327–8
delayed schedule for 295
equipment for 285
proposal for 270
reach Gulf of Alaska 319
retreat to Hawaii for winter 325
torching of Moorea 309–10
visits to: Cape Town 290; Christmas Atoll 313–14; Friendly Islands 297–8; Moorea 309; New Albion 316–17; New Zealand 294–5; Sandwich Islands 314, 327–8; Tahiti 306–10
Nœñez de Balboa, Vasco 88, 89

octant 94
'Olhemaroa' 156–7
Omai 267–8, 281, 283–5, 295, 306, 308–12
Ormsby Hall 14
'Orono' 331–2
Orton, Richard, incident 177

Pace, Grace 13, 17, 18
Pacific 89–9, 92–3, 126–8
Palliser, Captain Hugh 39, 43–4, 48, 69, 73, 75, 273
Panama Isthmus 88, 89
parallax, determining by transit observations 84
Paramour Pink 87
Paris 24, 34
Paris Commune 55–6
Parker, William 74
Parkinson, Sydney (Endeavour) 113, 123, 133, 137, 145, 158, 201, 212
Parmentier brothers 365
Patagonia coast 123
Patten, James (Resolution) 246
Pembroke, HMS 40, 41–9
Pension Petit Jesuit School 24
Pereira, Manoel 122
Perry, William (Endeavour) 108
Peru 153
Philippines 93, 102
Phillips, Molesworth (Resolution) 281, 337
photography, effect of 78–9
Pickersgill, Richard on Endeavour 108, 120, 136 on Resolution 213, 219, 221
Pickersgill Reef 186
Pitcairn Islands 102
Pitt the Elder, William 38, 41
plane charts 44
Point Danger 177
Point Hicks 164
Policy of Secrecy 93–4, 302
Polynesian society 240
Pool of London 59, 62
Pope Alexander VI 33, 230, 299 see also Line of Demarcation
Portland, HMS 204
Portugal 87 discovery of Australia by 354
Portuguese Spice Wars 91
postal service, Australia–Britain 258
Poverty Bay 149
Praval, Charles (Endeavour) 109
press-gangs 6, 35
Princes Island 201
Prince William Sound 320

Pringle, Sir John 277
prostitution 131, 239
Providential Channel 194–5
Prowd, Mary 30, 214

quadrant 90
Quakerism 17, 18, 59, 241
Quebec attack on 47–8 description of 48
Queen Charlotte Sound 154, 156, 235, 242, 251–2, 293
Queensland 302
Quirós, Pedro Fernández de 97, 249, 250 as discoverer of Australia 354

Raiatea 240, 248
railways 259–60
Raleigh 213
Ravenhill, John (Endeavour) 109, 201
Reclus, Elisée 262
Resolution on Great Southern Continent expedition 215 alterations to, for 216 Cook joins at Sheerness 221 crew for 213, 219–21 journal of 325 leaves on expedition 221 removal of alterations 216–17 repairs at cape Town to 256 supplies for 221
Resolution on Northwest Passage expedition 276, 278 condition of 290 crew for 279–81 masts snap 293 mood in 296 springs foremast 334, 340
Rhode Island Marine Archaeology Project 212
Rio de Janeiro 121
Riou, Edward (Discovery) 282
Risorgimento 31, 32
Roseberry Topping 14, 15–16, 37
Rotz, Jean 171, 367
Rowe, murder of 294–5
Rowland, William (tutor) 19
Royal Art Society 78
Royal Australian History Society 358
Royal Hydrographic Office 45, 50
Royal Society 74, 84, 87, 94–6, 101–2, 109–10, 119 running the 'gantlope' 72
'running survey' 69
Rurutu 145
Russian trading voyages to Alaska 273

'Sailing Directions' 46
St Helena 256
St Lawrence river 46–8, 271
St Matthew's Island 323
St Pierre island 67, 69
Samwell, David (Resolution) 282–3
Sanderson, William 27
Sandwich, Earl of 110–11, 112, 215, 262, 273, 276
Sandwich Islands (Hawaii) 314–15, 332
San Pedro 97
San Pedro y San Pablo 97
Santa Cruz island group 97
Satterly, John 202
sauerkraut 114, 127–8, 208, 324

Saunders, Patrick 178, 201
Savu 198
Schouten, Willem 124
Scottish coast 40
Scottish place-names 40
scurvy 41–2, 92, 114, 119, 146, 150, 153, 190, 235, 237, 246, 272 see also diet; health; sickness; voyages
seawater, freezing 254
Sedan, Battle of 54
Seven Years' War 38, 61, 82
sextant 85, 90, 94
sexually transmitted diseases 131, 137–8, 239, 240, 323, 327–8, 363 see also yaws
sexual relations with indigenous people 102, 131, 133, 135, 137, 239–40, 248, 312–13, 330 women banned from ships 328
Shadwell 59, 62, 63, 70
Shank, Joseph (Resolution) 213
Shepherd, James 62
sickness at sea 40 see also diet; health; scurvy; venereal diseases
Silesia, conflict over control of 38
Simcoe, Captain John 40, 43, 45, 46, 47
Skottowe, John 18, 204, 256
Skottowe, Thomas 14, 17, 27 character 17–18 furthering Cook's career 18
slavery 241
Smith, Adam 88
Smith, Isaac 350 on Endeavour 107, 109, 165, 204 on Resolution 219
Smoky Cape 175
Society Islands 129, 296
Solander, Dr Daniel Carl (Endeavour) 112, 160, 172, 262, 288
Solitary Islands 175
Solomon Islands 97, 152–3
Southern Alps 159
Southern Ocean 89, 92 lack of British colonies in 96 seeking westward passage to 91–2 see also Pacific; Spice Islands
South Georgia 253
South Island see New Zealand
South Land 101 see also New Holland
South Seas 85
'Southward' see 'voyage'
South West Cape 158
Spain 87
Sparrman (Resolution) 237–8, 255
Spice Islands 89, 99, 172, 224 division of 299–301 see also Southern Ocean; South Seas
spice trade 91, 226
Spøring, Herman 112, 133, 136, 201
Stáhlin, Jacob von 273, 324
Stainton-in-Cleveland 13
Staithes 27–8
Staten Island 124, 153
stealing see thieving
Stephens (Endeavour) 119
Stephens, Phillip (Admiralty) 199, 208, 262, 273, 347–8

Stewart Park 15
stingrays, giant 166
Strait of Juan de Fuca
Strait of Magellan 92, 124
Strait of Le Maire 123–4, 252
Sutherland, Forby 166, 208
Swallow 102
Swift, Jonathan 93, 94
swimming ability 186
Sydney, description of 168
Sydney Coffee House 78
Sydney International Exhibition 78
Sydney Mail 78, 168
Sydney Morning Herald 355

Tahiti 102
  Clerke returns to 268
  Cook attitude to treatment of
    women on 239–40
  description 129
  Fort Venus 133–4
  in Great Southern Continent
    voyage 213–14, 238–9, 247
  metal as favoured currency of
    131
  religious practices on 133
  rules concerning 131
  social structure and culture of
    131–2
  Spanish claims on 308
  trade with 131
  in Transit of Venus voyage
    103, 126, 127–8, 129–42
Taiata 141, 200
Tales of the Papal Zouaves
  (Collingridge) 33
Tasman, Abel Janszoon, 159, 163
  first voyage 99–101
  second voyage 101
Tasmania *see* Van Diemen's land
Tees, River 14
Tepau, chief 134
Terra Australis *see* South Land
Terra Australis Incognita 99, 102
  see also Great Southern
Continent
Terreeoboo 337
Thiers, Adolphe 55
thieving by indigenous people 124,
  132, 134, 138, 247, 297, 309, 319,
  335–7
Thirsty Sound 180
Thompson, John (*Endeavour*) 108–9
Three Brothers 175
Tierra del Fuego 123
Timor 198
Toleration Act 1689 17
Tonga 100, 145, 296
de Torres, Luis 97, 161
Torres Strait 98, 161–2, 194, 196
Town and Country Journal 78
Transit Committee 85, 87

Transit of Mercury 150–1
Transit of Venus 129
  location of observations for 85
  preparing for observation
    132–4
  setting up observatory for 132
  taking observations 136–7,
    220–1
Transit of Venus expedition 82–5, 94
  Admiralty Instructions, secret
    142
  animals on board for 112–13
  Articles of War 115
  on Batavia 197–200
  at Cape Town 202
  Cook's concern with diet and
    health 114, 119, 122, 150
  Cook relationship with crew
    109, 120–1, 122, 131, 138–9
  Cook selected to lead 95
  cost of voyage to observe 94–5
  crossing Atlantic 119
  crossing Equator 121
  crossing Pacific to Tahiti
    126–8
  diet 113–14, 131
  leaves Plymouth 116
  leaves Tahiti 141
  luggage for 113
  navigation problems of 117–18
  on New Holland 161–96
  preparations for expedition
    105–16
  provisions for 131, 145
  reach Tierra del Fuego 123–5
  return from 203–4
  round Cape Horn 125–6
  route of 115
  socialising with indigenous
  peoples during 141: *see also* sexual
relations
  on South American coast 122
  in Southern Ocean 143–60
  surveys by Cook on 139
  see also Cook, James;
    Endeavour; cartography;
    diet; exercise; New Holland;
    Great Southern Continent;
    natural history observations;
    scurvy; sexual relations
Treatise on Maritime Surveying
  (Mackenzie) 44
Treaty of Tordesillas 90, 94
Trevenen, James (*Resolution*) 282
Trinidad 92
Triton 39
Truslove, John 201
tuberculosis 285
Tupia 141, 142, 145, 200
Tuteha, chief 134–5
Tyne, River 29

Unalaska Island 322, 325

Vancouver, George (*Resolution*)
  219–20, 246
Vancouver Island 317
Van Diemens Land 100–1, 164, 293
Vanuatu 97, 249
Vaugirard 24
de Vaugondy, Gilles Robert 163
Verdi, Giuseppe 33
Vernon, Admiral 35
Victor Emmanuel 31–2
Viegas, Gaspar 303
Vierge, Daniel 64
Viollet-le-Duc, Eugène 25
Vittoria 92, 93
VOC *see* Dutch East India Company
'voyage to the Southwards' 75,
  82–103
voyages *see* Great Southern
  Continent; Northwest Passage;
  Transit of Venus

Wales, William (*Resolution*) 220,
  231, 236, 278
Walker, Henry 28
Walker, John 28–9, 30, 59, 62, 215,
  221, 269, 276
Walker, Mrs (tutor) 14
Wallis, Commander Samuel 96, 102,
  108, 129, 131, 145
Wapping High Street 59
Wardale, Frances 70, 115
watches 123
Watman, William (*Resolution*) 283,
  332–3, 334
Webb, Clement 140
Webber, John 281
Westminster Gazette 209
Whitby 28, 37, 211
Whitby 'cats' 29, 37, 95, 105, 213
Whitsunday Islands 180
Wilkinson, Francis 123
William I of Prussia 52
Williamson, James 368
Williamson, John (*Resolution*) 280,
  283, 339, 340
Will's Coffee House 210
Windward Group of islands 129
Wolfe, Archibald (*Endeavour*) 137
Wolfe, Brigadier 43, 45, 46, 48, 49
Wood, Arnold, Professor 357–8
Woolwich dock 215
Wright, Edward 44

yaws 138, 363
York Cape 196
Young Slaughter's Coffee House 277

Zouaves 33–4